THE REMINISCENCES OF

Captain David McCampbell
U.S. Navy (Retired)

INTERVIEWED BY
Paul Stillwell

U.S. Naval Institute • Annapolis, Maryland

Copyright © 2010

Foreword

I'm honored to write this preamble to the first-person story of the U.S. Navy's "Ace of Aces" in World War II, David McCampbell. And, it is most fitting to publish this U.S. Naval Institute Oral History to help commemorate the Centennial Year of Naval Aviation.

I first met David McCampbell as a junior ensign (read "nugget" Hellcat pilot) reporting to VF-15 in Air Group 15 on board *USS Essex* (CV-9). I had received my wings and commission in December 1943 and I joined VF-15 as a replacement pilot in June 1944. I was brand new and McCampbell was in his prime as a fighter pilot and leader. Only a few days earlier during the famed Marianas Turkey Shoot, he had shot down five Japanese "Judy" dive bombers, becoming an "ace-in-a-day." It was to be the first of two times he executed this feat, the only aviator in the war to do so.

As a "nugget" ensign I had limited contact with then Commander McCampbell, the Air Group Boss. But, I still considered him my shipmate, and I have vivid memories of my times with him.

As I settled into the squadron I learned that our ready-room conversations covered anything you could think of—past missions, future missions, combat tactics, family. We fliers spent a lot of time together, and we talked to kill time between missions. Naturally, we talked about our leaders; and McCampbell already had a considerable reputation. Whenever his name came up, the veteran pilots spoke with sincere admiration. He was highly respected by those in the squadron and was regarded as a hell of a pilot - a particularly good gunner/marksman. To put it plainly, he had a tendency to hit things he aimed at. But he was also obviously very thoughtful and meticulous in planning his air-combat missions.

My first personal encounter came when I was assigned to fly on his wing in the attack on Palau later that year. Prior to this particular strike, McCampbell himself came to the ready room and briefed those of us who would be flying on that attack. During our flight together he was very aggressive - a throttle-to-the-firewall kind of fighter pilot. I wondered whether he was testing my ability to stay with him (which I did). I can tell you it was pretty heady stuff for a young, first combat tour pilot to be flying wing with such a legend. But, I did pass my first test.

Subsequently, I flew in strike groups led by Commander McCampbell and other senior pilots, but that was the only time I had the honor of flying on his wing.

What I remember clearly about David McCampbell was his intensity. At times he was remote, but he was also aggressive, impressive, and one hell of a good air group commander. What struck me most as a naval officer was the general attitude of the pilots in that squadron. Their respect for McCampbell was reflected in their actions and feelings. They were dedicated and patriotic. But at the same time, they were also fun and generally a great bunch of guys.

Personally, McCampbell impressed me with the businesslike way he ran our air group and his general demeanor and interactions with the pilots. It is always a positive experience if you have served under somebody who is very good at what they do, and McCampbell was the best. He most definitely had a major impact on my overall experience as a naval aviator during that period.

In October after five months on board *Essex*, a dozen or so of us junior pilots were transferred to the USS *Enterprise* (CV-6). We had been at sea since June. So we had a great deal of experience, at least in our eyes. The *Enterprise* aviators had not been at sea as long as we had, and to us they looked less experienced. Maybe it was ego, maybe it was arrogance, or perhaps even some anger at having been transferred to the *Enterprise*, but we collectively did not think they were as sharp as the pilots on the *Essex* were. After all, we had been members of David McCampbell's "Fabled Fifteen."

Several years after the war, I went to a reunion where then Captain McCampbell was in attendance, and he still had that special commanding presence. I visited him personally again many years later when he was retired, living in West Palm Beach, Florida. I went to his home with a pilot who had been with the air group early on, prior to my joining the VF-15. McCampbell was a very gracious host, and we reminisced about our time in the squadron, Air Group 15, the war, and postwar period. By then, he was getting on in age, and time had dimmed his fires, but not in my eyes.

I'll always remember David McCampbell as a larger-than-life figure – the commander and supreme fighter pilot who tested me as his wingman, when I was with him on the *Essex* in 1944. I was a better aviator and naval officer because of David McCampbell. His personal story is unique in all the annals of naval aviation. We are fortunate to have it available for today's generation of naval aviators.

Jack C. Taylor
Former Lieutenant, USNR
December, 2010

Preface

On a sunny afternoon in mid-July 1987, I arrived at Captain McCampbell's home in Lake Worth, Florida. With me was Jim Gregory, a local businessman who had served as an enlisted man on board the light cruiser *Honolulu* (CL-48) in World War II. He had made McCampbell's acquaintance and was eager to have me interview this man who had shot down more enemy airplanes than any other U.S. Navy fighter pilot. By that time—more than four decades after he had earned a Medal of Honor and Navy Cross for his exploits—McCampbell had largely retreated from interaction with the outside. He didn't make demands on the world, and he preferred that it not make many on him. Thus, Gregory performed a valuable service in persuading the old fighter pilot to agree to an oral history.

As we settled down to business that afternoon, McCampbell was pleasant, but his answers were short and to the point. He volunteered little, though a number of the things he described were interesting, such as the fact that he and future Senator Barry Goldwater had been friends at the Staunton Military Academy back in the 1920s, before McCampbell went to the Naval Academy. He told also of his experiences as diving champion when he was a midshipman in the class of 1933, service as a junior officer, and flight training. One of the few times he opened up was when he related his diving proficiency as a midshipman to his maneuvers with an F6F Hellcat fighter in 1944.

The following day, I showed up to conduct a second interview and move the narrative forward. This time McCampbell was apologetic, explaining that he had broken off part of a tooth. His jaw was packed with cotton, so he wasn't able to do an interview. "But come on in," he said, "we can watch some television together." And so we did. It happened that Congress was right in the middle of its Iran-Contra hearings, so we watched and listened to the testimony of Oliver North and Robert McFarlane of the National Security Council. We also saw that evening's episode of "Wheel of Fortune."

Later, McCampbell played for me an audiotape in which three aviators told of their wartime experiences. One was Steve Ritchie, the Air Force's first fighter ace in Vietnam; he was smooth and polished as a speaker. George Gay, the lone survivor of Torpedo Eight's TBD Devastators at the Battle of Midway, described being shot down and then rescued. He had told the story so many times that he knew exactly when to pause and let the audience have a chuckle. Then it was McCampbell's turn. As I listened to the tape, it seemed that he had been ill at ease in speaking publicly and eager to be finished. So this was no pose I had encountered. He truly was uncomfortable about blowing his own horn. He preferred a quiet retirement in front of the television set. Sitting in an easy chair in his den, he was surrounded by framed photos and certificates depicting an exciting career.

Remarkably, though, that day we spent together, chatting, watching television, and sharing a couple of meals—broke the ice. The rest of the week he was much more loquacious, opening up about the remainder of his service, including the 1944 combat deployment of his Air Group 15 on board the brand-new carrier *Essex* (CV-9). He took out seven Japanese planes during the Marianas Turkey Shoot in June and nine in one flight on 24 October during the Battle of Leyte Gulf.

As he told what had happened, he painted vivid word pictures. Among them was the description of being aloft on 25 October when Admiral William Halsey took Task Force 38, the fast carriers and their escorts, north to meet a decoy force of carriers and battleships. As the Japanese and American forces steamed toward each other, McCampbell was able at one point to look down from his airborne vantage point and see both U.S. and Japanese ships heading toward each other before they turned back. When the cruise of the *Essex* ended, McCampbell had personally shot down 34 planes of the total of 315 amassed by Air Group 15.

During interviews later in the week, he shared recollections of his postwar career. He served in such career-enhancing jobs as executive officer of the carrier *Franklin D. Roosevelt* (CVB-42), Sixth Fleet operations officer, and skipper of the attack carrier *Bon Homme Richard* (CVA-31). Even so, he was passed over for flag rank. McCampbell was philosophical about it, calling to mind collisions in which his carrier had been involved. He also mentioned that he'd had multiple marriages, a real no-no for promotion in his era. Still, he was content as he passed the days of retirement with his fifth and final wife, Frieda, a cheerful, energetic woman whom he inevitably addressed as "Buffy" because her maiden name was Bouffleur. McCampbell died in June 1996 at the age of 86. A new destroyer, USS *McCampbell* (DDG-85) honors his achievements. The ship was commissioned 17 August 2002 and is now home-ported in Japan.

The person who produced the superb initial raw transcripts of the interviews was Deborah Reid (now Deborah Lattimore) of the transcription company Techni-Type. Unfortunately, for a variety of reasons, the process of turning the original transcript into the finished version in this volume took much longer than expected as other projects intervened. Captain McCampbell provided his changes and additions to the raw transcript. I did some additional slight editing for the sake of accuracy and clarity. I also added a number of footnotes to provide background information. Ms. Janis Jorgensen of the Naval Institute staff has coordinated the printing and binding of the finished product.

In completing this volume, the Naval Institute expresses its gratitude to the Tawani Foundation and the Pritzker Military Library of Chicago for their generous financial support of the oral history program that produced this memoir. Special thanks go to Jack C. Taylor, former naval aviator and founder and chairman emeritus of Enterprise Rent-A-Car, for generously underwriting this project. Just as Mr. Taylor honored his World War II ship with the naming of his company, he has honored the Navy's all-time fighter ace by enabling Captain McCampbell's recollections to reach a wide audience of historians and other readers.

Paul Stillwell
U.S. Naval Institute
December 2010

CAPTAIN DAVID MCCAMPBELL
UNITED STATES NAVY (RETIRED)

David McCampbell was born in Bessemer, Alabama, on 16 January 1910, son of Andrew Jackson and LaValle Perry McCampbell. He attended Staunton (Virginia) Military Academy and had a year at Georgia School of Technology, Atlanta, Georgia, before his appointment to the Naval Academy by Senator Park Trammell of Florida in 1929. As a midshipman he qualified as an expert rifleman and was active in athletics (baseball and swimming). He was Amateur Athletic Union Diving Champion, Mid-Atlantic States, in 1931 and was Eastern Intercollegiate Diving Champion in 1932. Upon graduation from the Naval Academy on 1 June 1933, because of congressional legislation limiting commissions in the U.S. Navy that year, he was honorably discharged and the same day was commissioned ensign in the U.S. Naval Reserve.

During the following year, while in inactive status in the Naval Reserve, he was employed by a construction company in Alabama and as an assembly mechanic with the Douglas Aircraft Company, Santa Monica, California. On 14 June 1934, he was transferred from the Naval Reserve to the U.S. Navy and was commissioned ensign to rank from 29 May 1934. Through subsequent promotions he attained the rank of captain, to date from 1 July 1952.

Upon recall to active duty, he joined the heavy cruiser *Portland* (CA-33) in June 1934 and in July 1936 was assigned to duty as aircraft gunnery observer with Scouting Squadron 11, the aviation unit of that cruiser. He was detached in June 1937 to report to the Naval Air Station, Pensacola, Florida, for flight training. He was designated a naval aviator on 23 April 1938. For two years thereafter he served with Fighting Squadron Four (VF-4), based on the aircraft carrier *Ranger* (CV-4). In May 1940, he was sent to Norfolk, Virginia, for duty with the air group of the carrier *Wasp* (CV-7). He subsequently served as landing signal officer on board the *Wasp* early in World War II, until that carrier was lost in enemy action in the South Pacific on 15 September 1942.

During his period of service on board the *Wasp*, that carrier rescued the crew of the schooner *George E. Klenck,* which was foundering in heavy gales off Cape Hatteras in March 1941; carried planes to the British forces on the island of Malta in the summer of 1942; and participated in scattered actions in the Pacific to keep open the supply lines to Guadalcanal following the Battle of the Eastern Solomons in August 1942. After his return to the United States, he had consecutive duty at the naval air stations in Jacksonville and Melbourne, Florida, from November 1942 until August 1943.

After fitting out Fighting Squadron 15 (VF-15), he commanded that squadron from September 1943 until February 1944. On 8 February, he assumed command of Air Group 15, based on the carrier *Hornet* (CV-12) and later the carrier *Essex* (CV-9). In addition to his duties as air group commander of "Fabled Fifteen," he became the Navy's highest-scoring pilot with a total of 34 airborne enemy planes destroyed, the greatest number ever shot down by an American pilot during a single tour of combat duty. His feat of destroying nine in one flight was unequaled in the annals of combat aviation. He was also credited with the destruction of 20 grounded planes.

Under his leadership, Air Group 15 ranged from the Central to the Far Western Pacific; participated in campaigns and attacks in the Marianas, Iwo Jima, Palaus, Philippines, Formosa and the Nansei Shotos; took part in the First Battle of the Philippine Sea, when Task Force 58 was under the command of Vice Admiral Marc A. Mitscher, USN, conducted the famous "Marianas Turkey Shoot," and destroyed over 400 planes in one battle, and continued its exploits up to and including the Battles of Leyte Gulf.

During the seven months and more than 20,000 hours of operations before it was returned to the United States for a rest period, Air Group 15 destroyed more enemy planes (315 airborne and 348 on the ground) and sank more enemy shipping (296,500 tons sunk and over half a million tons damaged and/or probably sunk) than any other air group in the Pacific War. Among the major combat ships sunk were the battleship *Musashi*, three carriers, and a heavy cruiser. Additional ships damaged included three battleships, a carrier, five heavy cruisers, four light cruisers, and 19 destroyers.

For his brilliant record in command of Air Group 15, Captain McCampbell was awarded the Medal of Honor, the Navy Cross, the Legion of Merit with Combat V, the Silver Star Medal, the Distinguished Flying Cross with two gold stars in lieu of the second and third similar awards, and the Air Medal. The citations follow, in part.

Medal of Honor: "For conspicuous gallantry and intrepidity at the risk of his life above and beyond the call of duty as Commander Air Group FIFTEEN during combat against enemy Japanese aerial forces in the First and Second Battles of the Philippine Sea . . . [He] led his fighter planes against a force of eighty Japanese carrier-based aircraft bearing down on our Fleet on June 19, 1944 . . . [and] personally destroyed seven hostile planes during this single engagement in which the outnumbering attack force was utterly routed and virtually annihilated. During a major Fleet engagement with the enemy on October 24, Commander McCampbell, assisted by but one plane, intercepted and daringly attacked a formation of sixty hostile land-based craft approaching our forces . . . [and] shot down nine Japanese planes and, completely disorganizing the enemy group, forced the remainder to abandon the attack before a single aircraft could reach the Fleet. . . ."

Navy Cross: "For distinguishing himself by extraordinary heroism and skill in operations against the enemy in the vicinity of Luzon, Philippine Islands, while serving as Target Coordinator for the combined aircraft of three task groups on 25 October 1944. His coolness, quick thinking, superior judgment and outstanding leadership resulted in the sinking of one medium aircraft carrier, one light cruiser, two destroyers, and the damaging of one battleship. By his outstanding performance not only was the maximum damage inflicted on the enemy but our own losses were kept at a minimum . . . ."

Silver Star Medal: "For distinguishing himself conspicuously by gallantry and intrepidity in action while serving as a pilot of a carrier-based fighter plane in an attack against the enemy in the Central Philippine Islands on 12 September 1944. When he so ably led the attack group as to cause maximum damage and destruction to the enemy and he did, personally, engage and destroy four enemy airplanes in aerial combat and, in the face of anti-aircraft fire, did strafe and cause serious damage to an enemy merchant ship . . ."

Legion of Merit: "For exceptionally meritorious conduct . . . while attached to the USS ESSEX, during action against enemy Japanese forces n the Philippine Islands from November 11 to 14, 1944 . . . [He] directed the operations of several attack groups during this period, skillfully deploying the forces under his command to strike at the enemy with devastating speed, power and precision in perfectly coordinated raids which resulted in maximum damage inflicted on hostile shipping and vital harbor facilities and in the complete destruction of a large Japanese troop convoy. . . ."

Distinguished Flying Cross: "For distinguishing himself by heroism while participating in an aerial flight . . . as Commander of an air group in operations against the enemy. He led his group against the strong fortifications on Marcus Island on 19 May 1944 and early in the attack was hit by anti-aircraft fire which seriously damaged the after fuselage and controls, and set fire to the auxiliary gas tank. Despite this heavy damage to his own plane, he remained in direct operations of his group until all ammunition was expended, then led them back to their carrier. . . ."

Gold star in lieu of the second Distinguished Flying Cross: " . . . while participating in an aerial flight against enemy forces on 13 June 1944. As Commander of a carrier-based Air Group, he led component parts of his group in an outstanding attack against an enemy convoy in the vicinity of the Marianas Islands . . . [resulting] in the destruction of upwards of fifty thousand tons of enemy merchant shipping, at least one enemy destroyer and three escort vessels, and damage to numerous others . . ."

Gold star in lieu of the third Distinguished Flying Cross: "For distinguishing himself by heroism and extraordinary achievement while participating in an aerial flight as pilot of a carrier-based fighter plane on 13 September 1944. When, as leader of a fighter sweep assigned to a mission against the enemy in the Central Philippines, he did engage and destroy in aerial combat three enemy planes and did, in the face of anti-aircraft fire, destroy two more planes on the ground by strafing. . . ."

Air Medal: "For distinguishing himself by meritorious achievement while participating in an aerial flight as Air Group Commander during carrier attacks against enemy aircraft and airfields on Luzon on 5 November 1944, when he successfully directed the attacking forces and so skillfully deployed those at his command as to destroy a large number of aircraft, both airborne and on the ground, two airborne being credited to him personally and to cause substantial damage to aircraft installations. . . ."

From March 1945 to January 1946 he was on duty at the Naval Air Station, Norfolk, Virginia, as chief of staff to Commander Fleet Air Quonset Point, and as Commander Carrier Air Groups, Hampton Roads, Virginia. He was next assigned to the

Armed Forces Staff College, Norfolk, Virginia, first as a student and later as a member of the staff (Intelligence Division). After attending Language School at Anacostia, D.C., he was sent to Buenos Aires, Argentina, as the Senior Naval Aviation Advisor to the Argentine Navy, and remained there from October 1948 to January 1951.

In February 1952 he joined the aircraft carrier *Franklin D. Roosevelt* (CVB-42) as executive officer, and then from March 1952 until July 1953 was planning officer on the staff of Commander Aircraft Atlantic Fleet, with headquarters at Naval Air Station Norfolk. In July 1953 he assumed command of the Naval Air Technical Training Center at Jacksonville, Florida, and a year later became Flight Test Coordinator, Naval Air Test Center, Patuxent River, Maryland.

In June 1956 he joined the staff of Commander Sixth Fleet in the Mediterranean as operations officer and in January 1958 was detached for duty as commanding officer of the fleet oiler *Severn* (AO-61). He commanded the aircraft carrier *Bon Homme Richard* (CVA-31) from February 1959 until February 1960. He was subsequently assigned to the Joint Staff Office, Joint Chiefs of Staff, Washington, D.C. He later served briefly in the Bureau of Naval Personnel and in September 1962 became Assistant Deputy Chief of Staff for Operations, to the Commander in Chief, Continental Air Defense Command, with headquarters at Colorado Springs, Colorado. He remained there until relieved of active duty pending his retirement, effective 1 July 1964.

In addition to the Medal of Honor, Navy Cross, Silver Star Medal with Combat V, Distinguished Flying Cross with two gold stars, and the Air Medal, Captain McCampbell was awarded the Joint Services Commendation Medal, the ribbon for the Presidential Unit Citation awarded Carrier Air Group 15; the American Defense Service Medal with bronze A; Asiatic-Pacific Campaign Medal with seven engagement stars; European-African-Middle Eastern Campaign Medal with one star; American Campaign Medal; World War II Victory Medal; National Defense Service Medal; and the Philippine Liberation Medal with two stars. He also received the Navy Expert Rifleman Medal.

Authorization

The U.S. Naval Institute is hereby authorized to make available to individuals, libraries, and other repositories of its choosing the transcripts of five oral history interviews concerning the life and career of the undersigned. The interviews were recorded on 13 July, 15 July, 16 July, 17 July, and 18 July 1987 in collaboration with Paul Stillwell for the U.S. Naval Institute.

The undersigned does hereby release and assign to the U.S. Naval Institute all right, title, restrictions, and interest in the interviews. The copyright in both the oral and transcribed versions shall be the sole property of the U.S. Naval Institute. The tape recordings of the interviews are and will remain the property of the U.S. Naval Institute.

Signed and sealed this 17TH day of MAY 1988.

David McCampbell
Captain, U.S. Navy (Retired)

Interview Number 1 with Captain David McCampbell, U.S. Navy (Retired)
Place: Captain McCampbell's home in Lake Worth, Florida
Date: Monday, 13 July 1987

Paul Stillwell: Let me begin by saying it's a real honor to meet you. I've read a great deal about you, and to see you in person is a considerable pleasure. That pleasure is doubled by the knowledge that we're having a chance to record the experiences of your life and naval career. We can begin at the beginning, with when and where you were born, and what you remember about your parents and your early days.

Captain McCampbell: I was born in Bessemer, Alabama, January 16, 1910. We left there in 1920 and moved to West Palm Beach, Florida.

Paul Stillwell: What sort of business was your father in?

Captain McCampbell: Well, in Bessemer, Alabama, he was in the hardware business. My grandfather had established the business: hardware, wholesale and retail. Then in West Palm Beach, my father was in the furniture business. He had three stores and was doing quite well until the Crash came in 1929.[*]

Paul Stillwell: Was the Crash what precipitated the move from Alabama to Florida?

Captain McCampbell: Yes. He bought the furniture store down here in West Palm Beach.

Paul Stillwell: Was Palm Beach still somewhat thriving, despite the Depression?

---

[*] Following the crash of the New York Stock Exchange in late October 1929, the United States was plunged into the Great Depression, from which it did not recover until the nation geared up for World War II at the beginning of the 1940s. The Depression was marked by high unemployment and many business failures.

Captain McCampbell: During the '20s, it was, until the stock market crashed in '29. Then the Florida boom burst.

Paul Stillwell: But to make the move he must have had some expectation that people would still be buying furniture.

Captain McCampbell: Yes. Well, he was in business till 1934, when he had to take bankruptcy.

Paul Stillwell: I see. What do you remember about your early years in Alabama?

Captain McCampbell: I don't really remember anything, except we had ten cows during World War I, and I used to deliver milk. We had a colored man working for us, and he would milk the cows. My mother and sister would put the milk up in bottles, and I would deliver. That was the most impressive thing that happened to me in Alabama. [Laughter]

Paul Stillwell: How much recollection do you have of following the news of the war in Europe?

Captain McCampbell: About the only recollection I have of that is I helped celebrate the false armistice day, which I think it was early November. I celebrated the actual Armistice Day too; that was 11 November 1918.

Paul Stillwell: Did you have any other jobs besides on the milk route?

Captain McCampbell: Cutting the grass.

Paul Stillwell: How good a student were you in school?

Captain McCampbell: I was a pretty good student up until the seventh grade. Now, in the sixth grade, I remember, I stood two in the class. I don't remember much else. Well, to go back, at Staunton Military Academy, which I attended for four years, I was mediocre, but I passed all my subjects and graduated with Barry Goldwater.*

Paul Stillwell: What do you think made a difference in the seventh grade? Why did you drop off at that point?

Captain McCampbell: Well, I guess, because the courses got a little stiffer. [Laughter]

Paul Stillwell: How early did your interest in swimming develop?

Captain McCampbell: I'd always been interested in swimming, even back in Alabama. Dad used to take us out to the lake about every weekend, when I was six, seven, eight years old. Then, when we moved to Florida, I would go over to the beach almost every day. I began to take up diving and swimming. I won a watermelon once over there for swimming the longest without breathing.

Paul Stillwell: How long was that?

Captain McCampbell: Across the pool, 25 yards.

Paul Stillwell: It's convenient for someone with an interest in swimming to move to a place right on the ocean.

Captain McCampbell: Right.

Paul Stillwell: Did you have any coaches in school who helped develop your skills in swimming?

---

* Barry M. Goldwater served as a U.S. Senator from Arizona from 1953 to 1964 and from 1968 to 1986. He was a pilot in the U.S. Army Air Forces in World War II and later an officer in the Air Force Reserve. In 1964 he won the Republican nomination for President but was defeated by Lyndon B. Johnson in that year's general election.

Captain McCampbell: Yes. At Staunton Military Academy, we had a good coach.[*] Here again, Barry Goldwater and I used to swim backstroke, and I was one of the two divers there.

Paul Stillwell: How did you happen to go to Staunton?

Captain McCampbell: Because I had a first cousin, three years older than I, who went to Staunton the year before I did, and my mother and dad decided I'd go to Staunton.

Paul Stillwell: What year was that?

Captain McCampbell: Nineteen twenty-three.

Paul Stillwell: I take it this was still when business was thriving, so they could afford to do it.

Captain McCampbell: Yes.

Paul Stillwell: What other recollections do you have of the military academy?

Captain McCampbell: Well, it wasn't as expensive in those days as it is now. I think it cost only about $1,200 a year at that time. Today you couldn't begin to touch that.

Paul Stillwell: Of course, those things are relative. Twelve hundred dollars was a year's salary for some people back then.

Captain McCampbell: That was big pay. That's about all I remember.

Paul Stillwell: How regimented was the military discipline there?

---

[*] Staunton Military Academy is in Staunton, Virginia.

Captain McCampbell: Modeled right after West Point. Our professor of military science and tactics was a West Point graduate, and his assistant was a West Point graduate. Two assistant instructors were sergeants in the Army, World War I, so everything was regimented and designed like West Point.

Oh, by the way, I got my second lieutenancy in the Army while I was at Staunton Military Academy. I had one summer in the ROTC at Camp Meade, Maryland, which now is Fort Meade.* Also, Barry Goldwater and I won expert rifleman at that summer camp. Those are about the only remembrances I have of Staunton, except for the good apples that they had in that area. [Laughter]

Paul Stillwell: That's the Shenandoah Valley area.

Captain McCampbell: Yes.

Paul Stillwell: What other memories do you have of Goldwater? Were you a fairly close friend of his?

Captain McCampbell: Yes, we were quite close, actually. He had Company B, and I had Company E, so we belonged to the little officers' club and shared experiences.

Paul Stillwell: Any specific incidents with him that you recall?

Captain McCampbell: Only in the camp. We went to camp in '27. We were mixed up with the college people in the ROTC work, and the college boys went on a sit-down strike. Barry Goldwater got us prep school boys together and said, "Look, we're not going to take part in this. We'll take a vote on it." So we took a vote, and we decided that we wouldn't take part in it. So we didn't. Finally, after two or three days, the college boys came back and went to work.

But I do remember at that camp a very tall, husky guy, and he used to drill us with full pack, and we'd run in the sand. He had us double-time around a track, in the sand,

---

* ROTC—reserve officers' training corps.

for 15 minutes. Then he'd give us five minutes' rest, and then we'd go double-time again.

Paul Stillwell: This was in that hot Maryland summer.

Captain McCampbell: That's right, it was hot in Maryland; it was in June and part of July. That's about all I remember there, except making expert in rifleman.

Paul Stillwell: What precipitated the strike that you mentioned?

Captain McCampbell: This running around with a full pack.

Paul Stillwell: I see. So they're related. How would you describe Goldwater's personality from that period?

Captain McCampbell: He had an excellent personality. I remember once he broke another strike. One day at Staunton Military Academy, a bunch of guys in the south barracks decided that they'd all throw their shoes in the quadrangle. Of course, nobody could go to school, and it just raised hell around there. General Patch came over and talked to them first, and then Barry Goldwater talked to them and got things back on track.[*] They all got their shoes out of the quadrangle.

Paul Stillwell: It sounds as if he was developing leadership qualities way back then.

Captain McCampbell: Right.

Paul Stillwell: And also very persuasive, another thing that he's noted for.

---

[*] Major Alexander M. Patch, Jr., USA, served as an assistant professor of military science and tactics at Staunton Military Academy from 1920 to 1924 and as professor of military science and tactics there from 1925 to 1928. In World War II he commanded the Americal Division in the Pacific and the Seventh Army in Europe. He was a lieutenant general on active duty at the time of his death in November 1945.

Captain McCampbell: Yes.

Paul Stillwell: Did you take readily to the military-type discipline?

Captain McCampbell: Well, after Staunton Military Academy, the answer is yes.

Paul Stillwell: How did you adjust to it there? Did you have problems with it?

Captain McCampbell: No, I had no problems with it. Barry Goldwater, by the way, did have problems there. He was called the "beat king." The "beat" was walking around in circles with your rifle on, hour after hour, as a punishment for various demerits.

Paul Stillwell: Did that experience at Staunton give you a desire to have a military career for yourself?

Captain McCampbell: Not particularly, because after that I went to Georgia Tech.

Paul Stillwell: What year was that?

Captain McCampbell: Nineteen twenty-eight.

Paul Stillwell: So you were five years at Staunton?

Captain McCampbell: Well, I had to come home in the middle of one year. I lost a year, because I had a terrible time with sinuses. The doctor couldn't do anything for me.

Paul Stillwell: What could you say about the value of the education at Staunton preparing you for the Naval Academy?

Captain McCampbell: Well, I can say this: I had no trouble in passing the exams to get into Annapolis, based partly on my work at Staunton. Georgia Tech accepted me without a pre-exam. So it helped me considerably.

Paul Stillwell: Was it geared specifically as a preparatory course for the Military Academy or Naval Academy?

Captain McCampbell: I think I'm the only one that went to the Naval Academy. It was a preparatory school for the Military Academy.

Paul Stillwell: What led you to Georgia Tech in 1928?

Captain McCampbell: Well, I wanted to go to University of Alabama, and my mother said, "No, you can't go there, because your uncle went there and graduated, was a big football hero, and all that, but he came back and was an alcoholic."

So I said, "Well, my second choice is Georgia Tech."

Paul Stillwell: Why Georgia Tech?

Captain McCampbell: It was primarily an engineering school in those days, and I decided I wanted to go into engineering.

Paul Stillwell: Why engineering?

Captain McCampbell: Well, our family business in Alabama was in engineering: building roads, schools, storm sewers, and that type thing. I figured civil engineering would fit in with that.

Paul Stillwell: How well did you do during that year at Georgia Tech?

Captain McCampbell: I did all right. I failed in Spanish, which brings up a story that goes even beyond Georgia Tech. I had had two years of Spanish at Staunton Military Academy. I took Spanish at Georgia Tech, and I failed. I had two years of Spanish at the Naval Academy later, and I had to take a re-exam both years, which I passed—finally. Then, before I was ordered to duty in Argentina, I had a six-week cram course.* There they didn't have "passing" and "not passing;" you just got what you got, and that was it. When I got to Argentina, I could speak Spanish a little bit, I'd say, but I couldn't understand it, because they talked so fast. But I took lessons down there twice a week for the whole two and a half years I was down there, and I got to where I was pretty good at cocktail Spanish, but not the grammatically correct Spanish.

Paul Stillwell: How did you do in the engineering subjects at Georgia Tech?

Captain McCampbell: I did all right, because most of them were the same subjects I'd had at Staunton Military Academy. I excelled in college algebra, and also we had advanced studies beyond college algebra. I'm trying to think of what they were.

Paul Stillwell: Did you get into calculus, for example?

Captain McCampbell: Not at Georgia Tech. We got into plane geometry and solid geometry, and that's as far as I went at Georgia Tech.

Paul Stillwell: Were your parents financing your education at Georgia Tech?

Captain McCampbell: Yes.

Paul Stillwell: That would have been up to the period of the Crash, I guess.

---

* From October 1948 to January 1951, as a commander, McCampbell was senior naval aviation adviser to the Argentine Navy.

Captain McCampbell: Well, I was at Georgia Tech the one year, 1928-29. I went out for football, freshman team, and I was suited up for about six weeks. Then one day the freshman team played the varsity team. There wasn't a guy on that varsity team's front line that weighed less than 220 pounds. I was weighing in at 156, so that's the day I turned in my suit.

Paul Stillwell: What position were you playing?

Captain McCampbell: I was playing at halfback.

Paul Stillwell: Did you swim at Georgia Tech?

Captain McCampbell: Yes, I was on the swimming team as a back stroker and diver.

Paul Stillwell: How was your social life with the Georgia belles?

Captain McCampbell: Pretty good. I had a couple of girlfriends there. I was fortunate—more fortunate than most—in that I had an automobile there. I had a Chrysler roadster, which was a real going car in those days, and which I enjoyed.

Paul Stillwell: What led you to shift in 1929 from there to the Naval Academy?

Captain McCampbell: The Florida boom had burst. I figured it was an undue burden on my family to continue my education, when I could get a free education at the Naval Academy. Also, I had joined the NROTC at Georgia Tech and made the reserve cruise that summer. That cruise was very enjoyable, and so I just decided I'd go to Annapolis.

Paul Stillwell: What ship did you go in on that cruise?

Paul Stillwell: Did you have to go through your congressman to get an appointment to the Naval Academy?

Captain McCampbell: Yes. I was appointed to the Naval Academy from West Palm Beach by Senator Park Trammell.* I remember that Park Trammell was on the reviewing committee that came to the Naval Academy every year.

Paul Stillwell: The Board of Visitors.

Captain McCampbell: Yes. I remember how embarrassed I was once when I had lunch with him. He had long, real senatorial hair, down to his shoulders. To us it was a disgrace, because, of course, our hair was always cut very short.

Paul Stillwell: Did your family have any political influence to help get the appointment?

Captain McCampbell: Yes, they did. They worked through some local people here. I'm sure Dad didn't know Senator Trammell personally, but I got on the appointment list. Some guy from Miami was the principal; I was first alternate.† The one from Miami failed his physical, so I was picked up.

Paul Stillwell: And you said that your background then stood you in good stead on the entrance exams. Did you have any problems on the physical at all?

Captain McCampbell: No, no problems. I had to take two exams, one of them arithmetic, the other in English. I barely passed the English exam. The arithmetic, I did very well on. I remember one of the questions was a long-division problem, and real

---

* Park Trammell, a Democrat, was governor of Florida from 1913 to 1917 and a U.S. Senator from 1917 to 1936. He was cosponsor of the Vinson-Trammell Act, passed in 1934, which authorized the increase in size of the U.S. Navy to existing treaty limits.

† The "principal" referred to here was the individual who received the congressman's principal appointment for a particular opening at the Naval Academy. Someone with an alternate appointment would get in only if the person with the principal appointment was found to be unqualified or if he decided not to accept the appointment.

long. I've forgotten the exact figure, but I think it was nine to the zero power. Now, do you know what that equates to?

Paul Stillwell: Zero, I guess.

Captain McCampbell: That's what I thought, but that's wrong. Anything to the zero power equates to one.

Paul Stillwell: I didn't know that.

Captain McCampbell: I didn't either. [Laughter] So I missed that question, but I got all the others correct, so I made it.

Paul Stillwell: What are your first memories of reaching Annapolis and getting started in plebe summer?*

Captain McCampbell: Well, they were not unfavorable, because I'd been used to military life. I accepted the fact that I was a plebe, and subject to a certain amount of hazing and that sort of thing, so I didn't really have any problem with it.

Paul Stillwell: Do you remember any specific examples of the hazing?

Captain McCampbell: They used to make us do what they called, "Simulate steam engine." The plebes at the table would alternate, going up and down, one side and the other.

Paul Stillwell: Like the cylinders.

---

* A midshipman in his or her first year is called a plebe; second year, youngster or third classman; third year, second classman; fourth year, first classman.

Captain McCampbell: Yes. And the man at the head of the table got caught doing this, although he hadn't directed us to do it. The one at the other end of the table did, Red Stroh, but Mush Dornin, who was the senior one there at the table, was sent to the prison ship for 30 days.[*] So that ended that episode of playing steam engine.

By the way, Smoke Strean was at that table, and two or three other plebes.[†] I remember Fig Newton.[‡] You don't know him.

Paul Stillwell: No. Interesting nickname.

Captain McCampbell: Well, we all had nicknames then.

Paul Stillwell: What was yours?

Captain McCampbell: "Soupy."

Paul Stillwell: That's understandable.

Captain McCampbell: All Campbells there at the Academy we called "Soupy."

Paul Stillwell: And all short guys were called "Brute."

Captain McCampbell: Yes. [Laughter]

Paul Stillwell: Did you ever get sent to the *Reina Mercedes* yourself?

Captain McCampbell: No. I had no trouble with the discipline there at all.

---

[*] Midshipman Robert J. Stroh, USN, was in the class of 1930, as was Midshipman Marshall E. Dornin, USN. USS *Reina Mercedes* (IX-25), captured during the Spanish-American War, served as a station ship at the Naval Academy from 1912 to 1957. Until 1940, midshipmen being punished for various disciplinary infractions slept and took meals on board the ship but continued to go to classes ashore.

[†] Midshipman Bernard M. Strean, USN, a classmate of McCampbell. The oral history of Strean, who retired as a vice admiral, is in the Naval Institute collection.

[‡] Midshipman Walter H. Newton, Jr., USN, another classmate of McCampbell.

Paul Stillwell: So you probably wound up with a pretty good grease mark.*

Captain McCampbell: Yes, I did. I remember only two incidents where I got demerits; one was for sunbathing on the roof. I got caught, and I think I got 20 demerits for that. One time the duty officer came by, and he was at my door when the bell for reveille stopped ringing. I was out of bed, but I hadn't yet turned the mattress back. So I got ten demerits for that.

Paul Stillwell: Both of those sound pretty trivial.

Captain McCampbell: Yes.

Paul Stillwell: How easily did you acclimate yourself to the academic routine? I would think that a year of college already would certainly help.

Captain McCampbell: Yes, but it didn't help enough. I had to take four re-exams when I was at the Academy—two in Spanish; one, mechanical drawing; and one in AC electricity.† I remember on the AC electricity exam I got a 3.98, which 4.0 is perfect. And the Spanish exam, the second one, anyway, I got 3.92 on.

Paul Stillwell: I'd say you did pretty well.

Captain McCampbell: [Laughter] I did pretty well, but a little late doing it.

Paul Stillwell: Are there any of your classmates that you have particularly strong memories of?

---

* "Grease mark" is Naval Academy slang for an individual's grade in the area of aptitude for the service.
† AC—alternating current.

Captain McCampbell: Yes, Ray Thompson, the swimmer, captain of the swimming team, and Jim Reedy, who was the captain of the football team.[*] And Smoke Strean, I've been closely associated with him all along through my naval career. As for my roommates. the senior year there were four of us to a room. Before that there were just two of us.

Paul Stillwell: Who were your roommates?

Captain McCampbell: A.C. Jones, Jimmy Ogden, Louis Majewski.[†]

Paul Stillwell: What are your recollections of Ogden?[‡] He was a man I got to know before he died.

Captain McCampbell: Jimmy was a good guy, a nice guy.

Paul Stillwell: Very friendly and outgoing.

Captain McCampbell: Right. I never called him that, but some of the other people called him "Sonny Boy." He was on the water polo team. That's about all I have to say about him; he was a nice guy.

Paul Stillwell: How much swimming did you do at the Naval Academy?

Captain McCampbell: I gave up swimming completely and went for diving. I was on the freshman team, and then three years on the varsity. I was the senior diver during the third and fourth years. I ended up winning the Eastern Intercollegiates in the third year, and the fourth year I was first runner-up. I also got to go to the national swimming and

---

[*] Midshipman Raymond W. Thompson, Jr., USN, was vice president of the class of 1933; Midshipman James R. Reedy, USN.
[†] Midshipman Arthur C. Jones, USN; Midshipman James R. Ogden, USN; Midshipman Lewis J. Majewski, USN.
[‡] Ogden, who retired as a captain, did an oral history with the Naval Institute shortly before his death in 1982.

diving championships in Ann Arbor, Michigan. I would have gotten a crack at the Olympics in '32, except that I was unsatisfactory in—that year I think it was Spanish.

Paul Stillwell: That's unfortunate. I think Thompson was involved in that as a swimmer, wasn't he?

Captain McCampbell: Yes, three from our class went to the Olympics. One was Tom Connolly.[*]

Paul Stillwell: He was the rope-climb specialist.

Captain McCampbell: Right. He took third or fourth in the Olympics. I think Ray Thompson took sixth in the 100-yard dash. And the other was Bill Denton, who was the rings champion.[†] He took second.

Paul Stillwell: It's quite an honor to have all those Naval Academy athletes represented.

Captain McCampbell: Yes.

Paul Stillwell: What specialties, if any, did you have in diving? Were there any that you were particularly good at?

Captain McCampbell: I was pretty good in all of them. You had the four compulsory dives; those were the front dive, back dive, the half gainer, and, I think, the jackknife. Then we had the four optionals. These were all on the one-meter board. I did the back one-and-a-half, the one-and-a-half, forward one-and-a-half with a half twist, the gainer one-and-a-half, and the double somersault. Those were the ones I did most often.

Paul Stillwell: Did you do any high-diving at all?

---

[*] Midshipman Thomas F. Connolly, USN, who eventually reached the rank of vice admiral.
[†] Midshipman William T. Denton, USN.

Captain McCampbell: Only in two meets. I won the Mid-Atlantic AAU championship from the three-meter board, and then I got into the nationals at Ann Arbor, Michigan, on the three-meter board; I took fifth in the nationals.[*]

Paul Stillwell: How many meets would you say you were involved in during a given year?

Captain McCampbell: Well, we'd usually run about eight, with Yale, CCNY, Harvard, Princeton, University of Pennsylvania, Rutgers, one or two others.[†]

Paul Stillwell: The *Lucky Bag* said you were also involved in baseball.[‡] To what extent was that a factor?

Captain McCampbell: I went out for baseball my freshman year, and I guess I was suited up for three or four weeks. One day I was playing right field when my left-handed classmate hit a ball that should have been a home run. But I reached over my shoulder and caught it like so. When I came in off the field, the coach, Artie Doyle, who later became an admiral, said, "What in the hell did you do that for?"[§] So that day I turned in my suit.

Paul Stillwell: Was this an intrasquad game?

Captain McCampbell: No, just amongst the plebes. I could see right then that he didn't think very much of me, so I gave it up.

Paul Stillwell: The *Lucky Bag* said you were also involved during your first-class year. Did you come back out again when he left?

---

[*] AAU—Amateur Athletic Union.
[†] CCNY—City College of New York.
[‡] *Lucky Bag* is the name of the yearbook for each Naval Academy graduating class.
[§] Lieutenant Austin K. Doyle, USN.

Captain McCampbell: No, because I was unsat. You see, they start making up that *Lucky Bag* along in, I guess, February, March, and I had intended to go out for baseball. But when the time came around, why, I was unsatisfactory, and I didn't.

Paul Stillwell: How much did you enjoy the competition? Was that an important factor in sports for you?

Captain McCampbell: Yes. At Staunton, I played football and baseball, in addition to swimming. I've had a lot of athletics, but I was never outstanding, let's say, except in diving.

Paul Stillwell: A number of people have tried to draw a correlation between skill in sports and skill as a fighter pilot. Do you see that correlation yourself?

Captain McCampbell: To a certain extent, among certain people. Like Killer Kane was a good fighter pilot, but he got shot down twice.* Joe Foss was, I'm sure, a good fighter pilot, although I never flew with him, but he goes around bragging about getting shot down four times.† So I don't know if he was as good a fighter pilot as the score indicates or not. [Laughter] Jim Reedy, a football player, was a good multi-engine pilot. Jimmy Smith was an athlete; he was a baseball player, a good pilot.‡ Smoke Strean wasn't an outstanding athlete, but I would consider him a good pilot.

Paul Stillwell: Reflexes and coordination are certainly two things that are in common in both and useful in both.

Captain McCampbell: Yes. As a matter of fact, I think my diving ability helped me get out of a bad scrape one time. It was over the Philippines, to the west of Luzon. I'd lead the flight in, attack the target, then my wingman and I would go and get out of the active

---

* Commander William R. Kane, USN, commanded Air Group Ten, flying from the USS *Enterprise* (CV-6) during World War II.
† Captain Joseph J. Foss, USMCR, was awarded the Medal of Honor in World War II. He flew in the Guadalcanal area in 1942-43 and was credited with shooting down 26 Japanese planes.
‡ Midshipman James A. Smith, USN, a classmate of McCampbell.

area.* Then I'd pick up the second flight coming in and direct them. This particular time, we were out west of Manila, and I saw a plane down low. We were up about 14,000 feet, and I saw this Betty cruising along.† He was probably 2,000 or 3,000 feet.

I called my wingman and said, "Roy, I'm going to make a run on him." I was going to pass over him and then go down on him. But I couldn't get him to go under me fast enough, and I kept pulling and pulling up. I ended up in an upside-down spiral. I was going around and around in what amounted to a flat spin upside down. Between whatever altitude I started at and the Betty's altitude, I flat spun down. Finally, I got out of it and came out right on his tail.

My wingman called me and said, "Hey, skipper, what the hell kind of run is that?" [Laughter] So I had to apologize for that one.

I said, "Don't try it."

Paul Stillwell: Did you shoot down the plane?

Captain McCampbell: Oh, yes, I came right out on his tail. I think that my ability to get out of this thing was perhaps due to my diving ability, because you don't practice those things. [Laughter]

Paul Stillwell: It would be a dangerous thing to practice.

Captain McCampbell: That's right.

Paul Stillwell: When do you think that incident took place?

Captain McCampbell: This was along in October '44, before the Leyte Gulf action.

---

* McCampbell's wingman was Lieutenant (junior grade) Roy W. Rushing, USNR. The action described here took place in 1944 when McCampbell was commander of Air Group 15 in the carrier *Essex* (CV-9).
† The G4M (known by the Allied code name Betty) was a Mitsubishi Type 1 two-engine, land-based torpedo bomber.

Paul Stillwell: We were speaking about competition. Certainly that's something that is fostered heavily at the Naval Academy.

Captain McCampbell: Yes.

Paul Stillwell: How conscious an effort did you make to stand well in your class?

Captain McCampbell: Not too much. I had kind of lost interest by my third year. I figured that I'd probably resign and go to work in the family business back in Alabama. Then, of course, the law came through that they'd commission only half the class.[*] Then, I guess, that pushed me down. I lost the incentive even more with that, because I knew I wouldn't be in the first half.

Paul Stillwell: Another of your classmates that we have in our oral history collection is Elliott Loughlin.[†] He said there were opposing reactions; some guys studied all the harder at that point, and some studied less.

Captain McCampbell: That's right. That's right.

Paul Stillwell: Did you have a particular interest in the professional subjects, such as seamanship, navigation, gunnery, and so forth?

Captain McCampbell: No. I just took them as they came. I remember this impression, for instance, in ordnance and gunnery—things like on an exam, drawing a diagram of a torpedo. That didn't do me any good at all in my service. We found out how lousy they were early in the war. The Mark XIVs were the early ones that were no good.[‡] The submariners found out that they were no good, and so did we. Fortunately, the only

---

[*] Because of economy measures resulting from the Depression, only the top half of the Naval Academy class of 1933 was commissioned that year. Many of the others were commissioned in subsequent years.
[†] Rear Admiral C. Elliott Loughlin, USN (Ret.), a submariner.
[‡] During the early part of World War II, U.S. torpedoes were notorious for running deeper than the designed settings and for malfunctioning or poorly functioning exploders in cases in which the torpedoes did hit their targets. For details see David E. Cohen, "The Mk-XIV Torpedo: Lessons for Today," *Naval History*, Winter 1992, pages 34-36.

experience my air group had dropping torpedoes was in the Battle of Leyte Gulf, and then we had the improved torpedo; I believe it was Mark 13.

Paul Stillwell: Did you have any interest in aviation while you were at the Naval Academy?

Captain McCampbell: Yes, I did.

Paul Stillwell: How did that develop?

Captain McCampbell: Well, aviation summer. During our second-class summer, they gave us maybe three or four flights in seaplanes. But I had had an interest in aviation even before that. Back in 1919, my grandfather bought one of the war-surplus Jennies.* I had a couple of flights in that, back when I was like nine or ten years old.

Paul Stillwell: I presume you followed Lindbergh's exploits as well.

Captain McCampbell: I was at the Staunton Military Academy when he came back.† Yes, I had an interest way back.

Paul Stillwell: What kind of planes were you flying during aviation summer?

Captain McCampbell: Seaplanes, twin-engine. I don't remember the designation.

Paul Stillwell: Did you get a chance to put hands on the controls then?

Captain McCampbell: No. These were just familiarization flights.

---

* "Jenny" was the nickname drawn from the Navy designation JN for a Curtiss-built plane. Following World War I many were sold as surplus to private owners and were widely used for barnstorming. The JN-4H model of the Jenny had wingspan of 44 feet, length of 27 feet, gross weight of 2,017 pounds, and maximum speed of 93 miles per hour.

† Charles A. Lindbergh became a national hero when made the first solo flight across the Atlantic Ocean in May 1927. The light cruiser *Memphis* (CL-13) brought Lindbergh and his plane back to the United States, arriving at the Washington Navy Yard on 11 June.

Paul Stillwell: Did that whet your interest? Was the sensation of flying itself something that appealed to you?

Captain McCampbell: Yes, it did.

Paul Stillwell: Who were the pilots on those? Were those lieutenants at the time?

Captain McCampbell: Artie Doyle was the senior pilot, and he was a full lieutenant.

Paul Stillwell: In addition to his work on the baseball team.

Captain McCampbell: Yes. I don't remember any of the others.

Paul Stillwell: How much contact do you remember having with the Bancroft Hall organization—the duty officers, company officer, battalion, and so forth?[*]

Captain McCampbell: I didn't have any contact with them. Of course, they assigned rooms, but that was about the only contact I had.

Paul Stillwell: What are your recollections of the parades and drilling?

Captain McCampbell: Well, I took them in my stride. They weren't all that bad. In fact, we didn't do as much drilling at Annapolis as we did at Staunton Military Academy, nowhere near as much.

Paul Stillwell: What are your recollections of Admiral Hart as the Superintendent?[†]

Captain McCampbell: Well, I never met him. I'd say he ran a pretty good school.

---

[*] Bancroft Hall is the large multi-wing dormitory that houses Naval Academy midshipmen. It also contains the offices of members of the executive department, including the commandant, executive officer, and battalion and company officers.
[†] Rear Admiral Thomas C. Hart, USN, was superintendent of the Naval Academy from May 1931 to June 1934.

Paul Stillwell: Did you continue your social interests with the hops and so forth?

Captain McCampbell: Yes, but my girlfriend at that time was up in New York. She was on the stage, and we didn't have much chance to go. I went to the hops, but I didn't have a date, usually. One or two along the line.

Paul Stillwell: Who was your girlfriend?

Captain McCampbell: Sara-Jane Heliker was the one in New York. I later married her; she was my number-two wife.*

Paul Stillwell: How had you met her?

Captain McCampbell: Here in West Palm Beach.

Paul Stillwell: You mentioned the cruise you made in the *New York* when you were in NROTC. What about the cruises from the Naval Academy?

Captain McCampbell: My youngster year, we went to Europe, and we hit Edinburgh; Cherbourg, France; Kiel, Germany; and Oslo, Norway. Those were the only four ports.

Paul Stillwell: Which ship was that?

Captain McCampbell: *Arkansas*.†

Paul Stillwell: And this is the cruise in which you were pretty much acting as an enlisted man.

---

* For a photo of McCampbell and his second wife, along with a detailed article about his background and World War II exploits, see David G. Wittels, "4-F Hero," *The Saturday Evening Post,* 14 April 1945, pages 17 and 109.
† USS *Arkansas* (BB-33), lead battleship of her class, was commissioned 17 September 1912. Following modernization in 1925-26 she had a standard displacement of 26,100 tons, was 562 feet long and 106 feet in the beam. Her top speed was 21 knots. She was armed with 12 12-inch guns and 16 5-inch guns. She was the oldest U.S. battleship in active service during World War II, eventually decommissioned in 1946.

Captain McCampbell: No, acting as plebes, ex-plebes. [Laughter]

Paul Stillwell: What do you recall about the duties you had in the *Arkansas*?

Captain McCampbell: Have you got George Miller?*

Paul Stillwell: Yes, we do.

Captain McCampbell: Well, George Miller and I were buddies on that cruise. Our job was to keep the dogs shined on the hatch, one of the hatches, or maybe two; I don't remember.† I've got a picture of George and me shining up the dogs.

Paul Stillwell: What do you remember about the liberty ports? Any specific incidents that stand out in your mind?

Captain McCampbell: Well, we went in Cherbourg. I took five days' leave and went to Paris, and we went into Kiel, Germany, and I took five days' leave and went to Hamburg. Those are the only two instances. I used as an excuse for the leave that my sister and her husband were on their honeymoon over there, and I was to meet them in Paris and Hamburg. [Laughter] You don't have to put that in.

Paul Stillwell: How well received were Americans by the Europeans in that period?

Captain McCampbell: Very well received. As a matter of fact, I was riding the train from Kiel to Hamburg, or vice versa, and I had a German tell me that, "Things are very quiet right now, but just wait for two or three years. Things are going to be popping over here." He was thinking of Hitler at that time.‡

---

* The oral history of Rear Admiral George H. Miller, USN (Ret.), is in the Naval Institute collection. Like McCampbell, he was in the class of 1933.
† A dog is a metal fitting used to hold a hatch closed. Each hatch usually has about half a dozen dogs around the edges.
‡ Adolf Hitler was Chancellor of Germany from 1933 until his death in 1945.

Paul Stillwell: That was a very prophetic statement.

Captain McCampbell: Yes. This was 1930. But he knew it was coming, or he thought he did. Speculated on it. That's about the only thing I can remember.

Paul Stillwell: Did you stand any engineering watches in that ship?

Captain McCampbell: Yes, I did, and bridge watches.

Paul Stillwell: Did you live in hammocks?

Captain McCampbell: Lived in hammocks. We didn't know they even had decent bunks on there.

Paul Stillwell: Another of your classmates I've talked to is Pete Galantin, the submariner.* Did you know him?

Captain McCampbell: Yes, he was in my battalion. He was a great guy. I've corresponded with him a little bit. I guess he still lives up there in Pinehurst, North Carolina.

Paul Stillwell: Was the second-class summer entirely in Annapolis?

Captain McCampbell: Yes, that was aviation summer.

Paul Stillwell: Then where was the first-class cruise?

Captain McCampbell: It wasn't to Europe, I remember. We hit Houston; Ponce, Puerto Rico; Cuba; and Bermuda.

---

* Admiral Ignatius J. Galantin, USN (Ret.).

Paul Stillwell: What ship was that?

Captain McCampbell: I've forgotten, but I think it was the *Florida.*

Paul Stillwell: And this was a time, I take it, when you had duties more akin to junior officers than you had the previous time.

Captain McCampbell: Yes.

Paul Stillwell: Did you take to the seagoing life? Did it appeal to you?

Captain McCampbell: Yes, I liked that. In fact, the first eight years I was in the Navy I spent in sea commands, except for the ten months I had at Pensacola. By the way, I was amongst the first five to graduate in my flight training class at Pensacola. The five of us got wings all at the same time.[*] I just happened to think of that. The others were Scoofer Coffin, who later became a torpedo pilot, Eddie Outlaw, Ray Doll, and Willie Martin.[†]

Paul Stillwell: Is there anything else from the Naval Academy years you want to discuss?

Captain McCampbell: No, I don't think so.

Paul Stillwell: What was your reaction, then, on finding out that you weren't going to be commissioned?

Captain McCampbell: I had expected it. We knew it back as early as maybe March or April. It wasn't final at that time, but we had an idea it was coming. By the way, we were the only class that was ever divided like that.

---

[*] McCampbell was designated a naval aviator on 23 April 1938.
[†] Lieutenant (junior grade) Albert P. Coffin, USN; Ensign Edward C. Outlaw, USN; Ensign Raymond E. Doll, USN; Lieutenant (junior grade) William I. Martin, USN. Outlaw retired as a rear admiral and Martin as a vice admiral.

Paul Stillwell: Was it a sense of disappointment?

Captain McCampbell: No, not really. Not really.

Paul Stillwell: In any event, it was a free education.

Captain McCampbell: That's right. I got a job almost immediately with our family business in Alabama. First, I was making $15.00 a week as a straw boss on a storm sewer job. Then I went from that into the hardware end of the family business, and I was paid only $11.00 a week. I worked in the Birmingham store, and I couldn't afford to drive back and forth from Bessemer to Birmingham. That's when I made up my mind to go to California. [Laughter]

Paul Stillwell: Did you have an awareness of opportunities out there?

Captain McCampbell: No, I was taken on at Douglas Aircraft, Santa Monica, as a riveter. I bucked rivets and did riveting work the whole six months I was with them.

Paul Stillwell: How did you find out about the job?

Captain McCampbell: I went out and looked for one. I applied at the Los Angeles *Tribune*—I think it was the *Tribune*—and they didn't take me. I applied at an oil company; they didn't take me. See, things were pretty tough in those days, '34, so I went and applied at Douglas, and they took me on. Then, when the Navy gave us a chance to come back in, I jumped at it. I was happy with it ever since.

Paul Stillwell: How was it that Douglas had work when other places didn't?

Captain McCampbell: They were building the DC-2 and later the DC-3.[*] I worked on the second DC-3 that was built.

Paul Stillwell: That's been a workhorse ever since.

Captain McCampbell: Yes, still flying a lot of places, South America particularly.

Paul Stillwell: How did you enjoy living in Southern California?

Captain McCampbell: Well, it was very pleasant. I got to be good friends with Buster Crabbe, the big swimmer in the '32 Olympics in Los Angeles.[†] He was the only American winner, by the way, in swimming in the '32 Olympics. It was the 400-meter freestyle that he won.

Paul Stillwell: The Japanese swimmers did well.

Captain McCampbell: Oh, yes. They cleaned up. And I got to meet Eleanor Holm, her husband Art Jarrett.[‡] Buster Crabbe got me into the Hollywood Athletic Club for free, and I used to dive there. But I was never in a meet representing them.

Paul Stillwell: How did your acquaintanceship start with him?

Captain McCampbell: Through Ray Thompson.[§] Ray was on the Olympic swimming team with Buster Crabbe. Ray was stationed there at Long Beach, and he'd come up. He's the one who introduced me to Buster and his wife Virginia.

---

[*] The DC-2 and DC-3 were superb cargo or passenger planes; the design was quite innovative for its time. In World War II the DC-3 carried the Navy designation of R4D and the Army Air Forces designation C-47.
[†] Clarence L. "Buster" Crabbe II was an American swimmer and actor. After his fame from Olympic success in 1932, he appeared in a number of movies and serials in the 1930s and 1940s.
[‡] Eleanor Holm, an Olympic backstroke medalist in swimming and a film actress, had married singer Arthur Jarrett in September 1933.
[§] Ensign Raymond W. Thompson Jr., a Naval Academy classmate of McCampbell, was then assigned to the heavy cruiser *Indianapolis* (CA-35).

Paul Stillwell: Did you get to visit any of the movie studios?

Captain McCampbell: Yes, a couple of them.

Paul Stillwell: There was an article about Buster Crabbe in *Sports Illustrated* at the time of the '84 Olympics, because that was the first time it had been in L.A. since '32. I guess he had just recently died at that point.[*]

Captain McCampbell: By the way, his wife Virginia stopped by to see me earlier this year, and I hadn't seen them since the war.

Paul Stillwell: He continued his swimming the rest of his life, I know.

Captain McCampbell: Yes, and was going around the country preaching how to stay in good health, and he up and died. He had a heart attack. Virginia told me about it. She said she went in and tried to wake him one morning. He wouldn't wake up, because he had died during the night.

Paul Stillwell: Then you said you jumped at the chance to get back into the Navy. Did you have a choice of duty at that point, coming in late?

Captain McCampbell: They didn't give me a choice; they assigned me to the *Portland*, which at the time was up in Portland, Maine.[†] I was out in California. Fortunately, I had an automobile. I drove across the continent, came here to visit my parents, then drove all the way up to Portland, Maine, and joined the *Portland* up there.

Paul Stillwell: What was she doing there?

---

[*] Crabbe died of a heart attack on 23 April 1983 at the age of 75. See William Oscar Johnson, "A Star Was Born," *Sports Illustrated*, special issue, 18 July 1984, pages 137-159.

[†] The heavy cruiser *Portland* (CA-33) was commissioned 23 February 1933. She had a standard displacement of 9,950 tons, was 610 feet long, and 66 feet in the beam. Her top speed was 32.7 knots. She was armed with nine 8-inch guns and eight 5-inch guns. She was eventually decommissioned in 1946 after service in World War II.

Captain McCampbell: Just a holiday visit.

Paul Stillwell: It would have taken you some time to get across the country and up to there.

Captain McCampbell: Well, I had 30 days to report.

Paul Stillwell: So you had some advance word on where she would be, I take it.

Captain McCampbell: Oh, yes. If I was smart, I guess I would have asked for a change in orders and gotten on a ship there in Long Beach.

Paul Stillwell: But you didn't.

Captain McCampbell: I didn't. Well, I wanted to come home first too.

Paul Stillwell: How did your seniority fall out then, as a result of coming in later than the rest of your class?

Captain McCampbell: Our bunch of non-appointees was tacked right on to our class, so we lost no seniority.[*]

Paul Stillwell: When did you report to the *Portland*?

Captain McCampbell: As I remember, it was 28 June 1934.

Paul Stillwell: What sort of duties were you assigned at the outset?

---

[*] McCampbell's official biography states that he was transferred from the Naval Reserve to the regular Navy on 14 June 1934 and commissioned as an ensign with a date of rank of 29 May 1934. That put him ahead of the men who graduated from the Naval Academy in the class of 1934.

Captain McCampbell: I was assigned to the engineering department as one of the assistants

Paul Stillwell: Did you enjoy that one?

Captain McCampbell: It was no strain. I had the E division, and I had a good electrician, a warrant officer, in the division. He did all the work. I was just for show. I'd muster them and that sort of thing.

Paul Stillwell: Did you stand watches down on the switchboard spaces, or how did that work?

Captain McCampbell: I stood watches down in the engine room almost the whole time I was aboard the *Portland*, which was three years.

Paul Stillwell: I guess you got to know those dials and gauges pretty well.

Captain McCampbell: Yes, but as I told you earlier, I was assigned all kinds of duties. When I left the ship, it should have taken three people to relieve me.

Paul Stillwell: So you were versatile.

Captain McCampbell: Catapult officer, deep-sea diving officer, electronics expert, so called. I stood underway deck and signal officer watches, and the last year I was on there I was aviation observer.

Paul Stillwell: You were mentioning earlier that you went to the USS *Utah* for a school. Could you give me some more detail?

Captain McCampbell: I believe they called it the "ECM machine" in those days, and that was to study it, take it down, take it apart, change the code, and that type thing. Just a week's school, really familiarization with equipment. But I did have occasion once to use the knowledge. Something got out of order, and I repaired it. I remember Lieutenant Ayrault was the communications officer, and he was very happy about that.* We got it working again.

Paul Stillwell: What do you remember of your association with Tiny McCorkle?†

Captain McCampbell: Well, he was my senior officer. He had one of the 5-inch batteries, and I had the other one.

Paul Stillwell: How much emphasis was there on antiaircraft gunnery in that period?

Captain McCampbell: Quite a lot. Quite a lot. We'd do both surface and air.

Paul Stillwell: Did you have the 5-inch/25?

Captain McCampbell: Yes.

Paul Stillwell: And what about .50-caliber machine guns? Did you have those as well?

Captain McCampbell: No, we didn't have any around the ship. In the airplanes we had .30 caliber.

Paul Stillwell: Do you have any specific memories of McCorkle from the time you worked with him?

Captain McCampbell: Yes. After one of these air exercises, and I've forgotten just when it was, but somebody had to work up the reports to turn in, spotting the shell bursts a certain distance from where they should have been. He assigned me that job, and I spent

---

* Lieutenant Arthur D. Ayrault, Jr., USN, served in the *Portland*.
† Lieutenant (junior grade) Francis D. McCorkle, USN.

quite a few nights aboard ship. I couldn't go ashore, because he kept my nose to the grindstone, but I got over it.

Paul Stillwell: The gunnery officer was Gordon Sherwood.* What recollections do you have of him?

Captain McCampbell: Well, very good. We used to play golf together. He and Admiral Rassieur—have you got him?†

Paul Stillwell: No.

Captain McCampbell: He was the senior aviator on board. He's still kicking. He's, I guess, about 87 now.‡ He lives out in Rancho Santa Fe, California. Rassieur, Sherwood, and Frank Marshall, and I used to play golf.§

Paul Stillwell: It sounds as if you were quite a versatile athlete.

Captain McCampbell: Yes, but I was never really any good, except in diving. I'm very proud of that, actually, particularly when they just inducted me into the International Swimming Hall of Fame down in Fort Lauderdale two years ago.

Paul Stillwell: You were good enough to be invited to the Olympics also.

Captain McCampbell: Yes, but that's the only thing I ever was really good at.

Paul Stillwell: What do you remember about the skippers, Captain Le Breton and Captain Bradley?**

---
* Lieutenant Commander Gordon B. Sherwood, USN.
† Rear Admiral William T. Rassieur, USN (Ret.); during his time in the *Portland* he was a lieutenant.
‡ Rassieur was born 15 March 1900. He died 14 May 1993, six years after this interview.
§ Ensign Frank G. Marshall, Jr., USN, was also in the *Portland*'s aviation detachment.
** Captain David M. Le Breton, USN; Captain Willis W. Bradley Jr., USN.

Captain McCampbell: Le Breton was a pretty tough guy. He was really very distant from the crew and from the officers. Willis W. Bradley was just the opposite. For instance, when I was a young ensign, he once left me as the officer of the deck, under way, to take the *Portland* under the Golden Gate Bridge. We went to San Francisco to celebrate the opening of the Golden Gate Bridge.*

Paul Stillwell: That was 50 years ago this year, because I was just out there, and they had the celebration.

Captain McCampbell: I'll never forget that. He left me to take charge. He went back in the chart room while we were going under the bridge. The communication officer was on the bridge, and then later, after we were under the bridge, the exec came up.

Paul Stillwell: You had the conn?

Captain McCampbell: I had the conn.†

Paul Stillwell: That's a real boost for one's ego.

Captain McCampbell: That's right, for a young ensign. By then, I was kind of an old ensign. [Laughter]

Paul Stillwell: What do you remember about the quality of the enlisted men in the *Portland*?

Captain McCampbell: Well, I can't say enough for them, particularly the ones I had in the E Division, and the crew of the port battery of 5-inch guns.

    As I mentioned, I was also the catapult officer. We had two catapults, and I had one of them. The assistant gunnery officer had the other one. So in addition to my other

---

* Construction on the Golden Gate Bridge, one of the largest and most spectacular suspension bridges in the world, began in 1933 and was completed in 1937. It opened for traffic on 27 May 1937.
† The individual with the conn—normally an officer—directs the ship's movements in course and speed.

jobs, I had that job. I had a lock shot one day. Bobby Jones was the aviator.[*] You turn the plane up to full blast, ready to go, and I would give the signal to go. That meant, "Take the pins out," but the pins didn't come out. They call that a lock shot. So Jones had to sit up there till we bled down the cylinder, a good five to six, seven minutes, with the engine turning full blast. Because the pins might come out at any time, he had to stay ready to go.

Paul Stillwell: That was a compressed-air catapult?

Captain McCampbell: Yes.

Paul Stillwell: Did you experience any cat shots yourself in that ship?

Captain McCampbell: Oh, yes. I was the aviation observer for a year, my last year on the ship. I went off many times. My pilot was Jimmy Smith.[†]

Paul Stillwell: Did you ever experience blackout just at the time of the shot?

Captain McCampbell: No.

Paul Stillwell: How did you get shifted over to that role, from the straight duties in engineering, deck, and so forth?

Captain McCampbell: I applied for it when a vacancy turned up. George Pittard was an observer ahead of me, and he got his fingers caught in the hook that would go down and pick up the plane.[‡] He lost most of a finger, about two joints, doing that job. So he quit, and I took over.

Paul Stillwell: Did this grow out of the interest in aviation that you had already?

---

[*] Lieutenant (junior grade) Robert F. Jones, USN.
[†] Ensign James A. Smith, USN.
[‡] Ensign George F. Pittard, USN.

Captain McCampbell: Not so much that as the additional pay. You got 50% over your base pay, and I was married then.

Paul Stillwell: When had you gotten married?

Captain McCampbell: In '36.

Paul Stillwell: Who was your wife? You told me about the other one that you had met on the stage. Who was this one?

Captain McCampbell: Susan Rankin. She was from West Palm Beach also. We spent our honeymoon in Honolulu when the ship was in there for overhaul.

Paul Stillwell: That's awfully convenient.

Captain McCampbell: Except I had to pay her way. Of course, I rode the *Portland* over and back.

Paul Stillwell: Did you observe that custom of calling on the skipper, the social calls?

Captain McCampbell: Oh, yes. We weren't so formal then. I called and got his permission to get married. We did the whole overhaul under Bradley, so it must have been him.

Paul Stillwell: Pearl Harbor then was not yet as nearly developed as a shipyard as it later became.

Captain McCampbell: It's long been a shipyard, but it got bigger, of course, during the war.

Paul Stillwell: What do you remember of Hawaii during that period in the '30s?

Captain McCampbell: I remember living in a beach house. Fortunately, I ran into an old friend from Wilmington, Delaware. He was an architect who had retired and moved to Honolulu. I ran into him the day that my wife arrived by ship, because he had gone down to the ship to meet his future wife. When they got married, he left his Packard with me. I was at Waikiki Beach, and it's about eight or nine miles to Pearl Harbor. So that car gave me transportation while I was there.

Paul Stillwell: What other operations of the *Portland* do you remember from your time on board? Where else did she go?

Captain McCampbell: One time we were the escort cruiser for the *Houston*, which was carrying the President. And we picked him up in San Diego, and then we went down to the Cocos Islands, and from there we stopped in Panama, as we went through the canal.[*] Then, on the Atlantic side, we went down to the San Blas Islands. The natives lived in huts built on stilts out in the waters around there. I remember we went ashore once to visit one of the native huts, and they had wild parrot for dinner. It was a very unusual tribe. They were definitely heathens and lived, you might say, in the dark ages. From their huts they'd go ashore to do their fishing and hunting for food. I remember in those days they had what they called a "sport" in the tribe. Almost all of these natives were brown-skinned, but this was a sport from the tribe. He was almost completely white-skinned and had pink eyes, an albino.

Paul Stillwell: I guess the *Houston* had been fitted out especially to take President Roosevelt, because he couldn't walk unaided.

Captain McCampbell: Yes. They had an elevator on there to go from the main deck up to his quarters, which were either the next level or two levels above the main deck.

Paul Stillwell: Did you get any fishing done yourself on that trip?

---

[*] President Franklin D. Roosevelt was in the *Houston* (CA-30) as the two cruisers left San Diego on 2 October 1935. After the stops in Panama and elsewhere, the ships went to Charleston, South Carolina, where Roosevelt disembarked.

Captain McCampbell: No, I didn't. All I got in on was a picnic. They'd surveyed it for a picnic spot and built a platform for the President. But by the time the picnic came off, the tide had risen, and we stood there eating our lunch in knee-high water.

Paul Stillwell: I presume that the President was gotten out of the water somehow.

Captain McCampbell: Yes, he came in a boat and went right up to the platform.

Paul Stillwell: What island was that on?

Captain McCampbell: Cocos. That's on the Pacific side.

Paul Stillwell: It sounds so different from today's atmosphere, for a President just to be able to take a long fishing trip on board a Navy ship.

Captain McCampbell: Right. Yes.

Paul Stillwell: But apparently that was an accepted way of life then.

Captain McCampbell: Well, of course, he did some work, I'm sure, while he was on the trip.

Paul Stillwell: And it gave him a chance to catch up on the latest from the fleet too.

Captain McCampbell: Yes. As I recall, he made two such trips, but that was the only one that went through the canal. The other was on the East Coast, and I've forgotten the year even.[*]

---

[*] In 1934 Roosevelt was on board the heavy cruiser *Indianapolis* (CA-35) to review the fleet as it approached New York City.

Paul Stillwell: He had another one that went out to Hawaii in the *Houston*. That was one of his favorite ships.

Captain McCampbell: Yes. Another time the *Portland* went to Midway Island. I remember I was the boat officer for a boat that landed a "landing force" on Midway. This was in late '34 or early '35. That was another duty of mine; I was in charge of a boat. We made landings on the island of San Clemente off the California coast. We landed there a couple or three times.

Paul Stillwell: What sort of landings were these?

Captain McCampbell: We had an organized landing force on the *Portland*, and we would put them ashore periodically, to give them the exercise.

Paul Stillwell: They were separate from the Marines?

Captain McCampbell: Yes.

Paul Stillwell: Any specific memories you have of the Marines on board the ship?

Captain McCampbell: I remember the names of two of them. Captain Rosecrans was the first one, and Bob McGill was the second one.[*] Bob McGill was one of four of us that failed our eye exam at Pearl Harbor. In 1936 four of us from the *Portland* went over to Ford Island to take eye exams. All four of us failed our eyesight, because we were accused of having hyperesphoria.[†] I had a good friend, John Murphy, out of the class of '30, who was already an aviator.[‡] He was in the hospital with hyperesphoria, so I went over to see him, and we talked about it a little. Then Frank Marshall and I decided to go out into town and be examined by a civilian optometrist.

---

[*] Captain Harold E. Rosecrans, USMC; Second Lieutenant Robert A. McGill, USMC.
[†] Hyperesphoria is a tendency of one eye to deviate upward and inward as a consequence of muscular insufficiency.
[‡] Lieutenant (junior grade) John W. Murphy, Jr., USN.

The civilian optometrist declared that our eyesight was perfect, so I asked him to put it in writing, the type of equipment he used, and so forth, which was a later and more sophisticated type than the Navy used, and he did. So then we took it back to the flight surgeon on Ford Island, who had failed us, and asked him if he'd give us a re-exam. That was on Friday. He said, no, he had below-deck inspection that day, and he couldn't give us a re-exam. So then I said, "Well, how about Saturday morning?"

"No," he said, "we have parade inspection Saturday morning."

I said, "Well, we're leaving at 8:00 o'clock Monday morning. Can you give it to us any other time?"

He said, "No, I don't work on Sundays." So we were delayed by one year in getting a flight physical so we could go to Pensacola. I didn't have any trouble getting the permission to attend the flight training once I passed my physical. Of course, we had to take another one at Pensacola, and I passed that, no strain.

Paul Stillwell: What do you think the motive was for this doctor turning you down?

Captain McCampbell: In those days, you could get a flight physical only in Pearl Harbor, Norfolk, Coco Solo, Panama, or aboard the *Saratoga*. I think the reason for his failing the four of us on hyperesphoria was proffered by my surgeon on board the *Portland*, Dr. Robertson.[*] He said he thought that maybe the reason the flight surgeon at Ford Island failed us was to get even with him, because at one time Robertson had kicked him out of his quarters down in Panama.[†]

Paul Stillwell: But you, rather than the doctor, were the victims.

Captain McCampbell: Yes.

---

[*] Lieutenant Commander Carl J. Robertson, MC, USN.
[†] Ford Island is in the middle of Pearl Harbor, Hawaii. At the time it was the site of a naval air station.

Paul Stillwell: What do you remember about the ship's executive officers, Commander McCandlish and Callaghan?*

Captain McCampbell: McCandlish was a son of a bitch. Dan Callaghan was a great guy. No comparison at all. Dan Callaghan used to come out and play deck tennis with us, and in other ways, he showed himself to be an outstanding officer.

Paul Stillwell: Well, being a son of a bitch is part of the executive officer's job, so some of that's understandable.

Captain McCampbell: Yes, that's right, but he carried it a little too far.

Paul Stillwell: Do you remember any examples of his toughness?

Captain McCampbell: Yes, but I don't care to mention those. They're personal.

Paul Stillwell: What were your specific duties during that time that you were an observer in VS-11?†

Captain McCampbell: Well, aside from being an observer, I was an in-port watch officer, and I was still standing engineering watches. I stood engineering watches the whole time I was aboard.

Paul Stillwell: What were your duties when you were in the air?

Captain McCampbell: Observer.

Paul Stillwell: Did that include spotting or scouting?

---

* Commander Benjamin V. McCandlish, USN; Commander Daniel J. Callaghan, USN.
† VS-11—Scouting Squadron 11 had detachments of floatplanes on board various cruisers.

Captain McCampbell: Spotting for antiaircraft—well, for all types of gunnery, including the main battery.

Paul Stillwell: You would spot the fall of shot, I presume, and give corrections?

Captain McCampbell: Right.

Paul Stillwell: Was this in Morse code or voice radio?

Captain McCampbell: Morse code.

Paul Stillwell: Was the Morse code a standard thing that naval officers mastered during that era?

Captain McCampbell: Yes, even at Pensacola. We practiced Morse code all through our tour of duty at Pensacola.

Paul Stillwell: Do you recall any specific incidents from that time as an observer?

Captain McCampbell: Yes, there was one incident. It was out at San Clemente, and we had been launched. There were two of us, and the other plane went down in the water, just off San Clemente Island. Jimmy Smith, my pilot, circled the other plane so he could relay the messages to the ship about the one that was down. We stayed so long that we couldn't get back to the ship ourselves. We ended up landing at night, and the *Chicago* picked us up. So we spent the night aboard the *Chicago*. The *Portland* eventually got to the plane that was down, and picked up the pilot and the observer. But that was about the only incident of any significance.

Paul Stillwell: Was fog a problem in those days before radar?

Captain McCampbell: No. I remember a lot of fog, though, later, when I was a fighter pilot. But off the coast of California, apparently you don't get so much fog. It's when the air hits the California coast that you get all the fog.

Paul Stillwell: Well, ships operate farther north, though, too, San Francisco, up around Seattle and Bremerton.

Captain McCampbell: All along the coast.

Paul Stillwell: Do you recall any operations in those areas, other than the Golden Gate experience you related?

Captain McCampbell: Yes. We made an extensive trip to Alaska.

Paul Stillwell: The fleet problem went up there in 1937.

Captain McCampbell: Well, then we were on it. I don't remember the fleet problem so much as that we hit three or four ports up there—Anchorage, Sitka, and Valdez, the place that's now the southern terminus of the Alaska pipeline. I panned for gold in a creek there at Valdez. We ran into an interesting thing there at Valdez. There was a man there that had a gold mine up in the mountains, and he used to commute back and forth to the gold mine by airplane. The tide up there would run sometimes 18 or 20 feet, but he would arrange it so he would take off at low tide. He'd go down a little ramp, and hit the mud flats. He had skis on his plane. He would take off, fly up to his gold mine, pick up a load of gold ore, and he'd come back again at low tide, and land on the mud flats and taxi on to shore. I don't know how much money he was making out of it, but I thought that was a pretty clever arrangement.

Paul Stillwell: You wonder how much gold ore he could carry in a plane.

Captain McCampbell: Yes, that's right. The other interesting thing up there—the assistant engineering officer and I went up in the mountains there one day, and we caught a salmon up in one of the creeks, just with our bare hands. I guess it was spawning time for them, and they get pretty lazy or something. Also, the skipper took us around to a bay there, where there was a big avalanche, and we fired three or four 5-inch shells into the avalanche, to make it crash down, which was quite a fantastic shot.

Paul Stillwell: Was this Captain Bradley?

Captain McCampbell: Yes. My pilot and I took a rather extended flight over this avalanche one day. I can't think of anything in particular. We hit, as I said, Anchorage, Sitka, Valdez, and it seems to me one other spot, but I can't remember.

Paul Stillwell: Where did your wife live after you got back from the honeymoon in Hawaii? Was that in Long Beach?

Captain McCampbell: Yes, temporarily. Then she came back to Florida. I believe we were based in Long Beach the whole three years I was on there.

Paul Stillwell: Did you have a separate JO mess, or did all the officers eat in the wardroom?[*]

Captain McCampbell: All the officers ate in the same wardroom.

Paul Stillwell: What do you remember about the atmosphere and camaraderie of the wardroom?

Captain McCampbell: Well, some of us played cribbage, and some of us didn't. The exec wouldn't allow any gambling, but we could gamble with cribbage, keeping score.[†]

---

[*] JO—junior officer.
[†] Exec—executive officer.

But we didn't have any poker or bridge in those days.

Paul Stillwell: The exec would have been president of the mess, I take it.

Captain McCampbell: Yes.

Paul Stillwell: Any specific recollections you have of Callaghan, other than the deck tennis?

Captain McCampbell: No, I don't think there were any. He was just generally a good naval officer.

Paul Stillwell: Did the *Portland* undergo any other shipyard periods besides the one at Pearl Harbor? Did you go up to Bremerton, for example?

Captain McCampbell: Yes, we did go to Bremerton. An interesting thing happened up there. My father had been in a bad accident and was not expected to live, so I got 30 days' emergency leave and came down to West Palm Beach. Then I was to rejoin the ship at a certain date in Long Beach, California. So when they took the *Portland* out of the shipyard at Bremerton, somebody forgot to close the seacocks, and as the ship came off the skids it damn near sank. Fortunately, I was on leave then, and I wasn't involved in that. But that created quite a furor for the ship.

Paul Stillwell: Presumably, there was an investigation afterward.

Captain McCampbell: Oh, yes. I don't know who got hung, but probably some poor enlisted man.

There was another incident up in Bremerton. I shot a great game of golf one day in the rain. Now, it wasn't a championship course, but it was a long course, and I had a 76. That's the best game of golf I ever had.

Paul Stillwell: Certainly respectable.

Captain McCampbell: In the rain, yet. And it can really rain up there.

Paul Stillwell: I know. I've been through a shipyard period up there also.

What do you remember about the competitive exercises and the competition for the E in that era?

Captain McCampbell: Not too much. There was not as much competition or excitement about E's in those days.[*] I don't think the *Portland* ever had one; I just don't remember anything about E's.

Paul Stillwell: Do you remember the athletic competitions between the enlisted men—the Battenberg Cup and football and baseball and so forth?[†]

Captain McCampbell: We participated in the rowing cup. I don't remember a baseball or football team aboard the *Portland*.

Paul Stillwell: A number of ships did have them.

Captain McCampbell: Yes, but they were mostly battleships, which had bigger crews.

Paul Stillwell: Anything else about the *Portland* that you particularly remember?

Captain McCampbell: No. I can end up by saying I was glad to get off. That's about all I can say for it.

Paul Stillwell: A sense of relief, after all that.

---

[*] An "E," for excellence, is generally awarded to a ship or component of a ship as a result of top performance in competition with other ships during a given time period.
[†] The Battenberg Cup was presented annually to the fleet's best race-boat crew.

Captain McCampbell: Yes. Get out of all those jobs.

Paul Stillwell: Well, by then, you had probably developed a very real desire to go into aviation too.

Captain McCampbell: Right.

Paul Stillwell: What do you remember about the experience when you first got down to Pensacola to begin flight training?

Captain McCampbell: Nothing spectacular happened there. I was the first person to finish Squadron One. That meant I was the first guy to solo out of my class. In Squadron Five, we were into stunts, and the instructor that was grading me on my stunts gave me a 4.0, which he said was the only one he had ever given. That was Fitzhugh Lee.[*] Other than that, I don't remember anything.

Paul Stillwell: What types of planes were you flying in that early training?

Captain McCampbell: Oh, we flew quite a few different types. We first started out in floatplanes. The NY was the one I soloed in. Then I think we graduated to the N2N. That was Squadron One. Squadron Two was the N3Ns. Squadron Three was land planes, the OS2U, on wheels, and Squadron Four was seaplanes, multi-engine torpedo planes. Squadron Five was SNJ and F4B-4.

Paul Stillwell: You mentioned you were the first to solo. How would you account for that?

---

[*] Lieutenant Fitzhugh Lee, USN, who eventually retired as a vice admiral. His oral history is in the Naval Institute collection.

Captain McCampbell: Well, I had a good instructor, Captain Holmberg, a Marine, and he put me through ahead of everybody else.*

Paul Stillwell: Now, don't be too modest here. There must have been some ability on your part too.

Captain McCampbell: Well, the main thing was that I was comfortable in the air. Having been an observer for a year helped with that aspect, and other than that, it was just following instruction.

Paul Stillwell: Well, there has to be an aspect of natural ability too. Some people are just better at things than others.

Captain McCampbell: Right.

Paul Stillwell: And you must be one of those.

Captain McCampbell: Well, yes, aside from being comfortable in the air, I had had my own automobile for years. I got my first one when I was 16, and I'd had one ever since. So I was a good automobile driver, which I think helped. And then my pilot on the *Portland*, when I was an observer, Jimmy Smith, would let me take controls every now and then.

Paul Stillwell: That would certainly help too.

Captain McCampbell: Yes. I'd do simple things like turns—nothing fancy.

Paul Stillwell: What about the takeoffs and landings? How easily did that come to you?

Captain McCampbell: No strain.

---

* Captain John S. Holmberg, USMC.

Paul Stillwell: I have a feeling at the other end of the spectrum that there were men who never got comfortable in the air.

Captain McCampbell: That's right. And they usually would bilge out. Bob McGill, the Marine off the *Portland*, was one of those, and there were others.

Paul Stillwell: Are there any of the other instructors you remember from flight training?

Captain McCampbell: Yes, I had a good instructor in Squadron Four, Frank Turner.[*] He's passed on now. But he was excellent. I got to fly with him later when I was on the *Wasp*. He had one of the squadrons.

Paul Stillwell: What sorts of maneuvers were done in these various planes? For example, how would what you did in a fighter differ from the training you'd have in a patrol plane? Was it mission oriented?

Captain McCampbell: Well, patrol planes didn't do much of anything, except fly straight and level, take off and land, a little navigation.

Paul Stillwell: For example, in the fighters, did you go beyond just flying the plane to get into tactics?

Captain McCampbell: Not tactics. Not really. I don't remember formation flying either. We got into stunts, and we got into a phase there that they called jumping rope. They'd string a rope between two poles, and the rope was about 10 feet high. Then we'd come in. Part of the program was that you'd have to do a slip for about 1,000 feet going down, then level off just before you crossed the rope, land, and then take off again.

Paul Stillwell: To see how close you could come to the rope?

---

[*] Lieutenant Frank Turner, USN.

Captain McCampbell: That's right. And also they judged your slip. I mean, you couldn't cheat very much, flying in straight and do it. You had to slip, come down on it, then level off, and get off again. That was a damn short runway, with big pine trees sitting right up in front of you. If your engine quit on you, you'd had it.

Paul Stillwell: Whom do you remember of your fellow students during that period?

Captain McCampbell: Well, Frank Marshall; George Pittard, off the *Portland*; Bob Camera, classmate at Annapolis; and Scoofer Coffin; Ray Doll; Billy Martin; Eddie Outlaw.[*] Those were the main ones.

Paul Stillwell: Was there a sense of competition there, as you experienced, say, at the Naval Academy, trying to finish at the top of the class?

Captain McCampbell: No, no, I didn't see that. There may have been some, but I didn't experience it.

Paul Stillwell: Was there any classroom instruction in addition to the flying itself?

Captain McCampbell: Yes, we had engineering every day, half a day, usually. I guess that only lasted about four or five months, and we had radio, dit-dot-dash-type thing, most every day, for months on end.

Paul Stillwell: What about instrument flying?

Captain McCampbell: No, we didn't get any.

Paul Stillwell: How about aerodynamics—the effect that the wind has on the airplane?

---

[*] Lieutenant (junior grade) Frank G. Marshall, Jr., USN; Lieutenant (junior grade) George F. Pittard, Jr., USN; Lieutenant (junior grade) Robert S. Camera, USN; Lieutenant (junior grade) Albert P. Coffin, USN; Ensign Raymond E. Doll, USN; Lieutenant (junior grade) William I. Martin, USN; Ensign Edward C. Outlaw, USN.

Captain McCampbell: Yes, we had a little of that at ground school, very little. I remember my instructor, when we got into the SNJ, said, "Now get in that plane and see how high you can fly."[*] Now, we had had nothing on the use of oxygen at that point, and I didn't have an oxygen mask. I got up to 22,500, and I began to get a headache, so I dove out. I got down around 10,000, and the headache went away. But they gave us no instruction on oxygen, and I didn't know anything about it. I knew about deep-sea diving, the pressures and all, but I'd never been instructed in anything on the use of oxygen.

Paul Stillwell: Was the purpose of that just to give you the feeling of what it was like to be deprived, so you'd recognize it?

Captain McCampbell: I don't think that was his purpose. I think he figured I'd get up maybe 17,000 or 18,000. I don't know what his purpose was. But that could have been, to give me that experience.

Paul Stillwell: Do you have specific memories of Captain Halsey as commandant of the station?[†]

Captain McCampbell: No, no, I don't. Now let's take a blow. It's after 6:00 o'clock.

---

[*] The SNJ Texan was a training aircraft manufactured by North American Aviation. The Navy first ordered a version of the airplane in late 1936; the Army designation was AT-6. Versions of the Texan continued in use for Navy training well into the 1950s.
[†] Captain William F. Halsey Jr., USN, later a fleet commander in World War II and five-star admiral.

Interview Number 2 with Captain David McCampbell, U.S. Navy (Retired)
Place: Captain McCampbell's home in Lake Worth, Florida
Date: Wednesday, 15 July 1987

Paul Stillwell: Captain, when we left off the other day, we were talking about your time in flight training in Pensacola. I wonder what your recollections are of the city of Pensacola from that period. It's been called the mother-in-law of the Navy, among other things.

Captain McCampbell: I didn't get to go into town very often. The only thing I remember is the San Carlos Hotel, right down in the center of town. And there was a roadhouse—as we called them in those days; you'd call it a pub now—about halfway from the air station into town. I went there a few times, but not too often. I was married at the time, and I didn't have too much free time. We had dances—I believe it was every Friday night, or maybe it was Saturday night—and we always attended those down at the officers' club.

Paul Stillwell: Legend has it that naval aviators and particularly fighter pilots are a hard-working, hard-fighting, hard-playing crew.

Captain McCampbell: Hard-drinking, yes. That's pretty much true. Once in a while down at the officers' club, late in the evening, some of us would go skinny-dipping. It was right down on Escambia Bay. Those were about the only memories I had.

I had a fairly easy time. As I told you, I graduated with the first five. We got our wings together, and I kind of breezed through there, except for one period. I got two downs, which kept me there to get extra instruction over Christmas leave.[*] Well, I wouldn't have gone anywhere anyway. It was just, I think, six days. Being married, we wouldn't have left town, I'm sure.

---

[*] A "down" was an unsatisfactory grade given by an instructor pilot during a check flight.

Paul Stillwell: Those two downs were out of how many check flights, would you say, altogether?

Captain McCampbell: Oh, God, I must have had at least 20, probably more, but I don't remember. We had a check for each phase. There were five squadrons, and so we had two or three or four in each squadron.

Paul Stillwell: Do you remember what you got the downs for?

Captain McCampbell: One time I got a down before I even took off, because I couldn't get the tail wheel to lock, and you're supposed to get it locked before you take off. So we sat there, and me trying to get the tail wheel locked. I couldn't, so the instructor just said, "Well, take me back to the hangar." And the other one was when we were restricted on altitudes between certain places, and I got below a certain altitude.

Paul Stillwell: So neither one of them really had anything to do with your flying ability per se.

Captain McCampbell: No.

Paul Stillwell: I take it you had a great deal of confidence in your flying ability right from the beginning.

Captain McCampbell: Yes, I had confidence in myself. By the way, the son of one of the instructors that gave me a down works in Annapolis now.

Paul Stillwell: Who's that?

Captain McCampbell: Tuzo. Do you know him?

Paul Stillwell: Yes, he's with the Naval Academy Alumni Association.*

Captain McCampbell: The other one, I can't remember his name. I didn't have any trouble getting the permission to attend the flight training once I passed my physical. Of course, we had to take another one at Pensacola, and I passed that, no strain.

Paul Stillwell: Didn't you tell me that Captain Le Breton was trying to discourage you from going into aviation?

Captain McCampbell: Yes, he was. I've forgotten whether he put my request through or not. In fact, I don't know.

Paul Stillwell: I've heard some individuals say that senior officers were telling people who wanted to go into aviation that they were hurting their career chances by doing that. The seniors didn't think there was a future in it. That proved to be very poor advice, as it turned out.

Captain McCampbell: That's right. [Laughter]

Paul Stillwell: I see by the record that you got your wings on the 23rd of April 1938. Was there any special celebration connected with that?

Captain McCampbell: The five of us got our wings at the same time, and then we went over to the officers' club and whooped it up a little bit. Other than that, there was no celebration.

Paul Stillwell: Did you have any say in the orders that took you to the USS *Ranger*?†

---

* Commander Lamar W. Tuzo, USN (Ret.), was then a fund-raiser for the Alumni Association in Annapolis. His father, Lieutenant Paul B. Tuzo Jr., USN, was at Pensacola in the late 1930s.
† USS *Ranger* (CV-4) was commissioned 4 June 1934. She had a standard displacement of 14,575 tons, full load of 17,577, was 769 feet long, 80 feet in the beam, an extreme width of 110 feet on the flight deck, and had a draft of 22 feet. She had a top speed of 29 knots and could accommodate about 75 planes.

Captain McCampbell: No. I had requested a fighter squadron, and since I stood high in my class, they honored my request.

Paul Stillwell: That proved to be a very fortuitous assignment.

Captain McCampbell: Yes, it did.

Paul Stillwell: What do you remember about VF-4 once you got on board?

Captain McCampbell: When I got to Fighting Four in the *Ranger*, I was assigned as the wingman for Joe Clifton.* I flew wing on him for about a year, and I always tell people that I learned how to fly, really, by flying on Joe Clifton. He had a nervous tic; we'd be flying along, and I'd be on his wing, and he'd push on the dashboard, sometimes with two hands. You can imagine what the plane was doing! Anybody that could stay with a guy that had that kind of a tic had to be good. [Laughter]

Paul Stillwell: Is that why they called him Jumping Joe?

Captain McCampbell: I guess so. [Laughter]

Paul Stillwell: What plane were you flying in that squadron then?

Captain McCampbell: F3Fs.†

Paul Stillwell: How would you describe the performance of that aircraft?

Captain McCampbell: It was like the F4B-4, very maneuverable, good rate of climb. It was a good stunt plane, good gunnery platform, and we even did a lot of dive-bombing in

---

* Lieutenant (junior grade) Joseph C. Clifton, USN. He eventually became a rear admiral.
† Grumman F3F fighters first entered fleet squadrons in 1936. The F3F-3 was 23 feet, 2 inches long; wingspan of 32 feet; gross weight of 4,795 pounds; and top speed of 264 miles per hour. It was the last biplane fighter in any of the U.S. armed services.

those days. I think I was the only one in the squadron that got both the gunnery and bombing E's assigned to my plane.* In those days, you were assigned a plane, and you kept that all the time.

Paul Stillwell: So it sounds as if you were very good from the very beginning.

Captain McCampbell: Yes. They used to call me a hotshot, but I wasn't really that hot. [Laughter]

Paul Stillwell: Well, you'd had the basic training, of course, at Pensacola. How much more did it take once you got to the ship to make you a good fighter pilot?

Captain McCampbell: Well, it took a lot of training, and we had two very good skippers, Admiral Switzer and Admiral Morehouse. They made admiral later; they were lieutenant commanders then.†

We had the privilege of being in the Cleveland Air Races one year. I believe that was '37. We performed as a squadron. I remember we used to land and take off with the nine planes at the same time. The first division and second division would be nine planes each. We did a dive-bombing demonstration for them and a formation flying demonstration.

Paul Stillwell: Did you normally fly in three-plane sections at that time?

Captain McCampbell: Yes, three planes.

Paul Stillwell: What do you remember about the training in air-to-air tactics?

Captain McCampbell: There wasn't so much training in that department. We used to act as the aggressor against seaplanes, I remember, and we used to act in fleet operations as

---

* An "E," for excellence, was generally awarded to a ship or airplane as a result of top performance in competition during a given time period.
† Lieutenant Commander Wendell G. Switzer, USN; Lieutenant Commander Albert K. Morehouse, USN.

escort for the bombers and torpedo planes on a number of occasions. We used to train in dive-bombing; we dropped practice bombs on the *Utah*.[*] They were little bomb-like devices about a foot long.

Paul Stillwell: What were they made of?

Captain McCampbell: I guess they were lead and had little shotgun in it so it exploded when it hit the deck of the *Utah*. I guess you could call them smoke bombs.

Paul Stillwell: But at least you could see where they hit on the ship.

Captain McCampbell: Yes.

Paul Stillwell: Well, presumably when you escorted the bombers, you had to be prepared to meet enemy fighters.

Captain McCampbell: Right.

Paul Stillwell: Was there training in the tactics for that?

Captain McCampbell: No, not really. I certainly don't remember any, but, of course, in escorting the bombers, we'd often have aggressors, fighter planes, come in. We would attack them, but more or less individually.

Paul Stillwell: Had fighter tactics been covered back at Pensacola, such things as the altitude advantage, getting behind, and that sort of thing?

---

[*] USS *Utah* (BB-31) was commissioned as a battleship in August 1911. In 1931-32 she was converted to a mobile target ship. On 1 July 1931 her hull number changed to AG-16.

Captain McCampbell: I guess there was a little of that. It was kind of a natural thing. I don't remember anything specifically. Oh, we used to do a lot of camera-gun fighting within the squadron and inter-squadron.

Paul Stillwell: How did that work?

Captain McCampbell: Well, each plane had a little camera in it, and you would dogfight each other and take pictures. Then you'd come back to base and analyze who shot who down.

Paul Stillwell: I think the camera took a picture of a clock at the same time, didn't it, so that you could see the relative positions of both planes at the same time?

Captain McCampbell: Yes.

Paul Stillwell: And did you have umpires then to rule on who got whom?

Captain McCampbell: I guess we had umpires within the squadron, the gunnery officer usually. Inter-squadron, I don't remember who refereed that.

Paul Stillwell: So occasionally you might take on other ships' planes?

Captain McCampbell: Yes, other squadrons. Frequently. Every year we'd have an exercise to see who could beat who.

Paul Stillwell: What was your relative standing within the squadron on that kind of performance?

Captain McCampbell: Well, as I said, I was awarded an E for excellence in gunnery, which included the dog fighting.

Paul Stillwell: Did that mean you were the number-one fighter pilot in the squadron?

Captain McCampbell: No, I was one of the ones that got an E. They had a way of scoring it so they could tell who was eligible for the E and who wasn't.

Paul Stillwell: What was your role in relationship to Joe Clifton, as his wingman? Did he teach you some of the tricks of the trade?

Captain McCampbell: He taught me how not to fly. That's a little facetious, I guess, but I was glad to get my own division.

Paul Stillwell: How soon did that happen?

Captain McCampbell: The second year I was in the squadron, due to seniority.

Paul Stillwell: Was that completely a matter of seniority, or was demonstrated skill a factor also?

Captain McCampbell: A little of both.

Paul Stillwell: What characteristics do you remember of the two skippers you've mentioned, Switzer and Morehouse?

Captain McCampbell: Well, I think Lieutenant Commander Switzer was seen to be the better pilot. I guess he'd had more training or whatever, but I would say he was the better of the two. Morehouse was a little distant from squadron operations when he got there. Of course, he got acquainted real quick. He had trouble, I remember, particularly in dive-bombing. I happened to drive him home one day, and he asked me what I did to keep from blacking out when in dive-bombing. And I said, "Well, when I have a hard pullout, I'll tighten up the gut muscles so that blood won't flow out of the brain."

I did black out one time early in the squadron. We were attacking seaplanes, and one day I got a little too aggressive, I guess, and I pulled up after shooting him with a camera gun. Then I pulled up into a half of a loop, and I blacked out. I actually had a little dream in that period, and finally I pulled out into an Immelmann that got my blood back in my system, in my head.[*] But that was the only experience I've ever had of blacking out. You could do it, I know; if you tightened your stomach muscle, you could take a little more G.[†]

Paul Stillwell: Another future admiral in that squadron was Ned Hannegan.[‡] Do you remember him?

Captain McCampbell: Oh, yes. He was the gunnery officer when I first joined. I joined them out in the Pacific, out of San Diego, North Island, and we were based there about six months.[§] Then the *Ranger* came around to the East Coast, and we were based on the East Coast the rest of the time I was with them, for about a year and a half.

Paul Stillwell: Was this at Norfolk?

Captain McCampbell: Yes, in Norfolk.

Paul Stillwell: How did the operations differ between the two fleets? What was the purpose in sending her around?

Captain McCampbell: It was political. There'd been some complaints about the fleet, most of it from the West Coast, so the Navy decided, "To hell with 'em. We'll go around to the East Coast." So we got in on that. In those days, you changed the homeport from North Island to West Field, it was called there, out of Norfolk, just a small grass field.

---
[*] An Immelmann turn is one in which an airplane in flight first makes half a loop and then rolls over to make the second half.
[†] G refers to the force of gravity. In various aircraft maneuvers a pilot may be subjected to several G's.
[‡] Lieutenant Edward A. Hannegan, USN.
[§] North Island Naval Air Station is on the end of the Coronado peninsula, across the harbor from San Diego.

And in those days, you had to pay for your wife's transportation; the government didn't pay for it, even though it was a change of homeport. So I remember that as a young jaygee then, it was quite a burden expense-wise.*

Paul Stillwell: The new carriers of the *Yorktown* class were coming out. Were any of them in commission yet that you could operate with?

Captain McCampbell: No. I was transferred from the *Ranger* squadron to the *Wasp*, and it was just coming out. I was on it when they commissioned it in Boston, and I was on it when the Japs decommissioned it in the South Pacific, after about two and a half years.

Paul Stillwell: What else do you remember about the time in the *Ranger*? What about the skipper, for example?

Captain McCampbell: John Sidney McCain was the skipper.† I remember O. B. Hardison was the executive officer, and those are about the only people I can remember now.‡ We weren't aboard all the time, of course. We were shore-based about half the time, either on the West Coast or East Coast. It was a happy ship under John Sidney McCain.

Paul Stillwell: Any particular incidents you recall involving him?

Captain McCampbell: Yes, involved Joe Clifton. Joe was quite a polo nut, horse polo, and he had married a quite wealthy woman. She bought him a couple of polo ponies, or one at least. Every time he'd come back from a mission, when he came back to the ship, he would have his mech give him a blanket, and he'd go out and put the blanket over the engine on his plane. [Laughter]

Paul Stillwell: As if it were a horse?

---

* Jaygee—lieutenant (junior grade).
† Captain John S. McCain, USN, commanded the *Ranger* (CV-4) from 1937 to 1939.
‡ Commander Osborne B. Hardison, USN.

Captain McCampbell: Yes.

We spent quite a lot of time in Guantanamo, Cuba, always training, the ship training or the air group training.* I remember we cleaned up a field. I've forgotten the name; it didn't have a name when we first went in there. It was the *Ranger* air group. And we set up tents. I guess the tents belonged to the landing force; I don't remember where they got them. Well, at that time, we didn't live in the tents; we'd go back to the ship every night. We'd operate out of the field and go back to the ship, but we had tents for the operations officer, guards, and that sort of thing. We had to make a landing signal officer who went ashore in a boat, he and a crew. I don't remember how many, six or so, and they had to come over and comb the field for rocks, clean the rocks out of the field before we could land. Then after we landed, the landing signal officer brought us in where they'd cleaned out the rocks, and then the whole air group made a sweep of the field and cleaned the rocks off for the whole field.

Paul Stillwell: Why so much operation around Cuba—just because of the weather?

Captain McCampbell: Mainly, yes, the weather. That had been an operational base for many years now, still is. I spent a lot of time there. [Laughter] My first eight years in the Navy, I think I spent about two years down in Guantanamo, always attached to a ship. Later on, the *Wasp* spent a lot of time down there. But I think it was because of the weather primarily.

Paul Stillwell: Anything you remember specifically about the operations while you were in the Atlantic? Was it more of the same types of things you've described—the dive-bombing and escorting and dog fighting?

---

* Guantánamo Bay, on the south coast of Cuba, near the eastern end of the island, for many years provided a fleet anchorage and training area for U.S. Navy ships.

Captain McCampbell: Yes, that sort of thing. We had one nice trip to New York to open the world's fair up there.* I believe that was in 1939.

Paul Stillwell: I suspect that the sailors from the ships were very well welcomed by the people there in New York.

Captain McCampbell: Yes, yes, they were; they enjoyed that. We were there for about a week.

Paul Stillwell: McCain was a colorful character. I'm wondering what you remember about him as the skipper. How much involvement did you as a fighter pilot have with him?

Captain McCampbell: Well, I was low on the totem pole. I didn't really have any involvement with him. I met him, but just briefly once on the ship, and then the next time I saw him, he was Commander Fast Carrier Task Force, the fast carrier forces in the Pacific. He took over from Admiral Mitscher during World War II, and I met him again out there.†

Paul Stillwell: Another one of your shipmates in the *Ranger* was Les Gehres, who was later skipper of the *Franklin* when she was hit.‡ Anything you remember about him from the *Ranger*?

Captain McCampbell: No. I think he was assistant air officer then. Have you interviewed him?

---

* The New York World's Fair of 1939-40 was held in Flushing Meadows an area of the borough of Queens. It was the largest-ever world's fair. President Franklin D. Roosevelt gave the opening-day address on 30 April 1939. The fair closed on 27 October 1940, more than a year after the start of World War II.
† Vice Admiral Marc A. Mitscher, USN, served as Commander Task Force 58, the fast carrier task force, in 1944-45.
‡ Lieutenant Commander Leslie E. Gehres, USN. The carrier *Franklin* (CV-13) was hit by bombs near Japan on 19 March 1945, resulting in great damage and loss of life. After her fires were extinguished, she was able to return to the United States under her own power, though she never did go back into active service. Gehres was then a captain.

Paul Stillwell: No, I haven't. The air officer was Lieutenant Commander Kendall.[*] Anything about him that you recall?

Captain McCampbell: No.

Paul Stillwell: And the air group commander was Commander Seligman.

Captain McCampbell: Mort Seligman.[†] Yes, I remember. Have you interviewed him?

Paul Stillwell: No. He was the exec of the *Lexington* when she was sunk.[‡]

Captain McCampbell: Yes, he was. I think he got a black eye from that.[§]

Paul Stillwell: He did, yes.

Captain McCampbell: The only thing I remember about Mort was when he was air group commander, we were based in North Island. He came to one of our squadron parties, and he had a couple of drinks and sat down on a chair and passed out. But since, I've met his wife; I know her quite well. She still lives in Coronado there. And, as a matter of fact, my daughter married one of her sons, Mrs. Eleanor Ring. She was married to Mort, and they were divorced, and she married Admiral Ring.[**]

Paul Stillwell: A later skipper was Captain Wood, and the exec was Commander McFall.[††] Any recollections of either of those?

---

[*] Lieutenant Commander Henry S. Kendall, USN.
[†] Lieutenant Commander Morton T. Seligman, USN.
[‡] USS *Lexington* (CV-2) was sunk 8 May 1942 during the Battle of the Coral Sea.
[§] Seligman apparently passed information from decoded Japanese messages to reporter Stanley Johnston, whose article appeared shortly after the Battle of Midway. Seligman's career did not advance any farther after that. For details on the publication of the Japanese order of battle by *The Chicago Tribune* on 7 June 1942, see Grant Sanger, "Freedom of the Press or Treason?" *U.S. Naval Institute Proceedings*, September 1977, pages 96-97.
[**] Rear Admiral Stanhope Ring, USN.
[††] Commander Ralph F. Wood, USN; Commander Andrew C. McFall, USN.

Captain McCampbell: McFall, yes. I don't believe I met him. Andy McFall. He was the exec after O. B. Hardison.

Paul Stillwell: Right.

Captain McCampbell: Later he was Com Air Patrol Force Atlantic or something in Jacksonville. But I didn't meet him then. I ran into him in 1957 in Rome. I was checking in a hotel there for the night, and just as I was getting in the elevator, he came in to register, and although I didn't know him personally, I recognized him, and I went up and introduced myself to him. Andy McFall.

Paul Stillwell: Any specific memories of him from the ship?

Captain McCampbell: No.

Paul Stillwell: How about the navigator, Ernest Litch?*

Captain McCampbell: Ernie Litch; yes, I ran into Ernie Litch later. He was the chief of staff for the operational command here in Florida; he was in Jacksonville.† On the *Ranger* I never met him there. He was a navigator. But after the *Wasp* was sunk, I came back and conducted a landing signal officer school here in Melbourne, and Ernie Litch was chief of staff for the operational command. After being in the landing signal officer business for three and a half years, I got a little tired of it, and so I kept trying to get out. I appealed to the detail officer in Washington. He said, "No, we need you. The carriers are coming out faster than we can train people to man them," which was true. But I got caught there in the landing signal officer job, and I was basically a fighter pilot, I thought.

Oh, I went first to David McDonald.‡ He was on the staff as second assistant operations officer, but I got to know him a little. So I asked him if he could help me.

---

* Commander Ernest W. Litch, USN.
† Litch was then a captain.
‡ Commander David L. McDonald, USN. As a four-star admiral McDonald served as Chief of Naval Operations from 1963 to 1967.

And I remember his words. He said, "Dave, when I get out of this job, I'll help you get out of yours." [Laughter] Well, now, in connection with that, not quite a year later, when I joined the *Essex*, he was the executive officer.

Paul Stillwell: Both of you succeeded.

Captain McCampbell: [Laughter] Yes. But I got out of my landing signal officer job before he got out of his, through Ernie Litch. I went to him, told him I'd been in that job for three and a half years and I was real tired of it. His advice to me was, "Well, Dave, I'll tell you what you do. You go back and train two guys to take your place, and I'll tell the detail officer that you should be transferred, or request your transfer."

I said, "Captain, I've already got two volunteers trained to take my place." So he got on the phone right then and called the detail office, and within a month I was transferred. That was my contact with him. But I just found out the other day, he had the *Lexington* out there the same time I was out in combat in 1944.* I didn't get to see him out there, but I read this *Confessions of a Squadron Commander* by Hugh Winters.†

Paul Stillwell: Winters was her air group commander.

Captain McCampbell: Well, he inherited it from Karl Jung.‡ Jung crashed one day, and I heard it was when he took off of the ship. But according to Hugh Winters, it was later, as the result of antiaircraft fire.§ Anyway, after he crashed, he was no good any longer, so they kicked Hugh Winters up to command the air group. In the latter part of our air group's tour out there, Hugh Winters was the air group commander, the guy I dealt with.

Paul Stillwell: And you were on a number of joint strikes together.

Captain McCampbell: Yes.

---

* Captain Ernest W. Litch, USN, commanded USS *Lexington* (CV-16) from April 1944 to January 1945.
† T Hugh Winters, *Confessions of a Fighter Squadron Commander* (Mesa, Arizona: Champlin Fighter Museum Press, 1986).
‡ Commander Karl E. Jung, USN.
§ Commander T. Hugh Winters Jr., USN.

Paul Stillwell: Back on the *Ranger*, that was one of the smallest carriers. Did that pose any difficulties as far as takeoffs and landings?

Captain McCampbell: No, not really. Of course, the planes were a little slower in those days. I didn't have any trouble. The only trouble I had was when I was qualifying at night, I told you about it.

Paul Stillwell: Yes, but the tape recorder wasn't running then.

Captain McCampbell: We were qualifying. We went out by three-plane divisions, and this was our initial qualification. We came in, and I landed. No strain, except I landed a little bit long. Then I took off, and the number two-guy in my division came in and landed. He crashed, hit the barrier. Then it took some time to clear his plane out of the area. Then the number-three guy and myself were circling that time while they were cleaning up the flight deck, and then the number-three guy happened to be in the right spot. They took him aboard, and he crashed, and took more time to clean the flight deck up. I had to circle, waiting for the deck to get clear, and I'd raised my wheels and my tailhook. Then when I got the green light to come aboard, I came down. I put my wheels down and forgot to put my hook down. So I crashed into the barrier. So all three of us crashed that night. [Laughter] But they counted that as my second qualification landing. You were only required to make two, and I never had to do another qualification.

Paul Stillwell: I think you told me also that there was an enlisted man with the LSO that was supposed to shine a light on your tailhook, but he hadn't done it.

Captain McCampbell: That's right. They had the wheels-and-hook-down man, hook and wheels down. In fact, I just saw a tape called that, "Hook and Wheels Down." He was supposed to shine a light, to check on my wheels and tailhook, and he missed the tailhook, so the landing signal officer went ahead and landed me, gave me the cut.

Paul Stillwell: What does the sensation of running into that barrier feel like?

Captain McCampbell: Well, not too pleasant, because I hit the gunsight, which was sitting right up there in front of me, a big long tube, about like this, half of it inside the cockpit and the other half out.

Paul Stillwell: So it was about a foot and a half long, maybe?

Captain McCampbell: Yes, about that. I remember when I crashed in the barrier. It excited the flight deck officer, because when I crashed, I immediately pulled the fire extinguisher, and it makes a pretty loud noise and sends CO_2 all over the place. He thought I was blowing up. He told me that himself. I've forgotten his name; it slips my mind at the moment.

Paul Stillwell: I can see that you still have a scar on the bridge of your nose from that night's encounter.

Captain McCampbell: That's right. That's where I first got the scar.

Paul Stillwell: Did that happen in the F3F?

Captain McCampbell: F3F.

Paul Stillwell: Would that have been about the spring or summer of 1938?

Captain McCampbell: In the fall, before we moved from San Diego.

Paul Stillwell: Fairly soon after you reported aboard.

Captain McCampbell: Yes.

Paul Stillwell: How did the assignment to the *Wasp* come about?[*] Was that just filling up the new ship's company?

Captain McCampbell: No, not exactly. They had already chosen a landing signal officer and an assistant. The landing signal officer was Fred Reeder, and the assistant was Ed Konrad.[†] Fred Reeder decided he would retire, so that left the opening.[‡] Ed Konrad moved up to the landing signal officer, and they picked me out of Squadron Four for the assistant. So that's the story on that, over my objections. I didn't want the job. [Laughter]

Paul Stillwell: Did that mean you flew less frequently or not at all?

Captain McCampbell: Much less frequently. About all the flying I got in was flying to and from an outlying field, where we would conduct the field carrier landings.

Paul Stillwell: So you spent quite a bit of time working ashore with the air group before they went to the ship.

Captain McCampbell: Yes. But I didn't participate in any of their flight programs or anything, just flying back and forth from the field. I did that for three and a half years. I was very efficient and competent in the Taylor Cub.[§] That's what we used in Melbourne when I was running the landing signal officer school. Except the latter part of my tour there, I checked out in F4Fs, but I had done no gunnery or dive-bombing or anything in it.[**] For about a week there in Melbourne, I'd go out on gunnery flights, and I myself qualified in the F4F on landing signals on the field. When I went to take over Fighting

---

[*] USS *Wasp* (CV-7) was commissioned 25 April 1940. She had a standard displacement of 14,700 tons, was 741 feet long, 81 feet in the beam, and extreme width of 109 feet. She had a top speed of 29.5 knots and could accommodate approximately 80 aircraft.
[†] Lieutenant Frederick M. Reeder, USN; Lieutenant (junior grade) Edmond G. Konrad, USN.
[‡] Reeder went on to other duty; he did not retire until 1946.
[§] The Taylor Aircraft Company's Cub was a small light monoplane used for utility work. It was a forerunner of the famous Piper Cub. Melbourne, Florida, about 60 miles southeast of Orlando, was the site of a naval air station used from 1942 to 1946 for training naval aviators.
[**] Grumman F4F Wildcat fighters first entered fleet squadrons in late 1940. The F4F-4 was 28 feet, 9 inches long; wingspan of 38 feet; gross weight of 7,952 pounds; and top speed of 318 miles per hour.

15, I was all checked out also in the F6F, which we got just the latter part of my tour at Melbourne. In fact, one of my assistants and I flew up to Glenview, Illinois, to check the F6F out over the carrier up there.*

Paul Stillwell: The *Sable* and the *Wolverine* were up there.†

Captain McCampbell: Yes, right.*

Paul Stillwell: Did Konrad teach you how to be an LSO?

Captain McCampbell: Yes.

Paul Stillwell: What do you remember about him?

Captain McCampbell: Cleaned up? Ed was a nice guy. He was class of '32; he was a year ahead of me. The way you teach one landing signal officer is by watching another one, and there's not much except to learn the signals, which was no strain, and the rest of the training consists of watching another landing signal officer who's qualified.

Paul Stillwell: So it's really on-the-job training.

Captain McCampbell: On-the-job training. You might say completely.

Paul Stillwell: Did you have a radio to the pilots then, or was it strictly with the paddles?

Captain McCampbell: On the *Wasp* I don't recall having a radio to the pilots. We had an intercom system to everything else, the bridge, the air officer, and so forth, but I don't recall having a radio to the pilots.

---

* Glenview, Illinois, north of Chicago, was the site of a naval air station.
† USS *Sable* (IX-81) and USS *Wolverine* (IX-64) were former Great Lakes passenger steamers that were fitted with flight decks and commissioned in the Navy during World War II to provide landing platforms for pilots' carrier qualifications. Being inland protected them from enemy attacks. For details see Duane Ernest Miller, "Aircraft Carriers on Lake Michigan," *Naval History*, Winter 1988, pages 42-43.

Paul Stillwell: In addition to knowing the different planes in the air group, I would think you'd have to know the different pilots as well, because they'd have different characteristics.

Captain McCampbell: That's right. You've got to learn the pilots, and after each landing, you went to the ready room and debriefed them on what you saw, whether they were consistently too long in their landings or consistently too high or too fast, or whatever. That was after each landing, practically, until you got all of them pretty well trained.

Paul Stillwell: That's certainly one of the hardest things to do in carrier aviation, so you had an important responsibility there.

Captain McCampbell: Yes, but to go a little further, you had to learn to judge the speed of the plane and the attitude, which, of course, go together more or less. The idea is to come around in the full-stall attitude with the engine about three-quarters revved up, and this would go in daytime as well as nighttime. Nighttime, you had lights to indicate whether they were fast or too slow on the plane. And that's a question of judgment, which comes by training, and also to get to know the pilots personally.

Paul Stillwell: And they have to have a lot of confidence in you to be able to follow your directions.

Captain McCampbell: Yes. We even went so far on one occasion, we were in Bermuda, and one of the pilots either fell overboard from a launch, or else he jumped in, but we were trying to get him out of the water. He said, "Nobody can take me out of the water except the landing signal officer." [Laughter] I happened to be in the boat, so I pulled him out.

Paul Stillwell: Was the ship in port, or what had happened?

Captain McCampbell: Yes, we were in port in Hamilton, Bermuda, when we were doing the Neutrality Patrol in early 1941.*

Paul Stillwell: What do you remember about the Neutrality Patrol? That was sort of a euphemism for aiding the British, wasn't it?

Captain McCampbell: Yes. We had a lot of unusual experiences. We went out on one occasion to search for the *Bismarck*.† In those days, the President had declared a line in the Atlantic—I don't remember the longitude or latitude—which we were not to go beyond. This was before the war started. But we went out to the limit of that—you might say U.S. area—in search of the *Bismarck*. We didn't find it; she got sunk.

On another occasion, I believe that I was on the *Ranger* then, we went out to Barbados. There was a French cruiser in there, and we were to prevent it from getting out. We even loaded bombs and rockets and whatever, bullets, to attack her if she came out. She didn't, so we put our bombs away and went back home.

Paul Stillwell: In the LSO business, how much night flying were you doing in the *Wasp*?

Captain McCampbell: Aside from night qualifications, we actually did very little at night. On occasion, a plane would get caught out at night, and we'd have to bring him in. But operations generally were not night operations.

Paul Stillwell: With you and Konrad, did you split the time between the two of you? Is that how that worked?

---

* In the period from 1939 to 1941—when the United States was not yet an active combatant in World War II—the American republics maintained what was called a Neutrality Patrol of a zone in the Western Atlantic. Ostensibly neutral, it in fact aided Britain in its war against Germany.

† In May 1941, the German battleship *Bismarck*, accompanied by the cruiser *Prinz Eugen*, entered the Atlantic to operate as a surface raider. In a gun duel on 24 May against the British, she sank HMS *Hood* and damaged HMS *Prince of Wales*. The *Bismarck* herself was damaged on the 26th by British torpedo planes and sunk on the 27th by gunfire from the British battleships *Rodney* and *King George V*.

Captain McCampbell: Once I got trained, yes. Then we had an NAP, naval aviation pilot, aboard, Walter Gregg.* I remember his name. He was first the hook-and-wheels-down man for us, and then he said he'd be very interested in training for landing signal officer. So we trained him, and he became very good at it. I don't know if he was the only one, NAP, that became a landing signal officer or not. Of course, he was aboard to fly the J2F utility plane, and the OS2U we had was used.† That was his primary purpose.

Paul Stillwell: I would guess very few enlisted men qualified as LSOs.

Captain McCampbell: Very few. We did, on the *Essex*. We had a non-aviator that worked his way up through qualification and was the number-one landing signal officer.

Paul Stillwell: I never heard of that before.

Captain McCampbell: Yes. A good guy. I can never remember his name. He came from Boston. Barrett Tillman, do you know him?

Paul Stillwell: Yes.

Captain McCampbell: He's written a number of books. But he did an article for one of the periodicals on landing signal officers, and he mentions Gregg in that, and also the other guy from Boston. Iarrobino was the landing signal officer when my air group first went aboard the *Essex*, and he fleeted up and let this guy take charge.‡ He was very good.

Paul Stillwell: Was that a frustrating job for you in the *Wasp*, not being able to fly more?

---

* NAPs were enlisted men who had earned their wings as naval aviators. The category no longer exists; all U.S. Navy pilots are now commissioned officers.
† The Grumman J2F Duck was an amphibian utility plane with a center float. The J2F-5, powered by a propeller-driven engine, had a wingspan of 39 feet; length, 34 feet; gross weight of 6,711 pounds; top speed of 188 miles per hour. The Vought OS2U Kingfisher was the principal floatplane used by U.S. battleships and cruisers in World War II. It was 34 feet long, had a wingspan of 36 feet, gross weight of 6,000 pounds, and maximum speed of 164 miles an hour.
‡ Lieutenant Charles A. Iarrobino, USN.

Captain McCampbell: No, it wasn't. I didn't get much flying in, but it wasn't really frustrating once I got into it. We had Eddie Konrad. He left after my first year, and then I fleeted up to senior landing signal officer, and we trained Gregg, and then later I trained a guy named Savage, Doc Savage, who was a jaygee.[*]

Paul Stillwell: You mentioned that you were present for the commissioning of the *Wasp*. Was there the usual big ceremony connected with that?

Captain McCampbell: Yes, but I was not present.

Paul Stillwell: Oh, I see.

Captain McCampbell: That was in Massachusetts.[†] I was not present. I was in Norfolk then, but we had the air group. I was the landing signal officer assistant.

Paul Stillwell: How soon after commissioning did the air group report?

Captain McCampbell: Well, it was quite a considerable length of time, because the ship had to go out on the trials and that sort of thing, came back to the yard. It wasn't until, I would think, around late May or early June before the air group went aboard.

Paul Stillwell: Do you remember Commander Hall, the air group commander?

Captain McCampbell: Yes, G. B. H. Hall.[‡]

Paul Stillwell: What do you recall about him?

---

[*] Lieutenant (junior grade) George E. Savage, USNR.
[†] The carrier *Wasp* (CV-7) was commissioned 25 April 1940 at the Army Quartermaster Base, South Boston.
[‡] Lieutenant Commander Grover B. H. Hall, USN.

Captain McCampbell: Yes. [Laughter] He was a little on the stupid side. He was also a communication expert, and how he ever got to be where he was, I don't know. Kind of like Leigh Noyes.* He was also a communications expert. At any rate, G. B. H., I became quite friendly with him, and, as I say, a little on the stupid side.

Paul Stillwell: How did that manifest itself in the ship?

Captain McCampbell: Well, we shifted, I think, to the SB2U, and he, of course, was assigned one.† He would run around in the plane leading the air group, and he was either all high pitch or all low pitch. He didn't know it was adjustable propeller on the plane. [Laughter] The scouting squadron commander, Charlie Crawford, finally told him, "Commander, we have a hard time following you in the air group. You're running high pitch or low pitch all the time. When you want to cruise, why, you ought to put it about halfway or two-thirds or something."‡ So he finally got the news on that. But he hadn't been properly checked out in the plane, obviously.

Paul Stillwell: How was he as the leader of the air group?

Captain McCampbell: He's dead now, so I guess I can speak my peace. He was not popular; put it that way. Kind of a hard man to get along with—mainly, I think, because of his ignorance in aviation.

Paul Stillwell: Was he a latecomer to aviation?

Captain McCampbell: No. I don't think so. He must have taken his communications PG before he went into aviation, so he may have been a little late for his class.§ He later

---

* Rear Admiral Leigh Noyes, USN, was on board the *Wasp* when the ship was sunk in September 1942. He had served as Director of Naval Communications from September 1940 to June 1942.
† The Vought SB2U Vindicator was a monoplane scout-bomber that first entered fleet squadrons in late 1937. The SB2U-3 model had the following characteristics: length, 34 feet; wingspan, 42 feet; gross weight, 9,421 pounds; top speed, 243 miles per hour. The Vindicator was in limited combat service against the Japanese in 1942.
‡ Lieutenant Commander Charles W. Crawford, USN, commanding officer, Scouting 72.
§ PG – postgraduate education.

became admiral and at one time had the *Enterprise*.* I think it was the time when they shifted over to all-night air group in the Pacific under Willie Martin, air group commander.†

Paul Stillwell: I think that was Air Group 90.

Captain McCampbell: Yes, I think that's right. Have you interviewed Willie Martin yet?

Paul Stillwell: My predecessor did, Dr. Mason.

Captain McCampbell: Oh.

Paul Stillwell: You also had a tough skipper of the ship in Captain Reeves.‡ What do you recall about him?

Captain McCampbell: I recall so much about Black Jack Reeves, it would take me a week to tell you.

Paul Stillwell: Take some time, if not a week.

Captain McCampbell: Well, the things I remember most are on the funny side, the comic side. He used to call on me to get up a foursome to play badminton on the hangar deck. And I remember one day, we were playing—it was with B. J. Semmes and Doug Fuller and Black Jack and myself, and I was playing with Black Jack.§ He always chose me, for some reason. [Laughter] He was facing the bulkhead at the forward end, he and I, and he hit a bird over, and Doug Fuller called it out. And Black Jack exploded. He said, "Goddamn it, that wasn't out! It was in! It was on the line!"

---

* Captain Grover B. H. Hall, USN, commanded the aircraft carrier *Enterprise* (CV-6) from 14 December 1944 to 25 September 1945.
† In the last year of World War II, Commander William I. Martin, USN, commanded Night Air Group 90 on board the USS *Enterprise*. It was the Navy's first carrier air group specialized for night operations.
‡ Captain John W. Reeves Jr., USN, commanded the aircraft carrier *Wasp* (CV-7) from 25 April 1940 to 31 May 1942.
§ Lieutenant (junior grade) Benedict J. Semmes Jr., USN; Lieutenant (junior grade) Harold D. Fuller, USN.

Doug Fuller said, "No, sir, it was out." And with that, the captain slung his racquet up against the bulkhead. [Laughter] He broke it all to pieces, and stomped off the court. He never played after that, and he got in a rage over that one point, but I shifted and got Frank Turner, B. J. Semmes's partner.* Then we continued playing, and we didn't have Doug Fuller in there anymore. Doug Fuller's still kicking. He's now president of the class of '34.†

Paul Stillwell: Same class Semmes is from.

Captain McCampbell: Yes, B. J. Semmes is still kicking, too.‡ Frank Turner, he's passed on, and Black Jack has passed on.§

Paul Stillwell: What else do you remember about Reeves? Did he specifically deal with you as LSO?

Captain McCampbell: Well, one instance he did, yes. He wanted to qualify on the ship in the worst way. He was one of your "latecomers," you know; he was originally a battleship admiral.

Paul Stillwell: I think he was a commander before he went to Pensacola.

Captain McCampbell: I think so, yes. So he came on the scene very late in aviation, but he was given command of the *Wasp*, and wanted to qualify landing aboard. He asked me one day if I'd take him on the field, qualify him on the field. I said, "Sure, Captain, I'll be delighted." The ship was then up in Boston Navy Yard. So I went over to NAS Squantum, and he appeared in the F3F.** We discussed what you do beforehand, about making the turn around, making the U and coming in. So he came around. The first time he was way too high and too fast, and I kept giving the "too high and fast" signals, too

---

* Lieutenant Commander Frank Turner, USN, was commanding officer of Scouting 72 (VS-72).
† Fuller, who retired as a captain, died not long after this interview with McCampbell.
‡ Semmes, a retired vice admiral, died 4 June 1994.
§ Turner, a retired rear admiral, died 26 January 1978. Reeves, retired four-star admiral, died 15 July 1967.
** Naval Air Station Squantum, Massachusetts, was on a peninsula in Boston Harbor.

high and fast, and nothing happened. So I gave him a wave-off, and he went around again. This went on for at least three times, and I'd have to wave him off. Finally, he got a little of the news, and he came in a little bit lower, and I think his speed was about the same, though. So I cut him way back, gave him the "cut" signal. He came in, touched his wheels, and took off again real quick, and I never saw him again. [Laughter] So that was the end of that exercise. He never did qualify in landing aboard.

The other amusing incident, we were up in Scapa Flow, and he wanted to play softball.* He thought of himself as a great athlete. He'd often leave the ship to play tennis. He'd pick somebody to play tennis ashore. This time he wanted to play softball, so we worked up the team in the wardroom, and we were playing the chiefs, chief petty officers. And Gus Lentz, I remember, a great big, about 6-feet-6 ex-all-American football player, was the umpire.† I believe Black Jack was playing shortstop, and the first time he came up to bat, and Gus Lentz, the umpire, called him out on strikes. Now, we had brought ashore about 12 cases of beer. It was supposed to be a beer party and softball game. But Black Jack said, "Goddamn it, that wasn't a strike!" He threw his bat down and said, "All right, fellows, we're all going back to the ship!" So we took the 12 cases of beer back to the ship, and that was the end of the softball game. In fact, that was the end of the season. We never got together again.

Paul Stillwell: Sounds like a man who hated to lose.

Captain McCampbell: Yes. [Laughter] Oh, Gus Lentz, the umpire, had a horrible cauliflower ear, and I remember I was on the bridge the day he reported to the captain for the first time. Gus Lentz was a big, tall guy, and Black Jack, I guess, was 5-8 or 5-9, and when Gus reported to him, Black Jack couldn't take his eyes off of that cauliflower ear. [Laughter] Gus suffered through it, but Black Jack used to call him "the mythologist," instead of the aerologist. Gus, the poor guy, died when the ship was sunk; he got caught

---

* Scapa Flow was the main base of the British Home Fleet in World War II. Located in the Orkney Islands, north of mainland Scotland, it provided easy access to the Atlantic and command of the North Sea. The *Wasp* operated with the British Fleet in April-May 1942.
† Lieutenant Commander August W. Lentz, USN.

down below deck in his cabin, I guess, and was just off of the wardroom, aft of it.* He must have been standing up, because, as I heard the story from the doctor—his cabin was right across the little passageway—he suffered two broken legs, which indicated he was standing up when the torpedoes hit almost directly under him. And the rumor was that the doctor had given him a couple of shots, morphine probably, and left him there when the ship went down. That was rumor now. I asked the doctor about that on the way home as survivors, and he neither agreed nor denied. So I don't know.

Paul Stillwell: The fact that Reeves would give him that kind of nickname indicates that Reeves had some sense of humor.

Captain McCampbell: Yes. [Laughter] And then another incident on the bridge. Mike Kernodle, who'd fleeted up to air officer, came on the bridge one day.† I don't remember what the argument was or the contention. But it ended up pretty quick. Black Jack said, "You ugly son of a bitch, get off of this bridge and don't ever come back!"

Mike Kernodle responded, "Well, if you think I'm ugly, Captain, you ought to see my wife!" End of conversation. He walked off the bridge, and I know for a fact he didn't go again on that bridge for at least three months, till just before he was relieved.

Paul Stillwell: You told me when the tape wasn't running that that was an accurate description of his wife.

Captain McCampbell: Yes, that's right. [Laughter] And he was pretty mean in that sense of the word. There was another instance when the new navigator came aboard. Wolf Wolf Smith was the first navigator, and then we had the new one come aboard, Dashing Don Smith.‡ He'd recently been the skipper of Floyd Bennett Field on Long Island, and he had grown himself a senatorial bob.§ When Black Jack saw that, hardly a word was spoken till he said, "Commander Smith, you go down and get a haircut and

---

* The *Wasp* was torpedoed and sunk on 15 December 1942, as McCampbell describes later in the interview.
† Commander Michael H. Kernodle, USN.
‡ Commander Walton W. Smith, USN.
§ Commander Donald F. Smith, USN.

then report back to me." So Don Smith scurried down the ladders and got a haircut. He came back up, and all he'd gotten was a trim. [Laughter] He still had this long bob of hair. Black Jack said, "Damn you, Smith. I thought I told you to get a haircut!"

So Don Smith went back down the ladders and got a closer cut, and then came back and reported to the captain. He was kind of mean in that respect.

Paul Stillwell: Others have told me he was also very demanding on professional-type things. Did you see that in the demands he made on the performance of the air group and ship's company?

Captain McCampbell: No, it didn't filter down.

Paul Stillwell: Certainly he believed in a taut ship.

Captain McCampbell: Oh, yes. We had muster and inspection every morning, except Sunday. I believe the time was 8:00 o'clock in the morning, every day, muster and inspection. Of course, the working crew—like engineers, whatever—they had to go down afterwards and change to dungarees. That didn't bother him. That went on for as long as he was aboard, unless it was a very unusual circumstance. Like when we took planes to Malta, he didn't require it. There were other occasions when he didn't call muster and inspection, but the average day he called it, every day. He'd go down and inspect a division or something.

Paul Stillwell: How was the morale in the ship with a skipper like that?

Captain McCampbell: It got pretty low at times. Got pretty low. Although there were enough comical things that happened that kind of kept morale up a little bit.

Paul Stillwell: Do you recall any others?

Captain McCampbell: Offhand, I can't think of any of it. Oh, yes, I can too. He had machine gun racks installed on the wings of the bridge—one machine gun, but he had an installation on both wings. One day, for some reason, I don't know why, he had the machine gun on the rack, and it was pointed down to the flight deck, and it went off. [Laughter] Oh, it was kind of comical in the sense that Wallace Beakley, the air group commander, one day came aboard, and he had forgotten to turn off the gun switches.* He landed and started spraying the bow, the flight deck, the front end of the flight deck. But I think Black Jack had the first encounter with that.

We had one other occasion where a gun got loose down on the hangar deck, sprayed a few. We didn't lose any people either time.

Paul Stillwell: Was Reeves himself connected with this machine gun on the bridge?

Captain McCampbell: Oh, yes, it was put there specifically for his purpose.

Paul Stillwell: But it fired accidentally.

Captain McCampbell: Yes. Some reason, I don't know why. Maybe it was when he was putting it in the rack.

Paul Stillwell: So he couldn't be too hard on Beakley as a result.

Captain McCampbell: That's right. And then I think they had one other instance on the flight deck, Lieutenant Monk Russell, and I know his came after Beakley's.† You haven't interviewed Monk, have you?

Paul Stillwell: No.

---

* Lieutenant Commander Wallace M. Beakley, USN.
† Lieutenant Hawley Russell, USN.

Captain McCampbell: He's quite a character. He's, last I heard, in Paris. I can't offhand think of any other—I do believe that if Black Jack Reeves had been aboard when we were hit with the torpedoes, that he would not have evacuated the ship. He would have stuck with it.

Paul Stillwell: The consensus of people that I've talked to is that even though he was demanding, he was the kind of skipper they'd want to go to war with.

Captain McCampbell: Yes. Right. Yes, he was tough. Oh, after the incident at Squantum, where I tried to qualify him on the field, he never imposed on me at all—never ever. Everything I did on my landing signal officer platform, he was right behind me. So, really, I never had any trouble with the guy, but I saw a lot of these comical incidents.

Paul Stillwell: What do you remember of Commander Sallada as exec?

Captain McCampbell: Oh, yes, Slats Sallada.[*] Is he still kicking?

Paul Stillwell: No, he's not. He's dead now.

Captain McCampbell: Yes, I remember him, but I really never had anything to do with him.

Paul Stillwell: He wouldn't need to be a tough guy with a captain like that.

Captain McCampbell: No. [Laughter] In fact, I would think he was kind of a counterbalance probably.

Paul Stillwell: Right.

---

[*] Commander Harold B. Sallada, USN.

Captain McCampbell: But we got Fearless Fred Dickey after him, after Sallada.*

Paul Stillwell: Any recollections of him?

Captain McCampbell: Yes, he was a good guy. He used to spend most of his time up in what we called the ready service room. I kind of felt like I owned it, because in between landing and waving planes off, I spent most of my intervals in the ready service room.

Paul Stillwell: Was that near the fantail?

Captain McCampbell: No, no, that was right in the superstructure, but on the flight deck level.

Paul Stillwell: I see.

Captain McCampbell: Fearless Fred and the senior surgeon used to spend most of their time up in my ready service room. We had a coffee urn, and they could get a drink of coffee. Somebody made the remark that when the ship got hit, that the exec and the senior surgeon couldn't get out the door fast enough, and knocked each other out, but I don't believe that. It was kind of an anomaly of their always being up topside. Both of their duty stations, of course, were way down below.

Paul Stillwell: Of course, the surgeon doesn't have anything to do until somebody gets hurts, so he can, I guess, pretty much go where he wants.

Captain McCampbell: Yes, right.

Paul Stillwell: How would you compare Beakley with Hall as air group commander?

---

* Commander Fred C. Dickey, USN.

Captain McCampbell: I would say Beakley was a better air group commander all the way around. After the ship got hit, I remember I tried to stay clear of him, because he wanted me to come back with the air group, and I could just see myself being landing signal officer for another year. I was anyway, as it turned out, almost a year, but I didn't know it at the time, so I refused to come back on the ship with him and the air group. The ship's company came on another ship.

On the *Wasp* it got to be where I held down three jobs on there, kind of like on the *Portland*. Three guys were flight deck officers, and they begged out of the job, because their feet couldn't take it. The first one was Dutch Close, class of '32, and then Skinny Innis, class of '32, and then a warrant officer took over the flight deck.[*] All three of them begged out on account of their feet couldn't take it. So that elevated me to flight deck officer, so I had the flight deck division, the V-2 division, my landing signal officer job. As flight deck officer, I'd wave them off. My third job was repair four on the flight deck. So I was holding down three jobs when the ship was hit. I was kind of glad to see it get hit [laughter] and get sunk. Or I'd have never gotten out of those as long as—oh, maybe some day I would have, but I was holding them.

Paul Stillwell: It says something for your ability that you would be given all that responsibility and be able to carry it off.

Captain McCampbell: Well, I didn't feel that way about it at all.

Paul Stillwell: You felt sort of beleaguered, probably.

Captain McCampbell: Yes. [Laughter] I felt I was being picked upon. A fall guy, in other words.

Paul Stillwell: How could that come about? If somebody begged out, why wouldn't the ship get another man to take his place?

---

[*] Lieutenant Burdette E. Close, USN; Lieutenant Walter D. Innis, USN.

Captain McCampbell: Well, all the men were placed. I don't know where they'd have gotten another man, unless they got a new one aboard, but this was kind of all that accumulated, kind of between being in the States and not. We were gone an awful lot of the time during the neutrality patrol, and then we operated out of Portland for about three months on the convoy work, and then we were sent right over to Scapa Flow to operate with the British Home Fleet. So we were gone an awful lot.

Paul Stillwell: Your boss, I presume, was the air officer. Commander Cassady later became a vice admiral.[*] What do you remember of him?

Captain McCampbell: Well, he didn't last too long. Neither did Sallada. He and Sallada left about the same time. Mike Kernodle took Cassady's place. By the way, Cassaday's passed on, and I saw him about a week before in the hospital down here at Bethesda.[†] He looked awful. I don't know what his problem was; I don't know if it was booze, cigarettes. I remember he was quite a smoker. Whether it was his heart or just what.

Paul Stillwell: What do you recall about Kernodle as air officer?

Captain McCampbell: Well . . .

Paul Stillwell: Aside from not going on the bridge.

Captain McCampbell: [Laughter] Kernodle wasn't a bad guy. I only flew him one time; it was up at Scapa Flow. We flew over to Hatston Airfield in a J2F.[‡] They lowered it by crane from the ship, put it in the water, and . . .

Paul Stillwell: That was an amphibian, wasn't it?

---

[*] Commander John H. Cassaday, USN.
[†] Cassaday, a retired four-star admiral, died 25 January 1969.
[‡] Royal Naval Air Station Hatston was on the island of Mainland Orkney, near the naval base at Scapa Flow.

Captain McCampbell: Yes, Grumman. He cranked it up for me and then got back in the rear seat, and I flew him over to the field there to Hatston. That was about the only connection I had with him, actually. He had an assistant air officer that I dealt with directly most of the time.

Paul Stillwell: Who was that?

Captain McCampbell: Jack Shea.* He was killed when the *Wasp* was sunk.

Paul Stillwell: I guess if you were doing your job well, he didn't have too much reason to interfere.

Captain McCampbell: Right.

Paul Stillwell: You mentioned the convoy work. What was it like operating a carrier and an air group in the North Atlantic?

Captain McCampbell: Horrible! It was cold as hell, and even when the temperature was like zero or maybe a little lower, it was still cold because of the winds. I got myself an electrically heated suit to work out on that flight deck. Being from Florida, I guess my blood was kind of thin. But I had the full suit and boots, all electrically heated.

Paul Stillwell: Did it have a wire that ran to it?

Captain McCampbell: I had a plug-in at my landing signal officer station.

Paul Stillwell: My goodness.

Captain McCampbell: I operated with that thing on, and even then, I'd get cold, mainly the feet.

---

* Lieutenant Commander John J. Shea, USN.

Paul Stillwell: I would think that the ship pitching would make it more difficult, too, to get the aircraft aboard.

Captain McCampbell: We had some rough weather, but not too much in the North Atlantic. Mostly we had to deal with fog.

Paul Stillwell: I would think that was a big problem, yes.

Captain McCampbell: Yes, that was the worst thing.

Paul Stillwell: How did you cope with that?

Captain McCampbell: Well, I remember we were headed east once with a convoy, and we had a battleship with us, and a guy named Admiral Wilcox.[*]

Paul Stillwell: He was in the *Washington*.

Captain McCampbell: Yes. Fell overboard or something, got washed overboard, I guess. He himself had told the skipper of the *Washington* to keep all people off the topside. I don't know how much later, but a little later, he was lost. So we sent up two planes that day, the scouting squadron commander, Frank Turner, and a wingman, to search for the body. They searched around for an hour or so, and then the fog started closing in. We recalled the planes. On the way in to a landing, Frank Turner, of course, was leading, and I was signaling to him, and I saw his wingman was hanging pretty close in there. I figured when Frank landed, why, the wingman would pull out and shove off. Well, he did, but he had to go around the stack. [Laughter] He didn't know that Frank was landing. I guess that was the problem. Anyway, he took off, started around. We never

---

[*] Rear Admiral John W. Wilcox, Jr., USN, Commander Battleship Division Six, was lost overboard from his flagship, the USS *Washington* (BB-56), on 26 March 1942, while she was en route to the British Isles. The circumstances of his death were never satisfactorily explained. See Winston Jordan, "Man Overboard," *U.S. Naval Institute Proceedings*, December 1988.

saw him again. Apparently, he had gotten in the fog, and what happened to him, we don't know, but we lost him. So I remember that incident. That was convoy.

Paul Stillwell: There's some speculation that Admiral Wilcox jumped over the side.

Captain McCampbell: Yes. Rumor.

We went into Reykjavik. We took each convoy as far as Iceland, and then the British would pick them up.* We went to Reykjavik one night, and I remember I had the 4:00 to 8:00 watch, and I went on deck to relieve Monk Russell. He was the officer of the deck. While he was turning over the job to me, the information that he had, where we were, what was anchored in the area, where we were anchored, the various checkpoints to check whether or not we were dragging anchor or not. And just about then, some ship passed us close aboard, and it was going about five or six knots. It turned out to be one of the hospital ships that was dragging anchor, and he passed us. I said, "Monk, I can't relieve you in a condition like this. You'd better call the captain, get him up here, and let him make the big decision." So he did, and the captain came up in his pajamas and saw what was happening. Of course, he had them check our anchor, make sure it wasn't dragging, take bearings again, make sure we were in the right spot and so forth. But finally, I relieved Monk about, I guess, 45 minutes later.

Paul Stillwell: That's quite a current to move a ship along at five or six knots.

Captain McCampbell: He was going like a bat out of hell. We were standing still, of course.

Paul Stillwell: Right. Well, that was still another job you had, then, as officer of the deck.

Captain McCampbell: Oh, yes. Always in port I took my turn as officer of the deck.

---

* The *Wasp* was involved in convoy escort operations in 1941, during the period when the United States was still officially neutral. Her operations with the British Home Fleet were in 1942.

Paul Stillwell: Did you ever take it under way?

Captain McCampbell: Not the *Wasp*, no. I got my underway training on the old *Portland*.

Paul Stillwell: Had you stood deck watches in the *Ranger* at all?

Captain McCampbell: No. Oh, *Ranger*—we had boat watches. Every liberty boat would carry an aviator as a boat officer. I caught that a number of times.

Paul Stillwell: Why an aviator?

Captain McCampbell: [Laughter] To give them something to do, I guess.

Paul Stillwell: I see. Presumably, you would need some antisubmarine capability on these convoys. How good were the planes on the *Wasp* at that?

Captain McCampbell: Well, the only incident I remember—one of the antisubmarine planes took off in Casco Bay, up in Portland, Maine, and lost its depth charge as it took off. We'd just gotten under way and were making the first launch. I just saw in the paper here a year or so ago where they had recovered a depth charge up at the entrance to Casco Bay. That may have been the one we dropped.

We did antisubmarine patrols all the time, but our planes never sighted one.

Paul Stillwell: Captain, I wonder what you recall about the operations of the *Wasp* with the British Fleet.

Captain McCampbell: Well, we did some training out of Scapa Flow, but not very much. Mainly it was to go out and exercise our pilots for takeoffs and landings, and I don't know what they did in the air. There was no activity. About the only thing I remember about Scapa Flow was the softball game. The fact that the Germans used to fly a reconnaissance plane over every day, of course, checking the number of ships that were in the Scapa Flow Harbor. Other than that, we went out two or three times or more.

Then we were assigned the job of taking Spitfires to Malta.[*] We sailed into Glasgow, Scotland, picked up on the first trip 47 Spits, and took them on down around the southern coast of England and then through the Strait of Gibraltar, and into the Med. We'd go about halfway in from Gibraltar to Malta, and then launch the Spitfires. Before we left, of course, we took all our planes off except 20 fighters. We kept 20 of our own fighters aboard. Then we'd launch the Spitfires, then turn around and quickly exit the Med. The first time we got all the Spitfires into Malta, but then they got in right into the middle of a German attack, and they had action in the air before they even landed, some of them. Then when they landed, about half of those were wiped out by the German bombing attacks. The Germans decided to knock out Malta about that time. There were no other fighters on the field when the first 49 went in.

The second trip, we came out, went back to Scapa Flow, and then we got orders to take another load of Spitfires to Malta. We got the same routine, and we got 50 of those Spits ashore. There was one of them lost his belly tank on takeoff, and we lowered the barrier. Our fighters were in the air; all the planes were off the ship. We lowered the barrier and gave this pilot all the wind that we could, and then we gave him the option of landing in the water and being picked up by a destroyer or landing back aboard. He chose to land back aboard. Of course, we knew he didn't have a hook, but somebody up the line was confident enough that he could get back aboard, so I was asked my advice.[†] I said, "Yeah, I'll take him if you want to take him aboard."

Fortunately, I'd given them a little talk the first day they were aboard, to acquaint them with our operational procedures primarily. And I did mention during the course of the talk, "If you see me jumping into that net alongside my landing signal officer platform when a plane's coming in, you know there's something wrong." In that case the pilot is supposed to take off and go around and come in again. So, sure enough, this guy

---

[*] In April and May 1942 the *Wasp* delivered Royal Air Force fighter planes from Britain to the Mediterranean, then launched them to beef up the defenses of Malta. The planes had an instrumental role in protecting the island. British Prime Minister Winston Churchill sent the ship a message: "Many thanks to you all for the timely help. Who said a *Wasp* couldn't sting twice?"

[†] The land-based Spitfires did not have tailhooks of the type attached to carrier planes. The Tailhook was used to grab a cross-deck arresting wire at the stern of the carrier and bring the plane to a stop.

had lost his belly tank, so he couldn't get to Malta from the ship, and he couldn't get back to Gibraltar or any Allied-owned territory. The Germans controlled all of North Africa at that point, or at least as far east as Malta. He couldn't get into Southern France, so that was the reason we chose to land him back aboard.

The first time, of course, he was high and fast, which is natural for one not accustomed to landing aboard a ship. He wouldn't answer my "too high and too fast" signals, so I jumped in the net. Then he got the news real fast, and he pulled up and went around again. So he came in on the second attempt, and he was still high and fast, but he wasn't as high or as fast as he had been previously, on the first approach. So I just decided to outguess him, and I cut him about 500 feet from the after end of the flight deck, though usually I'd give the pilots a cut about 50 feet or 100 feet back. But he took the cut, and then he landed, but he held off until he'd gotten about halfway up the flight deck. Then he applied his hand brake, which is not a very strong brake, specially designed so that novices flying a plane couldn't nose it over and damage the prop. So he applied his hand brake and went on up to the bow. At that point, I didn't think he was going to make it, but he did. He stopped just short of the forward end of the flight deck.

I rushed up to congratulate him, rather facetiously, on the fine landing. When he got out of the plane, I asked him his name, because I didn't know the British pilots. He said he was a sergeant; they called them sergeant/pilots. I took my hat off and gave it to him, and I said, "By the way, Sergeant Smith, you must have a lot of time in the Spitfire to pull this off, because it's, to my knowledge, never been done before."[*]

He said, no, he had 127 hours. Then another question. I said, "Well, you must have had a lot of time in the Spitfire."

He said, no, he'd never flown one before. So to do what he did was most unusual in many ways, lack of flying experience and lack of flying in that particular plane.

Paul Stillwell: And no carrier experience.

---

[*] Pilot Officer Jerrold Alpine "Jerry" Smith, Royal Canadian Air Force.

Captain McCampbell: And no carrier experience whatsoever. He'd never seen a landing before that trip. So that night in the wardroom, we gave him a pair of Navy wings and pinned them on him.

Paul Stillwell: How close would you say he got to the forward end of the flight deck before he stopped?

Captain McCampbell: Just 6 feet. I measured it off. It was about two and a half steps, 6 feet from the end of the flight deck.

Paul Stillwell: And presumably, if he hadn't stopped then, he would have rolled on over the forward end, into the ocean.

Captain McCampbell: Right. Right. He did have it lined up on the centerline, but he was, of course, high and fast. I didn't realize that their brake was just a hand brake either, so all those circumstances taken together, why, it was a most unusual feat. The *Eagle* was with us on that second trip, a small British carrier. I had three letters from Britishers who were on that carrier that saw the whole operation, and all three said they thought he'd choose to land in the water. They didn't think that the *Wasp* would take him aboard.

Paul Stillwell: Did he then get a new belly tank and go on to Malta?

Captain McCampbell: No, he went to Gibraltar when we passed through the straits. The Britishers sent out three Swordfish to pick him up; they had a couple of mechs plus the pilot, Smith, and flew them back into Gibraltar.[*] Some way they got Smith down to Malta, and he was killed later.[†]

Paul Stillwell: So you dropped him off on your way out again, is that right?

---

[*] The Fairey Swordfish was a torpedo bomber used by the Fleet Air Arm of the Royal Air Force during World War II.
[†] Smith was lost on 10 August 1942 while chasing a German Ju 88 toward Sicily.

Captain McCampbell: Yes, as we went out of the Mediterranean, after we'd launched and taken him aboard. The Britishers sent out the three Swordfish to pick him up.

Paul Stillwell: How much hazard was there to the *Wasp* herself during those operations in the Mediterranean?

Captain McCampbell: Well, we thought it was quite hazardous both trips, particularly after we'd been in there once, and then two weeks or so later, we made a second trip. But we didn't have any contact with the Germans, either by air or submarine.

Paul Stillwell: One of your shipmates for a brief time there in the *Wasp* was Douglas Fairbanks Jr.[*] Do you have memories of that?

Captain McCampbell: Yes, but I didn't have anything to do with him, except I knew he was aboard. I saw him two or three times. He was an aide to Admiral Hall at the time.[†] That was on the second trip.

Paul Stillwell: Did any members of the British Royal family come aboard to inspect the ship?

Captain McCampbell: No. I remember Douglas Fairbanks Jr., got a Legion of Merit for that trip he made in there, in which he did nothing to deserve it. I saw that in the paper here not too long ago.

Paul Stillwell: Did the rest of ship's company get medals for the operation?

Captain McCampbell: No one. Maybe the captain did, I don't know. But we did get a commendation straight from Churchill, and the message said, "Who said a *Wasp* can't

---

[*] Douglas Fairbanks Jr., a movie actor, served as a Naval Reserve officer during World War II. See his memoir *A Hell of a War* (New York: St. Martin's, 1993).
[†] Rear Admiral John L. Hall Jr., USN, was on board as a liaison officer from Commander U.S. Naval Forces Europe.

sting twice?" Well, he had it a little mixed up; it's the hornet that can't sting twice. The wasp can sting you innumerable times. But it was a congratulatory message. He didn't say what the operation was, but just "Who said a *Wasp* can't sting twice?"

Paul Stillwell: What do you remember about the collision with the destroyer *Stack*?[*]

Captain McCampbell: I don't remember too much about that, except the command duty officer sounded the fire alarm, because the smoke coming from the destroyer *Stack* was coming back and hitting the bridge. I got up, of course, with the fire alarm. I know we searched for three or four hours and made many attempts to contact the destroyer on the bullhorn, with no favorable results. We found out later that the *Stack* had taken off and gone up the Delaware River to Philadelphia Navy Yard for overhaul or to be repaired.

Paul Stillwell: Do you have any other memories of the *Wasp* from your time in the Atlantic?

Captain McCampbell: We had a few delightful days in Bermuda.[†] We were operating in and out of Bermuda on the neutrality patrol, and we'd go out for two weeks and then come in for one week, out for two more weeks and back for a week. We were in Bermuda, anchored there in either Grassy Bay or in Hamilton, enough for the crew, and particularly the officers, to make a few friends there in Hamilton. The British operated a censors' bureau, at which they had 300 or 400 people in that censor bureau, and censored some letters back and forth from the United States to Great Britain and vice versa. That's about all I remember.

Paul Stillwell: That was quite a contrast with Iceland and Scotland.

Captain McCampbell: Yes, that's right.

---

[*] The destroyer *Stack* (DD-406) collided with the aircraft carrier *Wasp* (CV-7) at 0550 on the morning of 17 March 1942. The ships were part of a task group steaming from Casco Bay, Maine, to Norfolk, Virginia. For firsthand accounts, see the Naval Institute oral histories of Vice Admiral Thomas R. Weschler, USN (Ret.), and Admiral Harold E. Shear, USN (Ret.).
[†] The ship went to Bermuda several times in 1941, prior to the onset of war in December of that year.

Paul Stillwell: Any special memories of the trip around to the Pacific, going through the Panama Canal and so forth?

Captain McCampbell: When we came from Scotland, we came direct to Norfolk, and we only had about three days there to pick up supplies, about three days in Norfolk, and around through the canal, and up to San Diego.*

Paul Stillwell: Previously, when carriers had gone through the canal, there had been subterfuges employed to try to prevent enemy agents from knowing which ship it was. Was anything of that sort done?

Captain McCampbell: Yes. We painted over the *Wasp* on the stern of the ship and painted "Stinger" on there, so it would confuse the Japanese or Germans or whoever happened to see it going through the canal. In fact, the Stinger is the name of our reunion group.

Paul Stillwell: What happened once you got to North Island at San Diego?

Captain McCampbell: We had about four days, three or four days there. The staff there at North Island came out and briefed our people.† They briefed the air group, I know. I took two days or three days off and went to Los Angeles to see my parents, and I wasn't there for the briefings, but I understood later that Jimmy Flatley was the one that came out to brief the air group, the fighter squadron.‡ I don't know who else came out.

Paul Stillwell: Certainly you'd be going into a different type of operations in the Pacific and needed some update.

---

* The *Wasp* departed Norfolk on 6 June 1942 in company with the battleship *North Carolina* (BB-55), cruisers *Quincy* (CA-39) and *San Juan* (CL-54), and six destroyers. The *Wasp* went through the Panama Canal on 10 June and arrived at San Diego on the 19th.
† North Island Naval Air Station is on the end of the Coronado peninsula, across the harbor from San Diego.
‡ Lieutenant Commander James H. Flatley Jr., USN, had been executive officer of Fighting Squadron 42 during the Battle of the Coral Sea in May 1942. He was a noted fighter tactician.

Captain McCampbell: Yes. And we caught up on the latest tactics they were conducting in the Pacific, like dive-bombing.

Except for the briefings we got there at North Island, we went from San Diego direct to the Guadalcanal area, to join up out there.* We took a convoy with us, the first Marines that were to go ashore at Guadalcanal. We launched them, as I recall, to Efate, and then they went up from Efate to Guadalcanal.

Paul Stillwell: And you got a new skipper in the process, too, in Captain Sherman.

Captain McCampbell: Yes. Captain Sherman came aboard before we left Norfolk.†

Paul Stillwell: Did you have much chance to observe him personally?

Captain McCampbell: No, I had no contact with him until I met him later, when the ship was sunk.

Paul Stillwell: The captain sets the tone for the ship. Could you notice any change in morale or atmosphere?

Captain McCampbell: No, not really. He was supposed to be a pretty good guy, and he came with a good reputation, anyway, Forrest Sherman. But I had no contact directly with him.

Paul Stillwell: When did Admiral Noyes come aboard?

Captain McCampbell: Admiral Noyes came aboard in Norfolk too.

** The ship stopped for a few days en route, arriving on 18 July at Tongatabu in the Tonga Islands. She supported the Marine Corps invasion of Guadalcanal in the Solomon Islands on 7 August.
† Captain Forrest P. Sherman, USN, commanded the *Wasp* from 31 May 1942 to 15 September 1942, the date she was sunk.

Paul Stillwell: Well, even though tactics and so forth might be different in the Pacific, your job as LSO would remain the same.

Captain McCampbell: Yes, that's right.

Paul Stillwell: Did you work the air group a fair amount on that long trip out to the South Pacific?

Captain McCampbell: We did some flying, but not too much, actually. Oh, we had some engineering problems or a problem. We must have picked up a bent propeller shaft operating out of Bermuda. I know we did run aground there once. We weren't fast aground, but we hit a reef or something going out. I remember our condensers were full of coral, and we had to flush those. It must have bent the shaft, because we had to stop in Tongatabu, an island out in the middle of the Pacific. I don't know where we got a new shaft, but somehow they fixed the problem.[*] The Pacific Service Force came aboard, and they fixed whatever the problem was. I understood it was a bent shaft. Then we went on out to Guadalcanal to join up with the task force out there.

Paul Stillwell: Some of those early carriers had the capability to take planes coming in on the bow in addition to the stern. Did you do that while you were LSO?

Captain McCampbell: Yes, we did. We did at one time. I remember you were supposed to take your wave-off to the right if you were landing over the bow, instead of to the left, which they routinely did, if you were landing on the stern.

Paul Stillwell: So would the circle be in the other direction too?

Captain McCampbell: Yes, you would take off to the right, do a right-hand turn, come in, instead of a left-hand circle. I remember Ernie Snowden was one of our scout-bomber

---

[*] The ship's official history reported the problem as a defect in a high-pressure steam turbine.

pilots.* He came in, and got a wave-off, and took off to the left as he routinely did when landing over the stern. He did about a quarter spin, but he only went down about 100 feet, and then he pulled out and made it. But it was the only incident we had landing.

Paul Stillwell: I gather that was strictly an emergency-type maneuver that you were practicing.

Captain McCampbell: Yes, and we never had to do it actually; just test them out.

Paul Stillwell: That time you were off Guadalcanal, of course, the four cruisers got sunk in one night.† What do you remember about that aboard ship?

Captain McCampbell: Well, I don't remember anything. We didn't know anything about it. I don't remember whether that was before we were sunk or not.

Paul Stillwell: Yes, it was in August, and you were sunk in September.

Captain McCampbell: Right. But we didn't learn of that, to my knowledge.

Paul Stillwell: Admiral Weschler said that there was some concern on board the *Wasp* that she wasn't closer and giving more support during that period.‡ I wonder if that filtered down through the ship.

Captain McCampbell: Well, I never heard that complaint. I really don't know. I remember some comment that some of the support ships, if not all, that were in protecting the transports and the cargo ships that had gotten into Guadalcanal, they were all pulled out for a day or two, something like that. I don't remember. No, we didn't

---

* Lieutenant Commander Ernest M. Snowden, USN, of Scouting Squadron 72.
† On the night of 8-9 August 1942, between Guadalcanal and nearby Savo Island, a Japanese surface force surprised Allied forces and sank four cruisers, the USS *Astoria* (CA-34), USS *Quincy* (CA-39), USS *Vincennes* (CA-44), and HMAS *Canberra*.
‡ Ensign Thomas R. Weschler, USNR, was in the crew of the *Wasp* then as an officer of the deck. He eventually retired as a vice admiral. His Naval Institute oral history contains considerable detail on his service in the *Wasp*.

know too much about the operations at Guadalcanal other than what we learned from our pilots that flew over there.

Paul Stillwell: What do you remember about that month or so of operations before the *Wasp* was sunk? Certainly it was a lot different from the North Atlantic.

Captain McCampbell: Yes, it was. [Laughter] The waters were good, calm; the weather was good, warm. But nothing very unusual aboard ship, anyway. Mostly our pilots had some activity over Guadalcanal and Florida Island. But I just don't remember too much about it. I remember one day a four-engine Jap patrol plane flew directly over the ship, and B. J. Semmes and his gunners missed him, didn't shoot, didn't even man the guns, as far as I know. And he just clearly came right on top of the ship at not too high altitude, maybe 1,000 or 1,500 feet. One of the fighter pilots shot down a four-engine bomber a day or two after that. Our fighters didn't run into any air opposition over Guadalcanal and Florida Island, around there. I don't think, to my knowledge, except for that four-engine patrol plane, we didn't shoot down a single plane.

Paul Stillwell: Now that your ship was finally in combat, did you find yourself wishing you could get up in the air as well?

Captain McCampbell: Well, I always had that desire, even when we weren't in combat. But I remained aboard as a ship's officer. We can, I think, go right into the sinking of the *Wasp*.*

Paul Stillwell: All right. What do you recall of that day, when, as you put it, you were with her until she was decommissioned?

Captain McCampbell: I had been down in my cabin taking a little nap, which I occasionally did in the daytime after I got the planes launched. Until they returned, why,

---

* The *Wasp* was torpedoed and sunk by the Japanese submarine *I-19* on 15 September 1942. For details, see Ben W. Flee, "Whodunnit?" *U.S. Naval Institute Proceedings*, July 1982, pages 42-49.

I had a chance to lie down a little. Because I was getting a little tired in those days. I just had come out of my cabin, which was on the deck above the hangar deck, and climbed up a little ladder to the flight deck, and was crossing the flight deck when the first torpedo hit. I at first thought it was a bomb attack. I had the chief arresting gear officer with me, and he wanted to show me where one of the arresting wires was badly frayed, and he thought it should be changed. But before we got to that, the torpedo hit. Then both he and I scrambled to get under the flight deck, because we thought it was a bombing attack. Then I peeked up and looked to see where the bomb hit, and I didn't see anything. But at that time, I guess, the second torpedo hit or the third, and the number-two elevator was blown up about 10 feet in the air, because the torpedo hit right under the mid-deck elevator, number two.

Then after I saw that, then I started aft on the flight deck, and I remember the ship was vibrating. The vibrations ran to the bow and then back to the stern, and it went back and forth. During one of these vibrations, it knocked me to the flight deck.

Paul Stillwell: When you said you got under the flight deck, did you go into a catwalk?

Captain McCampbell: Yes, just under the overhang.

Paul Stillwell: I see.

Captain McCampbell: On the catwalk. So I worked my way back to landing signals aft, which was my abandon-ship station. The first torpedoes hit about 2:20 in the afternoon, as I remember, and then I never heard the captain—well, the loudspeakers were out. Even the sound-powered telephones were out. The regular telephones, of course, were out. So I had no communication with the bridge or the air officer at that point. But the captain decided to abandon ship, and I believe it was about 40 minutes later, after we were first hit, as I recall. But when I saw people going over the fantail, even though I had heard no "abandon ship" on the loudspeaker or no one passed the word back to me—the captain didn't use the bugler, who was up on the bridge. He could have abandoned ship over the bugle, but he didn't use the bugle. But I saw people going over the stern voluntarily, off of the fantail, so most of my flight deck crew had gathered around our abandon-ship station.

I remember one guy in particular, Downs Wright, who was an aviator, had come back there, and he and I lowered one of these big—oh, I think it was an 18-man life raft that was hanging from the overhang of the stern of the ship.* We lowered that, and as we were lowering it, he saw we were coming to the bitter end of his rope, and he turned the damn thing loose, and I was jerked up into the pulley, up as high as wherever it was, up here. I was jerked off my feet. Of course, I finally got rid of it. The thing fell into the water, and I don't know if it hit anybody or not.

Paul Stillwell: How far did it fall, would you say?

Captain McCampbell: I guess the line, really, was about 6 or 8 feet too short. Anyway, we got rid of it. I went back up to the landing signal officer platform, and we had put lines over all along the side of the ship, and I directed people. I told them they could either go down below to the hangar deck and go over the side, or they could go down the lines. Some of them took to the lines.

I remember watching some that were right there. We had a line down from the landing signal officer platform, and they'd go over from there, and then the guy would get tired down here, and he'd stop, and the next guy would come down on him, and bounce off him into the water. [Laughter] This happened two or three different occasions.

Paul Stillwell: These are the guys that are going hand-over-hand down the line.

Captain McCampbell: Yes. Then I got most of my people either over the side or directed down to the hangar deck. Anyway, none were lost, which I was very proud of. Then I decided it was time for me to go over the side, so I took my shoes off, and I took my shirt off. I kept my pants on, because I had always planned to do a lay-out one-and-a-half with a full twist.

---

* Lieutenant (junior grade) Spencer D. Wright, USN, Scouting Squadron 71.

Paul Stillwell: Do it with style, huh?

Captain McCampbell: Being an ex-champion diver, you see. But when the time came, I stood up on the loudspeaker that we had back there, a box about that long and about that wide, round on top, and I stood up there and contemplated, and decided I wasn't going to dive. There was too much debris in the water, and people, and I decided to jump. So I held my nose with one hand and my family jewels with the other, and I jumped. By now, I figured later—I didn't think of it then—the flight deck was normally about 45 feet above water, depending on how heavily loaded we are with fuel and planes and whatnot. But now the ship was listing to starboard, and later I figured out that the flight deck must have been up about 56 or 58 feet. But, anyway, it was quite a shock. I remember going down, I had time to think about whether all my insurance was paid up and that sort of thing. And then when I hit the water, I must have gone down a good 18-20 feet in the water. I made a perfect jump shot. But I scrambled back up and got on top. When I jumped, the ship was steady; it wasn't turning. I started out swimming away from the ship. There were a lot of explosions going on aboard, and I wanted to get out of that. I found the ship was drifting down on me faster than I could swim to get away from it.

Paul Stillwell: So you were downwind of it.

Captain McCampbell: Yes, downwind. And also, by then, the wind had blown the gasoline fire on the water around to the port side of the ship. I decided to swim back to the ship, and part of the way, I swung on the lines we had over the side, and part of the way I swam. But I got around the ship, around the stern, to the starboard side, and I ran on to three guys on a makeshift life raft. We'd thrown lumber over the side, and they had taken their belts and put it together. Fitzpatrick was one; Elmo Runyan was another.[*] I don't remember who the third one was. I remember Elmo Runyon, who was a chief machinist's mate, aviator, warrant officer. He kept trying to scramble on top of the little raft. Of course, it just turned over with him, but he persisted, and I said, "Well, enough of this." I had gotten over the side with my emergency rations. They were well wrapped.

---

[*] Chief Machinist Elmo D. Runyan, USN.

I don't remember exactly, but I think I had a couple of boxes of K rations.* So I saw a water beaker floating by, and I swam out and got that, and brought that back to the raft, and decided that my best bet was to give them the water beaker and the emergency rations. I struck out for a destroyer, which had come to within 300 or 400 yards away.

I forgot to mention that I didn't have a life jacket I when I went over. Normally, in the South Pacific, in the combat area, we were all required to wear these kapok life jackets, but it was really hot, was most uncomfortable. That morning I'd seen the executive officer. I saw that he was not wearing a kapok jacket up in the ready service room. He had on a little life belt that had one CO_2 bottle in it, and was supposed to sustain you. I said, "Commander, is that life belt you have on legal instead of the kapok jacket?"

At this Fearless Fred Dickey said, "Well, I'm wearing it." Actually, it was against the law.

I said, "Well, I have one." So I sent my messenger down and got mine from in my cabin. So I discarded the kapok and put this little life belt on.

Well, back on the abandon-ship station, there was some guy didn't have a kapok or belt, so I took my life belt off and gave it to him, and I went over to one of the fighters that was still sitting on deck, wheels all busted and everything. I knew they had little life rafts that they'd sit on, about that square. So I went over and got myself one of the life rafts. Of course, I didn't inflate it before I hit the water, but after I was in the water, I had to scramble to get this little life raft from some other guy who saw it when it hit the water. Well, I got it, and then I started feeling around for the toggle to inflate it, and I found the toggle all right, and I pulled it, but nothing happened. So later I found out that the fighter pilots found they were too hard to sit on, so they'd taken the CO_2 bottles out of these life rafts. So there I was with a deflated life raft. Well, I quickly gave that up, and that's when I started swimming.

I left the little makeshift life raft that I had stopped on, and I started swimming for the destroyer. But before I got to the destroyer, it had taken off. But I did get to one of the large life rafts that were full of people. I remember Ensign Hipp was sitting in the

---

* The K ration was a U.S. Army field ration used in World War II. A day's ration contained three small cardboard boxes, each enough for one meal.

middle of this thing with a paddle, and people were trying to climb aboard to get inside of it, and he'd beat them off.* But the people were two and three deep all around that raft, and I was number three in my spot. So I said, "Well, this is no good either." So the big life raft had attached to it, it looked like a four-man rubber life raft, and one guy was laying up on it, on his back, and he had a big flap of scalp. And every time the water would wash up there, why, it would flick it. I recognized him. He was a warrant gunner's mate, but I had known him back when I was in the outfit on the *Portland*. I'll think of his name in a minute.

But, anyway, I left my position on the life raft and started swimming for another destroyer that came within the area. En route, I ran onto the captain, Sherman, and he was lying up on one of the mattresses that we had thrown over the side. In fact, I know where it came from. The Marines had the only floatable mattresses, water-repellent, let's say. It'd float for a while. But he was lying up there taking a nice sunbath, so I rested with him for a while.

Paul Stillwell: What kind of mood was he in?

Captain McCampbell: Then another destroyer came by, and I left the captain and his mattress and took off after this destroyer. It was the *Farenholt*, I later found out. En route, I ran into the little motor whaleboat they'd put over the side, and they picked me up. In all, I was in the water about three and a half hours. It was getting almost dark. In the little motor whaleboat that picked me up, the admiral was standing in the stern sheets, and he had on his overseas cap, a flight shirt, leather flight jacket, and long under drawers, which down in that hot climate he didn't need at all.

Paul Stillwell: This was Admiral Noyes?

Captain McCampbell: Yes. Anyway, I directed him to where the captain was lying up on this mattress out there, so we scooted over and picked him up, and then returned to the destroyer *Farenholt*. I remember later I went into the shower. I was covered with oil,

---

* Ensign Jacob E. Hipp, USNR.

and I went and showered down, and then they gave me some kerosene to get the oil off my body. Of course, being a very hairy character, that oil was pretty sticky. I had a hell of a time getting off what I did. It was still in my ears a month or so later.

Anyway, as I walked out of the shower room and went on deck, I saw this guy I'd run on to on the rubber raft, which was tied up to the big raft.

Paul Stillwell: The warrant gunner.

Captain McCampbell: Yes. He was still on the raft. The raft was alongside the destroyer, and nobody was doing anything to get him aboard the destroyer. I had no clothes on at that time, so I just dove over the side and then hollered for them to send me down a stretcher. I either called for one before I went over the side or when I got in the water, one or the other. Then the chief engineer of the destroyer took his clothes off, and he dove over. Between the two of us, we got him into the stretcher. He fell out of it once. We needed a holding line in the center of the stretcher to keep it from tipping. We had one line on each end. The warrant gunner fell off of the stretcher into the water. He went down 2 or 3 feet, I guess, and the chief engineer and I got him up, finally got him into the raft, and we asked for a small line, a holding line, I guess you'd call it. They took him aboard.

Then the executive officer was an old friend of mine. A. G. Beckmann was his name.[*] He was a big fat guy. I'd say he weighed 280, 285, 290 pounds. He offered me his in-port cabin. He had another sea cabin up topside. I guess he did. I didn't know execs rated a sea cabin.

Paul Stillwell: I didn't either.

Captain McCampbell: But the skipper does, so maybe they'd play a hot bunk arrangement; I don't know. Anyway, he gave me a pair of shorts that I could wrap around me almost twice. He gave me a pair of jodhpurs that I'm sure were too tight for him, because they weren't badly worn, but they were too tight for me also. And he gave

---

[*] Lieutenant Alcorn G. Beckmann, USN.

me $10.00 so I could go down and buy me a pair of pants and a shirt in the small stores they had there.

Then we were transferred to the cruiser *Helena*, which went into Espiritu Santo and discarded the wounded there. I remember one guy was very badly wounded, Ensign Mitchell, who had been blown up from the 5-inch gun mount, and ended up draped over the railing to the wing of the bridge.[*] Courtney Shands got him off of there and took him below, but he was badly wounded.[†] He was one of the people who got off at Espiritu Santo. Then the *Helena* went on in and took us to Noumea, New Caledonia. And then we transferred from the *Helena* to the troopship that was to bring us back to the States.

Paul Stillwell: And that's where you deliberately got separated from Commander Beakley.

Captain McCampbell: Right.

Paul Stillwell: Did that warrant gunner survive, the one that you brought on board?

Captain McCampbell: Oh, no. I forgot to tell you. Of the wounded that were brought aboard the *Farenholt*, 11 of them died during the night. I don't know about the other ships. The biggest rescue destroyer turned out to be the *Duncan*. They had about 900 people on there. We had around 400 on the *Farenholt*. They had so many on the *Duncan* that they had to send a lot of them below to sit in the corner or wherever and not move from there during the night.

Paul Stillwell: Just for stability.

Captain McCampbell: Stability of the ship.

Paul Stillwell: And the captain, I guess, asked you to preside over the burial service.

---

[*] Ensign John J. Mitchell, USN.
[†] Lieutenant Commander Courtney Shands, USN, was the commanding officer of Fighter Squadron 72.

Captain McCampbell: Yes. The next morning, word came down that the captain wanted me to do the burial ceremony, and I begged out of it, and somebody else did it. But that's about all that happened.

Paul Stillwell: You mentioned that because of the list, it was a longer jump down into the water than if the ship had been level. Why did you go off the high side instead of the low side?

Captain McCampbell: I wasn't thinking very clearly. [Laughter] At 45 feet, I'd never dived that high or jumped that high, but I figured that I could do it okay. I guess, too, I perhaps was trying to get some of the other people to go over the side, either dive or jump.

Paul Stillwell: Just by example, to show that it could be done?

Captain McCampbell: Yes. But most of the people there at my abandon-ship station had already disappeared; they'd gone below or gone down a line.

Paul Stillwell: What sort of mood or mental frame of mind did Captain Sherman seem to be in when you encountered him?

Captain McCampbell: He was very calm, cool, and collected. As I say, he acted like he was just out for a sunbath. Although he was on the *Farenholt* with me. I didn't see him again after that.

Paul Stillwell: Were you still around when the *Wasp* was finally sunk with the friendly torpedoes?

Captain McCampbell: Yes, yes. The *Farenholt* participated in that. It was finally sunk about 9:00 that night. They had a hard time sinking the thing.

Paul Stillwell: Yes. I think the *Lansdowne* was in on that also.

Captain McCampbell: Yes.

Paul Stillwell: What is the sense of emotion you feel, seeing your ship go down?

Captain McCampbell: Well, I had so many senses or feelings then that it didn't bother me terribly much. I figured that there were some aboard, some wounded, that were not evacuated. That's about the only thing I thought.

There was only one guy in the whole outfit, the crew and officers and everything, that didn't get his feet wet. That was the ship's service officer. He was a lieutenant in the reserves and called to active duty, and a Naval Academy graduate in 1922. But in all that time, he'd never learned to swim, and he wasn't about to get in that water. He tried to lower both lifeboats, I'm told, and we only carried lifeboats out there, and he couldn't get either one of them down. So he lowered the gangway, and he went down the gangway and got to the bottom and stood there until a little motorboat cruised around the ship to pick up survivors, and they picked him up off the gangway. [Laughter] Lieutenant Millett was his name, ship's service officer.*

Paul Stillwell: Did you get compensated for the personal effects you lost in the sinking?

Captain McCampbell: Yes, I put in a claim, as I recall, around $1,450, and I got about $1,200. I had everything aboard. I even had my full-dress uniform, my tails. Willis W. Bradley on the *Portland* required all of us to get frocks, so I had my frock coat also. I had a boat coat, which was a cape, and I had a couple of small Oriental rugs. I had my watch in my safe, I lost some money in the safe. I've forgotten now how much money, a nice amount. In the time we had had out of port, you couldn't spend it, except for gedunks, and I didn't subscribe to that too much.† But all my uniforms, golf clubs. So I had just about everything I owned.

---

* Lieutenant Charles R. Millett, USNR.
† Gedunk is a Navy slang term for candy, ice cream, and sodas—snack-type food.

Paul Stillwell: Then you went back on the transport. Had you gotten a set of uniforms down in Noumea?

Captain McCampbell: No. All we had was just underwear, shirts, pants, socks, and shoes, except I had these jodhpurs on. As survivors, we went back to the Hotel Del Coronado, and we stayed there until we settled up our accounts, got our pay and accounts of claims of lost uniforms and so forth.*

I remember the first night we were there at the Del Coronado, about five of us wanted to go out for dinner. Of course, we didn't have any transportation, so we decided to go there in the hotel. So we got to the door, and the man on the door there said, "You're not dressed. You can't go in here." The dining room.

I said, "Look, for chrissakes, this is all the clothes we've got. We're survivors." And they finally let us in.

No, I didn't have any other uniforms, just the one shirt and pair of pants, socks, till we got back to Norfolk. My wife was still in Norfolk.

Paul Stillwell: When did you get your assignment for a new duty station after that?

Captain McCampbell: Well, I had 30 days' leave, survivor leave, and then I was assigned to the operational training command there in Jacksonville. They further assigned to me— I first went out to Cecil Field, which was one of the outlying fields there in Jacksonville. I operated over there for two or three weeks. Ed Konrad then, the ex-landing signal officer, had command of the fighter training at Cecil Field. By the way, he's still kicking. He lives over at Sanibel, on the west coast.† I saw him over there three or four years ago.

Then from Cecil Field, I went to Fort Lauderdale for a couple of weeks. By then they had established NAS Melbourne, so then I went direct to Melbourne.

Paul Stillwell: The aviation training was just growing very rapidly at that point. I guess they were opening a lot of new fields and needed experienced people for the instructors.

---

* The hotel is in Coronado, California, near San Diego.
† Konrad, who retired as a rear admiral, died on 5 March 1997.

Captain McCampbell: Right.

Paul Stillwell: Did you teach flying at all, or was it strictly the LSO business?

Captain McCampbell: Strictly LSO. All the time at Melbourne, I had four or five or six people there, teaching them how to be landing signal officers. So I let them do most of the work, and I'd supervise every day.

Paul Stillwell: Were there any changes or refinements in the technique of that as the war went on?

Captain McCampbell: Not to my knowledge. I know there have been many changes since, but I know the technique system was the same when I went aboard the *Essex*.

Paul Stillwell: There were a number of these escort carriers coming in at that time. Did that require any difference in technique?

Captain McCampbell: No, not as far as landing signal officer was concerned. Well, not as far as the pilots were concerned. I qualified my whole fighter squadron on a jeep carrier in the Chesapeake Bay.[*]

Paul Stillwell: You still tried to get in the middle of the deck.

Captain McCampbell: Yes.

Paul Stillwell: Was that essentially just a repetitive-type operation, not too challenging, there at Melbourne?

Captain McCampbell: Yes, definitely.

---

[*] "Jeep" carriers was the nickname for the escort carriers, CVEs, which were considerably smaller than the large attack-type aircraft carriers.

Paul Stillwell: And you've already expressed your conversations in an attempt to get back out to the combat theater.

Captain McCampbell: Yes.

Paul Stillwell: When did that finally come about that you "escaped"?

Captain McCampbell: I commissioned and later trained Fighting 15 in Atlantic City.[*] My orders read to be there the first of August, and we started out with about 11 or 12 pilots and, as I remember, eight enlisted men, which is all we ever had. The others had gone to the CASU system then.[†] The members of the CASU, who would maintain our planes, were all ground-based. There were six or eight people; that included a couple of surface officers, one administrator, and one intelligence. So anyway, that's what we started out with. Eventually we filled out to 45 pilots, with 36 planes.

Paul Stillwell: That's a big squadron.

Captain McCampbell: Well, we didn't go into combat with all of the 45; we had to eliminate down to 40. We had to eliminate five of those people.

Paul Stillwell: How many experienced officers did you have in that number?

Captain McCampbell: I had two. One was a jaygee, and the other was an ensign.

Paul Stillwell: Who was your exec?

Captain McCampbell: The exec was Jimmy Rigg.[‡]

Paul Stillwell: He's the man who eventually commanded the squadron.

---

[*] Naval Air Station, Atlantic City, New Jersey.
[†] CASU – Carrier Aircraft Service Unit.
[‡] Lieutenant Commander James F. Rigg, USN.

Captain McCampbell: Yes.

Paul Stillwell: And how much experience did he have?

Captain McCampbell: No combat experience. I got him off of the *Wolverine*, up in the Great Lakes.* I got three or four officers out of operational training that I had known at Melbourne, to help fill out the squadron.

Paul Stillwell: Was there any set training syllabus for a fighting squadron, or did you pretty much just develop that yourself?

Captain McCampbell: Well, I trained them in what I had been trained in, primarily—gunnery and formation flying, night flying, that type of thing. For anything beyond that, why, we kind of made up as we went along, like tactics, dive-bombing, we did. Although I went to call on the skipper, Miles Browning, who was over in Newport News, still in the shipyard with the new *Hornet*.[†] He told me he didn't want me to train my fighters to do any dive-bombing. But I knew they were being used for that out in the Pacific to a certain extent, so I went ahead anyway, and we did a brief training in dive-bombing.

Paul Stillwell: Did you have F6Fs from the very beginning of the training?[‡]

Captain McCampbell: Yes.

Paul Stillwell: That was a help.

---

* USS *Sable* (IX-81) and USS *Wolverine* (IX-64) were former Great Lakes passenger steamers that were fitted with flight decks and commissioned in the Navy during World War II to provide landing platforms for pilots' carrier qualifications. Being inland protected them from enemy attacks. For details see Duane Ernest Miller, "Aircraft Carriers on Lake Michigan," *Naval History*, Winter 1988, pages 42-43.

† USS *Hornet* (CV-12) was commissioned 29 November 1943 after being built at Newport News Shipbuilding and Dry Dock Company, Newport News, Virginia. Captain Miles R. Browning, USN, was the first commanding officer.

‡ Grumman F6F Hellcat fighters first entered fleet squadrons in early 1943. The most commonly employed version of the airplane was the F6F-5, which was 34 feet long, wingspan of 43 feet, gross weight of 15,413 pounds, and top speed of 380 miles per hour.

Captain McCampbell: Oh, yes.

Paul Stillwell: You presumably had to learn the plane yourself, because it was new to the whole fleet at that point.

Captain McCampbell: Right. But I had checked out an F6 at Melbourne, before I left there, and, as I told you, I think, one of my assistants, a landing signal officer, and I flew Hellcats up to Glenview, and we checked out in the Hellcat on the carriers.* We had both the *Wolverine* and the *Sable*.

Paul Stillwell: Of course, your tactics depend in part on the capabilities of the plane, and the Hellcat surpassed anything the Navy had had previously.

Captain McCampbell: Yes, and it was an easy plane to learn to fly, easy to land, particularly. It was not like the Wildcat, which some people found very difficult to land, until I taught them better. That was when you were landing, stay off of the brakes, because if you applied, say, the starboard brake in landing, the plane would tip over to the starboard, and subject you to a possible ground loop, which many of them did. But if you stayed off your brakes, you had plenty of directional control through your rudder.

Paul Stillwell: I presume you had checked out in the F4F at some point, so you could land it aboard the *Wasp*.

Captain McCampbell: Yes, but, of course, landing on the *Wasp*—or on any ship—didn't make too much difference, because you'd hook a wire, see, which would straighten you out. But on land, they had to stay off the brakes. I found that way back in the primary training, SNJs, they were teaching people how to use the brakes. Well, it's all right to learn how to use them, but don't use them except in an emergency if you're landing.

---

* Glenview, Illinois, in the northern suburbs of Chicago, was the site of a naval air station.

Paul Stillwell: How well trained would you say these men were by the time they got to your squadron?

Captain McCampbell: Well, they'd all been through operational training, except the exec, Jimmy Rigg. The others had all gone through the training command. Some had been instructors. I got three lieutenants and one jaygee that had been instructors. There may have been others; I don't remember.

Paul Stillwell: Did you have to do any weeding out, or was this a good group to work with?

Captain McCampbell: They turned out to be a real good group of people. I got my nephew-in-law. He had been through Melbourne, and I asked for him and got him into Fighting 15.

Paul Stillwell: Was this your nephew-in-law Wayne Morris, the actor?[*]

Captain McCampbell: Yes.

Paul Stillwell: How much had you known of him previously?

Captain McCampbell: Not too much. I did get him out of Hutchinson, Kansas, where he was based as a primary instructor.[†] He had gotten his private pilot's license before joining the Navy. He took a short course at Pensacola, and then they assigned him as an instructor. I got him assigned to operational training command so he could improve and go to the fleet, and they first assigned him to big boats, on account of his size, I guess, mainly. He was in Jacksonville for a couple of months, and I got him reassigned to

---

[*] Lieutenant Bert DeWayne Morris Jr., USNR, was married to McCampbell's niece, Patricia Ann O'Rourke. Morris had a flourishing movie career prior to the war. He resumed his film career after the war, mainly as a character actor with lesser parts. He died of a heart attack in 1959 while visiting McCampbell on board the aircraft carrier *Bon Homme Richard* (CVA-31). See Barrett Tillman, "Wayne Morris: Actor, Naval Aviator and Fighting 15 Ace," *The Hook*, Summer 1984, pages 48-51.

[†] Hutchinson, Kansas, Naval Air station, near Wichita.

Melbourne for fighter training, which is what he wanted. Then after he finished at Melbourne, why, I asked for him and got him up at Atlantic City.

Paul Stillwell: How good a pilot did he prove to be in combat?

Captain McCampbell: He was, I'd say, not outstanding, but moderately good. Never got shot down. He got shot up pretty bad once.

Paul Stillwell: Did he shoot down any of the enemy?

Captain McCampbell: Oh, yes, he got seven and a half.

Paul Stillwell: That's certainly creditable.

Captain McCampbell: Yes, I say moderately good. Better than average.

Paul Stillwell: You had been out of the Naval Academy about ten years at that point, and this was your first command. What were the satisfactions that came with command?

Captain McCampbell: Well, you get so engrossed in what you're doing, you don't really think or appreciate any of the advantages. I know I did, in training the squadron, and later in the air group. It's better than being second on the list. You should have your own command.

Paul Stillwell: Well, especially in a role like that, where you can see tangible results over the course of a week or a month, and see people growing and developing, that must be satisfying.

Captain McCampbell: Right. And I even taught my people how to go down a rope from the gallery in the hangar. We put a rope just off the gallery, and then frequently I'd make them go down the rope to go man the planes.

Paul Stillwell: And you had good reason—your *Wasp* experience—to tell them why they were doing that.

Captain McCampbell: Yes, I did.

Paul Stillwell: Atlantic City is not known as one of the hotbeds of naval aviation. What were the facilities like there?

Captain McCampbell: They were all new, but very good. My squadron was one of the first to train there. They had good concrete runways and the regular Navy hangars. There were two of them. Good operations staff for the field.

Paul Stillwell: How many squadrons were training there at the time?

Captain McCampbell: Two. There was one squadron moved out just as we came in, but Fighting 14 and 15 were the two who trained.

Paul Stillwell: The gambling casinos weren't there yet, but it was still a resort area. Was that a pleasant place for liberty?

Captain McCampbell: Well, we were about, as I recall, 16 miles from town, and they had buses that ran there all right, but not too many would hit the beach. We had our parties at a country club, which was a little closer, I'd say. It was about 10 or 12 miles from the station, and we'd go there by bus.

Paul Stillwell: What was the place called Pungo?[*]

Captain McCampbell: That's down off of Norfolk. We went from Atlantic City to Pungo, and I guess we were there for seven or eight weeks, in the middle of winter. It

---

[*] Pungo was the name of a naval auxiliary air station at Virginia Beach, Virginia, not far from Oceana Naval Air Station.

was really crude. From the niceties of Atlantic City, we went to the basic necessities, the crude form of living. The barracks were the worst thing. In Atlantic City, we had nice barracks to live in. At Pungo they were just the Army type, enlisted men type barracks.

Paul Stillwell: Open bays?

Captain McCampbell: Yes, they were all open, except I had a cot at the end, and I put up a little screen there. And we had a pot-bellied stove in the center of the barracks. The barracks were about, I guess, 150 feet in length, and the one pot-bellied stove in the middle, it, of course, never covered all of it. I was cold most of the time.

Paul Stillwell: That would have a psychological advantage; it would get people that much more eager to go aboard ship.

Captain McCampbell: That's right. The guy that used to refresh the coal and stoke that stove would come in about 4:00 o'clock in the morning, and it seemed to us that he made as much noise as he could. [Laughter] But the mess hall was a regular enlisted-men mess hall. We did have a little canteen there, which was quite handy. You could get gedunks and cold drinks and things, toothpaste, things of that nature.[*]

Paul Stillwell: Did you get intelligence briefings on the Japanese planes that you'd be operating against?

Captain McCampbell: No, not at that time. We had an intelligence officer, and as I recall, we didn't start briefing, having recognition drills until we shifted from Pungo over to Norfolk.

Paul Stillwell: When did that take place? Was that early '44?

---

[*] Gedunk is a Navy slang term for candy, ice cream, and sodas—snack-type food.

Captain McCampbell: That was, as I recall, December of '43 and early '44. We were there for maybe a month. We had to replace a lot of the engines, and we did that. I think there were 16 of them we replaced. That was what we spent most of our time doing in Norfolk, reorganizing. We got rid of five pilots there. And then we qualified on the carrier. I think it was *Long Island*.*

Paul Stillwell: That was the first CVE.

Captain McCampbell: Yes, in the Chesapeake. We did our qualifications then.

Paul Stillwell: Why would you get rid of the pilots? Had they not measured up?

Captain McCampbell: Well, no. We had too many of them, so they whittled us down to 40.

Paul Stillwell: So all the people that came, you were able to take into the squadron, except the supernumeraries, really. I gather you didn't drop anybody because he didn't measure up.

Captain McCampbell: Most of the five were people who didn't measure up or didn't get along with the other people. I took a vote on them.

Paul Stillwell: I see.

Captain McCampbell: I took a census or survey, and every pilot got to vote who they'd like to go to combat with the most. In other words, I didn't ask for those they least wanted to go into combat with but the ones they wanted to go to combat with the most.

Paul Stillwell: So you took the top 40 on the basis of that vote.

---

* USS *Long Island* (AVG-1) was commissioned 2 June 1941 as the first escort aircraft carrier in the U.S. Navy. She was subsequently redesignated ACV-1 on 20 August 1942 and as CVE-1 on 15 July 1943.

Captain McCampbell: Yes. I reserved a final decision on it, but I didn't have to use it. I followed the survey.

Paul Stillwell: Was this a secret ballot?

Captain McCampbell: Oh, yes, I'm sure it was. Everybody was given a sheet of paper with a roster on it. But unless they collaborated with each other, I don't know.

Paul Stillwell: Then how soon did you get aboard the ship?

Captain McCampbell: We were in Norfolk about a month, and then we joined the new *Hornet* on a 17-day shakedown cruise, the shortest on record, I hear.* Most of them would go down to this bay off of Venezuela.

Paul Stillwell: The Gulf of Paria.

Captain McCampbell: The Gulf of Paria, right. And would take a month or so. But we just went out around Bermuda, for 17 days, and came back to Norfolk. Miles Browning was in a big hurry to get his ship out there. Everything worked pretty well except that he fired the air group commander and the bombing squadron commander after the shakedown.†

Paul Stillwell: Commander Drane was the air group commander.

Captain McCampbell: Yes. Well, he got fired, and the bombing squadron commander was Ike Dew. He was a classmate of mine at the Naval Academy. That's when I got boosted up to group commander.

---

* The *Hornet* (CV-12) had a standard displacement of 27,000 tons, was 872 feet long, 93 feet in the beam, and extreme width of 147 feet. Her top speed was 33 knots. She was originally armed with 12 5-inch guns and could accommodate approximately 90 aircraft.
† On 2 February 1944 Commander William M. Drane, USN, was removed as air group commander and Lieutenant Commander Irwin L. Dew, USN, as commanding officer of Bombing Squadron 15. McCampbell became Commander Air Group 15 on 9 February, and Lieutenant Commander Charles W. Brewer, USN, took over Fighting Squadron 15.

Paul Stillwell: Would it be fair to say that's as much a reflection on Browning as it is on them? I mean, in your estimation, did they deserve to be fired?

Captain McCampbell: Yes.

Paul Stillwell: Oh, they did?

Captain McCampbell: Yes. Drane, particularly. I'm surprised he even knew how to fly. We had practically no communication with him whatsoever, and he got fired primarily because he was responsible for training not only the enlisted personnel in the air group, but also for supervising training of the support unit aboard ship. And apparently he had done none of that. He didn't get his fingers into that. According to Browning, that was the primary reason why he was being fired.

Paul Stillwell: You said you had eight enlisted men initially. Did that build over time?

Captain McCampbell: Yes. It was either six or eight; I've forgotten. But we carried very few people, because we were more mobile, you see, and we wouldn't have to carry along all these extra maintenance people.

Paul Stillwell: So that the ship's company handled the maintenance?

Captain McCampbell: Yes, and on land they were a separate unit at the air station, whichever one you went to. Even at Pungo, they had a CASU unit there.

Paul Stillwell: Who handled it when you went aboard the *Hornet*?

Captain McCampbell: The people on the ship, although they were a separate unit; they were not part of the air group.

Paul Stillwell: What was your reaction when you got offered the job of air group commander?

Captain McCampbell: Well, I was very happy about it. More responsible position, and I'd been with the fighter squadron, of course, and I knew at least a part of it even before I went up to group commander. The bombers I didn't know very well. Of course, when they fired Ike Dew, the bombing squadron skipper, that created a problem. Miles Browning called me and said, "Look, get me a new bombing squadron commander."

I said, "Gee, I'm sorry, Captain. I can only think of one guy on the East Coast off the top of my head." Art Giesser was his name.[*] So Browning went to the detail officer and asked for Art Giesser as the new bombing squadron commander. Well, come to find out, Art Giesser bugged out. He claimed he had bad ears and couldn't dive-bomb, and yet he was up at a bombing squadron at Cape May training people to dive-bomb. So that threw him out. So Browning called me again. He said, "Well, that guy's a washout. Do you know anybody else?"

By then, I'd thought of someone else—Jim Mini.[†]

Paul Stillwell: Had you known him before?

Captain McCampbell: Never served with him. I knew him. He was a good football player, and I knew him.

Paul Stillwell: So mostly by reputation. Entirely by reputation.

Captain McCampbell: Well, no, he was class of '35, so I was there still at the Academy when he was playing football. He came out of Vallejo, California. So I nominated him to Browning. Browning went to the detail officer, and Jim joined the ship the day before

---

[*] Lieutenant Commander Arthur A. Giesser, USN.
[†] Lieutenant Commander James H. Mini, USN.

we sailed. He'd never flown the SB2C, but he had no other disabilities.* He had also had a training squadron. I believe it was Cape May, somewhere up the line. He had had combat experience in Fighting Five or Six; I've forgotten.

Paul Stillwell: Well, that was a definite plus.

Captain McCampbell: Yes. But he was pretty mad about the whole thing. He hadn't been ashore too long, and he had to leave a good job. His wife was most irritated. Anyway, he came aboard the day before we sailed to go out to Honolulu and qualified. As I said before, he had never flown the SB2C, and we had to qualify him aboard ship, in landing aboard. We'd had no chance to give him training on the field. So the first two landings he made, he cracked up, crashed the barrier. So I got hold of him, and I said, "Look, Jim. You're holding the plane off. Come on in. The signal officer will put you in a good position, and you just relax on the stick, and let the nose drop down, and kind of ease back on it when you actually touch down, and you'll be all right." Well, he caught on, and after that, he did okay. But he was part of the crashes that they had in the bombing squadron. Now it's true, they had changed planes from the SB2U to the SB2C three or four weeks before we sailed with them aboard.†

Paul Stillwell: So the air group had started out in the SB2U.

Captain McCampbell: Yes, the bombing squadron did.

---

* The Curtiss SB2C Helldiver dive-bombers first entered combat in November 1943. The SB2C-4 version was 37 feet long, wingspan of 50 feet, gross weight of 16,616 pounds, and top speed of 295 miles per hour. The Helldiver could carry 1,000 pounds of bombs internally and 1,000 pounds externally.
† The Vought SB2U Vindicator was a monoplane scout-bomber that entered fleet squadrons in late 1937.

Interview Number 3 with Captain David McCampbell, U.S. Navy (Retired)
Place: Captain McCampbell's home in Lake Worth, Florida
Date: Thursday, 16 July 1987

Paul Stillwell: I believe you want to start today, Captain McCampbell, by making the point about your record in combat and not being shot down or forced down.

Captain McCampbell: Yes, that's true. I'm quite proud of the fact that I was never shot down by the enemy in air-to-air combat or by antiaircraft. I came very close to it once on my second combat mission. It was over Marcus Island, and my plane was shot up pretty badly with antiaircraft fire.* I'd had a fire in my belly tank. My wingman called and told me, and I dropped that, but then I was able to get back to the ship, which was about 160 miles away. When I got back to the ship and prepared for landing, I found that I couldn't lower my wheels in the normal manner; I had to lower them down by an emergency method we had. I couldn't get the tailhook down in the normal manner; I had to crank it down. I had one of the flaps shot up pretty badly. I had a little difficulty in landing aboard, but I did get back to my ship. After I landed, one of the enterprising young mechanics took the good Hamilton standard clock out of the plane, and then they pushed it over the side.

I never had to parachute, fortunately. I missed a good opportunity on that particular flight that I just described, but I decided to stay with the plane, and we got back safely. Except for that situation, I never really had a forced landing. I always got back to the ship. Except one occasion, I was low on gas. My ship couldn't take me, but I was able to land on the *Langley*.

Paul Stillwell: And that was on the 24th of October 1944, which we'll get to during the course of today's discussion.

---

* This attack was on 18 May 1944, by which time Air Group 15 was operating from the carrier *Essex* (CV-9). For details see Edwin P. Hoyt, *McCampbell's Heroes: The Story of the U.S. Navy's Most Celebrated Carrier Fighters of the Pacific War* (New York: Van Nostrand Reinhold, 1983).

Captain McCampbell: Right.

Paul Stillwell: I think a point to be made in addition is that that reflects a considerable amount of skill on your part that you were able to avoid the antiaircraft.

Captain McCampbell: No, I would rather describe it as luck. I just was never in a situation where the enemy plane could shoot me down, I'd say. If I got in a situation, which I did on a couple of occasions, I actually had to run to get away from the enemy. But here again, I got back to the ship safely. Just as contrary to a lot of the pilots in those days, for instance, the group commander who was a classmate of mine at Annapolis, was shot down about three weeks after he relieved me on the *Essex*.* And most of the Marines at Guadalcanal were all shot down at least once, one of them four times. In fact, he goes around the country bragging about getting shot down four times and still living.

Paul Stillwell: Is that Joe Foss?†

Captain McCampbell: Yes. And various others. Even the famous German ace, Adolf Galland, was shot down twice, and another famous German ace was shot down nine times. So I considered myself pretty lucky to get away with it.

Paul Stillwell: Well, in addition to the luck, I'm sure there was an element of skill involved, and I think you're being too modest.

Captain McCampbell: Well, there was some skill along the line, I guess, but in line with my training, primarily.

Paul Stillwell: Just to follow up on your point about the air group commander who followed you, you mentioned to me when the tape wasn't running that a question you get

---

* When Air Group 15 left the *Essex* in November 1944, it was replaced by Air Group Four, commanded by Commander George Otto Klinsmann, USN, who was lost in action on 15 January 1945.
† Captain Joseph J. Foss, USMC, was the top fighter ace for the Marine Corps in World War II. He was credited with shooting down 26 Japanese planes in the Guadalcanal campaign and was awarded the Medal of Honor in 1943. He died on 1 January 2003.

asked frequently is, "What happened to the plane that you flew in Air Group 15?" This would be a point to answer that.

Captain McCampbell: It went to Otto Klinsmann, who relieved me as the air group commander.

Paul Stillwell: And so it was lost a few weeks later.

Captain McCampbell: Right.

Paul Stillwell: I presume that the rising suns on the side of the cockpit had been painted over by that time.

Captain McCampbell: I don't know whether they were or not. They may not have been.

Paul Stillwell: One other point that people would be curious about, the name Minsi III was painted on the side of the plane as well. What did that refer to?

Captain McCampbell: It was the third plane that I had. The first one was the one I just recounted the story about being shot up at Marcus Island. The second one had a deficiency in the engine when I'd get up around 18,000, 20,000 feet; the engine would cut out on me. I called for an emergency landing a couple of times. I found that when I got down around 10,000 feet, I could restart the engine, so I never actually had an emergency landing. The third one was the one I last flew and the one I turned over to the group commander that relieved me.

Paul Stillwell: How long did the second one last before you changed?

Captain McCampbell: Not very long.

Paul Stillwell: On that nickname painted on the side of your plane, Minsi III, I think it was more common, really, in Army Air Forces planes than Navy, wasn't it, to have a girlfriend's name?

Captain McCampbell: Yes, it was.

Paul Stillwell: How did you happen to do it?

Captain McCampbell: Well, my plane captain didn't give me the name, but the first plane that I flew—and he was plane captain—asked me if he could put up there on the side "Monsoon Maiden." Well, I was happy to get rid of that plane and scrub that off, and so that gave me the idea, and I named it after my girlfriend.

Paul Stillwell: We were talking yesterday about your work in putting together the fighter squadron and the air group for the *Hornet* when she was going to be commissioned. How much problem did you have with operational accidents during that time?

Captain McCampbell: Well, to go back to the early days of training, two of the pilots assigned to the fighter squadron were on familiarization flights in an SNJ. And for some reason, I guess they were stunting or something, they both got killed. So those were two of the operational accidents. Then the only accident in training is when we were qualifying aboard the *Long Island*. One of the pilots ended up off center and hit the gun gallery, the catwalk, anyway. Then we didn't have any more trouble with the fighters until we got to Maui for some additional training out in the Hawaiian Islands. We had a mid-air accident. They were practicing the Thach Weave and collided in midair, and the collision killed both pilots.* There was only one other operational accident. In combat, a pilot named Wolf took off, and shortly after takeoff, he landed in the water, for the reason

---

* The Thach Weave was developed shortly before World War II by Lieutenant Commander John S. Thach, USN, commanding officer of Fighting Squadron Three. It was a means of enabling the F4F Wildcat to counter the better-performing Japanese Zero fighter. Thach, who retired as a four-star admiral, described the origin of the maneuver in his Naval Institute oral history.

I'm not certain of, and the plane blew up, and he was killed. Those are the only operational accidents our fighters had.

Now, the bombers had quite a few—in fact, I can't remember all of them—both in early training and later in combat.

Paul Stillwell: Would you attribute that to the idiosyncrasies of the Helldiver?

Captain McCampbell: Yes, and the fact that they were not too familiar with the new planes, the SB2Cs, before going aboard ship. And the torpedo planes, they were quite fortunate. I can't recall any operational accident on their part.

Paul Stillwell: As the skipper, I'd think you'd have something of a dilemma. On the one hand, you want your pilots to be aggressive and adventurous, but on the other hand, you want them to be safe.

Captain McCampbell: Right.

Paul Stillwell: How did you walk that fine line?

Captain McCampbell: How did I balance it? Well, I just tried to give them the best that I could in training and hope that they'd come out all right.

Paul Stillwell: Did you have specific lessons on safety as part of your training curriculum?

Captain McCampbell: Yes, we would point out various things that had happened to other people in hopes that they could avoid them. That's about the only safety features that we discussed.

Paul Stillwell: The Bureau of Aeronautics hired this cartoonist Osborn to draw Grampaw Pettibone.*

Captain McCampbell: Yes.

Paul Stillwell: Was that a help to you? He illustrated examples of unsafe things.

Captain McCampbell: I don't think that we had that during the war, seems to me. I know it came on later. But, at any rate, the mail situation wasn't so good that we would get *Naval Aviation News*.

Captain McCampbell: I don't remember receiving a copy of that at all during the war.

Paul Stillwell: You mentioned the pilots killed working on the Thach Weave. How prevalent was the use of that in your squadron?

Captain McCampbell: When the two pilots were killed in the midair collision, we did away with the Thach Weave completely, except on rare occasions, when our pilots would maybe get caught and a couple of other pilots would try and protect him. One I remember distinctly was in the water off Guam. They might do that, because they were down low. They were in a dangerous position, trying to protect the pilot in the water.

Paul Stillwell: And protect each other.

Captain McCampbell: Yes.

Paul Stillwell: Do you recall the occasion when that was used? Was that in the Marianas?

---

* Robert C. Osborn (1904-1994) was a cartoonist who served in the Navy in World War II. He created a character named Dilbert, a pilot who was involved in many uinsafe maneuvers. Presumably, readers would learn from Dilbert's mistakes. After the war, he drew many cartoons for *Naval Aviation News* in which a bearded old naval aviator, Grampaw Pettibone, provided still more lessons to pilots.

Captain McCampbell: Yes, it was off Guam. I used it just one time. A little SOC from one of the cruisers was there to pick up a downed pilot. It was not one of mine, by the way, but I saw the two Zeros attacking the SOC, and so my wingman and I went in and protected them while they picked up this downed pilot.[*]

Paul Stillwell: Well, also, I don't think that you had as much need for the Thach Weave as with, say, the F4F, because you had more nearly comparable performance characteristics to the Zero.

Captain McCampbell: Right. Exactly.

Paul Stillwell: And Thach specifically devised that with a plane that had inferior characteristics.

Captain McCampbell: Right. And, of course, it was one of my propositions that I imparted to my pilots in the fighter squadron, that the fighters should never be put on the defensive if and when. So we used a more aggressive technique. Our fighters would fly in formation above the bombers and torpedo planes, if we were on an air group mission. Also, we were generally a little out ahead of them, so we could catch anything that was coming in before they got to the bombers and torpedo planes. Contrary to a lot of air groups out there, we never lost a bomber or a torpedo plane due to air-to-air combat. So our methods of protecting them proved out to be very good.

Paul Stillwell: What kind of guidance had you got from Miles Browning when he moved you up from the fighter squadron to be group commander?

Captain McCampbell: I didn't get any specific guidance from him.

---

[*] The Mitsubishi-built A6M Zero was the best-known fighter plane in the Japanese Navy in World War II. The standard A6M2 had a top speed of 317 miles per hour and was armed with two 7.7-millimeter machine guns and two 20-millimeter cannons.

Paul Stillwell: I was under the impression that he wanted you to concentrate more on air-to-air combat and not so much on bombing and strafing.

Captain McCampbell: That's right. That's correct.

Paul Stillwell: There have been so many stories about Browning and his personality and character. How do you remember him?

Captain McCampbell: Well, I remember him as a pretty tough customer, although I never had any difficulty with him. I remember when we were on our shakedown cruise, of the first four bombers that took off, three of them hit the water before they got airborne really. So he stopped the operation, and he called the exec and myself. I was then the fighter squadron commander and not yet the air group commander. He presented the problem, said, "What the hell's going on here? Why are all these bombers hitting the water as soon as they take off?" I told him that my experiences as a landing signal officer on the old *Wasp*, if we found that happening, we would give them more "run" down the deck, give them a longer deck to work with. So he adopted that. He gave them an extra 100 feet, and they had no more trouble that way. So that solved that. That was my only eyeball contact with Browning.

Paul Stillwell: Did you have a sense of the way he was running the ship, that he was very strict in that regard?

Captain McCampbell: Yes, he was very strict. Well, I remember he called the pilots all down in the wardroom one day and gave us a lecture. He said, "Now, we're in a hurry to get out there in combat. They need us very badly." That's understandable. And he said, "On this shakedown cruise, we're going to find out the guys that do the job and do it properly and the guys that don't. If you have one of those people under you that's not doing his job, you recognize it, then kick him aside and get rid of him when you get back to Norfolk," which was a pretty tough attitude. You can overlook some mistakes. If a guy just makes one mistake, you don't kick him aside; you try and instruct him and help him along. Because most of the crew—and that included the pilots—were really novices. Very, very few had had any combat experience. In fact, I had had none as a fighter pilot. My combat experience was on the *Wasp* as landing signal officer.

Paul Stillwell: One quality that really distinguished the Navy pilots from the Army's in World War II was the ability for long-range over-water navigation. How did you teach that?

Captain McCampbell: Well, I taught my people—the fighter pilots, anyway; I didn't get really a chance to get with the bombers and torpedo pilots too much—but I taught them to do their navigation in the ready room. They knew they were going out to attack a target in a certain place geographically, and you plot the course of where you're going, and when you get finished with a mission, turn around and do the reverse. I said, "Now, the ship won't likely be in the same spot that you took off from." But we what we called a Y-Z system, which consisted of the ship had the YE, like a pie plate, and they put it on radio, and they'd put out a signal, like AA, first 15 degrees of the compass, and every 15 degrees thereafter would give you a different signal, like AA, FF, ZZ, whatever. And in returning to the ship, as I said, it wouldn't always be in the same position; it would be somewhere within about 60 miles, anyway, depending on the length of your mission and time. I said, "You can pick up this signal from the ship, and then you change course as necessary and head for it."

Now, the fighters, during a shakedown cruise, we sent planes out on different quadrants, usually two to a quadrant, and tested them according to altitude. We found out on this experiment that we could pick up the signals from the ship, like whatever the code was, in that quadrant. At 6,000 feet you could pick up the ship about 60 miles away. At 8,000 you could pick up the ship about 80 miles away. And then on down the scale, of 40 miles out, you could pick it up at 4,000 feet. So this gave us a range that we could use in returning to the ship that, depending on your altitude, is how far out you'd be when you pick up the signal. I used that almost every time in returning to the ship. Four or five times it was very directive and caused me to change course significantly.

Paul Stillwell: How frequently did you have to operate when the ship was in a strict radio silence and have to get back?

Captain McCampbell: Well, when the ship was following radio silence, they'd still use this Y-Z system. They changed the pie plate every day, so you had different codes in different quadrants. If the Japs picked it up, I don't think they could ever use it.

Paul Stillwell: From what you say, it was relatively short range too.

Captain McCampbell: Yes.

Paul Stillwell: What else did you work on during that shakedown, as far as the squadron?

Captain McCampbell: For the fighters, it consisted mostly of just landings and takeoffs and formation flying. We did strafe a sled. Of course, dive-bombers dive-bombed the sled, and the torpedo planes too. I guess that was their main training. It was mostly takeoffs and landings, just operations.

Paul Stillwell: Was there a recognition at that point, in early 1944, that there probably wouldn't be that many opportunities to use torpedoes?

Captain McCampbell: Well, I never thought of it, actually. Of course, we had torpedoes aboard, and they didn't work very well for the people who had used them—submarines and planes. It was a World War I torpedo—I think Mark 13.

Paul Stillwell: Right.

Captain McCampbell: It wasn't until shortly before the Battles of Leyte Gulf that we got the improved Mark 18 torpedo. But the only time we used them was in the Battles of Leyte Gulf.

Paul Stillwell: But you must have had the recognition that they would have to do other things besides just torpedoes.

Captain McCampbell: Oh, yes. They did a lot of bombing and rocket firing. They had rockets, whereas the bombers and fighters didn't have them until, there again, just shortly before the Battles of Leyte Gulf. The fighters got rockets.

Paul Stillwell: Was Lieutenant Commander Lambert the CO of that squadron from the beginning?[*]

Captain McCampbell: He had the torpedo squadron, yes.

Paul Stillwell: What do you remember of him?

Captain McCampbell: I gave him an excellent fitness report. I didn't know him too well. We didn't have too much person-to-person conversation. I visited the torpedo ready room a number of times, but we didn't have too much in common to talk about.

Paul Stillwell: Evidently he got excellent fitness reports from a number of other people, because he eventually made flag rank.

Captain McCampbell: That's right. And so did the bomber squadron skipper make admiral—Jim Mini. He died of a heart attack, and he was out in Colorado Springs, where I was on duty.[†] He got up one morning, took his dog out for a walk, and then he climbed the stairs back up to the second floor, and keeled over, and never drew another breath.

The fighter squadron commander didn't make admiral. If you want to hear about him.

Paul Stillwell: Surely.

---

[*] Lieutenant Commander Valdemar G. Lambert, USN, commanding officer of Torpedo Squadron 15 (VT-15).
[†] Mini died 7 December 1963.

Captain McCampbell: He's still living—Jim Rigg. He came on initially as my exec, and then when the squadron commander was killed, why, he fleeted up to take over the squadron. But I had a number of occasions where he made claims that I couldn't approve, that I thought were excessive or that he really hadn't done. And so he was on occasions denied his claims as to shooting down planes and that sort of thing.

Paul Stillwell: I think you tended to have somewhat of a conservative outlook on that, even in your own achievements, because you probably got more than the 34 that were credited, didn't you?

Captain McCampbell: Yes. I had 11 probables, 21 on the ground, but we didn't give credit to destroying planes on the ground, and for good reason. I can go into that now if you want.

Paul Stillwell: Sure.

Captain McCampbell: It wasn't just in my air group that we didn't give credit for destroying planes on the ground. The only organization that gave credit to destroyed planes on the ground was the Eighth Air Force. The Marines didn't do it; the Fifth Air Force didn't do it; the Navy didn't do it. And because you come down generally from high altitude, and you strafe a plane on the ground, or two or three, and you may be hitting it all right, but it doesn't mean you've destroyed it. One air group had a pilot come in, and he had 123 bullet holes in his plane, but that didn't destroy the plane. And that was air-to-air combat. The only way you could positively claim one destroyed would be photographs taken right after, because if a plane's sitting on the ground, you don't know how many different people have attacked that same plane. That was my reasoning on it that we didn't give credit. But unofficially I claimed 21 destroyed on the ground and 11 probables in the air. The planes that I claimed probables were ones where I knew I hit a plane, and he would go smoking, sometimes spiraling, down towards the water, or land on occasion. But I never followed a plane down to see if I'd destroyed it.

Paul Stillwell: You had other things to do.

Captain McCampbell: Well, I didn't want to sacrifice my altitude, see, so I never followed them down. And I taught my pilots not to do that. In other words, you've got an advantage, hopefully, and you want to keep that advantage as long as you can. So those are the planes that we claim as probables. You know you hit him, you knocked him out of the formation, and he ran off or spiraled down or whatever, smoking generally.

Paul Stillwell: How far off the ground did he have to be to be considered in the air?

Captain McCampbell: As long as he was off the ground, that was it.

Paul Stillwell: If his wheels had left the surface of the runway.

Captain McCampbell: One of my fighter pilots, I know, George Duncan, we were over Negros, and we had arrived quite early in the morning before they were active there at that field, and he circled and waited for the planes to start taking off.[*] [Laughter] The plane he got was a twin-engine Betty, and he's the only one I know positively who delayed the combat action until the plane got off the ground.[†]

Paul Stillwell: A further point on that navigation. I would think you'd get at least somewhat disoriented from navigation while you were involved in a dogfight. How did you then figure out where you are to start back toward the ship?

Captain McCampbell: Well, you didn't get too far off of your course, whichever you were headed for. But I got well off course there once over Iwo Jima, and got into a dogfight there. I had to use Iwo Jima to orient myself and had no trouble flying back to the ship.

---

[*] Lieutenant Commander George E. Duncan, USN. The action described here was on 13 September 1944.
[†] The G4M (known by the Allied code name Betty) was a Mitsubishi Type 1 two-engine, land-based torpedo bomber.

Paul Stillwell: That was probably just before the invasion of Saipan, wasn't it?

Captain McCampbell: Yes. We made the first attacks on Iwo Jima back in June of '44.[*]

Paul Stillwell: You described the process yesterday whereby you came up with Lieutenant Commander Mini to take over the bombing squadron, after Commander Dew was relieved. How did you then get Commander Brewer to take your place in the fighting squadron?

Captain McCampbell: Well, Brewer had a fighter squadron in the Atlantic at the time, and I don't know how long, actually, he had had that squadron. It was aboard one of the smaller carriers. But he must have applied to get into a bigger squadron on an *Essex*-class carrier. And I guess Captain Browning must have raised it. When he boosted me up to air group commander, he must have told the detail officer there on ComAirLant staff, and he sent Charlie Brewer.[†]

Paul Stillwell: Brewer was with you only a few months before he was killed. What do you remember of him during that time?

Captain McCampbell: He was a good guy. He came to us just after the shakedown, and then he got in on the advanced training we had in Hawaii. So he was well prepared. He was a Fighting Four pilot in the *Ranger* in 1937 and was a good gunner and a good skipper.

Paul Stillwell: Had you known him before when you were in VF-4?

Captain McCampbell: Just barely. Just barely. He and I had lunch together one day at the officers' club, and that was all I knew of him until he joined the outfit.

---

[*] The attack on Iwo Jima was on 15 June 1944.
[†] ComAirLant – Commander Air Force Atlantic Fleet, the type commander.

Paul Stillwell: Did Captain Browning give you something of the understanding that you'd be both air group commander and fight with the fighters?

Captain McCampbell: No, he didn't discriminate or direct that type thing.

Paul Stillwell: But he wasn't going to prevent you from acting as a fighter pilot, was he?

Captain McCampbell: No. In fact, I asked if I could fly fighters in order to take on the air group, and he acquiesced.

Paul Stillwell: What had air group commanders been generally flying up to that time?

Captain McCampbell: Mostly the TBF.*

Paul Stillwell: What was the reason for the change?

Captain McCampbell: Well, I guess mainly because often we'd lead in one flight, and then there would be an interval until the second flight came in, working deck loads each time. And the group commander and his wingman would be sitting out there. At first I kept three guys with me, and then the admiral cut me down to just the one wingman, and he was sitting in the active area, and I guess that's why they gave the group commanders a fighter instead of a torpedo plane.

Paul Stillwell: Might as well make yourself useful.

Captain McCampbell: Yes. My reason was different. Mine was that I'd been trained in the fighter; I was comfortable with it; and I knew the people that were in the fighter squadron very intimately. I had flown the TBF. It was a good plane, but it didn't have the performance that the fighter did.

---

* The Grumman-built TBF Avenger was the U.S. Navy's standard carrier-based torpedo plane from mid-1942 through the remainder of World War II.

Paul Stillwell: I guess one of the real ironies is that you, as the most successful Navy fighter pilot of the war, were not in combat in a fighter squadron.

Captain McCampbell: Yes. [Laughter] But I considered myself a fighter pilot, and I was more with the fighters, of course, flying the fighter plane. So it was a very favorable spot, having trained the fighters and knew the people and then was flying with them.

Paul Stillwell: Did you work it out with Commander Brewer that he would follow essentially your same policies and doctrines that you'd established with the squadron?

Captain McCampbell: I didn't even discuss it with him. I considered him an experienced fighter pilot, and had combat experience in the Atlantic, and I never discussed tactics or anything. I may have told him how we performed group tactics, but that's about all.

Paul Stillwell: How much autonomy or individuality was left to an air group on group tactics? Was there a fleet standard, or could you vary some on that?

Captain McCampbell: You could vary it. We had our own. I wrote up a doctrine for air group actions, which consisted essentially of the fighters going down first on the target, and then come the bombers and the torpedo planes at the same time. The torpedo planes, of course, were low on the water, whereas our bombers came in overhead. But the fighters were preceding in strafing or dropping bombs as we did, and then rendezvous and give the bombers and torpedoes the protection while they were rendezvousing with the fighters.

Paul Stillwell: Was that initial strafing run designed to get the enemy's heads down before the bombers came?

Captain McCampbell: Yes. Right. And the best way, I thought, of doing it to get the fighters in the whole action. Particularly it would get them down and finish their strafing. They'd make one run when the air group was operating. And then get to the rendezvous point and be there to make it safe for the bombers and torpedo planes. And on occasion that worked out.

On October 25, in the Battles of Leyte Gulf, our fighters went down first, provided a rendezvous, and then in the meantime, they shot down three or four Japs. There weren't many Japanese fighters in the four carriers to the north. Later I found out there were 20 all told, and my fighters got either ten or 11 out of the 20. So the air groups that followed us in didn't have much air opposition. We were the first communication team, two fighters, that had been sent out 100 miles from the task force by Admiral Mitscher.[*] Jim Flatley was then the operations officer on the staff.[†] And these two communication fighters from my ship, from my air group, picked up the Japanese fleet to the north. The scout planes that had been sent out earlier all missed this big fleet sitting out there, which were only about 120 to 140 miles from our own fleet. But the scouts had had their sectors and they'd all missed him. But this little communication team spotted the whole goddamn thing. That was the way the action started.

Paul Stillwell: On that subject of communications, did you train in communications discipline as part of your training period?

Captain McCampbell: Oh, yes. We were very strong on it. When we first came aboard the *Essex* and I met Captain Ofstie, he said, "One piece of advice I want to give you, be sure you instruct your people to be very careful in their communications, to be as quiet as possible.[‡] We have one guy out here in the Pacific that you can hear him all over the Pacific, even without radio." [Laughter] And he said, "I don't want any of that." But that's about the only specific thing he told me when I first met him.

---

[*] Vice Admiral Marc A. Mitscher, USN, served as Commander Task Force 38, the fast carrier task force, during the battle.
[†] Commander James H. Flatley Jr., USN.
[‡] Captain Ralph K. Ofstie, USN, commanded the USS *Essex* (CV-9) from 6 November 1943 to 7 August 1944.

Paul Stillwell: After your shakedown in the *Hornet*, did you then come back to Norfolk for a period before the deployment?*

Captain McCampbell: Oh, yes. We came back. We had to change, I think, about 16 engines in our fighters. The bombers were okay; we didn't have to change any engines. I don't remember about the torpedo planes.

Paul Stillwell: Where did the training in the use of radar come in?

Captain McCampbell: Well, we had a few exercises. You're talking about ship's radar?

Paul Stillwell: I was thinking more of in the planes.

Captain McCampbell: Well, the torpedo planes were the only ones that had radar and the night fighters. But we had a few exercises with the ships. On one or two occasions, I remember, people got lost, disoriented or something, and the ship's radar brought them home.

Paul Stillwell: When did you get training in working with fighter director officers?

Captain McCampbell: We got that after shakedown and on the trip around to Hawaii. It was a big deal there. I can't remember any training at all with the fighter directors. As I say, it came after. That's about all I can say on it.

Paul Stillwell: You were due to go into combat in the *Hornet* but got held up in Hawaii. What were the factors involved in that?

Captain McCampbell: Well, mainly the bomber squadron concept. Captain Browning felt that they weren't well trained and prepared to go into combat, so they put the whole air group ashore for what they called advanced training. It helped us in the fighters a

_____
* The *Hornet* left Norfolk for the Pacific on 14 February 1944.

little, because we did do some bombing then, concentrated bombing. The training officer on the staff of ComAirPac said that, "The fighters are now doing a lot of bombing, and if you haven't had any or hadn't had much [we'd had a little back in Atlantic City], concentrate on that while you're here."* It was advanced training.

The other thing, we took advantage of the advanced training to do night field carrier landings, which, as an ex-landing signal officer, I conducted myself. I'd had considerable of that. For the fighters, that was about all it amounted to. We got a number of group gropes, we called it, where all the three squadrons would go out together and make a dive-bombing attack or make an attack on the island Kahoolawe.

Paul Stillwell: That was also a gunfire range for the surface ships.

Captain McCampbell: Yes.

Paul Stillwell: Were you based at Kaneohe during that period?

Captain McCampbell: No. Pu'unēnē, on the island of Maui.† Kaneohe was in operation.‡ We had a couple of air groups over there, or at least one.

Paul Stillwell: So that was a beneficial period for you.

Captain McCampbell: Yes, it was.

Paul Stillwell: How did it affect the handling of the Hellcat to hang bombs on it?

Captain McCampbell: It was no strain. Of course, it cut down a little bit on your maneuverability and rate of climb, but if there was group action the fighters would go in first and drop their bombs and strafe and then get out of there for the bombers and

---

* ComAirPac – Commander Air Force Pacific Fleet, the type commander.
† Pu'unēnē is an unincorporated town in the central part of Maui, Hawaii, near Kahului. It was the site of a naval air station from 1940 to 1947.
‡ Kaneohe was the site of naval air station on the eastern side of the island of Oahu, Hawaii.

torpedo planes. And even though they got to where later in our tour of duty, we sent out a fighter sweep, and equipped the fighters with bombs, and if they got into a situation of air-to-air combat, then the fighters knew they were free to drop the bomb and go ahead with the combat.

Paul Stillwell: Just essentially jettison them?

Captain McCampbell: Yes.

Paul Stillwell: The purpose of the fighter sweep, as I understand it, was to take out the enemy planes on the ground so they wouldn't be a threat in the air.

Captain McCampbell: Right.

Paul Stillwell: And that became especially important during the kamikaze period, which started in October 1944.

Captain McCampbell: Yes. To get into that kamikaze period, I to this day think that the day that my wingman and I got 15 planes, just the two of us, that those must have been kamikazes, because they give us very little fight.[*] Two or three of them tried to climb up to higher altitude. Of course, we picked them off in a hurry. The rest of the time, they were just sitting there flying along, taking it, and we were knocking them off right and left. Since they were headed back to Manila and away from our task group, we were in a position freely to strike them from the rear. There was no great hurry to get the leader. And we never did get him, by the way. Now, the real leader was a twin-engine bomber that led them in, and he was down. All the bombers were behind him; the fighters were above them. But it wasn't too much of a fight for us—just a question of taking our time

---

[*] Kamikazes were Japanese suicide aircraft that began showing up in the Philippines campaign in the autumn of 1944. The pilots attempted to crash their bomb-armed aircraft directly into American warships. Hundreds of them successfully hit their targets and inflicted great damage. The incident McCampbell described here took place on 24 October 1944. His wingman was Lieutenant (junior grade) Roy W. Rushing, USNR.

to make sure we got one. We didn't get one every time, but we pretty well took care of them.

Paul Stillwell: I think you told me that you made about 20 runs during that action.

Captain McCampbell: Made 20 coordinated runs, and my wingman went down with me each time.

Paul Stillwell: You got 15 planes, so that's an impressive score.

Captain McCampbell: And three probables. Most of the Jap planes were highly vulnerable, because they didn't have self-sealing wing tanks.

Paul Stillwell: Or seat armor.

Captain McCampbell: That's right. And we learned real early that if you hit them in the wing, anywhere near the wing roots, where the fuel was, they'd explode right in your face. So then after that, all of us, we learned to shoot for the wings instead of going for the pilot or the engine. And it turned out very successful.

Paul Stillwell: Well, on that particular occasion, the Japanese planes went into a Lufbery Circle for a while, which would suggest some element of self-preservation at work.*

Captain McCampbell: Yes. The five fighters that were with my wingman and me went down on the bombers, and almost immediately the fighters went into this Lufbery. They circled around there, I guess, maybe ten or 12 minutes. At least I had time to smoke a cigarette and sit up there and watch them. We made a couple of attacks and found it was very difficult. They were in a turn, and if you'd go in at them, you placed yourself in jeopardy, no matter where you'd attack them from, unless you'd go down below, but I

---

* The Lufbery circle is a defensive maneuver in which airplanes fly in a ring, each one protecting the tail of the plane ahead. It was named for Major Raoul Lufbery, a fighter pilot in World War I.

didn't want to sacrifice the altitude. So we made a couple of attacks, and I think we got two planes out of that. But I didn't like it, so we just pulled up above them about 3,000 feet and watched them go around until they came out of the circle.

Paul Stillwell: You told me that the reference to cigarette smoking was deleted from an account that was later written of that episode. How did that happen?

Captain McCampbell: Yes. Ed Sims wrote a book, *The Greatest Fighter Missions*, which is on Marines and Navy fighter pilots.[*] When they interviewed me, I had thrown that in about having a cigarette up about 18,000 feet, and Ed Sims accepted it, but when it got to the Navy reviewing officer, public information officer, he said, "You've got to strike that, because you can't smoke a cigarette at 18,000 feet." But you can do it, because both my wingman and I did!

Paul Stillwell: How did you do it?

Captain McCampbell: It was quite simple. You just pull the oxygen mask away from your face, put in a cigarette, and light it. You don't just light it; you're inhaling, and you get the cigarette lit, and you put your mask back on. Periodically you pull the mask away, take a puff on the cigarette, and then put your mask back on. And you do this until you finish your cigarette, then throw the cigarette butt out the window.

Paul Stillwell: You crack the cockpit a little to get it out?

Captain McCampbell: Oh, yes. You crack the cockpit so the smoke will go out too.

Paul Stillwell: I think also that you'd want to not get the flaming end too close to your oxygen mask.

---

[*] Edward H. Sims, *Greatest Fighter Missions of the Top Navy and Marine Aces of World War II* (New York, Harper, 1962).

Captain McCampbell: [Laughter] Right. Right. But it can be done. It was a little difficult, but we did it.

Paul Stillwell: One more point. You said you came on the rear planes in that formation. What was the normal procedure?

Captain McCampbell: Well, if the attacking planes are heading toward your ship or task group, you try to get the leader first, or leaders. The reason I say leaders, that's both the fighters and the bombers or torpedo planes. But if they're headed home after an attack on your ship or as in this case, whatever the reason was, I don't know, but after doing their Lufbery Circle, they formed up very neatly in formation. There were roughly 40 of them. I estimated 40. Actually, we can account for 38. When we ran out of ammunition and had to go home, I counted them. There were 18 left. Roy and I had gotten 15, and one other pilot, A.C. Slack, joined us for a couple of runs, and he claimed he was out of ammunition, because he had attacked the bombers before.[*] So the 18 and the 17, that comes to 35, and Roy and I claimed three probables, so that brings it up to 38. It's pretty close to the 40 that I estimated. The 40 I estimated, I reported back to CIC.[†] By the way, the fighter direction officer was John Connally, who later became Secretary of the Treasury and Secretary of the Navy, Governor of Texas for two terms.[‡] I called him, and I said, "Rebel base [which was the code name for the ship], my wingman and I are up here alone with about 40 fighters. What do you suggest that we do—attack them or not?"

He came back and said, "Well, use your best judgment." So I knew right then he was a damn good politician. [Laughter] He wasn't going to get caught in anything. But that was our fighter direction officer.

So Roy and ultimately did attack them, and it paid off.

Paul Stillwell: Did you get to know Connally on a personal basis?

---

[*] Ensign Albert C. Slack, USNR.
[†] CIC – the combat information center of the *Essex*.
[‡] Lieutenant (junior grade) John B. Connally Jr., USNR. He later served as Secretary of the Navy from 25 January 1961 to 20 December 1961; Governor of Texas from 15 January 1963 to 21 January 1969; and Secretary of the Treasury from 11 February 1971 to 12 June 1972. He was wounded in the attack that killed President John F. Kennedy in November 1963.

Captain McCampbell: Yes. I knew him very little aboard ship, but when he became Secretary of the Navy, I made a call on him a couple of times, and then later I saw him at a Medal of Honor reunion out in Houston, Texas. He was guest speaker for that. But that's about all.

Paul Stillwell: I've heard that the fighter director officers were very capable individuals that could manage a complicated picture in their heads.

Captain McCampbell: Yes. I wouldn't say they were all capable or good, but certainly we had some good ones on our ship. I don't even know how many fighter direction officers we had aboard ship. I didn't know who Connally was. I didn't even know his name until later. But he was very proud of the fact that he directed some of these people up there, originally about 60—40 fighters, 20 bombers, about. And the fighters all had belly tanks or what appeared to be 500-pound bombs. They had one or the other. I don't know. I tried to get close enough to identify what it was hanging underneath their planes once, and this third guy that joined us for two runs, he started firing way back while I was trying to get up close, and when I saw his bullets, his tracers going by me, I got the hell out of there. I thought somebody was shooting at me. The bullets were coming that close.

Paul Stillwell: If an enemy plane still did have a belly tank, would you aim for that?

Captain McCampbell: No. We still just aimed for the wings, because you're coming down on them primarily. But originally, this part of the tape started out talking about kamikazes. Now, the reason I think they were probably kamikazes, because the very next day, the 25th of October, the kamikazes started operating against the jeep carriers down off of Leyte. It was first reported officially as kamikaze attacks, but a number of instances out there during the war where they thought they must have been kamikazes because they dove right into the ship. But whether these were or not, I don't know.

Paul Stillwell: Well if they were hanging back, they must have been kamikazes who lost their nerve or directions.

Captain McCampbell: Either that, or by then we were running into some Japs who were poorly trained.

I don't know if you know it, but when the war started, all the naval aviators were six or seven years in training before they were sent to the fleet. Of course, they began to run out of those experienced aviators, and so we were getting then some of them after just a short training period. They taught them how to take off and land and fly formation, and that was about it.

Paul Stillwell: They had lost a lot of talent in the Battle of Midway and down at Guadalcanal.

Captain McCampbell: An awful lot in Guadalcanal, in the Solomons. Not just Guadalcanal, but all the way up the line—Rabaul, Bougainville, and some further south too.

Paul Stillwell: When you would go against the leaders of an incoming raid, was the idea that they would be less organized if, presumably, their best people were shot down?

Captain McCampbell: Yes. Well, just generally it would be a good idea to get the leaders; it might throw the rest of the pilots off a little bit, disrupt the formation. But we did. We made a practice, if they were headed toward our ships, we hit the leaders first, if we could. At the Marianas Turkey Shoot I missed the leader, and the first guy I got was one of the tail-enders.[*] I was going to go at him and then go under him, but he blew up in my face. I had to pull up and go above him, but I crossed the formation, and then came back in from the other side. Then I worked my way up, and I finally got the leader. I

---

[*] The "Great Marianas Turkey Shoot" took place on 19 June 1944 while U.S. carriers were supporting the invasion of Saipan. That day U.S. planes shot down more than 300 Japanese aircraft.

only had one gun to shoot by then, because I'd burned out the other barrels before that. But that was the flight where I got the five planes.

Paul Stillwell: How large a load of ammunition would you have with a full plane?

Captain McCampbell: Twenty-four hundred rounds to feed the six .50-caliber.

Paul Stillwell: So 400 rounds per gun.

Captain McCampbell: Yes.

Paul Stillwell: You were working in Hawaii after you'd left the *Hornet*. How soon did you get with the *Essex* then, to be her air group?

Captain McCampbell: I can't remember exactly, but it was about six weeks. Oh, I recall an incident while operating on Maui, Pu'unēnē air station. I went out on a gunnery flight, and I had eight people with me. The target that we used was a sleeve about 18 foot long, and I think it was three and a half or four feet wide, and it was flat like a canvas with copper wire running through it that held it together. And that would be towed by another plane. So this particular day, I started out with an overhead run, and I cut the target right in half. So I called my wingman, and I said, "Roy, take charge. I can't do any better than that." And then I went back to the base. [Laughter] They stayed out and trained on this half-sleeve.

Paul Stillwell: How did you happen to get hooked up with Roy Rushing as your wingman?

Captain McCampbell: He just volunteered for it, and the fighting squadron commander assigned him to me. I had lost one wingman on the Marcus Island to antiaircraft. So Roy was a replacement for him. But the original wingman was with me all through training and to the Hawaiian Islands, and it was our second combat mission.*

Paul Stillwell: What are the qualities that make for a good wingman?

Captain McCampbell: Well, one that'll stick with you.

Paul Stillwell: [Laughter] That's the main quality.

Captain McCampbell: Gives you moral support, if nothing else. Roy, the wingman I ultimately ended up with, went all through the rest of the tour with me. He'd stick so close sometimes I'd have to wave him back to give me a little more freedom to operate. [Laughter]

Paul Stillwell: How close would he get?

Captain McCampbell: Oh, hell, he'd get within 3 or 4 feet, his wing and my wing! It wouldn't have hurt me, I don't think, if he'd hit me flying formation. It'd disturb me, no doubt, but it kind of cramped my style as far as maneuverability. So I'd just wave him back and loosen up the formation.

Paul Stillwell: I would think that after two pilots had flown together a great deal like that, you wouldn't need much formal communication. He would almost instinctively know what you were going to do.

Captain McCampbell: We set up a system, a dot-dash type thing. If I had something to tell Roy, generally I'd just pound on my dashboard. I would pull him close in, and then I'd go ahead and pound on the dashboard—dit-dot-dot-dot, whatever, and communicate that way.

---

* Ensign W. T. Burnham, USNR, was lost on the Marcus Island raid of 18 May 1944.

Paul Stillwell: Morse code.

Captain McCampbell: Yes. And he'd do the same if he had to make an answer.

Paul Stillwell: So he could hear that over the radio or just by seeing it?

Captain McCampbell: Oh, no, just by seeing it.

Paul Stillwell: So that cuts down on radio communications.

Captain McCampbell: Tremendously. No, the dot was like that, and a dash, you'd leave the hand a little longer.

Paul Stillwell: But couldn't he also, just by your movements, ascertain probably what you were going to do?

Captain McCampbell: Yes.

Paul Stillwell: You got on board the *Essex*. Was that just because she was the next carrier coming out? Was she minus an air group? Or how did you happen to get aboard her?

Captain McCampbell: She had been out to combat with Air Group Nine.

Paul Stillwell: That was Phil Torrey's group.*

Captain McCampbell: Yes. Well, Phil came on later in Air Group Nine. But she had been in combat, I guess, six months, and gone back to the States for an overhaul. She had just come out of overhaul, hit Pearl Harbor, and then that's where we boarded her.

---

* Commander Philip H. Torrey Jr., USN.

Paul Stillwell: So that was just a matter of you being the next air group and she being the next ship.

Captain McCampbell: Well, both. Next ready ship and next ready air group to go.

Paul Stillwell: You described this meeting you had with Captain Ofstie about the communications discipline, but you didn't mention how you happened to meet when you did, and I think that's interesting.

Captain McCampbell: Well, we met on the accommodation ladder. I was just reporting aboard for the first time, and I just stepped on the accommodation ladder to climb up, and he had just stepped on topside to climb down. The first time I met him was about halfway up the accommodation ladder. And he gave me the few words of advice about radio silence and radio discipline. That's about all he ever advised me on, all he ever said. I saw him a number of times aboard ship, but we didn't have anything in particular to discuss. When I got to the top of the accommodation ladder, I ran into an old friend of mine, Dave MacDonald, who was there to see the captain off the ship.[*]

Paul Stillwell: He was the exec.

Captain McCampbell: He was the exec of the *Essex*.

Paul Stillwell: And you'd known him back in Florida.

Captain McCampbell: I'd known him back in the operational training command, yes.

Paul Stillwell: Did you have any reservations or hesitation or nervousness at all about going into combat, or was that just something you were eager to do?

---

[*] Commander David L. McDonald, USN. Later, as a four-star admiral, McDonald was Chief of Naval Operations from 1963 to 1967.

Captain McCampbell: Well, I was kind of eager to test out my ability, but when it came at me, it came all of a sudden. It was a surprise when the first guy came at me—practically head on.

Paul Stillwell: What was the circumstance? Where were you operating then?

Captain McCampbell: We were making the first strikes, my group, on Saipan. The other air groups were hitting Guam and Tinian. And we had finished bombing and strafing, and were forming up and heading home, and this guy came out of nowhere at me, as I say, almost head-on. So I let him have the .50-calibers and shot him down right then and there. No strain.

Paul Stillwell: Did you feel a rush of adrenaline?

Captain McCampbell: Yes, kind of, but you're too busy to think anything about it. Now I was alerted, looking for more, but I only got the one that day. It was 11 June 1944.

Paul Stillwell: Admiral Thach told me that if he was flying against a particularly good fighter pilot for the other side, he could admire that guy's skill, even though they were trying to kill each other. How did you view the enemy?

Captain McCampbell: Well, I viewed them all as equal, the fighters, because you could never know when you might run into a real topnotch fighter pilot. So I always gave them the benefit of the doubt of being a good pilot, and I engaged him in that fashion. In other words, I expected him to give his best, and I gave my best.

Paul Stillwell: Would that make you a little more cautious in your approach? What do you mean by that?

Captain McCampbell: No, that didn't make me more cautious. I knew, by virtue of the fact that the last gunnery run I made, I cut the target in half, that I was a pretty good shot. [Laughter] And so I was just doing what I had trained to do.

Paul Stillwell: But you say you gave them the benefit of the doubt. How did that translate itself into action?

Captain McCampbell: Well, I would, let's say, be not more aggressive, balancing one against the other. There was no way you could tell whether he was good or bad until you engaged him. If I found that he had a tendency to run maybe, why, I would be more aggressive. If he was more combative, I'd be less aggressive.

Paul Stillwell: It would also, I guess, keep you from getting lax and taking things for granted.

Captain McCampbell: Yes. Exactly.

Paul Stillwell: You mentioned this first one on the 11th of June. When was the Marcus raid, when you lost your first wingman?

Captain McCampbell: In those days, that was considered a training flight on our way out to Majuro in the Marshall Islands. In company with the *Wasp* and a couple of cruisers and destroyers, we went up to Marcus Island.* We hit that for two days. We didn't get any planes up there at all; there were none on the field. So all the fighters did was strafe trenches and antiaircraft guns and drop bombs. After two days Marcus, then we backed up and went to Wake Island, and we hit that.† And the same thing; we didn't get any planes there.

---

* This was a new *Wasp* (CV-18), commissioned 24 November 1943. She was a namesake of the carrier sunk in September 1942.
† The attacks on Wake occurred on 23 May 1944.

Paul Stillwell: I think you said Marcus was the second combat mission. Which was the first?

Captain McCampbell: That was the second one I'd flown that day.

Paul Stillwell: I see.

Captain McCampbell: The first day I flew three combat missions on Marcus Island, and the second day I only flew two. But then we went on down to Eniwetok and joined up with the fleet.

Paul Stillwell: What is the routine for a pilot—and specifically you, as an air group commander—on the day of a mission? Could you describe a day and how it went?

Captain McCampbell: Well, on the day of the mission, depending on what time of day the mission was to take off, I'd go up to my ready room and have a couple of cups of coffee. I never ate breakfast. Once in a while I'd stop by the wardroom and pick up a glass of orange juice. Then I would stay in the ready room. I always had work to do, paperwork, until time to man the planes. On some occasions, I would go to a fighter ready room and get the latest information, of maybe where the target was and what we could expect. Like when we first attacked Formosa, the fighter squadron intelligence officer had information was if we had a forced landing on Formosa, we could expect to encounter many types of poisonous snakes. [Laughter] So we actually had very little intelligence in those days at points like Formosa, Iwo Jima. Iwo Jima is quite small, so that wasn't a big problem. But we went on up to the Nansei Shotos north of Formosa, and we had no intelligence whatsoever there. That was in September.

We stuck around the Marianas there until the end of August doing support work. We supported the Marine landing on Guam, and there was some Marine and Army there. And we supported the landings on Tinian, Saipan first, and we were there for roughly three months. The other people went off somewhere else; I don't know where. In early

September, we attacked the Palau Islands, and we spent a couple of three days there.* And then we went on over and hit the Philippines.

Paul Stillwell: How were you prepared for striking a ground target? Did you get reconnaissance photos to look at before the mission?

Captain McCampbell: If it was the first strikes on that particular flight, we rarely had photoreconnaissance pictures, but one of our missions was to take photoreconnaissance and photo assessment of damage. So for that purpose we had four pilots qualified in two photo planes. So every operation we'd be taking pictures for damage assessment and for future use.

Paul Stillwell: Well, the first time you went in on a land target, how did you know what points to attack?

Captain McCampbell: Well, if they were main ones like Saipan, Guam, and certain points in the Philippines—Manila—we would have some information and frequently photo coverage of main targets. Main targets were always airfields for us.

Paul Stillwell: You'd probably work from charts, too, wouldn't you?

Captain McCampbell: Oh, yes, like *National Geographic* charts were real good in those days. [Laughter] That was all the information we had many times. For instance, I remember one flight we were to make a reconnaissance and take action where we ran into it, a flight over northern Mindanao. We had so little information even about where airfields were, this first attack of that area, that I was supposed to hit approximately six airfields, and most of them weren't even on our charts. So finally, I was briefing my fighter outfit that was going to be with me for the fighter sweep. As I recall, there were 12 or 16 planes, maybe 20. And it was so confusing, me trying to tell them what I wanted to do was have one division, as we attacked the airfield, count the number of

---

* These attacks were 6-8 September 1944.

planes on it, the approximate number we destroyed, what other damage, and have another division concentrate on another airfield, and another division on another one. There were six or seven in the group to make a reconnaissance of and to strafe planes or combat or whatever took place. But I got so confused trying to sort out these airfields, which some were there on the map, some weren't, that I told the pilots that were going with me, "I can't describe the targets that we're going to hit. Just follow me." So they did.

We didn't do much good there. One of my section leaders sighted a couple of planes down low over land, and I didn't see them. Anyway, I designated he and his wingman to go down and hit them. They got both of them. Took them a little time. We circled above. Then we went in on one of the little airfields. I caught a plane on the ground. It was a transport plane, like a DC-3 or whatever they used. So I took my little outfit down and we strafed on him. They must have been just getting ready to take off. They weren't on the field; they were in a secure area just off the field, lots of trees and whatever. And they had people running out of the planes while we were strafing them. I think they were just getting ready to take off and had loaded already.

Let's take a blow.

[Interruption]

Paul Stillwell: We were talking about the day in the life of a combat mission. You would go up and spend the time in the ready room. Did you talk to the squadron and give any kind of a pep talk or briefing before you'd go out?

Captain McCampbell: Briefing, usually, we'd get from our intelligence officers. If I had a few words to say, why, I might let go with the fighters. I never briefed the bombers, torpedo planes, because I'd get my intelligence usually from the fighter squadron intelligence officer, and that would amount to a briefing for whoever was on the flight.

Paul Stillwell: What was included in the intelligence that was briefed?

Captain McCampbell: Well, the main thing was recognition. Every day the fighters had recognition drill, where they'd flash various types of planes and ships on a screen, and just briefly, very briefly, flash it, and then people would answer what it was. I mean, the pilots themselves got to where they were answering, would call out what it was. At first, of course, the intelligence officer would have to tell them what it was. That occurred every day, which I didn't get in on, because I had other work to do. He also would look over whatever intelligence we had on targets that we were supposed to hit, and brief the pilots on it. Generally, it mostly boiled down to just location of various things.

Paul Stillwell: Did that include enemy antiaircraft sites and the amount of air strength that was expected?

Captain McCampbell: Yes, it did. Also on fleet movements he generally would give a rundown on where we were and what we intended to do and the plans for the future. Like we'd go into the Marianas, and all the pilots would be given a very thorough briefing on what we were going to attack and what the purpose was, and how we'd attack it.

Paul Stillwell: In addition to the recognition, was there a discussion of the characteristics and capabilities of the various enemy planes?

Captain McCampbell: Yes. Right. And the ships, what the armament amounted to. Just anything that came along, why, the intelligence officer usually would put together, and before we'd go out on a mission, he'd get from the fleet intelligence office whatever they had by way of intelligence, which, of course, was the basis of what the intelligence officers would put out. The fleet plans, I mean, like the invasion of the Marianas, we knew what the basic plans were for the fleet. That was about what it amounted to. And then the intelligence officers would debrief pilots and write down, make a script of what they had received, and from that, the intelligence officer and administrative officer would work up their aircraft combat action report, which they then submitted to me to review.

Paul Stillwell: Did the report go through the squadron commanders?

Captain McCampbell: I would sign it or the squadron commander would sign it before, but if it was an air group action, they didn't have the whole thing until I signed it and reviewed it. But if it was strictly like a fighter sweep, then only the fighter squadron commander would sign it. But it would still come through me. So the aircraft combat action reports that most of the book *McCampbell's Heroes* was based on had all been edited by me. That was my only part in putting out the book.

Paul Stillwell: I think a point worth making is that these were done on a daily basis, when events were still fresh in a man's mind.

Captain McCampbell: Right. They didn't all get completed in a day, but within three or four days they'd have them all done. So they were quite current.

Paul Stillwell: What was involved in your editing? Was that to see how plausible the claims were, among other things?

Captain McCampbell: Make sure that they were consistent. Like the three squadrons would make different determinations of what they attacked and what damage they'd done. I would try to put it all together so it would be consistent if there were any deviations.

Paul Stillwell: I've heard there's a natural tendency to be optimistic in claims.

Captain McCampbell: That's right.

Paul Stillwell: Did you notice that?

Captain McCampbell: And I usually made the determination. I turned down a lot of claims because there was no evidence. Where they had evidence, either visual or photo assessment or some other means, then I'd allow it.

Paul Stillwell: What kind of evidence would you look for in air-to-air combat?

Captain McCampbell: Well, by having another pilot visually see the action. That was the main source of intelligence. Initially, when we went out there, we had camera guns, and we discarded the camera guns for two reasons. The first good reason was the pilots had a tendency, as occurred on one or two occasions, to follow the plane down that was smoking and circling and whatever, he'd just damaged, to make sure he hit the water or hit the land. And they would forfeit their altitude to go down and get a picture of him blowing up or whatever. And this was, I considered, for the birds. He was not only breaking up the squadron formation or the flight formation, but also he was forfeiting his altitude, which altitude is a tremendous advantage in these engagements. And the second reason, they were very cumbersome and difficult to correlate with the actual action as to who got what. Two planes may be firing at the same plane that they knocked down, or also, we had considerable difficulty with vibration. When you're firing a gun, you get considerable vibration in the camera guns. I see a lot of good photos that were taken mostly by the *Yorktown*, because they had a special camera gun crew on board, and they even had colored photos. You've seen some, I'm sure. But we didn't have that; we had the initial installation. So we took camera guns out of our planes and discarded them.

Paul Stillwell: How early did you discontinue their use?

Captain McCampbell: I think about the time shortly after the Marianas Turkey Shoot on 19 June. They just weren't satisfactory for the purpose they were designed for.

Paul Stillwell: Sounds as if they were even counterproductive.

Captain McCampbell: Yes. Took a lot of time.

Paul Stillwell: Much has been made about the use of ultra for guiding submarines to targets.* Did that play any part in your operation at all?

Captain McCampbell: No.

Paul Stillwell: Once you got the intelligence briefings and so forth, what happened then? Did you go down to your plane?

Captain McCampbell: Up to the plane.

Paul Stillwell: Up to the plane. Where were the ready rooms, in the gallery deck?

Captain McCampbell: Yes, just one deck below the flight deck.

Paul Stillwell: So you'd meet your plane on the flight deck instead of the hangar deck.

Captain McCampbell: Yes. I was going to make a point, but it will come to me later.

Paul Stillwell: Let me follow up on something you said yesterday when we weren't recording, and that is that you didn't concern yourself in the details of the recognition, but it was up to your wingman, really, to identify what you'd shot down.

Captain McCampbell: That's right. Well, it just kind of worked into that. I was not anywhere near as sharp on recognition as he was, so I'd take his word for what I shot down. He was always that close to me when I was in air-to-air combat. The day we shot down the 15, for instance, I didn't dispute what he said we'd shot down. I suppose it was correct, but it was close enough anyway. We shot down three different type planes that

---

* Ultra—short for ultra secret—was a special security classification given by the British to information gained from breaking the code of the German radio enciphering machine. It has come to be used more broadly to encompass other information obtained from interception and decryption of German and Japanese radio communications.

day—the Zeke, the Oscar, and the Hamp.* He divided them up. I think there were six Zeroes or Zekes and three Oscars—no, I guess there were less—two Hamps, and I don't remember how he divided his up, but I'd depend on him. I got to depend on him.

Paul Stillwell: What Japanese plane did you have the greatest respect for?

Captain McCampbell: I shot down, by the way, 13 different types. I have a list. Barrett Tillman dug those out of the combat action reports, and he got a list for me.† But the Zeke was by far the most frequent plane that I met in air-to-air combat, and I guess that was the one I had the most respect for. Although I shot down different types, I considered the Zeke superior to the others.

Paul Stillwell: Interestingly, though, you liked to stay high for the altitude advantage. I gather that the planes were on more comparable performance terms down lower in heavier air.

Captain McCampbell: Not necessarily. Sometimes we'd go higher. We had combat action as high as 22,000, 23,000 feet.

Paul Stillwell: But didn't the Zeke have a relative advantage in performance when you got higher?

Captain McCampbell: No, a disadvantage.

Paul Stillwell: Oh, I see.

---

* "Zeke" was the Allied code name for the A6M carrier-based Japanese fighter plane also known as the Zero. "Oscar" was the code name for the Nakajima Ki 43 fighter plane. "Hamp" was the code name for the A6M3-32 variant of the Mitsubishi Zero fighter.
† Barrett Tillman is a prolific author on aviation operations.

Captain McCampbell: Zeke was better in maneuverability, rate of climb, up to 18,000 feet, basically, and from there on, the Hellcat began to get equal and then get better in maneuverability and climb, the higher you went.

Paul Stillwell: We were talking about you going out to the flight deck to meet your plane. Did you then inspect it or go through any pre-flight check with the enlisted crewmen?

Captain McCampbell: Very little. Very little. Generally, the only thing I would check would be my rudder and my elevators, and then get in the plane. I had complete faith in my plane captain. I had two. The first one wanted to get into aviation as a pilot, and I got him into it. So he left about shortly after the Turkey Shoot, 19 June. Then the other fellow took over from him, I found to be equally as good. In other words, I never went out and got in my plane and had a down plane. It was always ready. Of course, I was, generally, the only one that flew it. On occasion, they would be short on aircraft and maybe substitute mine, but generally, I was the only one that flew it.

Paul Stillwell: Did you ever go down to the hangar deck at night and just talk to the mechs for their morale and so forth?

Captain McCampbell: No, but my own mech would come frequently to my ready room and talk to me. We'd discuss things, like one thing, he said he'd like to do, if I wanted it, was put a cigarette pack holder in my plane for me. I said, "Yeah, that would be real neat." And so he fashioned a little holder out of aluminum and riveted it to the side, just under the cockpit cover, and every time I made a flight, he always had a fresh pack of cigarettes in there for me.

Paul Stillwell: Your kind of guy.

Captain McCampbell: I didn't smoke that much, but he'd always have a fresh pack in there.

Paul Stillwell: Did you make it a point after each flight to tell him any problems?

Captain McCampbell: Oh, yes, but I had very, very few. Except for the number-two plane, the one that cut out and kept cutting out on me at high altitude, I kept complaining about it, and finally, when we got some new planes aboard, I got me a new one.

Paul Stillwell: Was it a bad carburetor?

Captain McCampbell: I don't know to this day what it was. I don't even know if they fixed it. I know they tried on a couple of occasions when I'd complain about it, but the last time I flew it, it still cut out on me.

Paul Stillwell: Having a reliable plane can make a big difference in your confidence.

Captain McCampbell: Oh, hell, yes! Not only had a reliable plane, but a reliable plane captain. They took good care of me. They were very proud, took a lot of pride in taking care of the plane.

Paul Stillwell: Do you remember the names of those individuals?

Captain McCampbell: Yes. E. E. Carroll was the first one. He, after the war, got out of the Navy and became a highway patrolman out in California. Oh, and Chester Owens was the second one, a good fellow from Alabama. He came over on a couple of occasions and called on my family. Let's see. Those were the only two plane captains I had, Carroll and Owens.

Paul Stillwell: Once you got into the plane, what was the procedure to get off the ship?

Captain McCampbell: Oh, well, it was just routine. Usually, they'd spot me on the catapult, the number one catapult, because they'd bring my plane up from the hangar deck to the flight deck and then spot me right there on the catapult. We carried our own parachute harness. We put that on in the ready room, so we'd buckle up, and just four snaps to hook the parachute that we'd sit on, chutes that snap here, and then leg straps here.

Paul Stillwell: And fortunately, you never had to find out if those worked.

Captain McCampbell: No, I never did. Of course, we had the life jacket on underneath the shoulder straps. We all carried a .38 revolver and holster right here. So the only thing was just get strapped in, get the shoulder straps on, and the safety belt. I took off, oh, three or four or five occasions in such a hurry, I didn't even get my safety belt buckled and shoulder straps on. But shortly after, I'd get hooked up.

Paul Stillwell: In a coordinated strike, once you were in the air, would you orbit, then, while the other planes took off?

Captain McCampbell: No. We developed a system we called a running rendezvous. On a number of occasions, by using the running rendezvous, I'd take off, and then I'd make a half-circle and slow down so the other people could cut in and join up as they'd take off. If they didn't get joined up, then they could tail in behind me. I was still heading for the target or target area, and then they'd get joined up on me: the fighters, torpedo planes, and the bombers. That's one reason we preferred the deck load launch instead of the full air group launch. With the full air group, you'd have to circle and circle until they all got off and joined up. I don't know who else used the running rendezvous, but it allowed us to be usually the first at the target. Like the battles of the 25th of October, my deck load was the first one on the scene. I had orders from the operations officer, Jim Flatley, on Mitscher's flagship. He gave me direct orders to steer a certain course, and the target should be about 40 miles, something like that.

Paul Stillwell: Did you have to weave back and forth to avoid outrunning your bombers and torpedo planes?

Captain McCampbell: No, I'd just slow down enough to give them a chance to join up. I didn't circle or weave.

Paul Stillwell: Once you got over a target area, how did you exercise your functions as the group commander? Was that by radio, primarily?

Captain McCampbell: Yes, by radio. Usually, I would lead the fighters down into the initial attack, but if I had the mission of directing two deck loads, I didn't go down with them. I'd stay up and tell them what to attack and when to attack. The reason I didn't go down with the first strike, because I didn't want to get hit and have to go back and land on the ship.

Paul Stillwell: During an earlier break here, you mentioned that there was one additional item that you got briefed before a mission.

Captain McCampbell: Yes. Very often, whenever we had a rescue submarine in the vicinity, the intelligence officer would know approximately where it would be, and I know that there were many pilots rescued by submarine. One submarine, I think, picked up something like 18 pilots off Rabaul. They were very useful, but in my air group we only had one good occasion to use it, and he responded and rescued the pilot. It happened to be a torpedo pilot and his crewmen. The pilot was William Rising, who's from Pahokee out here, up near Lake Okeechobee.* What was your other question?

Paul Stillwell: We were talking about the business of you running the coordinated strike, and you said that you wouldn't go down with the first deck load; you would stay up high.

Captain McCampbell: Yes, if I had only the one strike and I was air group commander, I'd lead them in, and I would go down with that strike, make attack, whatever it was. But if I had to serve as target coordinator for two deck-load strikes, and frequently for other

---

* Lieutenant (junior grade) William S. Rising, USNR.

air groups, I wouldn't go down with them; I would stay up above and circle. And then in between strikes, my wingman and I would get out of the active area.

Paul Stillwell: Shoot down a few planes. [Laughter]

Captain McCampbell: Sometimes. [Laughter] And then come back for the second deck-load strike and/or other air groups. I'd bring in other air groups, because I was target coordinator for the Ormoc Bay mission, in which we sank the four troopships, one *Terutsuki* destroyer, and five patrol boats.[*] I directed other air groups there, and I directed other air groups in the Battles of Leyte Gulf on the 25th of October '44. So I didn't go down either of those times.

Paul Stillwell: When there would be more than one air group in the strike, was there competition between the two of them?

Captain McCampbell: Well, I was afraid there would be in the October 25 strike against the four Jap carriers up north, and I gave a little strike plan, you might call it. There were two other air groups. One was there with me, circling with me, made one circle, and he joined up right after we finished the circle, and there was another one coming in, and I told them that I would take the first carrier as our target, and it would be the one on the right, and the next air group was 19, take the one on the left in the formation. If they went in diving formation, I'd take the first one we came to, and he was to take the next one up the line. That's about all I recall.

As we were going in, though, on our target, the first carrier, I directed my bomber squadron commander, who was leading the bombers and the torpedo planes, to go for the aircraft carrier and pull out of the formation, and appeared to be launching planes. So my deck load went down on that carrier, and I found out subsequently that although I witnessed nine out of 11 1,000-pound bomb hits, the torpedo planes hadn't come in yet. I didn't see any of the explosions of their torpedoes, but they claimed four or five torpedo

---

[*] Ormoc Bay is on the western side of the island of Leyte in the Philippines. This mission was on 5 November 1944. The Japanese heavy cruiser *Nachi* was sunk by torpedoes in the battle.

hits. My fighters, of course, strafed ahead of the bombers, but I did not go down with them. I found out later that Air Group 19, against my desire, hit the same carrier, so he sank in about a half hour.* He was over hit.

Paul Stillwell: Sounds like it.

Captain McCampbell: Yes. [Laughter] The others I didn't see either. The other three, I didn't see any of those go down. I saw a couple of them hit, and I saw the hermaphrodite battleship *Ise* hit with bombs. The battleship had been converted partially to an aircraft carrier, so planes could take off but not land.

Paul Stillwell: The Japanese had two, the *Ise* and the *Hyuga*.

Captain McCampbell: Yes. I saw them hit.

Paul Stillwell: They both managed to escape.

Captain McCampbell: Yes. And that's about all I saw in that action.

Paul Stillwell: Going back again to a mission profile, after your group had done all its work, did you shepherd them together for the flight back, or how did that work?

Captain McCampbell: No, I didn't. I left that up to the bomber squadron pilot that led the bombers in. But my fighters were covered in for the rendezvous and shot down a couple of Japanese planes in that action. But I stayed over the target to direct the other air groups. I only stayed up there, and no one else was coming in, or if they did, they didn't report to me. I was out maybe two hours, a rather short flight, but I ran out of people to direct, and I knew Hugh Winters was coming on.†

---

* On 25 October 1944 planes from the carriers *Essex* and *Lexington* (CV-16) attacked and sank the *Zuikaku*, the last surviving Japanese carrier from the raid on Pearl Harbor in December 1941.
† Commander Theodore Hugh Winters Jr., USN, Commander Air Group 19.

Paul Stillwell: He was the *Lexington*'s group commander.

Captain McCampbell: Yes. He led the second deck load from the *Lexington*. And so I left and went back to the carrier.

Paul Stillwell: What procedures did you use to make sure that Japanese planes didn't slip into the returning formations?

Captain McCampbell: Well, that's where the fighters would come in for protection. While they were rendezvousing, you mean? While my people rendezvoused?

Paul Stillwell: Yes. And then did you squawk IFF on the way back?

Captain McCampbell: Yes. I think the standard procedure was that you'd turn your IFF on as soon as you took off.[*]

Paul Stillwell: What determined the sequence in which planes landed back aboard?

Captain McCampbell: Usually the fighters landed first, not that they were short on gas, but generally, when we got about halfway home, the fighters would take off and get out pretty far ahead of the bombers. We were out of the combat zone and headed home, and the fighters would land first, and they would all be landing, generally, by the time the bombers and torpeckers came home.[†]

Paul Stillwell: What was the reason for that?

Captain McCampbell: Just to expedite things.

---

[*] IFF – identification, friend or foe. This was an electronic feature that allowed friendly aircraft to have an additional identifying signature when they showed up on radar screens.
[†] "Torpeckers" was slang for torpedo planes.

Paul Stillwell: Was there some concern that they might need to get up quickest to protect the ship?

Captain McCampbell: No, because we would already have a combat air patrol in the air over the ship.

Paul Stillwell: Okay.

Captain McCampbell: Well, there was another reason, a good reason. The fighters, it turned out, were better on landings than the other planes. We had fewer accidents. In fact, we didn't have any accidents in the fighters during the whole combat tour, so they could expeditiously get aboard the fighters and then take on the bombers and torpedo planes.

Paul Stillwell: So that would also produce less risk of a foul deck too.

Captain McCampbell: Yes. Right.

Paul Stillwell: What happened after you landed aboard? Did you then go into the debriefings?

Captain McCampbell: Yes. My intelligence officer would debrief me, and the other squadrons had their own intelligence officers who would debrief their pilots.

Paul Stillwell: Did you typically touch base with the ship's captain after a mission?

Captain McCampbell: Not routinely, no, unless they called for me. Often, though, after I'd landed and got out of the plane, I'd go up to the air officer's level, to observe the landings of the other planes. And if the captain wanted to say something, I was right there.

Paul Stillwell: How much contact was there between you as the air group commander and the ship's air officer during routine operations?

Captain McCampbell: Well, quite a lot, quite frequently. I'd usually go up and observe the landings, and I was right there where I was available.

Paul Stillwell: Who was the air officer in the *Essex* then?

Captain McCampbell: Commander Stan Strong.[*]

Paul Stillwell: Anything in particular you remember about him or his capabilities?

Captain McCampbell: No. He was very good, a very good air officer. I never had any disagreements with him.

Paul Stillwell: What do you remember about Admiral Harrill?[†]

Captain McCampbell: We called him Whiskey Harrill. That nickname stuck with him for a long time before he ever came aboard ship.

Paul Stillwell: What was the origin of that?

Captain McCampbell: I don't know. I guess he was a good boozer. I just really don't know. I think I only talked to him maybe once or twice. He wasn't with us very long. He had an appendectomy shortly after the Marianas Turkey Shoot and was transferred back to the States.

Paul Stillwell: That's an amusing story. I'd appreciate it if you could get that one on the tape.

---

[*] Commander Stanley C. Strong, USN.
[†] Rear Admiral William K. Harrill, USN, Commander Task Group 58.4.

Captain McCampbell: No, let's don't.

Paul Stillwell: All right. Well, in any event, it's in the book *McCampbell's Heroes* in case anyone wants to look it up.*

Captain McCampbell: Yes.

Paul Stillwell: What was it about the F6F that made it such a good plane for that role?

Captain McCampbell: Well, as I've said before, I can't say enough good things about the Grumman Hellcat, F6F. We first had the F6F-3, and then later we got the F6F-5, with the rocket rails, so we were able to carry rockets. When we got the 5s, I either carried four rockets or a 500-pound bomb hung on the wing, because we always used the belly tanks. I remember the air officer told me shortly after we got into combat, he said, "Dave, you all are not using enough belly tanks." We were coming back in the first era there, our first period. We would attack targets and keep our belly tanks. We'd carry our empty belly tank back to the ship. The hangar deck was just full of belly tanks. So the exec was trying to get us to drop more of them so they could get rid of them off the hangar deck. I had them hanging from the overhead, hanging on the bulkheads, and some were on deck. So we started dropping belly tanks with the least excuse after that, and we got along with the exec fine.

But what were we talking about?

Paul Stillwell: We were talking about the capabilities of the Hellcat.

Captain McCampbell: Yes. Well, it had vastly improved capabilities over the previous fighter planes that had been in action, the F4F and the Buffalo.† The latter were only used by the Marines in the Battle of Midway. The Hellcat could climb faster, it was more

---

* See Hoyt, *McCampbell's Heroes*, pages 82-83. According to the book, Harrill was an indecisive leader, so when he complained of stomach pains, the skipper of the *Essex* had the surgeon remove the admiral's appendix in order to get him out of action.
† The Brewster F2A Buffalo was the first monoplane fighter to enter Navy operational squadrons, which it did in mid-1941.

maneuverable, slightly more maneuverable, it provided an excellent gun platform for the six .50-caliber machine guns. We had self-sealing gas tanks. I think the later models of the F4F did too. And we had armor plate behind the pilot. It was faster, equal at some altitudes with the Japanese Zero or Zeke, and better at higher altitudes performance-wise. The biggest advantage, I think, that it provided—over the Japanese, anyway—was the self-sealing gas tanks. It had tremendous firepower. You could shoot up 400 rounds per gun in 40 seconds if you held the trigger down. Of course, you'd burn out the barrels of the guns if you did. We were taught early on to shoot in short bursts, like three to four seconds, ease up on the trigger, and then let go another short burst, or repeated ones. I burnt out guns once there at Marianas Turkey Shoot, my first flight, and it was graphically displayed to me that the thing to do was not to hold the trigger down too long, so I never burnt out a barrel after that.

Paul Stillwell: When you held down that trigger, did that fire all six simultaneously?

Captain McCampbell: Yes. You could shut off a couple if you wanted. Some of the Marines down at Guadalcanal used to shut off two guns, they said, to come home on, but I always trained my people to fire all of them. If they wanted to save up a little ammunition, why, just stop shooting.

Paul Stillwell: Did you always use tracers?

Captain McCampbell: Yes. One tracer every third bullet. We had the incendiary, the ball bullet, and the tracer. We used that one-in-three combination all through combat.

An interesting thing also, I think worth mentioning, back in training, it was at Pungo, one of the two people who had had a little combat down in Solomon Islands, he didn't like the gun performance which, of course, had a pattern that the planes were coming out with. We called it Bureau of Ordnance gun pattern. So he went to work, and he developed a pattern for 1,000 feet. At 1,000 feet, the six guns would concentrate into a 3-foot-diameter circle, and he could get 92 to 94% of the shells in that 3-foot diameter circle at 1,000 feet. Now that contrasted with the Bureau of Ordnance pattern, which had the six guns firing parallel all the way out. But what this amounted to was a very concentrated fire at 1,000 feet, and the shells would cross each other, so you still had basically the same pattern for strafing which you do at much further distance. And we found that most effective for shooting down planes.

Paul Stillwell: So that was instituted in your fighters?

Captain McCampbell: In training, yes.

Paul Stillwell: What was the optimum range for firing at an enemy plane? Was that 1,000 feet?

Captain McCampbell: No, no, because your shells would cross. I would say around 3,000 feet or 1,000 yards, maybe more. For strafing, it was effective at greater distance.

Paul Stillwell: Why, then, was the pattern focused at 1,000 feet?

Captain McCampbell: To give us that concentrated fire. That was about the distance at which you would start firing in earnest. You may open fire a little further because in flying along, it's difficult to judge 1,000 from 1,200 feet or even 1,500 feet. But at that point, you had a very concentrated fire.

Paul Stillwell: Well, along with its other attributes, the Hellcat was a rugged plane.

Captain McCampbell: Very rugged.

Paul Stillwell: You mentioned the one that had to be pushed over the side. Did you get hit on other occasions?

Captain McCampbell: I took a couple of light-caliber bullets, and I've forgotten just where it was. It must have been Iwo Jima, because that Iwo Jima was surrounded by trenches full of soldiers when we first attacked it. And there was so much firing going on from some more guns and, I guess, machine guns, it delineated the trenches on both sides of the island, coming in and going out. It was the heaviest antiaircraft fire we went into, I think. We were fortunate, though, we only lost one pilot shot down by enemy aircraft, and we strafed Iwo Jima for two days, dropped bombs and strafed, got a lot of planes on the ground.[*]

I made three flights against Iwo Jima, one the first day because we attacked in the afternoon, and there was a heavy thundershower just moving over Iwo Jima when we set out to attack it, and we stayed under the overcast. I purposefully overshot. I changed course enough to overshoot Iwo Jima on the north side, between Iwo Jima and Chichi Jima, and after I was reasonably certain we were to the west of Iwo Jima, then I set course directly back to hit Iwo Jima. We were the first to attack them. The *Yorktown* air group came in high, and they had the night fighters lead them in. I don't think they actually hit the storm, but went up over it. They had considerable action topside, whereas ours just consisted mostly of shooting at planes on the ground or underneath; we did both.

Paul Stillwell: What was the purpose of overshooting?

Captain McCampbell: To make sure I didn't run into the damn island. [Laughter] They had a high peak on there, and we had to be so low to keep under the overcast, that I didn't want to run into that peak. Of course, we came in from the west, and by then the rain shower had moved on out, so it was perfectly clear when we hit them.

Paul Stillwell: Did you have any special techniques for avoiding antiaircraft fire?

Captain McCampbell: About the only special technique was not to go too low. We tried to do most of our strafing, if it was a heavily defended spot, to start pulling out at 1,500 feet. So we'd go down as low as maybe 700 or 800 feet at a strafing line, and then pull out. A little high for strafing, but not too bad. The gun pattern would accommodate it at that distance. So we had pretty good success. We claimed, although it is not official in

---

[*] The attacks on Iwo Jima were on 15-16 June 1944.

the records, that we had destroyed—it was fighters, bombers, torpedo planes, all together, an air group—442 planes, we claimed, which is more than we claimed in the air. The air group had 318 in the air.

Paul Stillwell: You're talking about the whole cruise.

Captain McCampbell: Yes.

Paul Stillwell: The dive-bombers would go down at a nearly vertical angle. Was there some maximum angle that you'd use for the Hellcat?

Captain McCampbell: We would shoot for about a 70-degree angle. We didn't always make it, but we tried to hit that.

Paul Stillwell: That's not too far off from vertical.

Captain McCampbell: That's right. In fact, it seems like it's vertical. But I remember distinctly that antiaircraft fire from around the perimeter at Iwo Jima. We just hit two sides. It's actually a triangular island, but we didn't hit the northern side.

Paul Stillwell: You had one other hazard besides being shot at, and that was that the pieces of planes that you destroyed would come back and hit yours, wouldn't they?

Captain McCampbell: In the air, yes. Yes. Oh, I did get some nicks, too, on the 24th of October flight when Roy and I got 15. I came back. The only damage I had was from the debris hitting the leading edge of my wings. And I had quite a few little dents in both wings. But normally you could avoid it. In fact, we'd try to get them a little further out so you could either mainly go over or around the debris.

Paul Stillwell: One thing we haven't talked about is the action against enemy ships. You had one convoy you worked against for the Saipan invasion.* What do you recall of that encounter?

Captain McCampbell: Yes, that was a pretty good-size convoy. The ships were only, let's say, medium size, around 6,000 to maybe 8,000 tons. My fighter squadron commander thought they were even less than that, maybe around 4,000 tons, but I think it went in the ACA report as 5,000 to 8,000.† All the staff had were approximations of where this convoy was. It had left Saipan the day before, but they calculated its speed and direction, and gave us an approximation of where the convoy was. They had one destroyer, and then about six little destroyer escorts along, a number of ships. I've forgotten the exact number now; it may be in my book. But about 12, 14 ships in the convoy. We launched a pretty good distance out, and the exact location was, of course, uncertain, but in order to accommodate that, I had my fighters form a scouting line approximately a mile between each plane, and then we'd go on out from there. That was the way we located them, but actually the initial direction that was given to us was pretty close to being right on him. The distance out was not very close, so we had to kind of extend ourselves a little beyond where we were supposed to pick them up. But we found them at about 275 miles from our ship.

I remember the CVL that was with us at that time launched an attack of nine torpedo planes, and we were launched before daylight. They were supposed to rendezvous with me, as I was target coordinator for the mission, but we could never get together, although I could see him up above me. I said, "Turn on your light." I could see his lights, but he couldn't see ours, so we never did get together. When I formed the fighters in a scouting line, he went on ahead and actually made the first attack on the convoy. Well, the air group commander was leading. I saw him when he was shot down. The Japs sent a couple of ships over to pick him up, and we thought better that our people pick him up, and so we strafed those ships, and they turned away. Well, it turned out that he had ten days in his life raft before the next strikes on Iwo Jim and Chichi Jima. No, it

---

* This attack was on 12 June 1944, when the *Essex* operated in concert with the light carrier *Cowpens* (CVL-25).
† ACA – after combat action.

was shorter than that, out of Saipan, about 150 or so miles. Jocko Clark went back up there.[*] They sighted him and picked him up, and said he had about ten days in the water, but he was not injured, just hungry and thirsty, I guess.

But carrying on, we strafed. The fighters didn't carry bombs on that occasion. We strafed repeatedly, not much antiaircraft fire, except from the destroyer. And we sank a good number of those ships. The bombers that were with me, they had bombs, and they bombed them. All told, the air group sank, we estimated, about 40,000 tons of shipping, which is quite a lot of shipping for two strikes. We had launched a second strike. And then we returned home. We rendezvoused and returned back to the *Essex*.

En route, I sighted a Betty down near the water. We were very close to the *Essex* by then, so I led all the fighters down and had a chance, most of us, the first of us did, had a chance to shoot at this Betty. I didn't get him on the first pass, because I shot at the rear gunner purposefully, to get him out of the way, so we could attack. And then the three other guys came down and made a run on him, and as soon as the third one completed his run, I made another run and shot him down. So I finished one Betty. Now that was the second plane that I shot down.

So then we rendezvoused, went on back to the ship. By then we had left the bombers and torpedo planes behind to get in ahead, to land and get out of the way for them, which we did. Then I was called to bridge; the admiral wanted to talk to me. Well, he didn't talk to me. This was Whiskey Harrill. But his chief of staff did, and just gave me "holy hell" for being late for the landing. We had to go out farther than we thought we would, than they thought we would, and so we were about a half hour late for the landing time. And he gave me holy hell, and that's one thing that the skipper, Ralph Ofstie, got so upset about. In other words, we'd gone out, found the convoy, sank a lot of ships, and did our job, and because we were a half hour late, why, they were giving us hell for it.

So, anyway, then the ship sent out a second deck load, and they got some more shipping, shot up a lot of cripples, and the squadron commander was credited with strafing the destroyer and hitting some depth charges, and blowing the tail end of the

---

[*] Rear Admiral Joseph J. Clark, USN, Commander Task Group 58.1 in the aircraft carrier *Hornet* (CV-12).

destroyer off, and sank it. So anyway, that was the main thing that his flight did, aside from hitting a bunch of cripples.

Paul Stillwell: I think Commander Brewer dropped his belly tank on one ship, too, didn't he? I think I read that in the book.

Captain McCampbell: I don't remember the belly tank. I know he supposedly hit a bunch of the depth charges on the stern. He may have dropped his belly tank on them; I don't know.

Paul Stillwell: That's an interesting weapon.

Captain McCampbell: Yes.

Paul Stillwell: Aside from the obvious difference that the ships were moving, how did attacking and strafing a ship differ from a land target?

Captain McCampbell: Well, generally, it's a lot more concentrated. Land targets like a hangar or barracks or something like that are generally a larger target.

Paul Stillwell: Does that mean you have to go in closer?

Captain McCampbell: For strafing purposes, yes. They're not as well defended, particularly merchant shipping, so you can afford to go down closer to make sure you hit it with either a bomb or strafing. But on that, that's about all. Well, no, you can often see more visible destruction results from your attack on a ship.

Paul Stillwell: Especially if you sink it.

Captain McCampbell: That's right. Right. So that's about all of that story. As I said, we made two deck-load strikes on the convoy. We pretty well finished them all off.

Paul Stillwell: Everybody has had an interest in the great Marianas Turkey Shoot, so please tell me your memories of that day.*

Captain McCampbell: Well, a few basic facts. I led the second group of fighters to take off from the *Essex*. Now, the fighter squadron commander led the first group from the *Essex*, and they did quite well. There were two in that first flight that shot down five planes. Charlie Brewer, the skipper, was one, and Ensign Plant was another one.†

Then as I said, I led the second strike. The enemy had been picked up about 120 miles away, which indicated to me that those early-warning radars were better than we had in the later part of the war, when they changed the surface ships' radar type, the carriers, anyway. But they picked them up, a nice, clear day, about 120 miles away. So we had plenty of time to launch our flight to go out and attack them. I guess we must have hit that second strike out about 60 miles, maybe more, maybe a little less. And we simply tore into them. They had Zeros, and they had Jills, torpedo plane, and Judys.‡ The Judy was a beautiful little bomber, not a heavy bomber, but a good-looking little bomber. For some reason, I missed the fighters. I never saw them.

I picked up first the Judys, so then I concentrated all my attention on them. Fortunately, the last division that was with me, of four planes, picked up the fighters and had a good time up there with them. But I led my rest of the people down on the Judys, and I had so much altitude advantage, that when I dove down, I would estimate we were maybe 20,000 feet above, and they were probably about 15,000 or 16,000. I dove down on them, and I had so much speed, I couldn't hit the leader, but I did hit one of the tail-end Charlies. I attacked him, thinking that I would knock him off, and then go under him, and go to the other side and come back with altitude advantage and hit them from the other side. But the Judy that I first went down on blew up in my face, and I pulled up above him to avoid the debris. So then I went across on top, and I remember thinking at the time, "Gosh, will I ever get across this formation?" Because I figured they were all shooting at me, see. There was no one out there waving binoculars or a sword at me, but

---

* This event was on 19 June 1944.
† Ensign Claude W. Plant, USN.
‡ "Judy" was the Allied code name for the Japanese Navy's Yokosuka D4Y carrier-based dive-bomber. "Jill" was the code name for the Japanese Navy's Nakajima B6N carrier-based torpedo bomber.

I had that feeling. I went across the other side and made an attack on another plane, and I worked my way up, and finally got the leader with just the one gun firing. I'd burned out the barrels on five of them. I still had one gun that fired, and with that, I dropped down to the flight of Jills, the torpedo planes below, and I shot a plane down. I shot at a plane, the leader, down there with the Jills, that I didn't claim him. I think I claimed him as a probable, because I knew he didn't blow up in my face. Then I went on back to the ship.

Now, this is all on June 19, the Marianas Turkey Shoot. Then I got new gun barrels first off, and I didn't go out again until the fourth flight of Japs coming in. There were five flights in all, and I hit number two and number four. They had gotten over near Guam by the time I got into them, and that was quite a melee. They were scattered somewhat preparatory to landing, and we blasted into them. I managed to get two planes out of that group, and, I guess, all in all, we only had seven planes on this flight. I was seventh. I don't remember, but I'd say we got about eight planes out of that bunch over Guam or very near Guam.

Then, as I was coming home, I saw this American seaplane down on the water that was trying to recover, pick up one of the downed pilots, and a couple of Japs were strafing him. So my wingman and I went down and ran them off. We didn't claim either one, but ran them off anyway. We circled a little bit, and then I ran into one of my pilots, Ray Nall, whose plane had been damaged.* He couldn't make anywhere near full speed, and there was at least one Jap attacking him. I ran him off, and that was one of the few occasions that I ever used the weave. I was weaving with him, trying to protect him from this Jap or two, and got him back to the ship, and then we landed. But as I was in the landing circle coming back to the ship, Charlie Brewer, the fighter squadron commander, had just taken off, and I heard him call in to the ship. He said to the fighter director, "Is this all the planes I get for this flight?"

The fighter direction officer said, "Yeah, that's all we got."

So I called Charlie, and I said, "Charlie, there's lots of Japs over Guam, so when you go in, you'd better go in high and fast and stay that way." He acknowledged.

Paul Stillwell: How many did he have with him? You say it was a few.

---

* Ensign Raymond L. Nall, USNR.

Captain McCampbell: Six with him.

Paul Stillwell: That was the same number you had on yours.

Captain McCampbell: Yes. And so he went in, and the result, he and his wingman both got shot down. We never heard from him again, and I questioned the exec, Jimmy Rigg, about it, which is one of the things I disliked about him. He was supposed to stay up high and protect Charlie Brewer and his wingman, and Charlie told him he was going down on this plane.[*] He must have had to go down quite a ways, and Jimmy Rigg never knew what happened to him. His main job was to offer protection for him in that case, and yet he didn't know what happened. So, even today, we don't know what happened to the two of them.

I strongly suspect, from the action I had had a couple of days before that, they dove from high altitude, like 22,000 feet, down to attack the plane, down low. I took the group that was with me—I've forgotten how many planes, maybe eight, and I got down about 4,000 feet. The enemy plane was lower than that. But my windshield fogged up on me. I had forgotten to turn my cabin heater on, and so I fogged up so bad, I had to pull up, and all the guys with me, they followed me, so that guy, he got away scot-free. But I suspect that may have happened to Charlie, and maybe he'd gotten so low by then, he couldn't pull up in time. He could have gone on instruments, but anyway, he may have gone on and hit the water, if he was bull-headed enough to stay in his dive, hoping it would clear up. I don't know. But except for the two, the rest of them got back to the ship safely. I've forgotten whether they shot down any planes or not. So that's June 19th for you.

Paul Stillwell: When you're in a melee like that, how do you keep track of all that's happening around? How do you avoid shooting down a friendly plane, for example?

Captain McCampbell: Well, recognition. You'd have to depend on recognition.

---

[*] Brewer's wingman was Ensign Thomas Tarr, USNR. Both he and Brewer were lost.

One unusual thing that day was the first time we'd ever done it, and we never had to do it again. We were getting so much business, Jap flights coming in at us, that as soon as a fighter plane would land, they'd take it aside, gas him up, fill him up with bullets, and send him off again. We were landing planes and planes taking off at the same time, practically all day. They wouldn't send just one plane off; they'd send eight or 12 or something. But the aspect of landing planes and taking off at the same time, that was very unusual.

Paul Stillwell: Especially for the straight-deck carrier.[*]

Captain McCampbell: Yes. Let's take a blow.

Paul Stillwell: We were talking about the Marianas Turkey Shoot. How do you protect yourself from behind, when you're going after an enemy plane?

Captain McCampbell: Well, you just hope nobody's on your tail, first, and second, if you have time, anyway, you'll zigzag a little bit and clear your tail, make sure nobody's back there. Or hopefully, if somebody's attacking you from the rear, they'll hit the guys in the rear first, the tail-end Charlie. But, other than that, you try to stay ahead of them. I had a couple of different times, people get on my tail, and I describe it as I had to run. In both instances, they were Zekes, and I knew that I could run faster than they could. In fact, I even caught one with a belly tank still on, one day over Guam, and he was one of the guys I had to run from, but not because I couldn't go faster than he could. But when I just almost got within shooting distance, firing distance, it was a Zeke, and he pulled up in a high wingover and real tight, and I followed him, but I could see he was gaining on me in the wingover, so when I got to the top, I just Immellmanned out, and took off back to where the rest of my people were.[†] So that way I had a little jump on him.

I got ahead of him, and then he came after me, but I was gaining on him all the time, and when I got near Orote Peninsula, which is on Guam, I called over the radio. I

---

[*] The U.S. Navy did not start putting angled decks on its aircraft carriers until the 1950s.
[†] An Immelmann turn is one in which an airplane in flight first makes half a loop and then rolls over to make the second half.

said, "This is 99 Rebel. Anyone not doing anything, please come down and get this Jap off of my tail. I'll pass about 1 mile off of Orote Peninsula to the west, and I'll be at 1,000 feet altitude in about two minutes." So, sure enough, I led him right into the mouths of two or three Hellcats that came down and knocked him off my tail. But that was the one occasion I was just tested out. The reason I chased him so far to see if I could catch him with a belly tank on. Of course, when he got on my tail, I quickly released that belly tank, and I set out to outdistance him, and I ran away from him.

Paul Stillwell: What did you have to do to get rid of the belly tank?

Captain McCampbell: Just pull a lever. No problem.

Paul Stillwell: Was it practical at all to have a rear-view mirror in a fighter?

Captain McCampbell: Not very. There's too much vibration. The Japs apparently had very good ones. There must not have been much vibration on them, because it was rather difficult to sneak up on them, unless you came from underneath.

Paul Stillwell: The next big event, then, was the long night chase on the 20th, when the strike was finally set out against the Japanese Fleet.

Captain McCampbell: Yes.

Paul Stillwell: What was your role that day?

Captain McCampbell: We didn't get in on that night action. We had been ordered to proceed to the east of Guam to replenish fuel and ammunition, bombs and so forth. So in my task group, none of us got in. All I can say, all I know about is what I've read since. It must have been a very confusing situation for them. The people who went out didn't accomplish too much, and it cost us about 120 of our own planes.* Not so many of the aviators and crewmen, because they were able to pick most of them up afterwards.

Paul Stillwell: That was a good one to miss.

Captain McCampbell: Yes.

Paul Stillwell: Now, Saipan was a case where the islands were softened up before the invasion, both by surface gunnery and by aircraft. How did you avoid running into those projectiles from the surface ships?

Captain McCampbell: Well, we made a deal with the surface ships to stop firing at a certain time, and we tried to be over the airfield or whatever, the beach, at those times. I know my air group did run into some fire from big guns at one time. That was on the invasion of Tinian. But none of our people got hit.

Paul Stillwell: You just have to give them a wide berth, I guess.

Captain McCampbell: Yes. Now, I did have one classmate who went in to Saipan after they opened the field. By the way, I was the first person to land in Saipan after they got the field in fairly good shape. It still had a lot of shrapnel on it, because the Japs were up in the mountains, they were still shooting down there on it. But this friend was Killer Kane, who was a classmate of mine at the Naval Academy, a hell of a good guy.† Our own antiaircraft shot him down as he was trying to come in and land at Saipan.

Paul Stillwell: He was off the *Enterprise*.

Captain McCampbell: Yes, I think so. He got shot down that day. They didn't open the field until about, oh, the 22nd or 23rd of June of '44, and then he still had a bandage on

---

* The Japanese fleet was so far away from the American ships at the time that the flights out and back resulted in many aircraft running out of fuel and ditching at sea.
† Commander William R. Kane, USN.

his head, where he was injured a little bit when he got shot down, and he made another flight, still had the bandage on his head and everything, and our own ship shot him down again. [Laughter] Two shootdowns in just a very few days, short time.

Paul Stillwell: There's a book about the *Enterprise* that has a picture of him with that bandage on.[*]

Captain McCampbell: Yes.

Paul Stillwell: What was the occasion for you being the first to land?

Captain McCampbell: I was to take some photos over to them. Our photo planes had shot some photos of the islands of Guam and Tinian, and I was delivering those. I had no strain getting in, as my classmate did, but when I started to take off, I suddenly got a flat tire while I was taxiing out. I thought, "Well, this is going to pose a little problem, but not too much, I guess, unless the other one goes flat." I figured I'd take off mainly on the one wheel, the still good tire, and I could make it all right. And I did. Of course, going back to land on the ship, that's not so important, having a flat tire.

Paul Stillwell: Why not?

Captain McCampbell: Because you're arrested by a wire. In those days, we had nine wires before you hit the barrier.

Paul Stillwell: The man in charge of that operation tactically, of course, was Admiral Mitscher, and his chief of staff was Arleigh Burke.[†]

Captain McCampbell: Right.

---

[*] Edward P. Stafford, *The Big E: the Story of the USS Enterprise* (New York: Random House, 1962).
[†] Captain Arleigh A. Burke, USN.

Paul Stillwell: I've seen pictures of you with both of them. What are your recollections of those individuals?

Captain McCampbell: Both very nice people. I didn't get to know them too well. Officially, on one occasion, I met Admiral Mitscher on the wing of the bridge, talked with him a little bit about the battles of Leyte Gulf. Also, I met with Admiral Burke, who was then a captain, of course, and his operations officer Jim Flatley. A classmate of mine was Tom Blackburn.* Why he happened to be aboard the *Lexington* at that time, I don't know, but he was there in the admiral's operations room. I had about, oh, a half hour, 45 minutes with Admiral Mitscher discussing the battles of Leyte Gulf. I had to take over our ACA reports, which, of course, all went through Admiral Mitscher, and also our recommendations for medals. I flew those over to the flagship.

Paul Stillwell: That's a great thing for morale, to recognize your people who have done well. What sort of program did you have in that regard?

Captain McCampbell: Nothing special. Each squadron handled their own recommendations, and I usually approved them. They'd work them up, an intelligence officer or administration officer.

Paul Stillwell: How was the administrative work handled for the air group? Did you have a specific person to specialize in that?

Captain McCampbell: Yes. He didn't have too much to do, except to help the intelligence officer write up these ACA reports.

Paul Stillwell: He'd have routine things—correspondence, I presume, and mail to route.

Captain McCampbell: Not too much. Most of it had to do with ACA reports, quite a few of them. I don't know, I guess he'd reach 70 or 80, anyway. I was trying to edit them

---

* Commander Tom Blackburn, USN.

and correlate the actions between the various squadrons. That was my principal paperwork. Very few letters, two or three recommendations. I would usually be the one to recommend the squadron commanders for medals. Of course, I reviewed all the other recommendations. But that principally was the paperwork that I had to take care of.

Paul Stillwell: Since you were an expert LSO, did you have any contact with the *Essex*'s LSO?

Captain McCampbell: Yes. I had known Charlie Iarrobino before in the LSO circles.* I frequently had talked with him.

Paul Stillwell: What about the mundane things—about sleeping and eating? Did you have any special quarters as the air group commander?

Captain McCampbell: Yes. I had the air group commander's cabin, which was like many of the others, but designated as the air group commander's cabin.

Paul Stillwell: Did you typically eat in the wardroom?

Captain McCampbell: Yes, and I guess each of the squadrons had a refrigerator in their ready room, which they could get a sandwich from. Had a little trouble with that. Paul Emrick was the navigator of the *Essex*, and I'd known him slightly before.† He was class of '32, a year ahead of me. He had been in the air group that was previously aboard the *Essex*, Air Group Nine. He was now the mess treasurer for the ship, and he objected to us having a refrigerator with food in it up in the ready rooms. It was his experience in Air Group Nine. They didn't have refrigerators. Whether they didn't have it or whether the exec wouldn't allow them, I don't know. But he appealed to the executive officer against having the sandwiches up there. But we were in so much action, close timing, that it was very helpful to us. For instance, on 19 June, we were coming and going all

---
* Lieutenant Commander Charles A. Iarrobino, USN.
† Commander Paul E. Emrick, USN.

day, and we didn't have time to go down to the wardroom. In fact, I don't think they even had a mess going down there at that day. But sandwiches were not unusual before we got the refrigerators. We would call down and order a bunch of sandwiches for the pilots. The mess boy would bring them up to the ready room. We just thought it was simpler than having a refrigerator stuffed with sandwich-type food.

Paul Stillwell: Did Commander McDonald support you on that?

Captain McCampbell: Yes, he supported us, and we got them.

Paul Stillwell: Sounds like a common-sense thing to do.

Captain McCampbell: Yes. Right.

Paul Stillwell: Did you have any opportunity to relax off-duty between missions? Did you have movies in the ready rooms, for example?

Captain McCampbell: Well, no. The only movies in the ready room were the identification, intelligence type. But we did have movies in the wardroom, nights when we were in the middle of nothing going on, practically every night. They weren't good movies or recent movies, but they were movies.

Paul Stillwell: Certainly a diversion from what you were doing.

Captain McCampbell: I remember we got ahold of one movie, a Wayne Morris movie, *Kid Galahad*, and they must have shown that six or eight times.

Paul Stillwell: Since he was on board.

Captain McCampbell: Yes. [Laughter] He got real fed up with that. He told the exec that he'd had enough of seeing his own movie, "Please get something else."

Paul Stillwell: Did you do any pleasure reading when you had off-duty?

Captain McCampbell: Didn't have time, frankly.

Paul Stillwell: Write any letters?

Captain McCampbell: Yes, a few. Personal letters.

Paul Stillwell: Well, I know that receiving personal letters is always a pleasure for men on board ship.

Captain McCampbell: Yes, I wrote a few, mainly so I'd receive some. I was courting two girlfriends at the time, so I checked off a few.

Paul Stillwell: But you had the name of only one on your airplane.

Captain McCampbell: Yes.

Paul Stillwell: What do you remember about Captain Wieber, who came along after?[*]

Captain McCampbell: He was a good guy. Old Admiral Sherman, though, used to beat him over the head all the time.[†] I never had any disagreeable words with him one way or another.

Paul Stillwell: Was your contact with him about as it had been with Ofstie, that is, very limited?

Captain McCampbell: Yes. Well, there was no reason to have frequent contact. I went to see Buddy Wieber after the war up in New York. He was commanding officer of the

---

[*] Captain Carlos W. Wieber, USN, commanded the *Essex* (CV-9) from 7 August 1944 to 1 July 1945.
[†] Rear Admiral Frederick C. Sherman, USN, Commander Task Group 38.3 during the Philippine campaign.

Floyd Bennett Field there, Long Island, and then I saw him again shortly before he passed on in Pensacola. I went over and called on him and his wife. He had had a malignant tumor of his ear, and he had to have that removed, and he had a false ear at that point.

Paul Stillwell: Well, since Sherman had such a strong personality, it would be tough to be his flag captain.

Captain McCampbell: Well, yes, and particularly since he was one of the latecomers in aviation. I don't know why, but we got a bunch of those people—Black Jack Reeves, Sherman, McCain, Halsey. Mitscher was an old-timer, and Browning was an old-timer.

Paul Stillwell: Sherman, by then, had a fair amount of experience as a task group commander.

Captain McCampbell: Oh, a world of experience. See, he had the *Lexington*, captain then.[*] Yes, he had a world of experience, but didn't make three-star admiral until very late.[†] He was out there the whole time.

Paul Stillwell: What do you remember of the events of that summer of '44, after Saipan had been assaulted and you were preparing to go into Guam?

Captain McCampbell: Well, that wasn't very long afterwards, but as I said before, I think, we supported the landings at Saipan, Guam, and Tinian, with just the one task group, my task group. I guess that was punishment for not being in on the strike in the nighttime on June 20.

Paul Stillwell: Are there any highlights of that period that stand out in your mind?

---

[*] As a captain Sherman was commanding officer of the first carrier *Lexington* (CV-2) until her sinking in the Battle of the Coral Sea in May 1942.
[†] Frederick C. Sherman was promoted to vice admiral in July 1945 when he became Commander Task Force 58.

Captain McCampbell: No. It was just more or less routine stuff.

Paul Stillwell: What do you remember about the logistic support of the carriers?

Captain McCampbell: Excellent. Really, they were excellent. They were a little bit slow in getting new planes out to us. I know the one time we were down in the fighter squadron, we only had about 22 planes left. Not because we were losing so many in combat—and we lost a lot in deck landings, not operationally—but the engines were getting old, and we were having more maintenance problems at that point, and also losses, like the one of mine that we pushed over the side. If they were badly damaged, they'd just push them over the side.

Paul Stillwell: Do you have any recollections of being in the anchorage at Majuro?

Captain McCampbell: We got ashore there once, but I think it was Eniwetok or Kwajalein, one or the other. And they had set up a little bar on the beach; they called it an officers' club. You could get beer, and that's all; maybe pretzels. [Laughter] But I only got ashore that once.

Paul Stillwell: Some ships had a practice of dispensing medicinal alcohol on board. How was it on the *Essex*?

Captain McCampbell: I only had one or two small bottles of brandy. I don't remember just when I had them, but it was a lousy brand, real cheap brandy. And so I flushed that; I didn't like the booze they were serving. But it was available through the flight surgeon, and on occasion, he'd dish it out when he felt somebody needed it, nerves getting on edge or something.

Paul Stillwell: How much contact did you and other members of the air group routinely have with the flight surgeons?

Captain McCampbell: Well, he would visit the pilots in their ready room quite frequently. He had no duties down below deck; his were all in the flight deck. I didn't have too frequent contact with him, but I know he would make the rounds of the ready rooms periodically. A very nice guy. I've had correspondence with him fairly recently. He's now a doctor up in North Carolina somewhere.

Paul Stillwell: Do you recall his name?

Captain McCampbell: For the moment, I can't. Of course, we always just called him Doc for short. He didn't have a long, difficult name; I just can't remember it.

Paul Stillwell: Did you have a concern about fatigue among the pilots in the air group?

Captain McCampbell: We only had one guy that claimed that he was petering out, so to speak, and his flying actions indicated that. He got shot in the thigh over Marcus Island, and he was screaming like a wounded eagle all the way back to the ship.[*] I escorted him back. He had had his air speed indicator knocked out and a few other instruments. So I told him, "Just get on my wing and follow me," and I'd take him back to the ship. We got to the ship, he didn't want to attempt a landing, so I ordered him to land. He made it all right with no strain. I led him in, to give him an indication of the airspeed, so on the follow approach, he could get the throttle set, then all he had to do, when he got the cut, was throttle it back. We had to put him in sickbay, and he was down there for a couple of weeks with his wound. It wasn't a terribly bad wound, but it scared the hell out of him. So we put him on as permanent squadron duty officer, and he didn't fly for about six weeks. But he finally got back to battery, and we let him fly. Well, he happened to be one of the two communications pilots that sighted the Jap Fleet, of all things. We put him on that job particularly to keep him out of combat.

Paul Stillwell: That was on the 25th of October.

---

[*] This was Lieutenant John J. Collins, USNR.

Captain McCampbell: Yes. Because he had lost a couple of wingmen in action after he got back to flying status, so we gave him jobs like communications coordinator, or whatever.

Paul Stillwell: Those planes served a relay role, too, didn't they, between distant stations?

Captain McCampbell: Well, that was the reason for it, yes.

Paul Stillwell: You were losing pilots here and there along the way. How did you go about working replacements into your organization, getting them trained and so forth?

Captain McCampbell: Well, I thought the replacements that we got, the fighters, anyway, were very poorly trained. One example: shortly after one of the replacement pilots reported aboard, he was on a mission, and he claimed he was running fast, running out of gas. Well, it turned out that he didn't realize he had a belly tank full of gas. So we got him back aboard ship, and he was about out of gas on the main tanks, but he hadn't used his belly tank at all. He possibly didn't even know about it, or it never occurred to him.

Paul Stillwell: Wasn't the standard doctrine to use that first?

Captain McCampbell: That's right. As soon as you got off, you got off on main tank, and then shortly after you got off, you shift to the belly tank. Then if you had to drop it, why, you still got your main tanks full.

Paul Stillwell: What do you remember about the first ventures toward the Philippines?

Captain McCampbell: That was after the Palau operation, which we worked over for two days.

Paul Stillwell: Well, maybe we could cover Palau, just hit that one.

Captain McCampbell: We didn't accomplish much there in Palau. The Japs were well dug in, there were no planes on the fields, and our only job was to bomb and strafe against antiaircraft and a few buildings there, but mainly the Japs were all dug in. So we in the air group were not successful, as far as we were concerned.

But then we went on, shortly thereafter, to the Philippines. The first attacks that my group made were on northern Mindanao, and we got a couple or three planes up there, and then the little convoy, which we cleaned up on.* And that was all that happened there. We attacked for two days, and then moved on up to the Visayans, they call them, that we hit. Then we started getting very fruitful missions, a lot of planes, all kinds in the air. Cebu, we hit all around Cebu, and then over to Negros, Panay. I guess my air group must have gotten 100, 150 planes in the Visayans. But there was nothing on Leyte when we first went in there. We were sent on one flight, my wingman and I, to survey what was on Leyte, and we found nothing. We found no ship concentrations, no airfields. We took pictures of it, and just nothing there. We later got up into Mindoro, another island to the west of Leyte, on the San Bernardino Strait, south of Luzon. We found nothing there, aside from mainly Cebu and Negros, where we got all the action.

Paul Stillwell: Is that where you ran into the Nates, the biplanes?†

Captain McCampbell: Yes, over in Negros.

Paul Stillwell: What were they like? How capable were they?

Captain McCampbell: Well, the one I tangled with was pretty capable.

Paul Stillwell: But that was more the pilot than the plane, wasn't it?

---
* The Mindanao strikes were on 9-10 September 1944.
† "Nate" was the Allied code name for the Japanese Army's Nakajima Ki-27 fighter.

Captain McCampbell: No, the plane was highly maneuverable, and, I guess, had a good rate of climb, a biplane. It was a training plane. And we got a few of those, along with other types—Bettys and a couple of patrol planes, that sort of thing.

Paul Stillwell: Then during about that period, you went and had a strike against Okinawa and one against Formosa.

Captain McCampbell: Well, we worked on up the coast, from south Mindanao, north. As I recall, we hit Manila, Clark Field, in that area, before we went to Formosa. We worked around there, I guess, around Manila, a couple of weeks before we went to Formosa. And we found that a quite lucrative area, too, as far as shooting down planes was concerned, shooting them down and shooting them up on the ground.

Paul Stillwell: Was it Admiral Mitscher who assigned which air groups would hit which targets?

Captain McCampbell: Yes.

Paul Stillwell: So partly, you just had luck of the draw on what you would be up against.

Captain McCampbell: Yes. But we had quite a few strikes. The whole task force would hit targets around Manila. There was an abundance of Japanese aircraft there, and we worked it over from south to north. And then we went on up to Formosa, and that was a real hotbed of enemy planes.[*]

Paul Stillwell: Well, that was really the farthest west the U.S. Navy had been up to that point.

Captain McCampbell: Farthest north.

---

[*] The Task Force 38 strikes against Formosa were on 12-14 October 1944.

Paul Stillwell: Well, closest to Japan.

Captain McCampbell: Yes.

Paul Stillwell: Then that really was what wiped out a good deal of their air strength, because you were so effective.

Captain McCampbell: Yes.

Paul Stillwell: What do you remember about that action?

Captain McCampbell: That they'd keep replenishing the planes on there. Well, we never did knock them all out, but we had a hell of a time when they could fly them down from Japan proper, direct to Formosa, without even stopping for gas. So they kept replenishing them; we kept shooting them down.

I took the air group on one mission to a group of islands called the Pescadores which are west of Formosa.* The mountains on Formosa are around 7,000, 8,000 feet, almost the entire length, and on this one flight we were in such a position when they launched us that there was a long ways to go around the south or the north end, particularly the north end. So I decided we'd go over more or less in the middle, and we ran into some clouds at about 5,000-6,000 feet. And so rather than take the dare of hitting the mountains, I decided to take my flight up through the overcast, and when I announced that was what we were going to do, I remember Lieutenant Commander Mini, the bombing squadron commander, called and said his people weren't trained to fly formation on instruments, to go up through the clouds.

I said, "Well, it's very simple. You just go up two or three at a time, and have your wingmen fly close, and you go on instruments, then go up through it." I would go up through first, and see how deep the cloud cover was, and I found it not too deep, maybe 1,000 feet or maybe more, and I called back and told him it was only 1,000 feet. The leader of each section would go on instruments, and the wingman simply followed

---

* The attacks on the Pescadores were on 11-12 October 1944.

on his wing. So they finally got up there, two at a time, and we got the torpedo planes. They didn't complain; they came right on up. But I had practiced in training with my fighters. I used to take them up through the clouds all the time, overcast.

Paul Stillwell: How capable were the Japanese pilots that you were encountering at that stage?

Captain McCampbell: They were all pretty good. I didn't get into too much action on Formosa. As I said, we went over and hit the Pescadores, and there was very little air activity. Mainly, they had a shipyard over there, and we strafed. There was a cruiser in dry dock, and we bombed and strafed the hell out of that cruiser. And some commercial shipping, we got three or four ships in there. I remember one of them, right at the entrance to the harbor. He was leaving, and our bombers got him, and he blew up. It looked like an atomic bomb blast, so he must have been full of either gasoline or ammunition or both. But there was a great fireball from that. He was a good-sized ship, too. Two or three, four ships, maybe, and the cruiser, that was about all the action we had.

Paul Stillwell: What do you recall about the venture to Okinawa?

Captain McCampbell: Yes, we found a lot of action there, too.

Paul Stillwell: Again, that's pretty close to Japan.

Captain McCampbell: Right.

Paul Stillwell: Any specifics that you remember?

Captain McCampbell: No. First, we got in some action. My fighters got into a lot of action, both Formosa and Okinawa. The bombers and torpedo planes didn't get too much action, mainly just bombing the facilities on the airfields and that sort of thing. But we had a lot of air-to-air combat in both places. We got one submarine tender up north at Nansei Shoto, and I've forgotten which one of the other islands it was, but the submarine tender was tied up at a dock in between two of the little islands, a very narrow passageway through there, and we sank him at the dock.* Other than that, it was just kind of routine operations.

Paul Stillwell: That certainly demonstrates the group mobility that the fast carriers had in World War II. That's why they were so important.

Captain McCampbell: The Nansei Shotos were the closest that my air group got to Japan.

Paul Stillwell: Any other preliminaries to cover before getting to the Battle of Leyte Gulf?

Captain McCampbell: Well, we worked up and down the coast in the Pacific from Mindoro to the southernmost Philippine Island, on out through Visayans, Manila, Formosa, Okinawa, I guess, about three months, at least two. And we'd hit and go back and repeat.

Paul Stillwell: How much intelligence word was there on what to expect going into the Battle of Leyte Gulf?

Captain McCampbell: Well, not too much that we didn't generate ourselves, except for the submarines. They were quite active during that battle. Before the southern Jap force came through Surigao Strait, and also the other force that came through San Bernardino Strait, and they sank one or two cruisers. It seems to me they sank only one cruiser and

---

* The Nansei Shoto strike was on 10 October 1944.

badly damaged another.* But they scouted these forces out and alerted Admiral Halsey as to what was coming, so we knew ahead of time, and we made attacks on the 23rd, to the west, the western side of the Philippines.†

Paul Stillwell: Was that the occasion that you and Dog Smith's group were flying together?‡

Captain McCampbell: No, as far as I was concerned, I didn't realize he was out there until a little later. But the 23rd, we sent out a bomber and a fighter into a team, more or less scout or reconnaissance and targets of opportunity, that type of thing. We sent out, I don't remember how many, but quite a few, on the 23rd. That takes care of the 23rd, as far as we were concerned. No big damage done. A fighter-bomber combination ran into—I know in one case, a cruiser, and I think a couple of merchant ships, and that was about it. And then, of course, we come to the 24th, and send in a large fighter sweep over Luzon. As I recall, we sent over 24 fighters for this fighter sweep, and I didn't make that flight.

Paul Stillwell: I think it would be useful to explain why not.

Captain McCampbell: The admiral called me up and specifically told me after June 19th, that he didn't want me taking part in any more scrambles or purely fighter-type missions.§ He wanted me to lead the deck loads of fighters, bombers, and torpedo planes on missions. So I didn't get in on that fighter sweep. But then, a couple of hours later, we got notification by radar that this flight was coming in on us. Now, some of them had had trouble all morning with Japanese hitting us there. We were right off Luzon. So we

---
* During the Battle of Leyte Gulf, the submarines *Darter* (SS-227) and *Dace* (SS-247) torpedoed and sank the Japanese cruiser *Atago* and damaged the Japanese cruiser *Takao*. Then they pursued the crippled cruiser through the channels of Palawan Passage in the Philippines. Just after midnight on 24 October 1944 the *Darter* grounded on Bombay Shoal. Efforts to free her were unsuccessful, so the crew evacuated to the *Dace* and rode safely to Australia.
† Admiral William F. Halsey, Jr., USN, served as Commander Third Fleet from 15 March 1943 to 22 November 1945.
‡ Commander Daniel F. Smith Jr., USN, Commander Air Group 20 in the *Enterprise* (CV-6).
§ This was Rear Admiral Frederick C. Sherman, USN, Commander Task Group 38.3.

only had seven planes left flyable. We thought we had eight, mine being one of them, but one of the guys couldn't take off for some reason. I never found out why, a malfunction of the engine or something. And we got notification of this raid coming in, and so we scrambled all the fighters we had left. The *Lexington* was short too. In reading Hugh Winters's book, those were all loaded and prepared to make a strike, as we were, I'd say, in the middle of our loading bombing and torpedo planes for a strike.[*] But this raid was right on us, and the first vector I got was like 290 degrees, 22 miles. That was just after I got in the air.

Paul Stillwell: Well, even before that, you were halted from getting into the air, weren't you?

Captain McCampbell: Yes. I got to the fighter ready room. I put on my parachute harness and my life jacket and my pistol, which I always carried but never used. It was mainly in case I got shot down over land or something. I was in the fighter ready room when I heard this announcement of a raid coming in, and I called to the air officer and asked him if he wanted me to take part in this flight or not, knowing that there were only seven planes ready to go, mine included, and he said, "Yes, the group commander is to go." Then I buckled up, was getting all set to go, and the next word came down shortly, "The group commander is not to go on this flight."

Paul Stillwell: Now, was that by telephone that that came?

Captain McCampbell: Loudspeaker. Intercom. So then I started taking off my flight gear, and then shortly afterwards, word came down and said, "The group commander is to go." I guess he found out by then that there were very few fighters left.

Paul Stillwell: It was Admiral Sherman who had found that out?

---

[*] T. Hugh Winters, *Skipper: Confessions of a Fighter Squadron Commander, 1943-1944* (Mesa, Arizona: Champlin Fighter Museum Press, 1986).

Captain McCampbell: Well, I thought that he'd probably gone to Admiral Sherman, but it turned out he didn't

Paul Stillwell: Captain Wieber.

Captain McCampbell: He must have gone to Captain Wieber. So then, in the meantime, I first told my plane captain to get my plane on the catapult. He had to bring it up from the hangar deck. And then word came I was not to go. I got in touch with him. I've forgotten how, but I told him, "No, I'm not to fly." So this was a delay. Then when I got the word to go, the plane captain had to get the plane on the elevator and get it topside. So when we were told to man our planes, my plane was on the catapult, ready to go, except it wasn't full of gas. We'd always degas it when we'd put it below, in case of bomb attack and fire hazard. So they were gassing it when I went out and manned my plane. Pretty soon word came down, "If the group commander's plane's not ready to go, send him below." I looked at my gauges and saw that my main tanks were only half full.

What they had done was gas the belly tank full. Of course, the first thing you do when you get in combat is drop that belly tank. Well, anyway, I waved the gasoline detail away, and I told them I was ready to go. So they launched me, and the other six planes followed, and we made a running rendezvous, and, as I said, shortly after I got off, the first fighter director direction was that the enemy was 22 miles away at 14,000 feet. The bearing, I believe, was 290. It later was changed to more like 298. And we intercepted them. I intended that second division to go down on the bombers and keep my division topside for the fighters. It turned out that number-three man in the bomber group was the second division leader. My second section leader couldn't take off.

Anyway, I called back to this guy, thinking it was the second division leader, and told him to go down and attack the bombers. Now, to this day, I don't remember who that was, but, anyway, he was only the third man in the rendezvous, and I thought he would be the fifth man. So five of the fighters went down and attacked the bombers, and that left my wingman, Roy Rushing, and me topside. So that's how we got into this action. We first made a couple of attacks on the fighters. We'd gotten the altitude advantage, and they quickly went into a Lufbery circle, and I guess that's when they made a couple of attacks.*

Then we saw that was not very fruitful, although I think we did get a couple of planes, and they went into a Lufbery. So Roy and I just preserved our altitude, got up about 3,000 feet above them, and circled, figuring that some were apt to come out of this Lufbery circle, and then we could go to work on them. So we had a cigarette apiece, and in about, I don't know, 10 to 15 minutes—it's kind of hard to judge time, but it was enough for me to smoke one cigarette, so at least eight to ten minutes. And then they broke out of this circle, and then headed for Manila. I don't think they ever sighted our task group at all. They headed for Manila and got strung out, and later formed up in a nice, neat formation, real tight, and that's when we went to work on them. So I've forgotten. Is this a repeat?

Paul Stillwell: Well, this is in sequence. I think this is the best place to tell it in detail.

Captain McCampbell: So we had the altitude advantage all the time we attacked the Japanese. We zoomed down, would shoot a plane or two. Roy and I each would take one, and I'd tell him which one I was going to take, if it was to the right or to the left, which one it was. By telling him this, that allowed him to know which way I was going to dive, and then allowed him to pull out after we attacked, which gave me freedom to go either way I wanted. This worked very successfully, and he got the news. I'd pick out my plane, then he'd pick out his. We'd make an attack, pull up, keep our altitude advantage, speed, and go down again. We repeated this over and over. We made about 20 coordinated attacks.

In the meantime, a third pilot joined up on us, and he made, he said, two attacks, getting a plane on each one, and then he said he ran out of ammunition, and he went back to the ship. But the guy didn't tell me he was going to leave us. It didn't make any difference, really, except that he should have called me and told me he was going to return to the ship. He may have been one of those that when we shifted frequency at the

---

* The Lufbery circle is a defensive maneuver in which airplanes fly in a ring, each one protecting the tail of the plane ahead. It was named for Major Raoul Lufbery, a fighter pilot in World War I.

fighter director's instruction, that he didn't get the word, or he didn't get the right frequency, and he had no contact with me. I didn't try to sort this out later.

But anyway, pretty soon, Roy called me. He said, "Skipper, I'm out of ammunition."

I called back, and I said, "Well, Roy, I've got a little left. Do you want to go down with me for a couple more runs, or do you want to sit up here and watch the show?"

He said, "Oh, no, I'll go down with you." So he followed me down for a couple more attacks, and then I looked at my gas gauges, and I saw I'd emptied one main tank. I was about on the second one, and I was beginning to get low. By then I was out of ammunition, too, getting low on gas, so I called Roy and said, "Well, we'll go back to the ship. I'm getting low on gas." By now, having followed this flight away from the task group towards Manila, we had gotten pretty far away from the ship. I'd estimate maybe around 100 miles, give or take a few.

So we headed back to the ship, and when I picked it up by YE on my ZB system, I was at about 6,000 or 8,000 feet in altitude. I figured was about 65 miles away, which turned out was about right, based on the length of time it took us to get back to the ship. I called the ship, when I first got the YE signal, and asked if they could take me as soon as I got back. They said, "Oh, yes, come on in." So we kept heading for the ship, and when I got over the ship, I found they had a flight deck full of planes, and I knew that to launch all those planes would take a good 20 minutes, and I didn't have that much gas left.

So I called the ship and told them that, and the admiral called the *Langley* and directed them to launch nine torpedo planes, so they could give me a clear deck to land aboard, which they did. When I saw the deck was clear, I came around and made a pass, but the LSO didn't cut me on the first pass. They still hadn't cleared the deck properly for landing. So I made a quick turnaround, came back again, and he gave me the cut, and I landed safely. But when I tried to come out of the landing gear, I gave it near full gun, and the engine conked out on me. So I ran out of gas on the deck. They had to push me out of the landing area. I found out from the mech who reammunitioned the guns that I had exactly six rounds left in the starboard outboard gun, and they were all jammed. But it worked out all right.

I went down to the fighter ready room. I remember the air group commander had just come back from a flight. I was in the ready room, having a sandwich and some milk, and he was all excited. I knew him. He said, "Dave, I just got five planes! How many did you get today?"

I was almost embarrassed to say. I said, "Well, I think I got 11, with a couple of probables thrown in there. You'll have to wait and talk to Roy Rushing." That took the wind out of his sails.

Shortly thereafter, the admiral had directed the *Langley* to launch me on a low combat air patrol, just by myself, no wingman, nothing, but we started getting a lot of low-flying torpedo planes, and so they sent me out about 20 miles from the ship at 3,000 feet, and I circled out there, doing left-hand turns for about an hour and a half or two hours before they would take me back aboard the *Essex*. So that completes the day for me.

A couple of other things, though. One, on returning to the *Essex*, I passed the *Hornet*. Now, the *Hornet* had a new camouflage on it, but I recognized the camouflage, because I'd flown from the *Hornet* on the way around from Norfolk to Hawaii. And they started shooting at Roy and me. I counted 12 bursts from the 5-inch guns. Fortunately, they were all behind us. We had slowed down, too. They would just lay off. One of my Naval Academy classmates was the gunnery officer, and I goosed him about that at some later date. Also, they directed their combat air patrol on us, and I saw him coming down, and I called on our frequency. They must have been on the same frequency, although they weren't in the same task group. I said, "For Christ sake, call off the dogs! We're friendlies!" I don't know whether that got to the combat air patrol people or not, but somehow he got the word, maybe by recognition.

So we proceeded on back to the *Essex*, and we passed the *Princeton*, which was in throes of sinking.[*] I can't remember which was first, whether we passed the *Princeton* before we were shot at, or after we were shot at. But anyway, we passed the *Princeton* close aboard before we got to the *Essex*.

---

[*] The light carrier *Princeton* (CVL-23) was hit by a Japanese bomb on the morning of 24 October 1944, during the Battle of Leyte Gulf. She caught fire, suffered massive explosions, and sank in the late afternoon with heavy loss of life.

Paul Stillwell: And Rushing got down okay, I take it, on the *Essex*.

Captain McCampbell: Yes. He had plenty of gas. He had been fully gassed, but I hadn't, so I had to land on the *Langley*.

Paul Stillwell: So how did it go after you had this combat air patrol, with nothing to do?

Captain McCampbell: Well, they laid off this, and we proceeded on to the *Essex*. No strain.

Paul Stillwell: Had you kept some sort of tally in the cockpit as all these enemy planes were going down?

Captain McCampbell: Yes. After Roy and I had gotten about five, I took out my pencil. We always carried a little pencil here. I started marking them down. I had one slot for the ones I shot down, and the other for the ones he shot down. I'd mark like this, and then cross them when I got to five, and that way kept score.

Paul Stillwell: And that's where your total of 11 probably came from?

Captain McCampbell: Well, I claimed two probables. Ray confirmed two probables out of the 11, and he claimed one probable. I gave him credit for one.

Paul Stillwell: So you were finally credited with nine certain?

Captain McCampbell: Yes.

Paul Stillwell: What kind of reception did you get back on board the *Essex* when you returned from the combat air patrol? Did they know of your exploit at that time?

Captain McCampbell: No, no. And I don't recall when the five people that attacked the bombers got back, whether they came back before me or after. I just don't know. Of course, they may have run into the same thing I did, with a full deck of planes.

Paul Stillwell: The 25th of October was also an exciting day. What do you recall of that one?

Captain McCampbell: Well, yes, it was exciting. The thing I recall most was that my day began very early on the 25th. I had hardly gotten in the bunk, when, about 2:00 o'clock in the morning, one of the staff officers called me and told me that I was to lead a flight the next morning. They were going to wake me at 5:00. The flight would be at maybe 6:00, 6:30. So I got little or no sleep that night. I went up to the ready room and got all rigged up for flying, and we took off on time.

To go back a little, the night before, that's on the 24th, we had a little bull session, Roy Rushing and I and my administrative officer, Wayne Morris. That was why I didn't get to bed till about 2:00 in the morning. But without much sleep that night, my wingman didn't make that flight. That was the first time in about six months that he didn't make a flight with me that he was supposed to. But he was supposed to because I was flying, but the duty officer didn't call him.

Anyway, I had a couple of cups of coffee, and we manned the planes. We had sent out two fighters ahead of us in time to act as a communications team positioned between the enemy and us. By the time we took off, the enemy hadn't been sighted, except by this communications team. In the meantime, we took off, rendezvoused, and we got directions from Admiral Mitscher to go out 100 miles and circle until they got the location of the Japanese fleet, which by then they knew was up north. But until the communication team reported their position, they didn't know just how far north. So they directed us out about 100 miles, to circle. The *Lexington* air group was supposed to rendezvous with us, but before they got there, Commander Smith and his air group from the *Enterprise* rendezvoused with us, just as we had completed the first circuit, making a circle, and he joined up the tail end of my group.

So we proceeded on out a little ways, and I sighted the Jap fleet. I told the people who were following, "I have the fleet in sight." I gave them the approximate location, about 40 miles from where we circled, and I gave them the disposition and approximate speed, and laid out a plan where the first group to attack would hit the ship on the starboard side, and the second group would hit the one on the port side of the formation, to keep them from trying to go in at the same time and get all mixed up in there. When I got a little closer, I could see this one carrier, the *Chitose*, was pulling out of formation to launch planes. I communicated this to the bombing squadron flight leader, and told him to attack that ship, which we did, and I was target coordinator, designated by Admiral Mitscher, or his staff. I circled over my group while they were attacking the *Chitose*. Of the 11 1,000-pound bombs that were dropped, they got nine direct hits on her. They also carried two 250-pound bombs, one on each wing in each plane, and I didn't count those. Some hit and some didn't. But I only counted the big bombs.

Then shortly after, or almost at the same time, we came in with torpedo planes, and I called the flight leader of the torpedo planes, who was V. G. Lambert, and told him if it was not too late, that he could see his way clear to divert his attack on the ship next door, which was the *Ise,* a battleship converted to a carrier with a half flight deck on the after end of the ship. I don't think they could land planes, but they could take off. And I said if he could see his way clear, why, pull off of the *Chitose* and get this battleship next door. He called back and said, no, he was too much committed to the *Chitose*. Of course, what they'd do in the torpedo planes, they'd go out to the sides, half one side and half the other, then they'd come in almost simultaneously on the ships.

Paul Stillwell: So she can't turn one way or the other to avoid.

Captain McCampbell: Right. Or if he goes straight, he gets hit by both sides. That also divides the antiaircraft fire. So I didn't actually see or count any torpedo hits, although he claimed later they had five or six. Then the fighters, which had gone in ahead of the bombers and torpedo planes, they had strafed the ship, dropped 500-pound bombs, and gone to the rendezvous point, which I had designated as 10 miles to the south, and waited for the bombs and torpedo planes to rendezvous with them. And so then they proceeded back to the *Essex*. I stayed over the Jap fleet about an hour and a half or 45 minutes. I directed Commander Smith's group on to another ship on the left side of the Jap fleet, but apparently he hit the same ship that we hit. But that ship, the *Chitose*, was hit so badly, it couldn't possibly last much longer, and so I tried to divert the torpedo planes off it. But anyway, I found out later that he hit that same ship.

Then along came Air Group 19. Hugh Winters was leading, and I directed them to the ship on the left side of the formation. And then after I did that, I left the area. I think he claims he hit the *Chitose*. But then there were two. There was the *Chiyoda* on the left flank ad the *Chitose* on the right flank. He said that he hit the *Chitose*. Well, they were sister ships, and you couldn't tell one from the other.

Anyway, I left the scene. As far as I was concerned, I'd done what I was supposed to do. I knew he was there, so I let him take over as target coordinator, and I came back to the ship and reported my actions. That was the end of the day for me. We did send out another deck load from my air group. Maybe they sent a third one; I don't think so. But, anyway, the final result, the combined actions of the various air groups, we sank the four carriers, heavily damaged a cruiser, and two destroyers. So the action lasted pretty much all day. When we sank the four carriers, Hugh Winters claimed he saw three of them go down. I didn't actually see any, but I know the *Chitose* went down first, and it went down real fast.

Paul Stillwell: That was the action in which Admiral Halsey got the message from Admiral Nimitz, "Where is Task Force 34?"[*]

---

[*] As Commander Third Fleet, Admiral William F. Halsey Jr., USN, had issued a preliminary plan that called for Vice Admiral Willis A. Lee Jr., USN, to form Task Force 34 of heavy surface combatants, including fast battleships. The intent was that they could stay and guard San Bernardino Strait to engage Japanese surface combatants attempting to enter Leyte Gulf and attack American transports. Instead, Halsey elected not to form Task Force 34 and instead took Lee's ships north with him to deal with the Japanese carrier force. The Japanese carriers were decoys, sent there to draw Halsey away from San Bernardino Strait. When the Japanese broke through and attacked U.S. escort carriers and destroyers, an urgent call went out for Lee's ships. Admiral Chester W. Nimitz, USN, Commander in Chief Pacific Fleet in Hawaii, sent a message to Halsey: "Where is Task Force 34?" That impelled Halsey to turn the fast battleships south before they could engage the enemy, and they wound up reaching the area of San Bernardino Strait after the battle was over.

Captain McCampbell: Yes. At one point, after a good five or ten minutes, I could see the Jap fleet and the fast carriers and the fast battleships at the same time; they were that close—I'd say about 30 miles apart.

Paul Stillwell: What direction were the carriers going when you finally got back aboard?

Captain McCampbell: Well, they must have been going eastward, because the wind, at least earlier in the day, was out of the east. A very slight wind, however, but normally, the carriers, when we'd land, would head into the wind.

Paul Stillwell: Now, if the American task force had not gone back south toward San Bernardino Strait, do you think you'd have launched another strike to finish the job on the Japanese ships?

Captain McCampbell: Very probably, yes. I think there would have been enough time in between, although the fast battleships, they could shoot 20 miles for certain, 25 possibly. I don't know with what accuracy, because those fast battleships weren't too well trained when they came out there. In fact, that precluded a possible night action with the Japanese fleet on the night of the 19th or 20th of June.

Paul Stillwell: Right. Admiral Lee decided not to engage, because his ships had been in the carrier screens and not operating as a battle line.

Captain McCampbell: Well, and because they'd had no night training.

Paul Stillwell: Right.

Captain McCampbell: Yes. So aside from being able to sight the Jap fleet and the fast carriers at the same time, then I saw and wondered at the time why they turned around. It was, of course, on account of the message from Admiral Nimitz. You remember the message?

Paul Stillwell: "Where is Task Force 34? The world wonders?" The last part was meant to be padding. The preceding part was "Turkey trots to water," and that was discarded, because obviously that was padding, but the communicator didn't know about the last part, so he left it in.

Captain McCampbell: Yes.

Paul Stillwell: And that enraged Halsey.

Captain McCampbell: Right. So he headed south and then got down there too late to tackle the central Jap force, where they raised hell with the jeep carriers.

Paul Stillwell: Did you see any of the remnants of that action when you got down there?

Captain McCampbell: No, because we didn't go with the fast battleships—at least not immediately. We joined them later. That about does it for the 25th.

Paul Stillwell: One little postscript. You mentioned this during a break. I enjoyed your story about the two Army Air Forces officers who came out to visit the *Essex* around the time of the Marianas campaign. If you could repeat that one, please.

Captain McCampbell: Well, two colonels came out to visit us during the Marianas campaign, and although they were full colonels, they were both very young, even younger than I, and were senior to the captain of the *Essex*. That was Ofstie then. The skipper, Ofstie, didn't recognize their being senior, so the Air Force officers, instead of eating in his cabin with or without Ofstie, they ate down in the wardroom with the lower-rank people.

Paul Stillwell: And you encountered one of them, I guess, later in your career.

Captain McCampbell: Yes. I ran into one of them later when I was on the Joint Staff for the Joint Chiefs of Staff.

Paul Stillwell: What was their purpose on being on board the *Essex*?

Captain McCampbell: Just to observe. I don't know exactly.

Paul Stillwell: Well, we can pick up the story tomorrow. Thank you.

Interview Number 4 with Captain David McCampbell, U.S. Navy (Retired)
Place: Captain McCampbell's home in Lake Worth, Florida
Date: Friday, 17 July 1987

Paul Stillwell: Captain, yesterday we wound up with the very dramatic Battle of Leyte Gulf and your activities on the 25th of October 1944. Your air group had been involved in strikes on Manila. I'd like to resume at that point, please.

Captain McCampbell: Yes. In all, we hit Manila six or seven different times. I don't remember anything very outstanding there, except that one time I led in the first deck load of planes to hit targets in and around Manila.[*] After the first strikes, my wingman and I went out to the west to get out of the active combat area and wait for the second strikes to come in. On this particular occasion, we were about, I guess, 14,000 feet, and I sighted a Betty, a Japanese bomber, down close to the water. I'd say he was maybe 2,000 or 3,000 feet. I called my wingman and told him I was going to make a dive on him. We were headed on opposite courses and I was trying to get him to go under me so I could make a dive on him. I kept pulling up and up, and finally went into a flat spin upside down. I'd never been in that situation before, but I came out of it finally and ended up right on the tail of this Betty.

Paul Stillwell: Was this the one that reminded you of the diving from the Naval Academy?

Captain McCampbell: Yes. I shot him down, and afterwards, my wingman called me and said, "Skipper, what the hell kind of a roll was that?"
 I told him, "Well, it was inadvertent, but it's the type of roll I wouldn't recommend to anybody else." I'd never been in a flat spin before upside down.

---

[*] McCampbell led the first strike on Manila on 13 September 1944.

Paul Stillwell: Was it easier to make a run on a bomber-type aircraft than a fighter?

Captain McCampbell: Well, yes, because you generally have altitude advantage, and you could position yourself either for an overhead run or a high side run.

Paul Stillwell: And the bombers were not as maneuverable.

Captain McCampbell: That's right. And also, of course, they're not as easy to shoot down either, as I found out once. But in this case, there was no problem. I had him all to myself, and I destroyed him.

Paul Stillwell: In what way are they not as easy to shoot down? Is it a tougher plane, more durable?

Captain McCampbell: Yes. I think they carry more of their fuel in the belly of the plane. Certainly it's not all in the wings like the fighters are.

But, anyway, then I went back over Manila, and we directed the second strike in. I've forgotten the targets in particular now. We also picked up a couple of our photo planes; they were over there to make photo strikes and reconnaissance. Then we made two or three runs on the Manila area. Most of the shipping was sunk by then. But they checked Nichols Field and another field there I've forgotten the name of. Runs on Manila itself, then they pulled out. There were two photo planes. Foltz was the pilot of the lead plane, and he called me and said, "Skipper, I've got six Zeroes cornered up here. Do you want me to attack them or not?"*

I called out and said, "No, you'd better wait for me," because they had already taken their photos, and I didn't want to take a chance of one of them getting shot down. They took out two of the .50-caliber guns so they would accommodate the photo equipment.

Paul Stillwell: That was interesting terminology: "I've got six cornered."

---

* Lieutenant (junior grade) Ralph E. Foltz, USNR.

Captain McCampbell: Yes. He was being a little facetious. So he waited for Roy and me, and we went up and we tangled with them. I think we knocked down three or four, the four of us did.

The only other interesting feature of that flight—when Roy and I had were going out west after the first strike hit, we ran onto a cargo ship, pretty good size, I'd guess 6,000 or 8,000 tons. They were tied up to a dock there at Olongapo, and some other air group was in there at the time and dive-bombing on it.[*] They sank that ship there in about two minutes. It happened to be Dog Smith's outfit, dive-bombers with him. So I called over the radio and congratulated the flight leader for leading such a successful attack on the ship. But that's about all that occurred on that flight.

Paul Stillwell: How well defended was the city of Manila by antiaircraft guns?

Captain McCampbell: They were darn well defended: an awful lot of antiaircraft around the city and around the dock area, particularly.

Paul Stillwell: I've seen pictures of that harbor, and it was just littered with half-sunk ships.

Captain McCampbell: Yes.

Paul Stillwell: You could see only the superstructure of the masts above the surface of the water.

Captain McCampbell: There was one cruiser sunk right there just off the docks, and he lay there in the water, half sunk. He had put up a hell of an antiaircraft fire. I remember him distinctly. As I say, that was about all there was to that mission.

Paul Stillwell: Just to go back to the Betty momentarily, you said that you had used the wing root as a point of aim for a fighter type. What was your point of aim for a Betty?

---

[*] Olongapo is a town on Subic Bay, island of Luzon in the Philippines

Captain McCampbell: Well, the first one I tangled with, I went for his rear gunner. But this one I didn't. I think I went for the pilot and the engine. There were two engines.

Paul Stillwell: After that Manila operation, you went after the convoys to Ormoc Bay. What do you remember of those operations?

Captain McCampbell: Yes, that came a little later. I think we had gone up to Formosa again, and then Admiral Halsey got a call from General MacArthur and said, "We've been getting a lot of Japanese convoys down here delivering soldiers, supplies. And we've got one coming in now which is up to the north and should arrive here in early morning."[*] He asked if Halsey could divert some of his aircraft down to attack this convoy, because all he MacArthur had were the fighter planes of the Fifth Air Force, and they were not accustomed to bombing. So he asked Halsey, who dispatched two task groups down to make the attacks.

Again, I was assigned as target coordinator, and I took in about, I guess, 16 fighters and maybe 12 bombers and six or eight torpedo planes.[†] We hit them, I believe, around 9:30. There were four troopships, one *Terutsuki*-class destroyer, and four or five destroyer escorts. My air group made the first attacks, and we sank three of the troopships real quick. I believe the *Lexington* air group had joined up in flying. Anyway, we sank two troopships real quick and then went to work on smaller ships.

About that time, Dog Smith's outfit came in, and I directed them to hit the *Terutsuki* destroyer, which she was doing about 30, 35 knots in that bay, inside, and so far he'd dodged every bomb successfully. But Dog Smith's people came in, and they started on him. There had been a lot of strafing of the destroyer, but there wasn't too much antiaircraft opposition. Dog Smith's outfit started dive-bombing on them, and they got him with two or three direct hits, which finished him off real quick. I think there was only one other destroyer escort that escaped being sunk out of that whole convoy. We found out later the soldiers, survivors on the troopships, and, I guess, some of the destroyer escorts, they started swimming to shore on a little island down to the south. We

---

[*] General Douglas MacArthur, USA, Commander Southwest Pacific Force, was in command of the amphibious forces that began invading the island of Leyte in the Philippines on 20 October 1944.
[†] This operation was on 11 November 1944.

heard that as they'd come up on the beach, the natives would clobber them with a club or a knife they used to cut cane with. And they just slaughtered every one of them that came ashore on that little island. Ilo Ilo, I think, was the name of it.

Paul Stillwell: Smith, I think, was senior to you. Why would you be assigned as the target coordinator?

Captain McCampbell: Well, I don't know. He was senior, yes, but I was senior in experience.

Paul Stillwell: I see.

Captain McCampbell: It was getting late in our tour, and generally it was because of my experience that generally I would be assigned as target coordinator. Now, it went so far even that when Hugh Winters became the air group commander on the *Lexington*, he flew over one day, came to me, and said, "Dave, you're always getting the good cushy job assigned as target coordinator. I'd like to do a little of that myself."

I told him, "Hugh, I don't really have anything to say. You'll have to go talk to Admiral Sherman and his staff." So he did, and that was just before the Battles of Leyte Gulf. Then we would alternate more or less as target coordinator.

Paul Stillwell: Did you come to any reconciliation with Admiral Sherman so that he would allow you a little more freedom of action?

Captain McCampbell: No, not really. I didn't ask for any reconciliation with him. I just obeyed his orders.

Paul Stillwell: And shot down an occasional plane. [Laughter]

Captain McCampbell: Generally. Yes. I didn't have too much to say to the admiral, nor him to me.

Paul Stillwell: You mentioned the Japanese in the water. Did the fast carriers have any doctrine of practice on shooting survivors in the water, either pilots or people off ships?

Captain McCampbell: No. Generally, we would pick them up. At one point, I remember, on the *Essex*, we picked up three Japanese survivors. They became survivors; we picked them up. I remember that they wouldn't eat our food, so we had to specially prepare rice for them. That's all they'd eat. Throw a little fish in there now and then and rice. But we only, I think, picked up just the three during our tour.

Paul Stillwell: So generally, your practice then was to strafe the ship while they were still on board, and leave them alone afterward.

Captain McCampbell: Right. Of course, there were always a number of survivors, the same as when our ships got sunk. We managed to rescue many of the people.

Paul Stillwell: I've heard also that a lot of the Japanese wouldn't allow themselves to be rescued.

Captain McCampbell: Let's say that they resisted it. The cases that I heard about, they ultimately were rescued.

Paul Stillwell: Some resisted less than others.

Captain McCampbell: But with some resistance, yes.

Paul Stillwell: The book *McCampbell's Heroes* talks about the casualties in the bombing squadron during the attacks on the Ormoc Bay convoy and that there was some revolt or hesitation on the part of the enlisted crew members who were concerned about their safety. How did you deal with that problem?

Captain McCampbell: Well, the squadron commander, Jim Mini, came to me with it. He was trying to do something to solve it. I told him simply I would take away their flight skins, their flight orders. We called them flight skins. And this he did, and I told Mini, "We don't really need them anyway. We haven't lost any of our bomber planes in air-to-air combat. So let's send them up and put them with deck crews, plane handlers, for a while." And so he did that. In about a week or so, they came around and went back to flying.

Paul Stillwell: Because that was hurting them in the pocketbook.

Captain McCampbell: Yes. Right. So that was about the end of that.

Paul Stillwell: How did the rest of the tour proceed? The kamikazes were becoming more active by that point.

Captain McCampbell: Well, we didn't get in into any of the kamikazes unless it was on the 24th of October, the fighters that Roy and I attacked. We know that they had either bomb or belly tanks. It could have been either, so I really couldn't say. There was something hanging underneath the belly of the plane. They may have been kamikazes; I don't know. But I do know that the next day on the 25th, the kamikazes started very actively down amongst the jeep carriers off Leyte.

Paul Stillwell: The *Essex* also made a trip to the fleet anchorage at Ulithi. Do you have any recollections of that?

Captain McCampbell: No, except there was a hell of a lot of ships down there in the bay, there for replenishment purposes, to pick up new planes and pilots and, of course, food and gas and oil, that type thing.

Paul Stillwell: It was a chance for the people to put their feet on land too.

Captain McCampbell: Well, yes, we had three or four days in there, and we had a little bar set up on the beach. You could get beer—no hard booze. It was a little diversion. I went ashore once there.

Paul Stillwell: Did the pilots in that kind of a situation tend to trade lessons learned and talk about their experiences and try to help each other do the job better?

Captain McCampbell: I don't know, but I didn't. About all we talked about was getting leave, because we'd been out there longer than most of the air groups. There may have been one air group, Air Group Eight, that was there longer than we were, but they didn't have anything near the action that we had. Most of them were getting relieved around four or five months, and we spent six and a half months in a combat role.

Paul Stillwell: Why do you think it was so long?

Captain McCampbell: Well, a couple of the air groups folded out there because of battle fatigue. We didn't report any battle fatigue. I know Air Group Eight was one that was the one that was out there longer than we were, but didn't have near the action that we had. And they were the longest air group out there that I know of. Battle fatigue hit a couple of the other air groups that I know of, but battle fatigue had to do with loss of planes and pilots, not so much the length of the tour in the combat activity.

Paul Stillwell: Another factor may have been hesitation to break up a winning team. You were doing so well, they wanted to get more out of you.

Captain McCampbell: I think that was part of it. But we should have been relieved earlier.

Paul Stillwell: The leadership of Task Force 58 changed. Admiral Mitscher was relieved by Admiral McCain.[*] Did that make a difference in the operation of the fast carrier task force?

Captain McCampbell: No, it was all pretty much the same. We had McCain just a little while; I think maybe a week or two.

Paul Stillwell: That wouldn't necessarily make that much difference to you at an individual air group level.

Captain McCampbell: No.

Paul Stillwell: Are there any other highlights to recount, then, before you got relieved and began the trip home?

Captain McCampbell: No. We had a little more action after Ormoc Bay. We made a few strikes again on the Manila area and got a little action from the 26th of October to the 14th of November, when we were relieved. I got four more planes. So we had a little action. Other than that, we were transferred to Captain Ballentine's ship that had formerly had Air Group Eight.[†]

Paul Stillwell: *Bunker Hill*, wasn't it?

Captain McCampbell: *Bunker Hill*, yes, was the ship. We were transferred at Ulithi and proceeded home. We had done a little flying going home just to keep a hand in, antisubmarine patrol.

Paul Stillwell: Was there any letdown as you stepped down from this furious pace to just a relaxing voyage home?

---

[*] Vice Admiral John S. McCain, USN, was Commander Task Force 38, the fast carrier task force, during the closing months of World War II.
[†] Captain John J. Ballentine, USN, was the first commanding officer of carrier *Bunker Hill* (CV-17).

Captain McCampbell: Well, it was boozed up.

Paul Stillwell: Oh, really?

Captain McCampbell: I remember the exec of the *Essex*, Dave McDonald, donated a bottle of Scotch to me. As I was leaving, he brought it to me in a brown bag. [Laughter] So I left with a bottle of Scotch. That's about all. We went into Bremerton.[*] *Bunker Hill* was due for an interim overhaul, and we got off there.

Paul Stillwell: How did you spend that time on that voyage home? Was there a taking of stock and writing up reports and so forth?

Captain McCampbell: Yes. Right. That's when we finished up all of our combat action reports.

Paul Stillwell: At what point did you get recommended for the Medal of Honor?

Captain McCampbell: I don't really know. They didn't tell me. No one told me until I got back to Washington. First, they sent me from Seattle to New York to appear at an event for the National Association of Manufacturers. They were having a meeting in New York at the time, at the Waldorf. They set me up in a suite there at the Waldorf-Astoria, and I appeared on the National Association of Manufacturers show. By the way, it was along with Mrs. Shea. Jack Shea, as you recall, was killed on the old *Wasp* when it got sunk. Mrs. Shea and their son were on that same show, by virtue of the fact that Jack Shea had, just shortly before we were sunk, written a very inspiring letter to his son. They were from Boston. But I stayed in my suite there in the Waldorf for about three weeks, all expenses paid, and I had a public relations man from the Navy and also one from Grumman there with me.[†] Finally, one day, I asked this guy from Grumman,

---

[*] Puget Sound Navy Yard, Bremerton, Washington.
[†] Grumman was the manufacturer of McCampbell's plane, the F6F Hellcat.

"Who in the hell is paying for all this?" We were eating at the 21 Club every night or a different club, but mainly the 21.

He said, "Oh, don't worry about it." So I didn't find out until much later that Grumman was footing the bill. Of course, they put it on their expenses and took it off their income tax.

Paul Stillwell: Did you enjoy being treated like a celebrity?

Captain McCampbell: Oh, yes, sure did. Yes, it was great. All expenses paid.

Paul Stillwell: Were you on leave status, or was this considered on behalf of the Navy?

Captain McCampbell: It was on behalf of the Navy. I got my regular pay. It was a public appearance type thing.

Then came the worst part of my whole experience. The Navy called me to Washington. That's when I found out that I had been recommended for the Medal of Honor. They had an appointment with the President to decorate me with it in the White House, and that occurred on 10 January 1945.

Paul Stillwell: Why do you say that was horrible?

Captain McCampbell: No, no, not that, but after that. The Navy sent me on a tour around the United States. Fortunately, I had with me—they provided it—the movie they had made, *The Fighting Lady*. I would carry that with me. I had a public relations officer and a pilot. Of course, I was a pilot, too, so I was the co-pilot. We toured the country in an SNB, the twin-engine Beechcraft. We took off from Washington, we flew to Glenview, Illinois, gave them a talk and an appearance there. What we'd do was show them the movie *Fighting Lady*, and then most of my business was question and answer.

From Glenview, we went to Ottumwa, Iowa, and from Ottumwa we went to California. We hit three places out there: St. Mary's first, which is college that had NROTC at that time.

Paul Stillwell: They also had the pre-flight there, didn't they?*

Captain McCampbell: Yes, I'm sure they did. We hit Los Angeles, but I'm not sure we did any show there, just refueled and went on to San Diego. We hit two airfields there, Miramar and North Island. Then we headed back east. We went to a place in Oklahoma; we stopped mainly to gas up. I didn't give a show. Then we went on down into Texas, to Dallas, Corpus Christi. We hit three air stations down there. From there we went to New Orleans, and then on into Florida, hit two or three stations around Jacksonville, Green Cove Springs, Cecil Field in Jacksonville, and then on down to Melbourne, and then to Fort Lauderdale. We headed back north, we hit the University of Georgia, and Chapel Hill, the University of North Carolina, and then back to Washington.

Paul Stillwell: Chapel Hill was also a pre-flight location.

Captain McCampbell: Yes. Right. So was the University of Georgia.

Paul Stillwell: It sounds like this was in part to give you an appearance before naval aviation audiences and perhaps to boost their morale and so forth.

Captain McCampbell: Right. We also hit Pensacola, a couple of stations there.

Paul Stillwell: How was the reception in these places?

Captain McCampbell: Very good. Very favorable, as far as I was concerned. But we would only spend like one night in each place, just put in one appearance, and we'd take off and go somewhere else. That was kind of a difficult job at that time, just back from a tour of duty, except for the three weeks in New York, which was a form of leave. I did a couple of radio shows there in New York. George Gay and I were on a Gulf Oil show,

---

* In the late spring of 1942 the U.S. Navy initiated the naval aviation V-5 pre-flight program at the universities of Iowa, North Carolina, Georgia, and St. Mary's College in Moraga, California. A fifth center started a year later at the Del Monte Hotel in Monterey, California, but closed within a year.

which they had, I think, once a week.* And I did a couple of other shows. I also made two appearances out at Grumman Aircraft, and one at Edo Floats Company. They were all in the defense business. But we did all that tour around the country there in three weeks, and that was pretty hard on me.

Paul Stillwell: A demanding pace.

Captain McCampbell: Yes. The flying was no big problem, but day after day after day, you got kind of fed up with it.

Paul Stillwell: Sure. Did you feel uncomfortable making the public appearances, the speaking?

Captain McCampbell: A little bit at first. The worst thing was to be on time, because they'd get these groups together in a theater, and to my recollection the only time we were late was at Glenview. We were an hour late getting there because of the weather. They had had the students sitting there in the auditorium for an hour until we got there, and that was kind of embarrassing. But every place else, as I recall, we were on time.

Paul Stillwell: I would imagine they'd ask the same questions over and over so you could pretty well work your answers.

Captain McCampbell: Yes. Right.

Paul Stillwell: We didn't discuss specifically the visit to the White House. I'd like to hear about that.

Captain McCampbell: Well, there wasn't too much to that. There were two of us called up at that time to be decorated by the President. The other man was Red Ramage,

---

* Ensign George H. Gay, USNR was the only crew member to survive from the 15 pilots and 15 air crewmen of Torpedo Squadron Eight TBD Devastators that attacked the Japanese fleet during the Battle of Midway in June 1942.

submariner.* He had three members of his family there, his wife and mother and father. He had his presentation, and then I was called in after him. He was senior to me, so I guess that's why that happened. I had my mother and my sister with me. We were ushered in to meet the President. I remember this was quite an exciting moment, and the President said to me, "Well, Dave, aren't you going to introduce your mother and sister to me?" [Laughter] So I had to turn around and introduce them. Then he said a few words to my mother, and he gave her the medal, and then she pinned it on me or snapped it on me, on a ribbon. That was about all.

Then we went off into an anteroom, and I guess I was in there, my mom and sister with me, for a good 15-20 minutes. I got to talk to Admiral King, who was there for the ceremony, and General Marshall, and General Hap Arnold.† I got to talk to each one of those individually. It was quite a thrill.

Paul Stillwell: Did President Roosevelt appear to have been briefed on what you had done to earn the medal?

Captain McCampbell: Oh, yes. Yes, they always were. I recall at that time, January 10, 1945, he looked ill. His eyes were sunken, with black rings around his eyes, and that sort of thing. He just didn't look in good health at all.

Paul Stillwell: He had lost weight too.

Captain McCampbell: Yes.

Paul Stillwell: And he didn't stand up to give the medal.

---

* Commander Lawson P. Ramage, USN. The oral history of Ramage, who retired as a vice admiral, is in the Naval Institute collection. The oral history describes his experience in receiving the Medal of Honor from President Franklin D. Roosevelt.
† Admiral Ernest J. King, USN, served as Chief of Naval Operations; General of the Army George C. Marshall, USA, was Chief of Staff of the U.S. Army; General of the Army Henry H. Arnold, USA, was Commanding General of the Army Air Forces

Captain McCampbell: No. Of course, we knew all about that. So that was about it. We went back to the hotel.

Paul Stillwell: Why was your father not there?

Captain McCampbell: Mother and Dad and Sister were out in California at the time, and the Navy made all the arrangements. They paid train fare for my mother and sister. My father had fallen and injured his face, and he didn't get to make the ceremony. He had a black eye, and his nose was buggered up, whatever.

Paul Stillwell: You told me when the tape recorder wasn't running that you objected to the term "Medal of Honor winner." So maybe we could put that on the tape, please.

Captain McCampbell: Yes. We prefer "awardee" or "recipient," which is used most, or some synonym for "winner," because a winner, the first thing you think, well, he won a race. That wasn't the object of our exercises. A lot of the people get it for injuries, like falling on a hand grenade or saving the life of one or two other people. I guess they figured that I saved lives by interrupting this air raid to the point where no plane actually got in to bomb the ship. One of the basic requirements for being awarded the Medal of Honor is to have saved somebody else's life as an individual action.

Paul Stillwell: It was a comparable situation to Butch O'Hare in 1942, when he staved off a raid against the *Lexington*.[*]

Captain McCampbell: That's right.

Paul Stillwell: I'm sure that was a very proud moment for you and your family.

---

[*] On 20 February 1942, while a member of Fighting Squadron Three, Lieutenant (junior grade) Edward H. O'Hare, USN, shot down five of nine Japanese bombers approaching the aircraft carrier *Lexington* (CV-2), thereby saving the ship. He was awarded the Medal of Honor for his exploit.

Captain McCampbell: Oh, yes, yes. We were very proud. I have a picture up here on the wall.

Paul Stillwell: I think one other point to be made in terms of saving the ship is that within a few days after you left the *Essex*, she was hit by a kamikaze.

Captain McCampbell: Yes. We're very proud of the fact that we never lost a bomber or torpedo plane that we were escorting due to air-to-air combat, and also our ship, the *Essex*, was never hit by enemy bomb or torpedo while we were aboard, which to us indicates that we gave the *Essex* good protection also. In combat, when you're in the active area, we always maintained a combat air patrol on the ship. We shot down many planes on that combat air patrol.

Paul Stillwell: When you went to Grumman, there was at that point no idea that the war would end as soon as it did. I'm sure that a satisfied customer coming back and testifying to the value of the Hellcat had to be a useful thing for building the morale of the workers.

Captain McCampbell: Yes. I think it was. I made two appearances out there, and subsequently, I made many others. We were great friends while the president, LeRoy Grumman, was still alive, and also with his second in command.[*] Well, let's take a break.

Paul Stillwell: Was it a relief, after making a tour of the country, to finally get back to a Navy job?

Captain McCampbell: Yes, and to be married.

Paul Stillwell: How did you get the assignment at Norfolk?

---

[*] LeRoy Grumman had founded the Aircraft Engineering Company in 1929.

Paul Stillwell: After my tour of combat duty with Air Group 15, I was assigned as deputy to ComFAir Quonset, and my location was at NAS Oceana, just out of Norfolk about 12 miles.[*]

Paul Stillwell: Virginia Beach.

Captain McCampbell: Yes. I operated from there, conducted surveillance more than anything else on the various air groups that were training in the area, in Chincoteaque, Oceana, Pungo, and another air station down south at Creeds, Virginia, where the bombers trained.

Paul Stillwell: So this was a chance for them to take advantage of your operational experience and expertise.

Captain McCampbell: Yes.

Paul Stillwell: Well, there were a number of new carriers being brought into service then, so this was developing the air group's program, I take it.

Captain McCampbell: Exactly.

Paul Stillwell: Was there any role beyond training involved in your job?

Captain McCampbell: No. Supervising, in general. I had nothing to do with the assignment of personnel. My dealings usually were with the group commanders and the squadron commanders. I had nothing to do with the active training, other than provide them with a syllabus.

Paul Stillwell: Was it primarily a desk job, or did you get out on the ships at the various bases?

---

[*] ComFAir – Commander Fleet Air.

Captain McCampbell: I didn't get on any ships. I went around to the various bases, air stations. But primarily a desk job.

Paul Stillwell: So what did you do, monitor the training of each group?

Captain McCampbell: Yes, as to flying hours, that sort of thing, and generally just how they were coming along. That only lasted about, I guess, six or eight months.

Paul Stillwell: That was essentially when the war ended.*

Captain McCampbell: Yes. Then I was assigned to ComAirLant staff in Norfolk, as the plans and intelligence officer.† I had that job I've forgotten how many months, probably about a year or so. From there I went to the Armed Forces Staff College there in Norfolk. I was the first class there.‡ [Laughter]

Paul Stillwell: I'd like to get more detail on how you spent that time before you went to the Staff College. What were your specific duties?

Captain McCampbell: The main thing that I did while I was there was to formulate plans for the re-supply of the Mediterranean fleet, the Sixth Fleet, in atomic weapons.§ During the period that I was there as plans officer, it was about a six-month period that we completed those plans for re-supply. It involved dealing with Fort Campbell Army base in Kentucky and with the capabilities of the DC-3—I think that's all we had to work with—as just how to do it.** We would have our planes ferried from Fort Campbell to the Azores, and then from the Azores to Port Lyautey.†† At Port Lyautey they had a

---

* V-J Day – Victory over Japan Day, marked the end of the war in the Pacific on 15 August 1945. Because of the time difference it was 14 August in the United States when combat ended.
† ComAirLant – Commander Air Atlantic Fleet, the type commander.
‡ The first class of the Armed Forces Staff College convened on 3 February 1947 on the site of a former Navy receiving station in Norfolk, Virginia.
§ This section on atomic weapons deals with Commander McCampbell's AirLant staff duty in 1952-53.
** The DC-2 and DC-3 were superb cargo or passenger planes; the design was quite innovative for its time. In World War II the DC-3 carried the Navy designation of R4D and the Army Air Forces designation C-47.
†† Port Lyautey, on the Atlantic Ocean, was in what was then known as French Morocco.

stockpile, so that the AJs could fly from the ships, pick up the weapon at Port Lyautey, and then fly back to the ship.*

Paul Stillwell: You had some very famous admirals you were working for—Admiral Bellinger and Admiral Bogan.† What do you remember about them?

Captain McCampbell: I had no problem with them. As far as I was concerned, they were nice people.

Paul Stillwell: What specific characteristics stand out from them as individuals?

Captain McCampbell: None, really, except that they all were not old at that point, but they had been in aviation for a long time, graduated from Pensacola in the early '20s. By the time they came to the staff, they were experienced aviators. I made a couple of trips for little vacations.

Oh, yes, one thing. Admiral Bogan resented his age and grade. I made a couple of trips with him, one to Miami, I remember. The first thing he did when he got on the plane, he took off for Miami. He took off his admiral shoulder boards and put on commander shoulder boards. I had to ask him. I said, "Admiral, what did you do that for?"

He said, "Well, I find I get along better with the girls at the commander rank than I do with the admiral rank." [Laughter]

Paul Stillwell: He'd have to change his hat too.

Captain McCampbell: Yes. But that's about the only thing I remember of any of them, the only unusual, funny thing.

---

* The AJ Savage was a propeller-driven carrier-based nuclear strike aircraft built by North American Aviation, Inc. It first entered the fleet in squadron VC-5 in September 1949.
† Vice Admiral Patrick N. L. Bellinger, USN, served as Commander Air Force, Atlantic Fleet, from 20 March 1943 to 2 February 1946. Vice Admiral Gerald F. Bogan, USN, served in the billet from 2 February 1946 to December 1948.

Paul Stillwell: What about the process of winding down after the war ended? There had been this great pipeline buildup of training and ships and planes and so forth, and that had to be turned off. How did you go about that?

Captain McCampbell: I didn't have anything to do with it, actually. It came out of BuPers to reduce the personnel, both officer and enlisted.* They had a kind of a bad time getting rid of the officers that had grown into commander, captain ranks. We instituted some changes there, like after you did 26 years, you had to be selected to continue for the four additional years to get your 30 years in. This applied to mainly captains and commanders. It was a way of eliminating some of the top rank.

Paul Stillwell: I think there were some captains from around the class of 1930 who got reverted to commander.

Captain McCampbell: I don't remember that. If they did, they were only in the captain rank temporarily.

Paul Stillwell: I'm sure that's true.

Captain McCampbell: Temporarily appointed, and then there were warrant officers who were promoted during the war. They had to revert back to their original rank, the rank before the war. Not all of them, though. Some were retained in their wartime rank. I remember we had one on the AirLant staff, Elmo Runyan, and he was retained under his rank which he had reached during the war.†

Paul Stillwell: Well, it would probably depend on the assessment of the individual.

Captain McCampbell: Yes, and his specialty.

---

* BuPers – Bureau of Naval Personnel.
† Lieutenant Commander Elmo D. Runyan, USN, a naval aviator who was subsequently promoted to commander in 1952.

Paul Stillwell: I'm curious why you were officially assigned to Commander Fleet Air Quonset Point when you were physically in Norfolk.*

Captain McCampbell: Well, because we had about five air groups training in the Norfolk area. Quonset was about 300 miles, and it was inconvenient for the commodore and staff to communicate or supervise all the air groups. Of course, they had a bunch of people training around Quonset too.

Paul Stillwell: So you were his on-scene representative.

Captain McCampbell: Right.

Paul Stillwell: This was Commodore Rowe, I think you told me.† How much communication did you have with him to report what was happening?

Captain McCampbell: Quite frequently. About once a month. I would fly up to Quonset Point if they had a banquet or a gathering. Once in a while he'd call us up there for a staff meeting.

Paul Stillwell: Did you continue to be called on for these public appearances once you settled into the job at Norfolk?

Captain McCampbell: Yes. I'm even doing some of it today. [Laughter] It's been almost continuous, but about once a week or so, but, for instance, just this past May, Memorial Day week, I had three engagements during that week. Various people, the local clubs, the Kiwanis Club, and that sort of thing, and they have me address the luncheon or something. But public appearances, I've made many of them.

---

* Quonset Point, Rhode Island, was the site of a naval air station until the mid-1970s.
† Commodore Gordon Rowe, USN. The August 1945 issue of *All Hands* magazine contained a photo of Rowe awarding McCampbell a medal at the Oceana Naval Auxiliary Air Station. All told McCampbell received four medals on that occasion for his exploits in the Philippines the previous year: Navy Cross Silver Star, Distinguished Flying Cross, and Air Medal.

Paul Stillwell: After the war, there was a slate of books and magazine articles from various participants, describing their experiences. How did you resist having some of that yourself?

Captain McCampbell: Oh, I assisted a number of people in writing books, like Barrett Tillman and *Hellcat*.* We had numerous communications, mostly correspondence. And various others, like Hoyt's book, *McCampbell's Heroes*.

Paul Stillwell: I was thinking more in terms of the late 1940s, when the books were coming out right after the war. Did people approach you then about doing books?

Captain McCampbell: Not very much, no. I did a number of radio show appearances and some television appearances. I was on the Bob Hope Show in San Francisco just after the end of the war. That was a good show. On the same trip, I did two radio shows in Los Angeles. On four occasions, I've been the grand marshal for parades, one in Winchester, Virginia, I believe, was the first one, Colorado Springs, Pensacola. I was in a big parade in Washington when Nimitz and Mitscher came back. I rode with Mitscher. I've been on other parades, but grand marshal for four of them. So those public appearances have occurred all along, and I'm still making public appearances, like these shows up at Maxwell Field.† For me, that's a public appearance. The show in Atlanta, seminar. Pensacola, I was up there for the opening of the new museum.‡ Even before that. So I've been called on to make public appearances all through the years. It's slacked off considerably now. The naval aviation's 75th anniversary, I was invited to that, but they didn't volunteer to pay my expenses.§

Paul Stillwell: So you didn't go?

Captain McCampbell: So I didn't go to that one.

---

* Barrett Tillman, *Hellcat: the F6F in World War II* (Annapolis, Naval Institute Press, 1979).
† The Air War College is at Maxwell Air Force Base, formerly Maxwell Field, in Montgomery, Alabama.
‡ The National Museum of Naval Aviation, Pensacola, Florida.
§ The anniversary was in 1986, the year before this interview.

Paul Stillwell: Well, people like Joe Foss and Pappy Boyington and so forth had autobiographies.* Did you have offers to do that and turned them down?

Captain McCampbell: I only had one offer for that, and I turned them down. I didn't want to do it.

Paul Stillwell: Was it a case of just avoiding the publicity? What was your reasoning?

Captain McCampbell: No, not so much that as just it would have been a real chore, as your interview here is a chore. It disrupts my entire routine. [Laughter]

Paul Stillwell: Well, I appreciate the imposition that you're willing to put up with it.

Captain McCampbell: And I appeared there on the *Yorktown* for the Carrier Aviation Hall of Fame.† I've skipped some of them. I've been invited to speak at the Air and Space Museum at the Smithsonian; I turned that down. They didn't volunteer to pay my way either. Generally, those that don't volunteer to pay my way, I don't attend if they're long distance. Locally, I accept.

Paul Stillwell: I think it's also fair to say that you certainly haven't sought to exploit your achievement.

Captain McCampbell: No.

Paul Stillwell: Otherwise, you certainly would have accepted more offers than you did.

---

* Joseph J. Foss and Gregory Boyington were Marine Corps fighter pilots during World War II and Medal of Honor recipients.
† The aircraft carrier *Yorktown*, which at various times carried the hull numbers CV-10, CVA-10, and CVS-10, was decommissioned on 27 June 1970 and placed in mothballs. In June 1975 she was towed to Charleston, South Carolina, to become the centerpiece of a naval memorial named Patriot's Point. She was formally dedicated in that role on 13 October 1975, the U.S. Navy's 200th birthday.

Captain McCampbell: Yes, I would have. I don't have a book to sell, like some of the celebrities. [Laughter] And I have attended a lot of reunions. The *Wasp* has one every year, the *Essex* has one every year, the *Portland*, the *Ranger*, and I've attended. The Congressional Medal of Honor Society—I attend all those gatherings. They have them all over the country, and the local people pick up the tab for the expenses. The airlines always give us free first-class transportation to wherever it is, even as far as Honolulu.

Paul Stillwell: To those who received the Medal of Honor?

Captain McCampbell: Yes, and their wives and girlfriends. [Laughter]

Paul Stillwell: That's generous.

Captain McCampbell: So those I always attend.

Paul Stillwell: That's different also, because it's the opportunity to see old friends and shipmates.

Captain McCampbell: Not shipmates, because no one on the *Essex* had the Medal of Honor except me.

Paul Stillwell: No, but I mean the ship reunions would be.

Captain McCampbell: Yes. But, of course, I know a lot of the Medal of Honor people. As a matter of fact, for air-to-air combat, Butch O'Hare and I are the only two who ever received the Medal of Honor.

Paul Stillwell: Well, that's a very select group. What do you talk about when you get together with others who had that award?

Captain McCampbell: Well, experiences. Various ones have written books, and we discuss those and critique the books. [Laughter] But we always have a principal speaker. We had Westmoreland at the last reunion up in Myrtle Beach, South Carolina.* We had the governor there; Senator Strom Thurmond was there.† They put on a big banquet there. Well, most panels do, except Washington. Washington, we get it for the inaugurations. I've been at the last five inaugurations, and there again, they pay all the expenses: hotel, food, and banquet and so forth.

Paul Stillwell: Is that the Inauguration Committee that picks up the tab?

Captain McCampbell: I don't know exactly who, but I presume it's the Inauguration Committee.

Paul Stillwell: Do you have any specific memories of any of those inaugurations that especially stand out?

Captain McCampbell: Yes, I do. The one for President Carter.‡ Well, the one before that, too, a couple of times before that. Before Johnson was Kennedy, and we were at that.§

Paul Stillwell: You were still on active duty then.

Captain McCampbell: I was still active duty. I was stationed at the Pentagon then, and I remember that usually the ceremonies were four or five days. And the first one, I was to attend the governor's ball. At the time of the Kennedy inauguration, I worked in the

---

* General William C. Westmoreland, USA, served as commander of U.S. Forces in Vietnam from 1964 to 1968 and as Army Chief of Staff from 1968 to 1972.
† J. Strom Thurmond, who represented South Carolina as both a Democrat and Republican, served in the Senate from 7 November 1956 to 3 January 2003.
‡ James E. Carter, Jr., who had graduated from the Naval Academy in the class of 1947, served as President of the United States from 20 January 1977 to 20 January 1981.
§ John F. Kennedy served as President of the United States from 20 January 1961 until he was assassinated on 22 November 1963. Lyndon B. Johnson served as President of the United States from 22 November 1963 to 20 January 1969.

Pentagon, and it just started to snow. I remember they let everybody go home early at 3:00 o'clock, I think it was, and I was due at the governor's reception at 5:00, 5:30. So I came home and changed to civilian clothes. No, I had civilian clothes on then, because we always wore civilian clothes in the Pentagon, on the staff. I came home, to the apartment, and I don't remember exactly changing clothes, but anyway, I started out about 4:30 to go to the governor's reception, and I wasn't married then, so I took my girlfriend.

We got just short of one of the big hotels out to the west. I can't remember the name of it. They had a little hill to climb up to go to the parking area, and it had snowed so much by then, the roads were getting slippery, and as we were climbing up this hill, we went into a skid and went into the gutter. I was out surveying how to get the hell out of there, and along came a black in a truck. He saw we were in trouble, and he parked the truck and got out and came back, said he wondered if he could help us. I said, "Yes, you sure can. I've got some chains in the trunk of the car. If you'll help me put them on, I'd appreciate it." So we got the chains out, and I noticed that he had on tennis shoes, and his big toe was sticking out of both of them. And here he is wading around in the snow. We got the chains on, and then I decided that it was a lost cause, trying to get to the hotel in that snow, and it would be even worse coming home. So the first chance I got, I turned around.

I gave the colored guy ten bucks, and I turned around and started back to the apartment. We got about halfway there, and the traffic was just horrible. What happened, we would be stopped in traffic, and it was cold, and we kept the heater going in the car, and I ran the battery down. So I happened to be in a spot about half a block from a friend's house, and I pulled off and parked, thought I'd go have a drink and give the battery a chance to charge. I went in and had a couple of drinks. By the time I came out, the car started, but it had snowed more. So thankfully, we did have a chain, but I figured the traffic was so bad, stop and go, stop and go. So the first chance I got, I took a sharp cut and went down a one-way street for about four blocks. The traffic leaving Washington central area wasn't anywhere as heavy as going to various functions that evening.

Anyway, I got partly back to the apartment, took me about three hours, after stopping and having a couple of drinks. In the paper the next morning, it said there were over 10,000 cars in the District of Columbia alone that were parked because they couldn't go anymore, whether it was the battery or just too much snow and no snow tires, no chains or anything. But over 10,000 cars in the district alone. I don't know how many were outside in Maryland and Virginia.

Paul Stillwell: Did you make it to the inauguration itself?

Captain McCampbell: Yes. I haven't finished yet.

So we got back to the apartment, and the next day we were supposed to go to the banquet, which was way across town in the auditorium, I think it was. This was for President Kennedy now. They told us the next day would be buses at Fort Myer to pick us up and take us across town, because a lot of the guys didn't have cars.[*] They'd come from out of town, whatever. So we made our way over to Fort Myer. My apartment wasn't very far from there. I'd say it was 1111 Army Navy Drive, a big apartment, within five minutes walking distance to the Pentagon. Fort Myer was maybe a mile and a half, two miles. We made our way over to Fort Myer and took the bus, so that's how we got to the event, which wasn't the banquet. I don't know if it was called a reception; it was more of a show. They had people like Frank Sinatra was there, and, of course, the President and his wife, various dignitaries were there.[†] They passed out bottles of champagne, maybe hard drinks too. I didn't get any; I got champagne. It was quite a prolonged show. I remember we left early and took one of their early buses over to the apartment.

But we made the inauguration, the actual swearing-in ceremony the next day. Of course, we had pre-arranged reserved seats for the ceremony, all in a group. We had coffee and doughnuts just across the street from the Capitol there. The United Services Organization provided coffee and doughnuts and sweet rolls. Then we walked over to where we were seated, and we got in there, and they had set up these aluminum chairs. It

---

[*] Fort Myer, an Army post, is in Northern Virginia, adjacent to Arlington National Cemetery.
[†] Frank Sinatra was a singer and movie actor who had connections with President Kennedy and his family.

had stopped snowing, but there were about 3 or 4 inches of snow on the ground. We sat down, and the preliminaries took a little long, I thought, relatively, sitting out there in that cold weather. [Laughter] I don't know what the temperature was, but it was below zero. My date had worn jeans, and she had a good warm jacket, but she had jeans on. After about a half hour of this, we were sitting there with our feet in the snow.

Paul Stillwell: And on a metal chair.

Captain McCampbell: And a metal chair. She finally said, "David, my ass is cold as a nun's fanny. I've got to leave." So we got up and left the ceremony. Kennedy was just coming out when we got up and left. We had a hell of a time bucking the crowd going out; they were coming in.

Paul Stillwell: So you didn't see the swearing-in.

Captain McCampbell: We didn't see it, no.

Paul Stillwell: Did you go to any of the inaugural balls that night?

Captain McCampbell: Oh, yes. They always had us a special ball. We made the inaugural ball.

Paul Stillwell: Did you wear your uniform to those occasions?

Captain McCampbell: Some did and some didn't; it was optional. I think I wore my evening dress to most of them, anyway, maybe all of them.

Paul Stillwell: That is an especially impressive uniform with the Medal of Honor around your neck.

Captain McCampbell: Yes. I don't think anything unusual occurred.

Paul Stillwell: You have on the wall here also a picture of yourself meeting President Kennedy in the White House Rose Garden. That was evidently another occasion. What happened then?

Captain McCampbell: I was on duty out at Colorado Springs in the Air Defense Command, and he called in all the Medal of Honor holders from all over the world. I know there was one there from Japan, there was one there from Okinawa, there were a couple there from Germany, and all those within the United States. And they flew us out. It was more like a brunch than anything else, except an opportunity to meet the President. It was kind of a reception-brunch type thing. That was my only occasion to meet President Kennedy. Most of the time at these inaugural balls, you get to meet the President, but we didn't at Kennedy's. But it was a very pleasant reception, and I got to meet the President.

Paul Stillwell: Do you have any impressions of him from that meeting?

Captain McCampbell: He had been briefed, of course, on each one of us, I guess. The only thing he said to me was, "Congratulations," that type thing. And he said, "I'll be seeing you out in Colorado Springs in a couple of weeks." And I got to see him again out there.

Paul Stillwell: He was aware of what you had done.

Captain McCampbell: Yes, I'm sure he had been briefed on all of us.

Paul Stillwell: Apparently, he had a very good memory, too, so he could assimilate this kind of information and probably had something personal for each individual that he met.

Captain McCampbell: Yes. Because we had about, I guess, maybe as many as 200 people there for that reception. Of course, we have had the Vietnam conflict since, but we still have 235 living. One died early this year, so there are 235. But on these occasions, the inaugurals and also Kennedy's reception, you could bring your wives. They didn't say anything about girlfriends. So I had a couple, good friends of mine there in Washington, and I didn't have a wife at that time, so this naval officer said, "Why don't you take me over to the lunch?"

Paul Stillwell: Who was that?

Captain McCampbell: Sam Lanier, a good friend of mine.* I'd served with him three times. I said, "No, but I can take your wife." She's an ex-movie actress. She's a cutie. She had injured her spinal cord earlier in life. She used to dance. She was a little crippled still, used a cane. So I took her with me to this reception. I drove the car into the gate, finally got permission to do that, and drove her right up to the White House and let her out right there in the Rose Garden. But then they told me I had to take the car back out and park it, so I did that, and came back in. She enjoyed the hell out of that. But she didn't get to meet the President; just the Medal of Honor people did.

Paul Stillwell: Did you have occasion to meet President Johnson subsequently?

Captain McCampbell: No, we didn't meet Johnson. I didn't meet Eisenhower as President, but I met him prior to that. He flew out to the ship, the *Franklin D. Roosevelt*, when I was exec there.

Paul Stillwell: That was probably when he was the NATO commander.†

Captain McCampbell: Yes, it was. He flew out, and I escorted him around the ship, down into the atomic weapons compartment, which he was very much interested in. I met him then, and I met him once at the Armed Forces Staff College, when we had him down as a guest speaker.

---

* Commander Samuel L. Lanier, USN, a naval aviator.
† General of the Army Dwight D. Eisenhower, USA, served as NATO's Supreme Allied Commander Europe from 2 April 1951 to 30 May 1952.

Paul Stillwell: What impressions do you have of Eisenhower?

Captain McCampbell: I don't have any particular impression. I just don't know. As a matter of fact, I did not vote for him, because I have a feeling that military people should not be put in that position, whether it's Army, Navy, or Air Force, I don't care. But most of the people disagreed, so he was elected.

Paul Stillwell: Did you meet President Nixon during his inauguration?[*]

Captain McCampbell: Yes, met Slippery Dick.

Paul Stillwell: I know he has great reverence for military people, so he probably put on a good show for you.

Captain McCampbell: Yes. When I say I met him, most of those people I just shake hands with, and they say, "Congratulations," and so forth, and that's it. But I was on the platform with Reagan and got to go up to the strategy session with him, had pictures taken with him, in '76, when he announced his candidacy for President.[†]

Paul Stillwell: This is when he was in the primary against Ford.[‡]

Captain McCampbell: Yes. Then later at the inaugural ball in Washington, I got to shake hands with him. That's about all. He impressed me very highly, he and his wife Nancy. We got to meet her. Of course, I kind of followed his career along, and I voted for him, but that was all.

Paul Stillwell: Any impressions of President Carter?

---

[*] Richard M. Nixon served as President of the United States from 20 January 1969 until his resignation on 9 August 1974.

[†] Ronald W. Wilson ran unsuccessfully for the Republican Party nomination for President in 1976. He did won the nomination in 1980 and was elected later that year. Reagan was President at the time of this interview.

[‡] Gerald R. Ford served as President of the United States from 9 August 1974 to 20 January 1977.

Captain McCampbell: Yes, Carter I never liked, I guess mainly because he was—I guess still is—a Trilateralist. You know that group, don't you?

Paul Stillwell: David Rockefeller and so forth.[*]

Captain McCampbell: That's right. And also the other group that Rockefeller controls. I forgot the name of it.

Paul Stillwell: I don't know.

Captain McCampbell: But most of the same people belong to both groups. For instance, I may not vote for George Bush because he's a Trilateralist.[†] That's called a government outside the government. So Carter I was not impressed with, and I didn't vote for him. That's about all my experiences with the Presidents.

Paul Stillwell: Did you meet President Truman?[‡]

Captain McCampbell: No, I didn't meet Truman.

Paul Stillwell: Whose inaugurations have you been to besides Kennedy's?

Captain McCampbell: Well, Kennedy. I'm not even sure I can name the Presidents. Kennedy, Johnson.

Paul Stillwell: Nixon was after him.

Captain McCampbell: I was at his.

---

[*] Rockefeller was the long-time head of the Chase Bank in New York.
[†] George H. W. Bush served as President of the United States from 20 January 1989 to 20 January 1993. He was Vice President at the time of the interview.
[‡] Harry S. Truman served as President of the United States from 12 April 1945 to 20 January 1953.

Paul Stillwell: Then Carter. Well, Ford didn't have an inauguration.

Captain McCampbell: No. He was appointed. Nixon. Kennedy, Nixon, Reagan, two for Reagan.

Paul Stillwell: Did you go to Carter's inauguration?

Captain McCampbell: Yes, I went to that, too, but I didn't get to meet him. He was busy walking down Pennsylvania Avenue. I saw it on TV. When we left his inauguration, that's one where it was snowing, also snowing. My last one for Reagan, he was inaugurated in the White House.

Paul Stillwell: It was so cold.

Captain McCampbell: Snowing again.

Paul Stillwell: Well, moving back to where we were chronologically after that tour in Norfolk on the AirLant staff, you went to the Armed Forces Staff College. I believe you told me that it was just getting started then.

Captain McCampbell: Yes. I was in the first class there. I applied for it when I heard it was going to be open. It was a good experience. And then they kept me on for a year as an intelligence officer, and that was a good experience also.

Paul Stillwell: What was the curriculum at that time?

Captain McCampbell: Well, it lasted six months, and most of it consisted of lectures and outside reading. Most of it was strategy and tactics. And then we would have a seminar, each class, developed in a specific area, like we had one on the Persian Gulf, we had another one over in China, Korea, in that area. They called it the Chinese Sea area. And one other one; I can't remember what it was. But the seminar we would work on all year, and we were divided up into various divisions: personnel, intelligence, planning, operations, logistics, communication, divided the students up in different classes, and they would prepare a part for the whole seminar. We'd have to get up on the stage and give our presentations. We'd have six or eight on the stage. It might be an operational mission presentation. As I said, it was very interesting.

Paul Stillwell: Had you specifically requested to go to a joint service staff college instead of the Naval War College?

Captain McCampbell: I just put in specifically for the Armed Forces Staff College, mainly because I owned a home there in Norfolk. It was convenient, only about half a mile from my house.

Paul Stillwell: The charge or specification or whatever has been made a number of times that the Army does better staff work than the Navy because the Army doesn't have to operate ships, of course. Was this your first real contact and detail with the Army and Air Force officers?

Captain McCampbell: Yes. Well, they attend more schools than the Navy. Most of their life is spent attending various schools. I'd been to the artillery school, for instance, for two weeks down in Texas somewhere. I believe it was in El Paso. And the Armed Forces Staff College, that was my first contact with the Air Force in a large group, Army and Air Force.

After the Armed Forces Staff College, I was assigned to Buenos Aires, Argentina.

Paul Stillwell: I don't want to jump ahead quite that quickly. One point that a number of people have made who have been to that staff college is that it gave them an insight into the way the officers of other services think, and that that was useful to them for the rest of their careers. Did you find that to be the case?

Captain McCampbell: Yes, somewhat, because I was later on a joint staff. There I had 25 Navy captains, Army colonels, and Air Force colonels, and Marine colonels under me. So it helped me, I guess, through that period.

Paul Stillwell: This was also a period when the Defense Department was being created, and unification of the services, the battles between the Air Force and Navy. Did that friction manifest itself in the staff college?

Captain McCampbell: Very little, if any. Very little. Which brings up another appearance I made—before the American Legion convention in Chicago. I believe it was '46 or '47. And that's when the unification thing was a hot potato. What I was told to do was to make a presentation to this particular group. The Air Force was trying to take over naval aviation, and we were very much against that, so my presentation was against the Air Force absorbing naval aviation. But I got off the subject a little there, but that's another one of the appearances that I have made through the years.

Paul Stillwell: There were some strong efforts on the part of the Air Force to recruit naval aviators and give them promotions to be Air Force officers. Admiral Radford, for example.[*]

Captain McCampbell: Admiral Radford headed up that committee that I worked for on that, and Admiral Forrest Sherman was also on that committee with me in Chicago.[†]

Paul Stillwell: This was the committee that sent you to the convention to speak on behalf of naval aviation?

Captain McCampbell: They had an op named to it, but I've forgotten what the number was.

---

[*] Admiral Arthur W. Radford, USN, served as Vice Chief of Naval Operations from 3 January 1948 to 16 April 1949.
[†] Vice Admiral Forrest P. Sherman, USN, later Chief of Naval Operations.

Paul Stillwell: Admiral Burke was in one called OP-23, and I think they were specifically trying to fight off the Air Force challenge.*

Captain McCampbell: Well, he was on the same committee, then.

Paul Stillwell: Did the Air Force make any overtures to you to try to get you to switch services?

Captain McCampbell: No.

Paul Stillwell: Another problem that was heating up at that time was the Mediterranean, with the Greeks and Turkey, trying to keep them from going over to the Communists. Was that a topic for study in the staff college?

Captain McCampbell: I don't think so. I don't recall.

Paul Stillwell: You had mentioned to me, when the tape recorder wasn't running, that you did a study on the Persian Gulf during that period. Could you discuss that in a little more detail, please?

Captain McCampbell: Well, the area that we were invading was the—I think they called it then the Green Triangle between the Tigris and the Euphrates Rivers. The invasion was through the gulf into what is now Iraq and Kuwait, not so much in Iran. It was up in the end of the gulf.

Paul Stillwell: Was this a full-fledged contingency plan? What was the character of the study?

Captain McCampbell: Well, it was like a contingency plan, yes.

---

* Rear Admiral Arleigh A. Burke, USN, later Chief of Naval Operations.

Paul Stillwell: What sort of thing might have triggered the invasion that you were looking at, if the Soviets had tried to move into the area?

Captain McCampbell: Yes.

Paul Stillwell: How detailed did the study get?

Captain McCampbell: It got pretty much in detail, although the whole thing, of course, was hypothetical. Number of troops, number of aircraft required, ship support, use of the Marines. It covered the waterfront. Of course, we didn't get down to the nitty-gritty details of it. Not being there, we couldn't.

Paul Stillwell: Well, that probably took into account also the fact that the U.S. had atomic weapon capability, and the Soviets didn't.

Captain McCampbell: Yes, it took in the world situation, too, in general.

Paul Stillwell: I think you mentioned to me also that students had individual papers to write, and you got the freedom of choice which later students didn't have. What did you write on?

Captain McCampbell: I wrote on the future of naval aviation.

Paul Stillwell: How did you envision it at that time?

Captain McCampbell: [Laughter] Well, I didn't get too far with it. I forget whether it was 10,000 or 20,000 words, a discussion of it. But it again was very hypothetical, and I could let myself go on it.

Paul Stillwell: Have you ever pulled that paper out to see how good it was as a predictor?

Captain McCampbell: No. I turned it in to the school, and they never returned it. They supposedly reviewed all those papers. We weren't given a mark on it or anything. I never heard anything about it after I turned it in, so I don't have a copy.

Paul Stillwell: Who was the commandant of the school at that time?

Captain McCampbell: General Emmons of the Army Air Forces.[*]

Paul Stillwell: Do you have any memories of him?

Captain McCampbell: No. My wife and I called on him after I became an instructor there, but nothing special. He seemed like a very nice gent. I played golf with him a couple of times.

Paul Stillwell: Was there a senior naval officer that you reported to?

Captain McCampbell: Yes. Rear Admiral Hall. I've forgotten his first name.

Paul Stillwell: It may have been the same one that Douglas Fairbanks came with to the *Wasp*, John Hall.[†]

Captain McCampbell: We had an Admiral Olds there first, and I think Hall came on after him.

Paul Stillwell: Was the school split on service lines, or pretty well integrated?

Captain McCampbell: It was split in service lines. See, we had an Air Force guy who was the commandant of the college, and we had a deputy, Navy, and a deputy, Army.

---

[*] Lieutenant General Delos C. Emmons, USAAF. Later in the year he became part of the newly established U.S. Air Force.

[†] It was indeed the same individual, Rear Admiral John L. Hall, who had been on board the *Wasp* in 1942. He became commandant of the Armed Forces Staff College in 1948.

Paul Stillwell: What specific role did you have then when you moved to the staff after being a student?

Captain McCampbell: I was assistant intelligence officer.

Paul Stillwell: What was involved in that?

Captain McCampbell: Well, the original intelligence officer, one of the assistants had worked up a command decision paper, and I essentially didn't change it, but I thought I improved on it, developed it a little further. Other than that, I would supervise the intelligence division for the seminars, the students that worked in the intelligence. So that was about all it was. It wasn't difficult at all.

Paul Stillwell: Were the seminars on a classified level?

Captain McCampbell: They were all either secret or top secret, one or the other.

Paul Stillwell: So presumably, you'd get the latest intelligence on various areas of the world, to keep them updated.

Captain McCampbell: That's right.

Paul Stillwell: Was there anything that you saw that foretold what happened in Korea a couple of years later?

Captain McCampbell: We did one seminar on that area. It wasn't specifically Korea; it was the war against China, the Shantung Peninsula. It's right across the Yellow Sea from Korea.

Paul Stillwell: Did you have prominent guest speakers come to the Staff College?

Captain McCampbell: Oh, yes. We would have at least one every week, and then I remember we'd take a vote on who we didn't want to invite back. [Laughter] We never told that particular speaker, but I remember one Air Force guy said nothing.

Paul Stillwell: Who was he, do you remember?

Captain McCampbell: I can't remember.

Paul Stillwell: Do you recall any who were particularly good?

Captain McCampbell: Yes. Eisenhower got a good mark. Pete Quesada got a good mark.[*] Most of them were just fair to middling. Some stood out.

Paul Stillwell: Did the students take any field trips during the course of the term there?

Captain McCampbell: No.

Paul Stillwell: That would be one major difference from the National War College, which has that as a regular part of the curriculum.

Captain McCampbell: Yes.

Paul Stillwell: Well, it sounds as if that was a very broadening experience in terms of your career as a professional service officer.

Captain McCampbell: Yes. My roommate was an Air Force colonel, and various other officers there I became quite close to.

Paul Stillwell: Any that you especially remember that went on to prominence later?

---

[*] Lieutenant General Elwood R. Quesada, USAF, became the first commander of the Tactical Air Command in the newly independent Air Force in 1947.

Captain McCampbell: Well, my office roommate went on to become a major general. I ran into him later in Wichita Falls, Texas. He invited me down there to be a guest speaker for a "dining in," the Air Force calls it. And I think now the Navy has some of that.

Paul Stillwell: They call it mess night.

Captain McCampbell: Yes. But I had hardly gotten there when this goddamned tornado came through there. We went out to play golf. We were in the middle of playing golf when a tornado alarm went off on the base, and this tore the hell out of one area just to the west of us, and knocked out the generator in the hospital at the base. While the tornado was there in the area, we spent most of the time in a storm cellar. There were about eight or ten people in the storm cellar. But it killed about, I think, six people. It was a full-bred tornado, I'll tell you.

Paul Stillwell: Who was that officer friend of yours?

Captain McCampbell: Bob Stillman.[*]

Paul Stillwell: How did the assignment to Argentina come about after the Staff College?

Captain McCampbell: Well, that was the best assignment I had in the Navy.

Paul Stillwell: Even better than being a fighter pilot?

Captain McCampbell: Yes, but different in many respects. I was still at the Armed Forces Staff College, and they pulled me out of there. The armed forces have a policy, generally, I found out, at least the Marines and the Navy and the Air Force, that holders of Medals of Honor would not be sent back into combat again.

---

[*] Lieutenant Colonel Robert M. Stillman, USAF, served 1946-47 as deputy chief of staff at Tactical Air Command headquarters, Langley, Virginia, near Norfolk. From 1963 to 1965, as a major general, he commanded Sheppard Air Force Base, Wichita Falls, Texas.

Paul Stillwell: I didn't know that.

Captain McCampbell: And the Korean War was coming on about that time, a year later.*

Paul Stillwell: It probably started when you were in South America.

Captain McCampbell: Yes, the whole time I was down there, practically. I was assigned as senior naval aviator to the Argentine Navy, and as instructor in the Naval War College. I had two hats. And they assigned me a Beechcraft, two-engine, and a pilot and radioman and a mechanic to go along with the plane. The plane was actually assigned to the naval attaché, but he was a non-aviator, so I had full use of it.

Paul Stillwell: Had you asked for that assignment?

Captain McCampbell: It went along with being the senior naval aviator down there. So my office was in the Naval War College down there. Aside from meeting a lot of the Argentine people, senior people, I met Peron and an individual who was like the Secretary of the Navy.† And they had an admiral in charge of the school, the Naval War College.

One of the Argentine naval aviators, Pio Baroja, took up with me, because he used to come around, and he spoke a little English, not very well, but, of course, I was in the middle of trying to learn to speak Spanish. He set up these fishing and hunting trips for us, and he always flew with me, so he'd get his flight time in and get to see some of his friends. We visited various places. I got to know him quite well, very well. In fact, when my tour of duty was over, we had to turn in my plane. He flew back to the States with me. The U.S. Navy flight crew all had families down there, and they wanted to go back by ship. That's a nice 18- or 20-day cruise with their families, and they agreed to

---

* The Korean War began on 25 June 1950, when six North Korean infantry division and three border constabulary brigades invaded South Korea. The troops were supported by approximately 100 Russian-made T-34 tanks. In New York that same day the United Nations Security Council adopted a resolution condemning the invasion.
† Juan Peron was the President of Argentina from 1946 to 1955.

pay our way back from the States. Of course, we were flying a government plane up, and that was all paid for. But they paid our way from Miami to Buenos Aires.

That came later, of course. While I was in the job, we made trips all over South America, practically. About the only place we didn't hit was Venezuela. We didn't hit Colombia or Ecuador until we came through going north, to take the plane over. But the first trip, as I recall, was down to Ushuaia, which is the tip of South America, on the Straits of Magellan. The Navy had a naval base there and an airfield, and that was about 1,800 miles. We flew down there, made a couple of stops. We stopped at one ranch down there, where each year they slaughtered one million sheep, and they shaved the wool off of five million. Menendes Bette is the name of the ranch, and that extended from the Atlantic to the Pacific, across—well, we were getting down to where Argentina is kind of small—but across Argentina and across Chile and to the Pacific. A tremendous big ranch. We were invited through this friend of mine, Pio Baroja, later an Argentine admiral.

We spent three days with them. He was a little isolated on this ranch, although he had a nice big house. He had a flower garden inside. It gets real cold down there and windy. And he had a pool table. We'd go fishing. About twice we went fishing. This ranch didn't go across the Straits of Magellan; it bordered it, a tremendous big ranch. Oh, ostensibly, we were there to fish and hunt, and they had so many geese, like Canadian honker type, come on the ranch. They would spoil the grass for the sheep, so they had a full-time, two professional hunters killing off these geese. So we got in on that and killed a couple of geese. They were so plentiful that it was almost like they were tame. It was a shame to kill them.

And we went fishing one time down in a little place across the Straits on this ranch owned by a guy named Green, who was a former minister who settled down there. The Argentines had killed off all the Indians that they could, kind of like we did, and this guy Green, as I recall, he had a son who was a little off balance, "loco," as they call it. He had his own plane, a single engine, and he would fly around various places until the Argentine Government found out he didn't have a license. He applied for a license and failed on his "license to fly." So before we went fishing, we had to go out and see his plane and watch him taxi around the field. All he could do was taxi; he wasn't supposed to fly. But he took good care of his plane, and maybe one day he got the permit), I don't know.

But then we went down this little stream, maybe 75 yards wide, just chock full of trout. I struck out down the stream there fly fishing, and I caught rainbow trout, brown trout, and brook trout. I caught about 20-some just walking down about two miles down the stream and fly fishing. I caught so damn many, it was getting rather tiresome, and also they were getting heavy. [Laughter] So I went back up to where the other people were, Pio and my good friend, Luis Ortiz Basualdo, and we had what they call an "osada," like a barbeque. They brought along some lamb, so we had a lamb osada, and took the fish back to the ranch.

Then we flew on down to Ushuaia, and nothing unusual happened there. The Argentines also have a big prison there, not just a Navy prison, but a national prison. We spent a couple of days there, and we thought of flying on down to Antarctica, but we didn't do it. Then we came on back home.

Paul Stillwell: Was it cold when you were that far south?

Captain McCampbell: No. We were there in their summer, which would be January, February, something like that.

Paul Stillwell: You say it was your most enjoyable tour of duty. Aside from the fishing and hunting, what else made it enjoyable?

Captain McCampbell: I got to travel all around the country, all around South America. We made a trip to Rio, made two trips up to Ascunsion in Paraguay, and we made, I guess, five or six trips to Bariloche, a big lake at the foot of the Andes. Pio's friend, later, of course, my friend—we visited him out there five or six times. They had a big ranch and raised cattle and horses, and they were across the lake from Bariloche, which is a nice little city. Now it's become a famous ski resort.

Paul Stillwell: What was the purpose of these trips to the various countries?

Captain McCampbell: Just to visit.

Paul Stillwell: But did you have a military mission as well?

Captain McCampbell: No, although we did discover through our friend there was something very unusual going on over on a little island in the middle of Lake Bariloche, which we later told the attaché, identified as an effort to manufacture plutonium. I conveyed the message to intelligence that there was something unusual going on there, and I guess he kind of followed up. But we'd go and visit him to go fishing or just to go visit. We'd take our wives. Pio didn't have a wife; he didn't get married till he was 54 years old. [Laughter] But he'd take friends, and he did have a girlfriend. We took her over there once.

On other occasions, we'd fly up north just to the west of Rosario, which is quite a large city there in Argentina, which is maybe 200 miles north of Buenos Aires. We'd go visit a ranch to the west maybe 30 miles. They didn't have paved runways; the owner of the ranch's handymen would go out and clear away a field for us, and we'd land in the tall grass—sometimes amongst chuckholes, but we never had the experience of hitting a chuckhole and nosing over. But my friend on the Air Force mission down there was flying a DC-3, and he landed on one of these unpaved fields, and he wrecked his plane when he hit a chuckhole.

Paul Stillwell: What was the specific focus of your duty? You say you were attached to the Argentine military. What were you doing for them?

Captain McCampbell: Well, giving advice, mostly when asked, but making speeches down there in Spanish. That brings up a little story. In prep school, Staunton Military Academy, I'd had two years of Latin and then two years of Spanish. At Georgia Tech, I had a year of Spanish, which I failed. At the Naval Academy, I had two years of Spanish, and one year I failed. I had to take a re-exam. So Spanish came difficult for me. But before they sent me down to Argentina, they gave me three weeks at Anacostia, a special language school, trying to cram me into Spanish.

Well, when I got down there and got off the ship, I found that we couldn't really communicate. I couldn't communicate with them because they talked so goddamned fast, like Italians. So the whole time I was down there taking courses, instructions, twice a week. I finally got pretty good at speaking mostly cocktail Spanish. We'd go on these trips, and my instructor would ask me, "Well, tell me about the trips. What did you do? Who did you meet?" So I'd recount activities and meeting people on these trips. It gave me something to talk about.

Paul Stillwell: Did you use interpreters part of the time?

Captain McCampbell: No. Pio was the interpreter, although his English wasn't too good. It never was. He's dead now. He died here last year.

I remember a trip. We hit three towns up in the northern part of Argentina, where they grow a lot of sugarcane, and some eat it with rice. We took our guns along and fishing rods, but we didn't do any fishing or hunting. We met people in Salta, JuJuy, and Oran—those three towns. We first stopped in Salta for gas, and Pio ran into one of his friends that wanted to go to Buenos Aires, so Pio said, "Well, I'll have to talk to Dave, who's the captain of the plane." I didn't agree at first, because we already had Pio, myself, and three passengers—Luis Ortiz Basuldo and a couple of others—and guns, fishing rods, and suitcases. Also, we had recently received a Navy directive that if you used a nose tank, three passengers was your limit. So that was my reason for first turning the guy down. Finally, I agreed to take him. So we picked him up on the way back from Salta, JuJuy, and Oran. Oran was the last one we hit and then back down the line.

We picked him up in Salta. The field was 2,000 feet high, they had a very short runway, and it was grass. So I told Pio, "Well, what I'm going to do is hold my brakes, turn up full blast on both engines, and take off." And I told him, "When I get about halfway down the field, lower the flaps one third." So I was able to get off, although we were fully loaded—overloaded. We took off, and I had to fly straight for about 20 miles. I was afraid to turn, because I had so little control. We sank pretty good, just going over the cliff, taking off. I flew along straight and level for about 20 miles, and finally, I very gently turned to go back in the other direction. That was an experience that I shouldn't have had to experience. I was a damn fool. But, anyway, we got back safely.

The second trip we made down to Ushuaia, and we got down to Punta Gorda. They were famous for shrimp; they had a shrimp fishing fleet there. So while Pio went over to arrange for some shrimp—on our way back, we'd pick them up—I inspected the plane, and I noticed on the left wheel, that the left engine was dripping oil. It was Pio's plane this time. He had a twin-engine Beechcraft, too, as operations officer for the Argentine fleet. So when Pio came back, I told him about this oil dripping very slowly on the wheel. He said, "Oh, the plane's in perfect condition. Just came out of overhaul." Very enthusiastic about it, "Nothing wrong with it."

I said, "All right." So we got in, and it was my turn as the left-seat pilot. We'd take turns, one leg each when I was pilot in the left seat, and the other one I'd fly. This was my turn. So we took off, no strain, and got headed down south, and we got about 45 minutes or an hour out of Rio Gallegos, which is where we were going to stop and gas again. But about 45 minutes or an hour out, I noticed the oil gauge flicking, and I tapped Pio. I said, "Pio, look."

He said, "Oh! You're going to have to feather that port engine." So we did, and now we were on one engine, which held its altitude all right. We went on now and flew about 45 minutes to an hour, and we got to Rio Gallegos, and asked Pio if he'd ever been in that field before.

"Oh, yes, frequently."

I said, "Well, I'm going to drag the field anyway. I want to see what's in there, whether there are chuckholes or whatever." By the way, there was a DC-3 parked on the field about halfway up. I guess he was fueling. So anyway, I drug over the field, then turned around, came back like making a carrier landing, and I got around to the crossing. I lowered the flaps a little bit, one third, and the one engine we still had working, almost full throttle. I got on the final leg straight in, and I told Pio to lower the wheels. With that, he lowered the flaps all the way and thought he was lowering the wheels. He hit the wrong lever, see. So I looked outside the plane, which was customary, and I still had my head out, flying one engine. I said, "Pio, no wheels!" Oh, shit. He quickly reacted. He raised the flaps and lowered the wheels. Oh, gosh, we were about 400 feet, and we went down like an elevator. So I finally caught it, thanks to my old Pensacola training, pushed the nose over to pick up a little speed, and here again, we had a cliff staring us in the face, and a barbwire fence. But I remembered that the Beechcraft had a tendency to bounce on landing, and so I got over the cliff, and I bounced short of the fence and jumped over the fence and rolled maybe 50, 75 yards.

Oh, I forgot to throw in there we were bucking a real strong wind. We saw the dust from the field a good 20 miles away, as we were coming into it. So with the wind resistance and the slow speed, I went 50, 75 yards.

Paul Stillwell: And your brakes, presumably.

Captain McCampbell: No, I didn't put my brake on. I didn't need them.

Paul Stillwell: I see.

Captain McCampbell: So then we had to taxi on up. We got out and ordered some gas. In the meantime, we had a mech with us. There was an oil leak in the pipeline. He sawed out about a 6-inch section of the pipeline and happened to have some rubber hosing with him, and he put the rubber hose where he sawed out the pipeline, and clamps on both sides, and away we went. But that was a case of real good field maintenance. He just happened to have that rubber hosing, or we'd have been sunk there. They had no facilities; just gas, you know.

Paul Stillwell: How capable would you say the Argentine Navy of that period was?

Captain McCampbell: Well, they were a skeleton Navy. They had one cruiser. I was instrumental in their getting a carrier; they later got a CVL.[*]

---

[*] The Argentine Navy purchased the British light carrier *Warrior* in July 1958, and she was delivered in December of that year. She was renamed the *Indepencia* in January 1959. In 1968 Argentina purchased the Dutch light carrier *Karel Doorman*, which had originally been HMS *Venerable*. She was renamed *Veinticino de Mayo* and was in the Argentine Navy at the time of the Falklands War in 1982.

Paul Stillwell: The cruiser Argentina got was the *Phoenix*, which was subsequently sunk in the Falklands Islands War of 1982.*

Captain McCampbell: I was aboard it in Philadelphia, when I was going to firefighter school up there, preparing to be exec of the *Roosevelt*. And one of the guys I had known in the War College down in Argentina was skipper of the *Phoenix*. I wanted to have some good Argentina beef and socialize with him a little bit.

Paul Stillwell: You say you were instrumental. What was the role there? Did you have a hand in the transfer?

Captain McCampbell: Before they even got it. When I was down there, they didn't have a carrier, but one of my lectures was on carrier aviation and how they should be employed. In the Falklands War, they wouldn't take my advice.† The carrier never got in the war. They were saving it; for what, I don't know. [Laughter] But no, you asked about the Navy in general. They had a pretty good Navy; it was a small Navy. They had a good naval base, and they had a good naval war college. Apparently, they had no recruiting problems. I would give them an overall "very good."

Paul Stillwell: Did you see rivalry among the various South American nations?

Captain McCampbell: Rivalry within Argentina. The Army and the Navy were very much rivals. In fact, on one occasion, shortly before I got there, the Army marched in from Camp DiMaggio, the part of the Army that was based there, just outside the city. They marched in, went down the main streets, and on the way, they fired bullets at the

---

* The *General Belgrano*, a light cruiser armed with 15 6-inch guns, had originally been commissioned as the USS *Phoenix* (CL-46) on 3 October 1938. She was decommissioned on 3 July 1946 and placed in reserve. She was transferred to Argentina on 9 April 1951 and commissioned as the *Diecisiete de Octobre* on 17 October 1951. She was renamed *General Belgrano* in 1956. The Argentine Navy also received the former U.S. light cruiser *Boise*. She was transferred in April 1951 and commissioned at Philadelphia on 11 March 1952 as the *Nueve de Julio*.

† The event that triggered the 1982 Falklands War was the Argentine occupation of South Georgia Island on 19 March 1982, followed on 2 April by the occupation of the Falklands. The British then mounted a long-range expedition that made an amphibious assault on the islands and recaptured them. Argentina surrendered on 14 June.

Naval War College. So that's how much rivalry there was; it was all based on their trying to get funds, money. The Air Force not so much. Their main base for training operations was up in Cordova, which is about 250 miles northwest, up in the mountains. We didn't see much of them.

Paul Stillwell: What impressions did you have of Juan Peron?

Captain McCampbell: Well, I know that the people in the Navy were all very much against him. I gathered that he was only popular, really, with the Camasados, "the shirtless ones." In other words, the common laborers. Their condition was really quite poor in that country, as in all the South American countries. As in all Central American countries, they had the very rich and the very poor. I've seen that in El Salvador, Nicaragua, and they had it in Argentina and still, to a certain degree, they still have it.

Paul Stillwell: What sort of living conditions did you have for you and your wife there in Buenos Aires?

Captain McCampbell: It turned out they were fantastic. First couple of weeks, we lived in a hotel. We were house hunting all that time we were there. We finally got our own house, had plenty of rooms, four bedrooms, because we took my wife's mother down, and we had two kids. Once we got there, we hired a nurse for the two younger boys. It was an old house, but plenty of room, as I've said. No central heating; we had to use little kerosene heaters. No air-conditioning, of course. In fact, there were no screens in the house. We had some trouble with mosquitoes at certain times of the year, the rainy season.

We hired the cook first, and she recruited the other people for us. We had an upstairs maid, a downstairs maid, and a washerwoman, and a cook. The cook's granddaughter lived with the cook, because she had a little building out behind the house. The nursemaid for our kids lived in the house. Then when we first started out there, we had a big yard, and we couldn't get one gardener full-time that could do the whole thing, so we ended up with three gardeners. They'd cut the grass with a scythe. Of course, it took longer to do that, but they got plenty of exercise, I'll tell you.

At one point, one of the gardeners died, and I got a couple of sheep, figuring that they would help mow the lawn. They were only $7.50 each, and if they could do the job, they were well worth it. But I found out that they liked the flowers better than the grass, and so I penned them up down there in the corner, and they would jump the fence, so I had to call in a butcher, and he took them away for free, and slaughtered them.

Well, we had a full household there, a lot of servants. These servants, all of them put together, except the gardeners—all the household servants, we got for $100.00 a month, which was pretty cheap for labor. Of course, we fed everybody except the washerwoman, who did our washing and ironing, and the gardeners; we didn't feed them. But the house itself, originally we were paying $300.00 a month for it, but by the time we left there two and a half years later, it was costing us less than $100.00 a month because of the currency devaluation.

Paul Stillwell: Did all this come out of your salary, or did you have an allowance too?

Captain McCampbell: What happened, I'd get my regular pay and flight pay, and then I got paid by the Argentine Government. I was a commander then; I got commander's pay from the Argentine Government.

Paul Stillwell: That was convenient.

Captain McCampbell: They took very good care of all of our household expenses, and food was delightfully cheap. We would usually fill up our freezer. The mech for my plane would go out to Swift's packing house and pick up a side of beef for me and a side for himself, so we kept our freezer full of beef. Oh, we used to feed the puppies beef all the time. Of course, the Argentines—the cook, the maid, and everybody—they're all beef-eaters. At the war college they had beef there three times a day—breakfast, noon, and dinner. I could eat breakfast if I wanted to get there early enough, and I always had lunch there. I guess they did have to serve dinner for the students, but most of the instructors ate at home.

Paul Stillwell: Did you have duties in the war college itself? Were you an instructor?

Captain McCampbell: Yes, I was like an instructor. My title was advisor. I communicated with the other instructors, and some of the students I got to know pretty well.

Paul Stillwell: Did you deliver any lectures in Spanish?

Captain McCampbell: Yes, I delivered two in Spanish. The lectures were relatively brief, but I would take questions and answers afterwards. I got to where I could speak Spanish fairly well.

Paul Stillwell: How well received were North Americans in Argentina in that era?

Captain McCampbell: Well, the Navy has had a mission down there for many years, advisors, people like myself. Actually, back in World War I, there were four Argentine aviators who took training at NAS Pensacola. To my knowledge, none of them ever got into combat in France, but two of them did go there. Even before World War I, they got to observe the naval battle of Tsushima.* They were guests of the Japanese. So the Argentine Navy and naval aviators have always been very close to us. Almost every year they send people up to Pensacola, or they did during that period.

Paul Stillwell: Is there anything else to mention about that tour of duty?

Captain McCampbell: Well, yes, there is. Along in the fall of 1950, in the Johnson regime—he was Secretary of Defense while we were there—he started cutting down on

---

* In the 27 May 1905 Battle of Tsushima Strait (which connects the Sea of Japan with the East China Sea), Japanese forces under Admiral Heihachiro Togo overwhelmed the Russian Baltic Fleet led by Admiral Zinovy Rozhdestvensky.

the number of aircraft assigned around the world.* I lost my plane. The Air Force had a DC-3 there that belonged to the attaché. So they had to turn my plane in at Norfolk, and I volunteered to fly there to turn it in. My good friend Pio Baroja, Argentine naval aviator, commander, my same age, by the way, volunteered to fly back with me. So we arranged with the flight crew of the plane, who all had families down in Argentina, who wanted to go back by ship, and we made a deal with them that if they would pay our way back from Miami to Buenos Aires, Pio and I, just the two of us, would take the plane back to Norfolk. So that worked out all right, except we did have a very interesting trip back to Norfolk.

The first leg of our trip, we flew from Buenos Aires to Santiago to Chile, nonstop. We hit some high winds and bad weather going over the Andes. In fact, when we got to Santiago, they told us that we were the only plane that got through the pass that day, whereas actually we hadn't intended to go through the pass, but because of the head winds that slowed us down, used more gas than expected. My friend Pio took a little shortcut, and we barely got over the hump at 18,200. Not many Beechcrafts had ever gotten up that high.

We had a spare wheel and tire; we had a six-man life raft and, of course, our suitcases, and some mail. We were just about ready to toss that out, when I saw we could make it over the hump at about 300 feet, maybe, 300 or 400, no more. But once we got over the hump, then we just cut the engine back and coasted into Santiago.

Paul Stillwell: Downhill all the way.

Captain McCampbell: Yes. We had about 15 minutes of gas left when we got there. We spent a day and two nights there, and then took off pre-dawn the next day for Lima, Peru. We got halfway, Antofogasta, and gassed up. Taking off pre-dawn, we forgot to raise the landing light, so we burned out a battery. The tower at Antofogasta called us and told us that our landing light was on and didn't think we needed it. So we cut it off real quick. Anyway, they got us started there at Antofogasta.

---

* Louis A. Johnson served as Secretary of Defense from 28 March 1949 to 19 September 1950. George C. Marshall served as Secretary of Defense from 21 September 1950 to 12 September 1951.

We made it on to Lima, Peru, and we spent two nights and a day there. I think by then we had ruined our generator. The mission there had to give us a new generator. Then we took off at pre-dawn at Lima. The ceiling was about 600 feet, but the visibility was good below that. We took off, and we got in the air, went through maybe 1,000 feet of overcast, got on top, and then Pio discovered that we'd forgotten our maps; we left them in Lima. I couldn't believe it. I went back and searched for the maps, the charts, and sure enough, we had left them in Lima.

Anyway, we went on up the coast. It wasn't too difficult. We had a bird dog direction finder, and as we went along by these towns, over them, beside them, the bird dog would point to a commercial radio station, and Pio would identify the town or city. So we worked our way on up the coast, and decided to gas at a place called Quito, Ecuador, and Pio said he'd been in there before. We had to cross a low range of mountains about 3,000 or 4,000 feet and follow up a railroad in a valley for a half hour or so and come to this little town, where there was an Ecudorian Air Force base, and we landed there to gas up. They would roll out the red carpet for us, practically. We had a delightful lunch and a glass of wine, and we got back to file our flight plan out, and I asked the operations officer if he could provide us with a map to Panama. He said, "Sorry, the only map or chart we have is the one on the wall there." [Laughter]

So we had to proceed on from there to Panama with no charts. All we had was a little guide to radio stations that was in a big, thick book about that long and so wide. In the back of it, it had a map of the whole of South America on it. Between that and identifying the radio stations, we made our way on up the coast to Panama, and we landed at Coco Solo, gassed up, and spent two nights and a day.

Then we flew out of there to Mexico City, and we stopped at Managua. It was called Managua City, the capital of Nicaragua. Anyway, we stopped and gassed up there. Then we took off across the Andes again, going east. We got on top of the clouds and cleared on top to Mexico City, and we flew from there to just a little ways out of Mexico City. We were still on top, and now we were running short on gas, and we hadn't found any hole to go down in. We were about to go into Mexico City, which, I think, the field's either 5,000 or 6,000 feet, and we weren't about to go in there on no instruments. We were thinking about heading for the water, the Gulf of Mexico, but we didn't, and we continued on.

Finally, a little hole in the clouds opened up for us, and I dove down. We got down below the overcast and saw a railroad headed north, heading in our direction, so I just followed it right into Mexico City, about 40 miles out. Mexico City was clear, but they had a high overcast, and we were on top. So we got in there and spent two nights and a day. The Argentine Embassy put us up for dinner one night we were there.

Then we flew from there on into Corpus Christi, Texas, spent two nights and a day. My ex-wife and her husband and my daughter were stationed there at Corpus Christi, so I got to see my daughter. Also while there, I had a flight physical, and I failed on my eyes. Well, I figured it was just I'd been flying for a long time the previous few days, and I'd been straining them, Long flights. The flights ran about four or five hours. So I asked for a re-exam, and they gave me one, and I passed it. So I got that over with.

Then we wanted to get off at New Orleans, and there was a heavy front just over Dallas, moving eastward, so we waited an extra day to give the storm a chance to go through, took off, landed in Dallas, and gassed up at Love Field, and then we took off for New Orleans. Unfortunately, we overran the front. I decided to go underneath. It was raining, a lot of rain, and we crossed Lake Ponchartrain there at about 50 feet, all overcast and rain.

Then we got to the air station there. We planned to land at the reserve naval air base, and they were closed. They trained their reserves mostly on the weekend, and we arrived Monday night. So I contacted the tower at the New Orleans airport, and they said, "Well, you can land here, and then you can taxi over to the naval reserve base." So that's what we did. Still raining, though. That Beechcraft didn't have any windshield wipers, and landing there, I had done it once before in Argentina, you had to open up a side window and kind of stick your head out there to see where the hell you were going. But no strain. So we spent two nights and a day there. I ran into my old wingman while there.

Paul Stillwell: Roy Rushing?

Captain McCampbell: Yes. He was being deactivated, resigning, and I talked to him for a little while. It was unusual, because just as I went to check out at the desk, this enlisted man on duty said, "Did you know you spent the night next to your ex-wingman?"

I said, "No, hell no, I didn't know he's here." Well, I went back and woke him up and talked to him a little bit.

Anyway, we went on from there right nonstop to Norfolk, with no strain. So we got to Norfolk, and it was after dark. I contacted the FASRon people, the man on duty.[*] They were closed for the night, of course. At ComAirLant was an old ex-skipper of Fighting Four, whom I'd served under. So I went over to his quarters and told him our situation. We just got in from Buenos Aires, we had a plane to turn in, and FASRon was closed up for the night. I asked him if he could do anything about it to help us, and he said, "Yeah." So he called the FASRon commanding officer, and he came down to the hangar, and we turned the plane in. We still didn't have our maps. We didn't have anything except that radio guide. Engine logs and all that stuff you were supposed to turn in, flight log. But I told them I'd try to get them through PanAm, which had somebody pick them up at the hotel there.[†] We had left them behind the afternoon the station wagon took us from the hotel to the airport in Lima. We ultimately got them, about three weeks later.

Paul Stillwell: Who was this old skipper of yours?

Captain McCampbell: Al Morehouse.[‡] So then Pio and I took off the next day from Norfolk, commercial, and flew to New York. We still had five days left, so we spent five days in New York, and then flew down to Buenos Aires.

Paul Stillwell: Commercially?

---

[*] FASRon – fleet aircraft service squadron.
[†] PanAm – Pan American World Airways, a commercial carrier that flew to South America among its many destinations.
[‡] Rear Admiral Albert K. Morehouse, USN.

Captain McCampbell: Yes. We paid our own way from New York to Miami, and then the flight crew paid our way from there to Buenos Aires.

Well, it's a long story, but that was essentially what happened to us.

Paul Stillwell: There was an interesting one you told me yesterday during the break, and this goes back to before you went to South America. I hope you will tell it again, please. That was the tale about you and your father, when you went to a Civil War prison camp and to the Naval Academy.

Captain McCampbell: Yes. My father came to visit me. Well, he stayed about a month with us, but I think this was along in either March or April of '48, just before I went to Argentina. He told me, "Dave, there's two things I want to see before I die. I want to see the old area or grounds where my father was imprisoned during the Civil War." It was out of Richmond and, I think, quite close to Yorktown. So I had to go to Washington. We went by the old prison area on the way to Richmond, and then went to Washington. I made my commitment there. The next day was Sunday. We drove down to Annapolis so he could see the school where I had graduated, because he'd never seen it.

Also, he wanted to see a bust which I knew had been done by the Navy, and the Navy advised me it was in the museum at Annapolis. So I drove him around the grounds of the Academy, and it must have been June. I drove around, and we saw the Academy, all we wanted to see, and we went to the museum to see the bust that had been done of me. The curator, or the guy that was on duty there that Sunday afternoon, said, "Well, we don't have a bust in here of a sculpture of Commander McCampbell." And so I took his word for it, and my dad and I went around to see what they had in the museum and so forth, a rather quick tour, and then headed back for Norfolk, where I was based through Washington.

But en route, we hit some spotty ice in the road, and I obviously was going too fast for it, and we rounded a curve and went down a little hill. I must have applied my brakes, because we flipped, rolled over once, and ended up right side up, but in a ditch. Fortunately, a salesman for Armour meat company came by and asked if there was anything he could do. I said, "Yes, my father's been hurt. You can take him and me back to Annapolis to put him in the hospital." So he did. He graciously took us to Annapolis to the hospital, and they put my dad up, took X-rays first to make sure there was no concussion. When I found that out, I told the doctor I was in school at Norfolk, and the doctor said that I could come back on the next Friday and pick him up, take him home, because he didn't seem to be hurt too bad, just a cut on the head.

I had to buy a new car. Our car was wrecked. So I stayed overnight with a friend there in Annapolis, and went out on Monday and bought a new car. It was a Lincoln, not a Lincoln Continental, but in those days we had a smaller car made by Lincoln. I've forgotten what the name of it was. But anyway, it was a show car, the only one they had in the shop, and I had a hell of a time begging him to sell it to me. I said I was in bad need of a car, and he finally relented and decided to sell it to me. So I bought it. I had to wire home to ask my wife to get the money and wire it to me. I was able to close the deal on Tuesday, and I then drove back to Norfolk.

On Wednesday, I got a call from the nurse in the hospital there, and she said, "If you want to see your father again, you'd better get up here in a hurry. He's lapsed into unconsciousness."

So I went over to FASRon and borrowed a seaplane. Annapolis didn't have an airport at that time, didn't have anything, so I got a seaplane and flew up there that Wednesday, landed over across the river, and got wheels from somewhere or other, and got to the hospital. By the time I'd gotten there, why, he had passed on. What he died of was a diabetic coma, and I didn't know that he was taking injections every day, which I found out later, and he didn't tell the doctor, and I didn't tell him, so he just went into a diabetic coma and passed on.

So I went up in the seaplane. We had his remains cremated, and I sent them out to Los Angeles, where my mother was, and they put his remains in a crypt out there. But I jumped in the seaplane and came on back to Norfolk.

Paul Stillwell: Another interesting sequel to that story is your correspondence about the bust, the sculpture.

Captain McCampbell: Oh, yes, I didn't finish that. So Dad didn't get to see my bust. It's a shame. Later on, I had had three requests to display my bust or sculpture, whatever you want to call it, and the last one came from the American Legion in San Francisco, California. I wrote back to the guy and told him that I didn't have the bust in my possession or control of it; it was in the museum at Annapolis. So I told him that I would write to the Annapolis Museum and see if they would send it out, put it out on loan, which I did. I told them I had three requests, and the latest one was from the American Legion, and would they loan it to them for three or four days. And when I first wrote to the museum, the curator was an ex-classmate of mine at Annapolis, Dale Mayberry.[*] But he had been relieved by another officer, and in answer to my request to display the bust, he said, "I'm sorry, but we don't allow our artifacts, paintings and busts and whatever, to be displayed until the subject to the artifact has died."

So I wrote him back a very terse note, and I said, "Well, thank you, Captain. You've been most helpful. You've certainly given me something to look forward to." That's the end of the story. [Laughter]

I told the curator at the Naval Aviation Museum in Pensacola about this, and he said, "I bet I can get it." So sure enough, he wrote and asked for it, and the museum in Annapolis allowed him to put it on display in Pensacola. And to my knowledge, it's still on display down there.

Paul Stillwell: When had the sculpture been created?

Captain McCampbell: 1945.

Paul Stillwell: Do you remember who the artist was?

Captain McCampbell: No. He was out of the public info office there in Washington, or they had hired him, I don't know.

---

[*] Commander Dale Mayberry, USN.

Paul Stillwell: There was one who did several Navy people, Felix de Weldon. Does that name sound familiar?

Captain McCampbell: No.

Paul Stillwell: How long a period did you sit and pose for it?

Captain McCampbell: About a week or maybe nine days.

Paul Stillwell: Was that done in Washington?

Captain McCampbell: No. Down in Norfolk, where I was based.

Paul Stillwell: One other thing that we mentioned during the break was the opportunity you had to fly the F8F, which, of course, you did not do in combat, but after the war.[*] I'd be interested in your reaction to that plane.

Captain McCampbell: Yes. I flew the F8F on three or four occasions, but most of those occasions was just checking out, familiarization with the plane. I had one trip to Aurora, Illinois, for a Navy Day celebration, and I took off from Norfolk and went over the top. I got my clearance over the top. So I was on top all the way until I got into the Chicago area, and I tried to tune into, first, Glenview, just to check in, because I knew that Aurora didn't have a tower or radio equipment to contact. I wanted to get a little more specific direction to Aurora. I couldn't find the radio in the cockpit, and I had a hell of a time. Looked all over for it—it was a small cockpit anyway, and I finally had to take my safety belt and safety harness off, and I found it way back over here in the corner on the right side. I had to do my tuning in a very unusual way, and I finally got Glenview and told

---

[*] Grumman F8F Bearcat fighters first entered fleet squadrons in 1945. The F8F-1 version was 28 feet long, wingspan of 35 feet, gross weight of 12,947 pounds, and top speed of 421 miles per hour. It was one of the best piston-engine planes ever to serve the U.S. Navy but had a short operational life because of the advent of jet fighters.

them I was on top in the Chicago area; I didn't know exactly where, and could they give me directions to land.

I saw that the weather was fogged in, socked in. First I asked if they could take me up at Glenview, and they said, "Well, no, we're socked in here solid. We can't even take you in by radio."

I said, "Well, can you tell me what the weather is in Aurora?"

He said, "Well, in that area it's generally overcast. We don't know how bad it is, but if you're at Chicago," and he gave me directions to it. It was something like 265-270, so I flew in the direction, on top, still. I had decided to keep flying west until I found a hole to go down in, and I finally found one. The overcast opened up for me, I dove down through the overcast, and found myself over a little river. I figured that it was so close that the river probably flowed into Lake Michigan, so I'd follow it in that direction. What had happened, I had overshot Aurora, and I was going back east. Sure enough, pretty soon, I came on a little airfield, and I thought I recognized it as Aurora, though I'd never been in there, but there were a couple of hundred people on the field, like school bands in various uniforms, and so I decided to land there anyway. If it wasn't the right place, I'd find out how to get to the right place. But it turned out that that was the Aurora airfield. I came in. I was overdue by 20, 30 minutes, but I was welcomed. That night I had no activities, but they warned me the next day that I had to visit various high schools and locations in the area, high school and grade schools.

The next day, in all, I made 13 appearances. I had to say a little something every place I went, but one of those I remember was Moose Heart, which is a community supported by the Moose Lodge for more or less destitute families of ex-Moose people who had died. So I went there, I made a little talk, and I believe that was the last place I went that day. But I had had 13 appearances, so I was pretty well tired out that night. And although I was invited to a cocktail party, I didn't stay too long. I went back to the hotel and turned in.

The next day, I left and went back to Norfolk.

Paul Stillwell: How would you compare the F8F to the F6F in performance?

Captain McCampbell: Well, I knew it to be a better performer all around, although it didn't get into combat. It was capable of better climb ability, a little better maneuverability, it was faster. The one thing that it couldn't do was carry bombs or rockets, at least not outfitted to do that. It was strictly a fighter, which was highly desirable in those days too. But that's about all I saw it. It had a very cramped cockpit. I described the trouble I had finding the radio equipment in the cockpit. Other than that, it flew just like any other plane.

Paul Stillwell: Had the war lasted a while longer, it might well have gotten into combat in World War II.

Captain McCampbell: Oh, yes, I'm sure it would have. I don't know that it would ever have replaced the F6F, which was coming out equipped with rocket rails and the ability to carry bombs. I even carried up to, on one occasion, a 1,000-pound bomb. Usually if it was hung with that much of a bomb load, why, you'd be catapulted and not take deck takeoff.

Paul Stillwell: We did not discuss the use of rockets during your deployment on the *Essex*. Maybe you could mention that now, please.

Captain McCampbell: Well, the last plane that I flew, the F6F-5, was equipped with rocket rails, and I had the torpedo squadron commander, V. G. Lambert, instruct me a little bit in the use of rockets. I had had no training with them and didn't know anything about them, but he had found them quite useful, and I figured that I would too. So ever after, I took off with four 3.5-inch rockets and/or a bomb load. Usually I had bombs in addition to rockets, but I retained the 2,400 rounds of ammunition.

  I had one occasion south of Manila, actually, more over Mindoro, the island in the Philippines, I'd been surveying the island for resistance, mainly aircraft, or concentration of troops.* I sighted this twin-engine plane well above me, a good 8,000, 10,000 feet up. I'd finished my survey of the island, so I started to see if I could go up and knock him

---

* McCain and his wingman, Roy Rushing, hit Mindoro on 21 October 1944.

down. I just had Roy with me, my wingman at that time, so we chased him for a good 15 minutes or so, and finally, I was able to catch up with him, get to his altitude. I thought, "Well, this is a good time to try out my rockets, see if they're any good in the air."

So I pulled up behind him; I let go with two rockets. Now, they didn't make a direct hit, but one of the rockets cut off part of his tailfin, vertical stabilizer. And with that, one of the crewmen jumped out, parachuted out, and then the first two I could see, the rockets were not very efficient in air-to-air gunnery, so I let him have the .50-calibers, and I shot him down. That's the only time I ever fired the rockets in the air. I did, on occasion, fire them at ships, and once at installations. I remember Cebu City, I fired them at an oil installation, a tank farm.

Paul Stillwell: How effective were they against the ground target?

Captain McCampbell: Well, my fighter pilots, I wouldn't say, were too keen about it. They were effective, all right, but they were used to the .50-calibers and the bombs, although as we got the F6F-5s, why, they started using them just like I did.

Paul Stillwell: What advantages had Lambert found from the use of rockets?

Captain McCampbell: Well, the torpedo plane didn't have much firepower, except for rockets. As I recall, they had two .50-caliber forward and one .30-caliber in the belly. No, not in the belly; that was the earlier version. They had it in the turret. They had, as I recall, twin .30s.

Paul Stillwell: That was aft of the cockpit.

Captain McCampbell: Yes. That's about all I can say for the rockets. They were useful, they seemed to be sufficient for certain purposes, but not for air-to-air gunnery.

Captain McCampbell: Well, we wrapped up your tour in Buenos Aires, and then you became the executive officer of the fleet carrier *Franklin D. Roosevelt* in early 1951.* That is another good job in the ladder.

Captain McCampbell: Yes, it was a good job. As a matter of fact, when Pio Baroja and I turned in my plane and had our little vacation in New York, we came back to Washington. I went to call on Admiral Forrest Sherman, who was then the Chief of Naval Operations, and had formerly been the skipper of the *Wasp*, my ship.† He wasn't in, but I left my card. In the meantime, the detail officer in Washington told me that he had inquired about my next duty, and I presume that by leaving my card with him, why, he made the inquiry.

Anyway, I went on to the *Franklin D. Roosevelt* as exec. We called the captain Little Bill Davis, William Davis, W.V. Davis.‡ And the ship was in the Med at the time. I flew over to Port Lyautey in a Constellation and then flew from there.

We took off at Port Lyautey to go to Nice, France, but just past the Spanish islands, the Majorcas, we lost an engine. This was a PB4Y-A, which was the amphibious type.§ We were closer to Barcelona than any other point that we knew had airport facilities, and, of course, at that time we weren't allowed into Spain at all. But he called for an emergency landing in Barcelona, and we were on one engine. We were just about ready to throw out the mail and any spare parts that we had, but it held at about 100, 150 feet off the water.

So we flew on in to Barcelona, landed safely, and then the problem was that since none of the crew spoke Spanish, for me to break out my Spanish and let them have it. So fortunately, my Argentine friend, Baroja, had given me two names if I ever got to Spain, he said, and be sure and look them up; they were good friends of his. And so I had my little address book with me, and I got on the phone and called one of these friends of his.

---

* USS *Franklin D. Roosevelt* (CVB-42), a *Midway*-class aircraft carrier, was commissioned 27 October 1945. She had a standard displacement of 45,000 tons, was 968 feet long, 113 feet in the beam, and had an extreme width of 136 feet. Her top speed was 33 knots. She had 18 5-inch mounts and could accommodate more than 100 aircraft.
† Admiral Forrest P. Sherman, USN, served as Chief of Naval Operations from 2 November 1949 until his death on 22 July 1951.
‡ Captain William V. Davis Jr., USN, commanded the *Franklin D. Roosevelt* from July 1950 to July 1951.
§ The PB4Y-2 Privateer was a four-engine land-based patrol bomber.

His name was Baron MacMahan, and in my best Spanish, I talked to him on the phone. I told him that we'd had a forced landing in Barcelona, main airport, and we were without any money or hotel accommodations or anything, and I asked him if he could help us out a little bit. And I went on a little more than that, I guess. Anyway, he came back in perfect English and said, "Dave, I'll be down there in ten minutes, and I'll bring you some money." He changed money.

He came right down, and I believe there were five in the crew and myself. He got us hotel reservations at the Ritz, a real fancy hotel with sunken black marble bathtubs and that sort of thing. And he took us all out to dinner in the hotel. He even got us lined up with a couple or three dates—I guess they were either call girls or bar girls, one or the other—and treated us royally.

I only had the one night there, because Port Luaytey flew over a spare engine the next day, and they were busy changing the engine. Then the plane brought the spare engine, picked me up, and took me on in to Nice. The ship was anchored off Cannes, so I reported aboard there.

Paul Stillwell: Did you get the feeling that Admiral Sherman's call had helped you get that job?

Captain McCampbell: Very possibly. It had already been decided, because the detail officer told him that they were going to detail me to the *Roosevelt*, but he was satisfied with that.

Paul Stillwell: That was one of the three newest carriers in the fleet at that time, and so it sounds like an ideal job for an aviation commander.

Captain McCampbell: Yes, I would consider it one.

Paul Stillwell: Whom did you relieve?

Captain McCampbell: I don't remember his first name. Chittenden was his last name.*

There was nothing very unusual about the *Roosevelt* in my tour—I only had one year on it—except the Eisenhower visit. And we had a bunch of Germans who came down at the invitation of—I guess, originally, it started with the Navy Department. But they were supposed to be guests of the Commander Sixth Fleet, but for the air demonstration there one day, we had them aboard.

Paul Stillwell: Did you have to take any special security precautions from having atomic weapons on board?

Captain McCampbell: Oh, yes. In those days, there was real, real tight security.

Paul Stillwell: Did the Marines run that?

Captain McCampbell: No, there were special crews. They had their own atomic weapons spaces. We called them special weapons in those days. And I remember ashore in Norfolk, whenever they would load or unload an atomic weapon, why, they'd close the gates. They had a special area, with a 10-foot-high chain-link fence, and very close. Even with their own people, they would cover up the atomic bomb and hide it from them, so that they wouldn't know what it was, supposedly. But the security was very tight.

Paul Stillwell: What do you remember about Captain Davis?

Captain McCampbell: He was a very good skipper and well known, one of the older aviators. He had formerly been a test pilot. He was the navigator on the first seaplane flight from San Diego to Honolulu. They had a pilot, copilot, and he was the navigator, as an aviator.

Paul Stillwell: Was he popular with the crew of the ship?

---
* Commander John L. Chittenden, USN.

Captain McCampbell: Not too much, I would say, because he was one of these people who never go below decks. He spent all his time up on the bridge or in his cabin. He was a fast operator for handling paperwork. Either a fast reader or just he'd glance at it and toss it aside, sign it if it called for a signature, in contrast to the next skipper. Anyway, we had nothing unusual happen to us; we did just routine Sixth Fleet operations.

While I was aboard, we got into Spain. We didn't go into Barcelona. We went into Valencia, Spain, for four or five days. Nothing particular, except it was a good experience for a naval officer.

Paul Stillwell: Well, that probably had some diplomatic connotations, since U.S. ships hadn't been allowed in previously, and Sherman had just been negotiating with the Spanish.[*] Were there receptions and so forth to mark the occasion?

Captain McCampbell: Not too much of that. Of course, when we'd go to these various ports, we'd always have an open house on the ship, and they usually reciprocated with some kind of reception.

Paul Stillwell: A ship that big probably couldn't go alongside the pier, so you'd have to run boats, wouldn't you?

Captain McCampbell: Oh, yes. We anchored out there.

Paul Stillwell: Which is one more complication in trying to have a reception on board the ship.

Captain McCampbell: Right. The one thing I remember, I had picked up some cloth in Gibraltar, or maybe I bought the cloth in Greece. Anyway, I'd picked up enough to make me a pair of trousers and a jacket. And there were a couple of Spanish aviators that had been sent out to ride and observe fleet operations on the *Roosevelt*, and when we got to

---

[*] Admiral Forrest P. Sherman, USN, arrived in Paris on 21 July 1951 after a tiring week of negotiations in Spain and Italy. At 10:40 the following morning he had a mild heart attack, then died in Paris at 1:05 that afternoon after two more heart attacks.

Valencia, one of these naval officers lived there. I told him I had this cloth that I wanted to get made into a jacket and a pair of pants. It was doeskin wool, and the jacket cloth was, I believe, vicuna. And so he said, sure, he knew a good tailor, his father's tailor, and, "I'm sure he'll do it for you," which he did. So I had a jacket, a nice jacket, I wore for years, and a pair of doeskin trousers made up.

Other than that—oh, I became acquainted with a dish called angoulas, which are small eels about this size.

Paul Stillwell: Three inches long, maybe.

Captain McCampbell: And they fry them in olive oil. And they are delicious, of course, with a little garlic in them. I guess the garlic gives it flavor.

Paul Stillwell: Was that in Spain?

Captain McCampbell: Yes, in Valencia.

Paul Stillwell: You probably also had to cope with the fact that they had a much later dinner hour than Americans are used to.

Captain McCampbell: Oh, yes, yes. We went to a nightclub there a couple of nights, and this naval officer—I've forgotten his name—who lived there, he and his mother and father put on a flamenco group, which they hired, that came to the apartment and did a lot of flamenco dancing. How the other people in the apartments stood it, I don't know. [Laughter] They had us all doing flamenco dances.

Paul Stillwell: Who was the captain that succeeded Davis and was a bug on paperwork?

Captain McCampbell: That was Fitzhugh Lee.[*]

---

[*] Captain Fitzhugh Lee, USN, commanded the *Franklin D. Roosevelt* from July 1951 to July 1952. The oral history of Lee, who later retired as a vice admiral, is in the Naval Institute collection.

Paul Stillwell: Who had been your old flight instructor.

Captain McCampbell: Yes. And he even got upset about all the paperwork, and a lot of it was useless, I admit. Of course, I had to review all of it and all the message traffic. But he got so upset about it that he got himself a counter, and he started counting every piece of paper he was supposed to read and some for signature. He got some phenomenal figure, and he complained about it to Com6thFlt.[*] He wrote an official letter and complained about too much paperwork for the captain of a ship. But nothing I can recall that was unusual about his tour.

Paul Stillwell: How was he as an operator?

Captain McCampbell: Well, as a ship handler, I think Captain Davis was better. I don't know how I got the idea, really, except we had one minor collision with a tanker once.

Paul Stillwell: Was this when Lee was the skipper?

Captain McCampbell: Yes. And of course, those are not too unusual, at least in those days. So that about takes care of my tour on the *Roosevelt*.

Paul Stillwell: I've got a few more questions. Lee, I gather, was a pretty smooth diplomatic type. Did you observe that?

Captain McCampbell: No. He had formerly been a naval attaché in Venezuela, but he couldn't speak the Spanish language. He mentioned on my fitness report that I was real good with communicating in Spanish with the various visitors that we had aboard ship.

Paul Stillwell: You had at least one admiral on board during that period—Admiral Pride.[†] What do you recall of him?

---

[*] Com6thFlt – Commander Sixth Fleet.
[†] Rear Admiral Alfred Melville Pride, USN, Commander Carrier Division Two, 1951-52.

Captain McCampbell: I didn't have any real contact with him. No, nothing really. I met him. I gave him a partial tour of the ship, when he was aboard. And when my tour ended, we went into overhaul at Portsmouth, in Virginia, so I didn't go through the overhaul period. Eddie Outlaw relieved me.[*]

Paul Stillwell: What do you recall of the internal administration of the ship—inspections, dealing with the crew and so forth?

Captain McCampbell: Fitzhugh Lee had formerly been the exec of the *Essex*. Dave McDonald relieved him. On one occasion, I mentioned to him that the *Essex* was the dirtiest ship I'd ever served on, having served on the *Wasp*, which was the cleanest ship that ever got sunk. Then the contrast was significant. Aboard the *Essex*, you'd find candy wrappers, cigarette butts thrown in the corner and passageways and that sort of thing. When I came aboard the *Roosevelt*, it was almost as bad. But now, the *Essex* was the best operating ship I was ever on. But I'd say the *Roosevelt* was just mediocre, but it was dirty too.

Paul Stillwell: Did you work deliberately at correcting that?

Captain McCampbell: Oh, yes, we did. I had appointed a special painting detail, and I had six people on it. And while I was aboard, the passageways, I had them to paint a little white line, both on the bulkhead and on the deck, in all the passageways, so that if somebody threw a cigarette butt in the corner, if it hit these white lines or near them, why, it was easily seen and could be cleaned up. We painted all the officers' staterooms—I think all of them. Well, we started on it, anyway. These six people in the painting detail had free gangway whenever we got in port. In other words, they didn't stand any other watches aboard ship. It was very successful. They did a lot of painting, but they were volunteers.

Paul Stillwell: Did you point this out to Captain Lee when he came aboard?

---

[*] Commander Edward C. Outlaw, USN.

Captain McCampbell: Oh, yes, yes.

Paul Stillwell: What about your administrative workload? You said the captain had a lot. You probably had a great deal also.

Captain McCampbell: I had more than he did, a voluminous amount of paperwork. That's about all I did.

Paul Stillwell: Did you have some administrative assistants to help with that?

Captain McCampbell: Yes, yes. But then it all had to funnel through me, and then things that I thought were necessary, I'd pass on to the captain.

Paul Stillwell: What do you remember about disciplinary problems involving the crew? That's certainly important in the Mediterranean.

Captain McCampbell: Fortunately, the *Roosevelt* crew was well disciplined. We had a few cases. I'd usually handle a preview mast before I'd pass them on to the captain. I couldn't render any punishment; the captain only could do that. But I'd handle the preview of mast, sort them out. Some I thought should go to the captain for decision, and others I'd throw out.

Paul Stillwell: What can you say about the level of talent, both officer and enlisted, in a ship like that? Did you have a good deal of good people to work with?

Captain McCampbell: Yes, I'd say we did. The heads of departments were all capable people, and the other key people on the ship were all capable, the navigators and so forth.

Paul Stillwell: What sort of operations was the ship involved in when she was not on deployment to the Mediterranean?

Captain McCampbell: Overhaul, for one thing, and other times, it was rest and recreation, liberty.

Paul Stillwell: Did you take part in any local operations in the Virginia Capes operating area?

Captain McCampbell: I don't remember Virginia Capes, but we had various planned operations by Commander Sixth Fleet we participated in. It consisted of more or less routine stuff.

Paul Stillwell: How much did you get to fly when you were executive officer?

Captain McCampbell: Not very much. I had a little difficulty getting in my flight time. Sometimes it would pile up on me; in two or three months I wouldn't get any, and I'd have to go out and fly like hell. We had utility planes, though, aboard, and usually if we went into a port where they had an airfield, why, we'd put a couple of utility planes ashore so we could get our flight time.

Paul Stillwell: After you left the *Franklin D. Roosevelt* as exec, then you came back to Norfolk. You were already in Norfolk, but moved to another command, ComAirLant, as planning officer. What was involved in that job for you?

Captain McCampbell: Mainly, I was involved in the resupply of atomic weapons to the Sixth Fleet. Most of the legwork was done by one of my assistants, but I had to put the whole plan together. We had dealings with Fort Campbell, Kentucky, which had the supply of additional atomic weapons, and it was like a depot for atomic weapons. And we had to deal with the transport command, and we had to deal with the squadron there in Norfolk that had the AJs that carried the atomic weapon, later the A3D. But it was just a question of planning and putting the whole process together.

The only other thing was that Admiral Moorer—he was a captain then—relieved me as the plans officer.* At that time, he didn't stay very long in that job before he was called in to be Admiral Burke's aide.† That's about all I can recall of any interest while I was plans officer. We did put on a couple of fleet maneuvers, one in the Mediterranean, and another one in the North Atlantic, but that's about all that occurred.

Paul Stillwell: Were there any war plans involved in the job?

Captain McCampbell: Yes, as to the disposition of the carriers that were under ComAirLant's control, I made a trip to England to attend a conference over there of NATO nations. About all I had a part in was in case war broke out, what could ComAirLant supply NATO in the way of aircraft carriers. Other than that, I can't remember anything in particular.

Paul Stillwell: Where were the atomic weapons manufactured before they were shipped?

Captain McCampbell: They all came out of atomic weapons storehouse or supply depot in Albuquerque. They were manufactured at a plant in the state of Washington, and another one in Tennessee. That's about all I know.

Paul Stillwell: So was Fort Campbell some kind of a storage depot?

Captain McCampbell: Yes.

Paul Stillwell: How were they physically transported to the East Coast?

---

* Captain Thomas H. Moorer, USN, later Chief of Naval Operations.
† Admiral Arleigh A. Burke, USN was Chief of Naval Operations from 1955 to 1961.

Captain McCampbell: By cargo plane and transferred from Fort Campbell to the Azores, and then on to Port Lyautey in Spanish Majorca. And then from there by AJ or A3D to the fleet in the Med.*

Paul Stillwell: Why wouldn't they just be put on board in Norfolk and carried across in a ship?

Captain McCampbell: Well, because they were resupply weapons designed for emergency.

Paul Stillwell: I see.

Captain McCampbell: By ship would take too long.

Paul Stillwell: Well, this was the emergency plan. How was it done routinely? Were they boarded at Norfolk?

Captain McCampbell: Well, we never did it routinely.

Paul Stillwell: Oh, I see. [Laughter]

Captain McCampbell: I guess if we were sending an additional carrier or something like that, why, they'd put them aboard that.

Paul Stillwell: Did you have to arrange for security in those foreign nations?

Captain McCampbell: No. We had a base then in the Azores, and we didn't even contact them. We just figured that we had liberty to pass through there.

Paul Stillwell: What they didn't know wouldn't hurt them.

---

* The Douglas A3D Skywarrior first entered fleet squadrons in 1956 as a carrier-based heavy bomber.

Captain McCampbell: No.

Paul Stillwell: The policy has long been to neither confirm nor deny that nuclear weapons are on board ships. Was it that way back then?

Captain McCampbell: We didn't seem to have any problems then. I doubt that all of the friendly European nations knew that we had atomic weapons aboard ship. Like when the Germans came to visit the ship, they were not aware that we were carrying nuclear weapons. At least we didn't show them those spaces.

Paul Stillwell: Well, from there you in 1953 assumed command of the Naval Air Technical Training Center at Jacksonville. Back to your old stomping grounds again in Florida. What did that command do?

Captain McCampbell: Well, we were part of the command, the headquarters of which was in Memphis, Tennessee, and was called the Technical Training Command. I had command of the Technical Training Center in Jacksonville. There was another center in Memphis, and I don't recall there being another one.

Paul Stillwell: Had you made captain by this time?

Captain McCampbell: Yes, I made captain while I was on duty in the ComAirLant.

Paul Stillwell: So this was your first shore command.

Captain McCampbell: Yes.

Paul Stillwell: What specifically was the command involved in? What phase of training?

Captain McCampbell: Well, I had over 9,000 people under me. I had enlisted men, Marine enlisted, and I had WAVES and I had BAMs under me at that time—over 9,000 total.* But the Marines kind of took care of their own people. There were maybe 1,500-2,000 Marines, including the BAMs, and the rest were all Navy enlisted. The Marines kind of took care of their own discipline and the people under their command. The top Marine was under me, but I never interfered with him.

Paul Stillwell: Were these like rate-training schools for enlisted people essentially?

Captain McCampbell: Yes, they were trade schools.

Paul Stillwell: Like aviation boatswain's mate or electronics technician.

Captain McCampbell: Like machinists, and then while I was there we organized and trained people in missiles, aircraft missiles.

Paul Stillwell: Who set up the curriculum?

Captain McCampbell: We had a lieutenant commander, or maybe he was a commander, in charge of that school. It was fenced off as a separate department of my command. I didn't have much to do with them. I wasn't trained myself in the use of missiles.

Paul Stillwell: Well, I was thinking about the overall curriculum, the missiles and these individual rate schools. Did that come out of BuPers perhaps, or from Memphis?†

Captain McCampbell: Well, out of Memphis. Memphis was the overall command. That was Admiral Switzer.‡

Paul Stillwell: One of your old skippers from the *Ranger*.

Captain McCampbell: Yes.

---

* WAVES was the term then used for Navy women; BAMs was a slang term for female Marines.
† BuPers – Bureau of Naval Personnel.
‡ Rear Admiral Wendell G. Switzer, USN, Chief of Naval Tactical Training, Memphis, Tennessee

Paul Stillwell: Well, was the idea that there would be standardized training, that people could get essentially the same thing at Memphis and at Jacksonville?

Captain McCampbell: Yes, except for the missile training.

Paul Stillwell: How did that happen to be set up at Jacksonville? Do you know?

Captain McCampbell: I don't know. Because we had the space. I was only there for about a year.

Paul Stillwell: The missiles were a new discipline in the Navy at the time, so I can see why you would need to train along with the students.

Captain McCampbell: Yes.

Paul Stillwell: Were these air-to-air missiles?

Captain McCampbell: Yes, air to air.

Paul Stillwell: Any surface to air involved?

Captain McCampbell: No.

Paul Stillwell: You probably would have benefited by having some of those in World War II also.

Captain McCampbell: No, not much. But this was between missile handlers, the people that arm the missile and install them on planes and . . .

Paul Stillwell: Probably work on the electronic circuitry too.

Captain McCampbell: Yes, right.

Paul Stillwell: Was your job largely an administrative one?

Captain McCampbell: Completely. I handled all the personnel matters, discipline, and that sort of thing.

Paul Stillwell: Did you get into budgeting?

Captain McCampbell: Yes, somewhat. The command in Memphis usually did most of the budgeting work, but we installed, shortly before I arrived, our own PX and the only other thing was the maintenance of the buildings for the students; we handled that. I remember one instance where we had money allocated out of Memphis for a new butcher shop, but I didn't see the need of it and at that time there was talk of folding up the command in Jacksonville so I turned the money back over to the head command in Memphis.

Paul Stillwell: What precipitated the talk about closing it up?

Captain McCampbell: Well, I don't know.

Paul Stillwell: It seems a little curious that there would be talk of reducing it, or getting rid of it at the same time a new school was installed for the missiles.

Captain McCampbell: Well, there was an interval in there of maybe nine months or maybe more.

Paul Stillwell: You told me also when the tape wasn't running that there was a new swimming pool inaugurated.

Captain McCampbell: No, it wasn't a new pool. It was there when I arrived, but they didn't have any of the buildings named, and I thought we ought to name some of them anyway. One was a natatorium or swimming pool, and I decided to name it after Admiral King.[*] He came down to the dedication ceremony, but he didn't talk. He stayed in the car and pulled right up in front of the speaker's platform. The speaker was me. I entertained him in my home quarters one evening for cocktails and dinner, and he wasn't saying much of anything at any time. He was getting rather senile. But, I wrote Albert Einstein who was at Princeton.[†] We wanted to name a building for him and he wrote back and said no, he wouldn't give us permission because it had something to do with military operations and he had divorced himself from that completely.

Paul Stillwell: Any other famous people that you named them for?

Captain McCampbell: We named five or six other buildings and I've forgotten offhand who they were.

Paul Stillwell: Did you have much of a contingent of civil service employees there?

Captain McCampbell: Yes. I would say at least half our instructors were civilian employees. And at least two of our supervisory personnel were civil servants. We had one GS-17, and I think the other was a 15.

Paul Stillwell: They work under different rules than the Navy people do so you probably had to get up to speed on that.

Captain McCampbell: They had to get down to speed. There was one letter to my boss in Memphis, to Admiral Switzer and it was written in a jargon that I couldn't understand.

---

[*] Fleet Admiral Ernest J. King, USN, had been Chief of Naval Operations and Commander in Chief U.S. Fleet during World War II. In 1947 he had the first in a series of strokes, and his health gradually deteriorated over the years.
[†] Albert Einstein (1879-1955) was a German-born physicist probably best known for enunciating the theory of relativity to explain the relationship of matter and energy. He was awarded the Nobel Prize in physics in 1922.

I've forgotten now what the subject was, but it had to do with the academic schools, and I called in the senior officer in charge of the educational department and I said, "Look, I'm the dumb sergeant, I can't understand this jargon. Take it back and rewrite it." And he admitted he hadn't written it, that the civil service GS-17 had written it. He claimed that the people in Memphis would understand it. I said, "I don't give a damn about the people in Memphis, but I don't understand it, so rewrite it." But just the one case and that squared that away.

Paul Stillwell: When you say down to speed, does that mean they were less productive than some of the military people?

Captain McCampbell: No, I meant down the speed, you asked if I had to get up to speed and I said no, they had to get down to speed.

Paul Stillwell: They had to get down to speed.

Captain McCampbell: Yes.

Paul Stillwell: What was your relationship with the Commander Fleet Air Jacksonville.

Captain McCampbell: None whatsoever. And the only relationship with the commanding officer of the air station, who, of course, senior to me—we didn't get along too well because, although we would generate most of the welfare funds out of our own PX and barbershop, he had his exec as head of the committee that was spending all these funds, and so we had our differences on that score.

Also, I don't know if he was directed to or not, but we were not getting any of the blacks in the barber shop, and he decided that the barbers had to start taking blacks. His barbers went on strike, and he tried to get me to change over. I said, "We already have a black barber, and he takes care of the blacks that come in. Something that works, don't try to fix it." So I never did try to do anything really to get additional black barbers or, I didn't even do anything to encourage the blacks that were in school to go to our black barber. And the white barbers wouldn't take them because the senior barber told me, "We don't know how to cut black hair." And I guess there is a little different technique. I don't think it would have taken them too long to learn if they had wanted to do it. But I didn't have any trouble with my barbershop. I had ten barbers in there. I also had five priests under me; I had eight or nine dentists. I had three chaplains and a bunch of doctors—I don't remember, about 10 or 12.

Paul Stillwell: Well, you needed all those people with 9,000 to take care of.

Captain McCampbell: We had the hospital down at the air station there. All the doctors did was to prescribe pills: "Take two aspirin and come back to see me tomorrow."

Paul Stillwell: Did the 9,000 include the students?

Captain McCampbell: Oh yes, yes.

Paul Stillwell: You mentioned the Marines that were there. What was their part in the whole operation?

Captain McCampbell: Well, they had students and they had their own little organization. And they had their own discipline.

Paul Stillwell: Were they a security force on the station?

Captain McCampbell: No, no, we didn't have anything to do on the station except we provided four people for the commissary on the station. Most of the enlisted men weren't married, and most of them used the commissary very little. So we figured four people would be about proportional to the officers that did use the commissary. Because they had Fleet Air there in addition to my training command. And they had the reserves there.

Paul Stillwell: Well, I wasn't thinking about your training command. They also trained student pilots there.

Captain McCampbell: Only the reserves.

Paul Stillwell: Oh, I see.

Captain McCampbell: The rest of them were trained, like Cecil Field, and Green Cove Springs and that sort of thing.

Paul Stillwell: Well, these Marines that were being trained there, was that because the Marine Corps didn't have facilities to train those particular specialties?

Captain McCampbell: Well, yes, I guess so. Of course, the Marine Corps had their own air force more or less.

Paul Stillwell: How much dealing did you have with the civilian community there?

Captain McCampbell: Well, normal. I attended the monthly meetings of the Chamber of Commerce. The director of the Chamber of Commerce and I had quite a few dealings, communications, anyway. On a couple of cases, they had their monthly Chamber of Commerce meeting in my mess hall. Of course that was a cheap, easy way for them to have it, because I think we only charged them about $1.25 or $1.30 for their meal.

Paul Stillwell: Who was the commanding officer of the air station?

Captain McCampbell: Captain McCaffree.[*] He was skipper of the new *Wasp*, which ran

---

[*] Captain Burnham C. McCaffree, USN.

into the destroyer in the Atlantic and killed about 125 people.[*]

Paul Stillwell: She ran into the *Hobson* in 1952.

Captain McCampbell: Yes, right.

Paul Stillwell: Anything else you recall about that command?

Captain McCampbell: No, I had nice quarters. I lived right on the St. Johns River. And I had a little fishing boat that I kept right there. I had two mess attendants assigned to me. It was kind of a nice setup for me.

Paul Stillwell: Did the ships at Mayport send people over for training?

Captain McCampbell: No, Mayport wasn't in operation then. They were developing it.

Paul Stillwell: From there you went to Patuxent.

Captain McCampbell: Patuxent River, Maryland. I was coordinator of tests. In other words, I had all the tests. There were five test divisions under me. There was flight test, service test, electronics test, arms test and the test pilot school. I just coordinated their efforts and conducted the Monday morning briefings. We'd all get together Monday morning for a short period.

Paul Stillwell: You worked for Commander Naval Air Test Center?

---

[*] On the night of 26 April 1952, during an eastward crossing of the Atlantic, the destroyer minesweeper *Hobson* (DMS-26) turned in front of the aircraft carrier *Wasp* (CV-18), collided with her, and sank. Of the *Hobson*'s crew, 176 men were lost, including the commanding officer, Lieutenant Commander W. J. Tierney, USN; 52 were rescued. See Winston Jordan, "Flank Speed to Eternity," *Naval History*, Spring 1988, pages 12-17.

Captain McCampbell: Yes, which was then Admiral Duerfeldt.[*]

Paul Stillwell: Any specific memories about him? What kind of a guy was he?

Captain McCampbell: Well, I'd been onto him; he was the exec of the new *Hornet*. And since my air group trained for the *Hornet*, we went around to Pearl Harbor on the ship when I knew him.

Paul Stillwell: Did you have a good relationship with him?

Captain McCampbell: Yes, I had a good relationship.

Paul Stillwell: What do you recall about that job?

Captain McCampbell: It wasn't too difficult. I had a lot of paper work reviewing reports from the various test centers. The test pilot training school I didn't have much to do with, except I was one year on a panel that selected the people for the school. Otherwise, I had nothing to do with the school.

Paul Stillwell: A number of the people who went through that school subsequently became astronauts and so forth. Do you remember any of them?

Captain McCampbell: Astronauts are aviators. Most of them are aviators. It seemed to me when they completed the training in test pilot school, they would have a tour of a year, or maybe two, in one of the test divisions and then they'd retire. I guess they felt they'd had it, and I believe that mainly those people were lieutenant commanders and commanders. None were captains but they had had little or no training as a ship's officer, and they didn't want any, and they saw they were coming up to get some of that. Even the captain of a ship, they apparently didn't want it because they had had little or no

---

[*] Captain Clifford H. Duerfeldt, USN.

training. Most of them came up during the war, and I believe that's the reason they resigned. Plus they could go out and get a job quite easily.

Paul Stillwell: Do you remember any of the test pilots who did stay in and became astronauts or who were otherwise famous?

Captain McCampbell: Yes, Senator John Glenn was one.[*] He was there when I was there. He was in flight test. The director of flight test, the second one while I was there, later became skipper of the *Bon Homme Richard*. I believe he shot down 11 planes during the war and lost a wife while he was out on combat. A black-shoe naval officer in Honolulu ran off with his wife. I'm trying to think of his name. He's the only one that I followed very closely. The flight test director, the one before that I just mentioned, was Harvey Lanham, and he made captain.[†] The director of service tests, whose name I can't remember, later was operations officer for the Seventh Fleet and also later got command of a ship.

Paul Stillwell: What was the difference between flight test and service test?

Captain McCampbell: Well, they all had their own peculiar tests, more particularly, I guess, the flight test was, the new players that came aboard did most of the earlier testing, they usually went to flight test first. And then they would go to service test. Service meant carry out suitability trials, that sort of thing. And they would do arrested landings and catapult shots and things like that on the field there. Armament test was strictly the armament that would go in the various planes and missiles, and electronic test was strictly for electronic training development, and they also had the deep freeze division of that business. They had a deep freeze over there where they could put the different planes under very severe weather strains.

---

[*] On 16 July 1957 Major John H. Glenn, Jr., USMC, broke the transcontinental speed record when he flew an F8U-1P Crusader from Los Alamitos, California, to Floyd Bennett Field, Brooklyn, in 3 hours, 22 minutes, and 50 seconds. On 20 February 1962, as a lieutenant colonel and astronaut, he flew the "Friendship 7" spacecraft on the first manned orbital mission by the United States. As a Democrat from Ohio, he served in the Senate from 24 December 1974 to 3 January 1999.
[†] Commander Harvey P. Lanham, USN.

Paul Stillwell: Do you remember any of the individual planes that were undergoing testing then?

Captain McCampbell: Yes, the F3H.*

Paul Stillwell: The F8U, was that one of them?†

Captain McCampbell: No, we didn't have the F8U. The F6F was still undergoing tests, although in service.

Paul Stillwell: Oh, really?

Captain McCampbell: Yes. They get it in that test command, and it goes on and on forever practically. The Bureau of Inspection and Survey had a small shop there with a captain and a commander assistant and a couple other areas. They had their tests, but they didn't come under my command.

Paul Stillwell: I think you mentioned to me that it was during that tour of duty that you became qualified in jets. What do you recall of that experience?

Captain McCampbell: Well, the commander of the armament test center invited me one day to come down and fly his F9Fs.‡ So I did and asked for a handbook, I read that over thoroughly and how to eject and all that jazz. So I went down and took off—no strain—and came around. I flew for about 45 minutes. The F9 was relatively short legged and not too much gas. I flew for about a half hour or so and came in and landed. The only unusual feature was I had been used to landing a plane with three wheels, but landing in a tail-wheel attitude. With the jets you had to land more or less nose down. So I eased up

---

* McDonnell's F3H Demon was a jet-powered fighter-bomber that first entered the fleet in the 1950s but was relatively unsuccessful in fleet service.
† The F8U Crusader was a jet fighter plane.
‡ The Grumman F9F-6/F9F-7/F9F-8 Cougar was first delivered to operational units in November 1952. The F9F-6 model was 42 feet long; wingspan of 36 feet; gross weight of 20,000 pounds; and top speed of 690 miles per hour. It was armed with four 20-millimeter guns. The Cougar had swept wings and was a substantial improvement over its predecessor, the Panther.

on the stick and landed too high and blew out one of the tires when I landed. But the unusual thing was I didn't even know I had blown out the tire until I tried to turn off from the runway. They have very small tires, I mean, about like that.

Paul Stillwell: Three inches in diameter.

Captain McCampbell: About all, yes.

Paul Stillwell: I've heard a number of pilots say that they found jets easier than propeller planes because they didn't have to deal with the torque, and they didn't have the distraction of the propeller in front of their face.

Captain McCampbell: Yes, a lot quieter, and that was the biggest difference, was the lack of noise. Otherwise, it seemed like most any plane except for the landing. You had to land nose down, or you'd come in almost to the deck before you began to ease back on the stick.

Paul Stillwell: How much did you fly that plane subsequently?

Captain McCampbell: Before I took over my tanker, I was assigned to Olathe, Kansas, for, I think it was three weeks and I flew daily in the F9F, two-seater.* I had an instructor except, I think, for the last hop I made. He put me off by myself.

Paul Stillwell: Was the idea that you'd eventually be taking over a carrier, and then you'd know what your pilots were doing?

Captain McCampbell: Right, plus they were going to have F9Fs. And we did some gunnery and bombing and plane-to-plane simulated combat and mostly landing takeoffs. I didn't do any simulated carrier landings. I had no difficulty.

---

* The naval air station at Olathe was the site of jet transitional training in that period.

Paul Stillwell: One thing that was noted about the test pilot business is that it is a dangerous job, and you're going to lose some people along the way. Did you have any hand in notifying the families of those who were killed or injured?

Captain McCampbell: No. In my tour there, we lost only one test pilot. I believe this was K. D. Smith, who had been on the *Roosevelt*, and I approved his request to become a test pilot. He was killed in an F9F. At that time he was testing the durability of the F9F in landing high. See how high he could land before he busted up the landing gear. And he must have been pretty high because he busted up landing gear and the plane, too, and he killed himself.

Paul Stillwell: I guess there's a question that goes back to when you were in the *Essex*. Did you write letters to families of pilots and air crewmen who were killed in your air group?

Captain McCampbell: Only when we were in the early stages of training, the fighters.

Paul Stillwell: Just as a squadron CO you did that?

Captain McCampbell: Yes, and after that I left it up to the squadron commanders.

Paul Stillwell: Not a pleasant job under any circumstances.

Captain McCampbell: Well, we had the administrative officer who would write the letter for you, and you'd sign it.

Paul Stillwell: What else do you recall about the time at Patuxent River?

Captain McCampbell: That's about all. From there I was assigned as operations officer of the Sixth Fleet.

Paul Stillwell: That was another good job.

Captain McCampbell: Yes, a good job. That was under Admiral Brown. I was first assigned to Admiral Freddie Boone, who had been recently just assigned to the Sixth Fleet. He interviewed me, and then his orders were changed, and he went to CinCNELM.* Then came Admiral Felt, who took over Sixth Fleet.† He was with us about four months, I guess, then he was assigned VCNO, and Brown relieved him.‡ So most of my two-year tour was with Brown.

Paul Stillwell: Okay. This was around the time of the Suez crisis.§ What do you remember about that?

Captain McCampbell: Yes, we were in on that. We were in the western Med. We sailed very quickly to the eastern Med. We were busy and did evacuate a couple hundred people out of Alexandria. We ran into the British fleet in that area, and Admiral Brown sent the commander of the British fleet a message that said, "I'll stay out of your way if you stay out of my way." And so we never actually sighted the British fleet. They agreed to it.

Paul Stillwell: There are a lot of interesting stories about Brown, and I'd certainly be interested in your perspective from observing him daily.

Captain McCampbell: Well, I knew him on the old *Essex* there. He was chief of staff to Admiral Frederick Sherman. He made a remark to Sherman, and it was after the 24th of

---

* Admiral Walter F. Boone, USN, served as Commander in Chief U.S. Naval Forces Eastern Atlantic and Mediterranean (CinCNELM) from May 1956 to February 1958.
† Vice Admiral Harry Don Felt, USN, served as Commander Sixth Fleet from 12 April 1956 to 4 August 1956. As a four-star admiral, Felt was Vice Chief of Naval Operations from 1 September 1956 to 28 July 1958. His oral history is in the Naval Institute collection.
‡ Vice Admiral Charles R. Brown, USN, commanded the Sixth Fleet from 4 August 1956 to 30 September 1958.
§ On 26 July 1956 President Gamal Nasser of Egypt announced that his country was nationalizing the Suez Canal Company. Israeli forces invaded Egypt's Sinai Peninsula on 29 October 1956. Britain and France then intervened militarily on behalf of Israel in an unsuccessful attempt to secure the Suez Canal, which was damaged and closed to traffic. Rather than support the British and French, the United States asked for a United Nations resolution to end the fighting. A cease-fire took effect on 6 November.

October when Admiral Sherman had gotten into that flight that I got the nine planes on. Sherman called me up to the flag bridge and "ate me out" for taking part in the "scramble." I remember Admiral Brown, who was then a captain, after Sherman more or less got through with me. He said, "Well, Admiral, we were sent out here to kill Japs, and that's exactly what Commander McCampbell did." So that may have softened Sherman up a little. Anyway, the staff recommended me for the Congressional Medal of Honor.

Paul Stillwell: Maybe Sherman signed it somewhat reluctantly.

Captain McCampbell: I don't know. I didn't even know of the recommendation until months later.

Paul Stillwell: What do you remember about Brown as a vice admiral and fleet commander? What was his operating style?

Captain McCampbell: Well, he used to tell everybody who came aboard that he had a lean, mean staff. And he considered himself lean and mean, but he wasn't lean. He had a stomach disorder; we found out later it was hookworm. Later on, they took a worm out of his belly almost as big as your forearm. But he had that little belly way down here, and that's what it was. Because he dieted all the time. And he always controlled the mess. He made a considerable amount of money on that mess, because when we left the ship, we ended up with a credit over and above what we had contributed to it. Every morning he had his aide bring him the menu for lunch and dinner. Breakfast you could have whatever you wanted, but the other meals were all set. And I know full well, because one day we had some guests aboard, and I think they had fish on the menu or something. And the senior Marine officer and I decided before we went in for lunch that we'd rather have scrambled eggs. So I told the cook to please serve us scrambled eggs, and old Brown hit the ceiling at that—boy. He called me in and dressed me down real good.

Paul Stillwell: What difference did it make to him?

Captain McCampbell: Well, he made out the menu, and he expected you to eat what was laid before you. Or if you didn't what to eat it, you didn't eat it, but that was what you were going to get.

Paul Stillwell: Could you go to the wardroom and eat there instead?

Captain McCampbell: I didn't, but he told me I could do that, though, if I wanted to.

Paul Stillwell: The fleet commander was in a heavy cruiser at that time, *Salem, Des Moines, Newport News*. What kind of quarters did you have on board?

Captain McCampbell: Not every elaborate, I'll tell you that, just the one cabin. I remember on the cruiser, on the *Salem*, I had a bed that would sink way down, put you like you were swinging in a hammock. I never could get that corrected. I got an extra mattress for it, and it'd still sink down. And as long as I was aboard, that was what I had to contend with. Very difficult to get to sleep at night.

Paul Stillwell: Brown, you said, liked to be in control. Did he want to control the carrier task force in the Mediterranean as well?

Captain McCampbell: Oh, well, he did. When I went to the Sixth Fleet, I took over with me, the guy that had been at Patuxent in patrol planes. He came to me and said he understood I was going to Sixth Fleet as operations officer, and would I please take him along. This was Jerry Denton, who later became a senator.[*] I said, "What's your specialty in?" He said his specialty was electronics. He had some ideas about the disposition of the fleet. Basically his idea was that instead of running around in the Mediterranean, which is an enclosed sea, more or less, in formation with the fleet

---

[*] Lieutenant Jeremiah A. Denton, Jr., USN. Denton, who was a naval aviator, later spent eight years as a prisoner of war during the Vietnam War. His memoir of that period is *When Hell Was in Session* (New York: Readers Digest Press, 1976). He subsequently served as a U.S. Senator from Alabama, 1981-87.

commander and carriers, and cruisers—in the normal fleet formation where the destroyers are protecting the carriers and the cruisers are protecting them—to scatter them all out. And we'd go into different ports for liberty, for rest and recreation.

So it was convenient in one sense that they could leave their port that they were in and go to a designated area or point. And when the time came, the fleet was assembled, more or less, they would be scattered all over the Mediterranean. We conducted exercises in that and got quite proficient at it. It was difficult, because you had to meet a certain schedule, like for replenishment. A tanker would have to be at a certain spot at a certain time on a certain day, and then the carrier would rendezvous on it and replenish the oil or gasoline. But we got pretty good at it. If we were in the western Med, we'd scatter over the whole area practically. If we were in the eastern Med, we'd scatter all over the whole area of the eastern Med.

Paul Stillwell: What advantage did that offer, doing it that way?

Captain McCampbell: Well, we had two exercises with the British. The heavy bombers, Lancasters or whatever, and we defied them to find our carriers primarily. Now they were flying out of England, and we'd be in the western Med, and both times they couldn't identify our carriers. They couldn't find them. And they had a new type radar; I've forgotten the features of it, but it was supposed to be excellent for locating formations of ships primarily. We'd have a critique afterward, and they'd admit that they couldn't find us. They could find individual ships, but from high altitude their radars couldn't distinguish between a merchant ship and a naval vessel. There's so much traffic in the Med, you see, that we can hide, really just hide amongst all the traffic.

Paul Stillwell: And obviously with a tight formation, you know the carrier's going to be right there in the middle.

Captain McCampbell: Yes, so they couldn't identify us.

Paul Stillwell: Did Admiral Brown tend not to give much autonomy to his carrier commander?

Captain McCampbell: Oh, no, he would give the usual amount of autonomy. He would kind of haul them up now and then. I remember Bob Pirie at one time was carrier group commander.[*] And he did a couple of things wrong, according to Brown. So Brown called him over and told him what he'd done wrong.

CinCNELM determined which ports we were going to for rest and recreation. And Brown was not at liberty to change those ports, because they all went through requests in diplomatic channels. So we had to go where CinCNELM told us to go. He directed the traffic of the Sixth Fleet from afar.

Paul Stillwell: Were you able to make inputs and recommendations to that schedule?

Captain McCampbell: No. I started to tell you about Admiral Pirie. At one point he was assigned to go to Valencia. And instead of going to Valencia, he wanted to go to Barcelona, which is a bigger city, and I think he had some friends there or something. Pirie called me over to his flagship and first made the request to me. I went back and carried the request to Admiral Brown, and Brown, unbeknownst to me, gave Pirie an extra four days in Valencia, instead of Barcelona. And that made Admiral Pirie very mad. But he should have known Brown better than that. He should have known that Brown couldn't change the schedule.

Paul Stillwell: No, but I'm wondering if there was a chance for the commander of the Sixth Fleet to make a recommendation to CinCNELM before CinCNELM set up the schedule.

Captain McCampbell: No, we didn't do that. CinCNELM held the whole thing, and we'd get our schedule on ports of visit like six weeks ahead of time, maybe even more.

---

[*] Rear Admiral Robert B. Pirie, USN. The oral history of Pirie, who retired as a vice admiral, is in the Naval Institute collection.

Paul Stillwell: The first of the super carriers, as they were called, came out during that period, the USS *Forrestal*.* Did that offer a change in working her into the rotation since she was a more capable ship?

Captain McCampbell: No, we didn't. While I was in Sixth Fleet we didn't operate with the *Forrestal* or any of the bigger carriers. We only had the *Franklin D. Roosevelt* and the *Coral Sea*. I think *Midway* was on the West Coast at that time. Then others were the *Randolph*, *Valley Forge*, *Leyte*.

Paul Stillwell: Any of the other members of that staff that you especially remember?

Captain McCampbell: Yes, I remember the first chief of staff I was under. He and I had quite a few run-ins. I'm not gong to say too much more about him. I think he's still living. He's class of '27, so he was six years ahead of me and quite senior, and he had been ComServFor Sixth Fleet, or ComServFor Mediterranean, one or the other. He had charge of the service force ships that had been in the Med. He'd been over there for a couple of years before he joined the Sixth Fleet staff.

Paul Stillwell: Who was that?

Captain McCampbell: Larry Freeman.† And he kind of thought he was the boss of the Sixth Fleet. Oh, he was at one time, for about two weeks before Felt got there. Ralph Ofstie, my old skipper of the *Essex*, had had to go to the hospital up in Germany for a colostomy, cancer of the bowels, large intestine.‡ He never returned. He died, and Larry Freeman was the chief of staff under him. He had charge of the Sixth Fleet there during the interim before Felt got there.

---

* USS *Forrestal* (CVA-59) was commissioned 1 October 1955 as the first of the U.S. Navy's big-deck carriers. She had a standard displacement of 56,000 tons, was 1,046 feet long, 129 feet in the beam, and had an extreme width of 252 feet. Her top speed was 33 knots.
† Captain Charles Lawrence Freeman, USN. He died 21 August 1995, several years after this interview.
‡ Vice Admiral Ralph A. Ofstie, USN, was Commander Sixth Fleet, 1955-56. He died of cancer on 18 November 1956 at the Bethesda Naval Hospital in Maryland.

Paul Stillwell: Felt moved up pretty quick.

Captain McCampbell: He got selected about the time Burke was; he and Arleigh Burke were moving up very fast. I think Felt wanted to get that experience under his belt before he came as assistant to Burke. I remember when the change of command came we were in Venice. When Admiral Brown came, Mrs. Brown came aboard for the change of command. She met him over there.

Interview Number 5 with Captain David McCampbell, U.S. Navy (Retired)
Place: Captain McCampbell's home in Lake Worth, Florida
Date: Saturday, 18 July 1987

Paul Stillwell: Captain, since we met yesterday, you were kind enough to lend me Captain Hugh Winters's book about his experiences as air group commander in the *Lexington* in World War II.[*] That has prompted some additional questions, and I appreciate your patience on these details. He talked about the use of the water injection system to give a temporary boost in power to the F6F. Could you explain how that worked, please?

Captain McCampbell: Yes, we first introduced that, as I recall, when we got the F6F-5. We'd formerly been flying the –3. It gave us about 15 minutes of extra boost that we were warned not to use for too long a period of time. So what we would do, we'd use it enough in an emergency situation, like to get away from an enemy plane or something like that; it would give us the 250 pounds of additional thrust. Use it for a short period, and then cut it off. It was activated very simply on the throttle quadrant. It had a wire stretched across so that full throttle would be up to the wire. Then you'd get the additional boost from the water injection if you broke the wire and went on through it. It came in use, I guess, infrequently. I don't know. The tank was 15 gallons, and I used about three refills on it. So it was used infrequently.

Paul Stillwell: How could water increase the power of the engine?

Captain McCampbell: Well, it's the same principle as an automobile engine that will run better in rainy weather than it does in clear weather. It's the water, I guess, mixed with the gasoline that gives it a little extra oxygen for the engine.

---

[*] T. Hugh Winters, *Skipper: Confessions of a Fighter Squadron Commander, 1943-1944* (Mesa, Arizona: Champlin Fighter Museum Press, 1986).

Paul Stillwell: Do you remember the specific occasions when you had to use it?

Captain McCampbell: Yes, I remember twice. Once was off Guam. I took off chasing this Zero, or Zeke, with a belly tank on to see if I could catch him, because usually we didn't chase away from the formation. Not that we stayed exactly in formation all the time, but from the area where our people were having combat action. But I intentionally did this to check to see if I could catch the Zeke with a belly tank on at low altitude. It had already been tested and proven that you could, but I didn't know that. So I caught him all right, but then that was the occasion where I was just getting ready to fire, and he whipped up into an Immelmann. I followed him and saw that I couldn't stay with him at low altitude, so I dropped my belly tank and headed back for the area where the rest of my people were. Three Hellcats came down as I passed, and he was chasing my tail.

The other time was the day I got my nine planes, and Roy and I got separated there once. He was late or slow in reforming after we had made attacks. I never asked him, but I figured that he probably got—I knocked my plane down, and he had a little more trouble with his. So I looked around, and I didn't see him. I saw a plane heading for me a little later, and I thought it might possibly by a Jap, so I broke the wire and used my water injection until I could get enough distance. Then I turned and called to Roy. I said, "Roy, if that's you behind me, wobble your wings." He did, so I throttled back with that, and we rejoined.

Paul Stillwell: How much extra speed could you get as a result of that for a short period of time?

Captain McCampbell: I don't know. I don't have any way of measuring it. It was supposed to give us an additional 250 horsepower, or approximately that.

Paul Stillwell: What was your normal top speed, do you recall?

Captain McCampbell: In level flight I really don't remember. I think it was reported to be 320 or 330 miles an hour, but I'm not sure that it would accomplish that top speed. Of course, in a dive you'd go much faster.

Paul Stillwell: We were talking the other day about the steep angle that the Hellcat would achieve in a dive. Now, the dive-bombers, of course, had specific dive brakes. How did you ensure that you would pull out in time?

Captain McCampbell: Well, we, of course, had no dive bakes, and our flaps we would use for landings primarily were spring-loaded. So that if you exceeded a certain speed they'd fold right back up into the wings. So they were no good in a dive. We just learned to observe. In a four-plane division I was leading, and I knew enough to—if we were strafing or dropping bombs, we'd start our pullout about 1,500 feet, and that gave me enough altitude to successfully, easily pull out.

Paul Stillwell: Would you judge that just by seaman's eye, or was that from the altimeter?

Captain McCampbell: Yes, just by seaman eye generally.

Paul Stillwell: He made brief reference in his book to the gunsight and that being reflected on the windshield. Could you explain, please, how the gunsight worked and how the bombsight worked?

Captain McCampbell: Well, the bombsight on the Hellcat was the same as the gunsight.

Paul Stillwell: I see.

Captain McCampbell: But the gunsight was projected from the dash up onto the windshield, immediately in front of the pilot. It consisted of three concentric circles. I believe they were marked off of 50 miles per hour, roughly, 50, 100, and 150 concentric circles. So if you were making an angled approach on an enemy plane, depending on what angle you were as to how much lead you would give him, and his approximate speed and angle of attack. And you can find it really by seaman's eye as to how much lead to give him. You can go 50, 100, 150.

Paul Stillwell: That's on a deflection shot?

Captain McCampbell: Yes.

Paul Stillwell: Now, how about if you were coming in behind him? How would you do it then?

Captain McCampbell: Well, you'd put him on the pipper then.

Paul Stillwell: What's the pipper?

Captain McCampbell: Well, the pipper's the center of the gunsight, a little mark in the center. But you rarely attacked one from directly behind. The best way to attack was from within a 20-degree cone directly astern—somewhere in that 20-degree cone around the tail.

Paul Stillwell: Why would you prefer the 20-degree angle, let's say, as opposed to coming in directly astern?

Captain McCampbell: Because it gave you a larger target. Also it gave an opportunity to shoot the wing root, whereas from dead astern, you can hit the wing root, but it's a little smaller target.

Paul Stillwell: How did you use the same sight for dropping bombs?

Captain McCampbell: About the only part we used with the gunsight would be the pipper. Just center it on the target, whatever you're aiming at.

Paul Stillwell: And then the bomb is going to have some forward momentum after it's dropped.

Captain McCampbell: Well, you get that by training. You learn how much it's going to hit—well, if you're not on target exactly, it will go to one side or the other, or it will fall short or long. My wingman was a better dive-bomber than I was, actually, although I'd had more training. It came natural to him. He would follow me in, and on one occasion over Guam we'd gotten a special call from the Marines to attack a blockhouse. It was blocking a road intersection, and the Japanese were holed up in the blockhouse. We'd gotten a special request to come knock out that blockhouse. It was up in the north end of Guam, and I had some other people with me. I broke them off to attack another target, and Roy and I went in to attack this blockhouse. I dropped, and I missed; my bomb went over. Roy hit it right in the center and knocked it out. Later we got a message from the Marines thanking us for such expert bombing, so I recommended Roy for an Air Medal for that incident.

Paul Stillwell: What techniques did you use for close air support of the Marines with your guns?

Captain McCampbell: No particular technique, just strafing. They would give us a target. We'd try and hit it with our strafing.

Paul Stillwell: And, of course, you have to use care so you don't hit the friendly troops in that situation.

Captain McCampbell: Oh, yes. We had charts that were marked off in sections, latitude and longitude. I guess we didn't always hit the exact target, but they would designate the target, and a small section of the chart was blocked off.

Paul Stillwell: Did you talk directly by voice radio to the forward air controllers on the ground on those occasions?

Captain McCampbell: Yes, there were three or four occasions. I don't remember specifically any of them.

Paul Stillwell: Another thing that Captain Winters talked about in his book was how badly he felt when members of the air group were shot down, lost in other kinds of accidents. You know that's going to be inevitable. How do you keep that from affecting your ability to do your job?

Captain McCampbell: Well, I guess I, too, felt badly every time we lost a pilot, but I tried to throw that out of my mind—not really forgetting it, but just push it aside and go on with my usual business. I rarely attended a burial over the side, because, there again, I figured it would begin to prey on me so I couldn't sleep at night and things like that. I just tried to stay away from it as much as I could.

Paul Stillwell: Fortunately, when you're in the air, you've got so many other things to think about, that's not too much of a problem.

Captain McCampbell: Well, and usually you don't know it until it's over. Particularly the leader doesn't; he doesn't see too much of what's going on behind him. Which is one reason I'd really rather go out with just two or no more than four planes, because you have a lot more flexibility in what you do. And you have less responsibility for what's behind you. Roy and I did very well all through the latter part of the war on our combat tour with just the two of us out there.

Paul Stillwell: A name he mentioned in his book that's become quite prominent since is Justice Whizzer White of the Supreme Court, who was on Admiral Mitscher's staff.[*] What do you recall of him?

---

[*] Byron R. White served as an Associate Justice of the Supreme Court from 16 April 1962 to 28 June 1993.

Captain McCampbell: I didn't meet him when we were out there. I met him since then at the carrier aviation dedication up in Charleston, South Carolina, and had a nice long talk with him. I found him to be a very easy man to talk to, and very knowledgeable about naval aviation and what we did out there. He remembered me by name. And I didn't know he was on Mitscher's staff, actually.

Paul Stillwell: I suspect nearly everybody out there knew you by name.

Captain McCampbell: Yes, they got to know me. Well, I had landed on the *Lexington* there one time. And, of course, at that particular time I had 30 Jap flags on the side of my plane, so that always created a little stir on whatever ship I happened to land on.

Paul Stillwell: Sure. He mentioned in there, on the .50 calibers, that he had them bore-sighted about 300 yards, which was close than the figure you mentioned. Was that pretty much left up to the individual squadron commander or group commander?

Captain McCampbell: No, it came with the plane, a BuAer bore-sight pattern, and we changed ours.* As I told you, we discussed the other day, it was about the same. We changed ours to 1,000 feet. And he said, what, 300 yards? Pretty close.

Paul Stillwell: So you just lengthened it out a little bit?

Captain McCampbell: Yes. Well, I don't know how accurate he is on his. He didn't mention anything about having developed a new gun pattern, did he?

Paul Stillwell: Well, I don't remember specifically. I think he said he wanted to get it pretty close, because he felt that was the optimum range for hitting.

---

* BuAer – Bureau of Aeronautics.

Captain McCampbell: Well, really no optimum range, but if you're between, let's say, 800 feet and 1,200 feet, that's a very good range to have your guns bore-sighted at. It works out to about 1,000 feet.

Paul Stillwell: It's all in the same ballpark certainly.

Captain McCampbell: Yes, right.

Paul Stillwell: He talked also about the value of squadron parties and building the cohesiveness of the squadron and sense of oneness. Did you do some of that also in building your air group?

Captain McCampbell: Oh, yes. Yes.

Paul Stillwell: Any in particular that you remember?

Captain McCampbell: Yes, at Atlantic City. I don't recall the name of the golf club now, but there was a lovely clubhouse and golf course. I played there numerous times, and they would allow us to hold our parties there. That was just the fighter squadron, usually on Saturday night, and they wouldn't charge us for it. They gave us free admission to the golf course, play golf, no greens fees or dues or anything, and also allowed us to have our parties there. At Atlantic City in about three months we had maybe four or five squadron parties. And on Maui, Pu'unēnē Naval Air Station, we had an officers' club there that served beer and wine and booze. I don't know exactly how they kept it stocked so well, but they usually had most everything you'd want. We would have little get-togethers there in the officers' club, and at Atlantic City too. So we had no restrictions, nor did I have any trouble with alcoholism, people that would over-booze. Most of the kids were young, anyway. I'd say the average age was 20-22, in there.

Paul Stillwell: Well, there's also a notion that a guy's not a real fighter pilot if he doesn't cut up a little bit.

Captain McCampbell: Yes. That's right. At Pungo, there outside of Virginia Beach, we had a Christmas party. There was an ex-warrant officer who'd been promoted to full lieutenant, and he was in charge of Pungo Naval Air Station. He would get booze for occasions like Christmas party and New Year's Eve party. As I recall, we only had two parties there. At Norfolk we had none, because we were only there a short time.

Paul Stillwell: Did you find that civilians were especially gracious and hospitable to men in uniform?

Captain McCampbell: Atlantic City was, yes, and in Maui too. We would only got to see a few on Maui, but there was a woman, Polish descent, Countess Alexis von Tempsky, who entertained. I don't know if she entertained Hugh Winters's squadron or not, but she entertained our air group people. She couldn't entertain all of them. I wouldn't say she was wealthy, but she was well off, had a nice place up in the mountain. Some of the other people from Kailua mentioned her name and Mr. Hoyt, too, mentioned her in the book *McCampbell's Heroes*.

Paul Stillwell: In his book, Captain Winters talked about a couple of pilots who didn't seem to have a stomach for going out on strike missions. They were sent back, and one was disqualified as an aviator. Did you have a problem with that sort of thing?

Captain McCampbell: Only the one with the pilot who got shot in the thigh over Marcus Island, which I discussed earlier. He got, you might say, gun-shy after he got out of sickbay, and so we put him on as a permanent duty officer.

Paul Stillwell: Well, you mentioned the officer was in the radio relay plane too.

Captain McCampbell: Yes, that discovered the Jap fleet up north. We put him on permanent duty for a month, six weeks, anyway.

Paul Stillwell: The unsung heroes of the carrier war were the plane handlers and the flight deck crews. What can you say about those people?

Captain McCampbell: I can't say too much, but what I have to say is all good. As I mentioned before, the *Essex* was the finest operating ship that I'd ever worked with. It wasn't the cleanest ship by any means, but it was the top operating ship. It was a fairly new ship; they'd only made one earlier combat tour in the Pacific. They had Air Group Nine on it, which is a good air group, apparently, from their record. So, the flight deck crews were well trained.

I remember shortly after we got aboard the *Essex*, the executive officer called the crew together and over the loudspeaker, amongst other things, he said, "I want you people to realize we have a new air group here. They're not accustomed to combat as the air group we previously had. They may not be as perfect in the operations as the last group who's had experience out here, but it's a new air group, and I want you to treat them just the same as you did the old air group. Their air group, our air group, belongs to the *Essex*, and they'll improve with time." But he gave them a good speech along those lines, and we had perfect coordination and cooperation.

Paul Stillwell: Well, that's interesting because Winters said that he initially, and his people encountered some coolness on board the *Lexington,* and it took a while for them to be accepted by the ship's company.

Captain McCampbell: Yes. Well, that was the same point that Dave McDonald was talking about, to accept us right away.

Paul Stillwell: Well, that was certainly an advantage for your group.

Captain McCampbell: Yes.

Paul Stillwell: Those flight deck crews had a dangerous, physically demanding job and long hours, so they deserve all the recognition they can get.

Captain McCampbell: Right. Yes, they had long hours. Of course, we aviators would get relief now and then. We'd get to fly off, but they spent many hours on battle conditions, general-quarters type thing. They'd have to eat lunch, and sometimes their dinner, at their battle stations. The ship would serve them at the battle stations, sandwiches, that type of food, and coffee. They spent many long hours at battle stations.

Paul Stillwell: Really, their participation in the air battle was sort of vicarious. They were living through you in that sense.

Captain McCampbell: Yes, they got occasions to cut loose with their guns. They claim they shot down about 11 or 12 planes at various times.

Paul Stillwell: What can you say about the enlisted air crewmen as a group—the rear-seat men, the radiomen?

Captain McCampbell: Well, I didn't have too much to do with them. They were in the bomb and torpedo squadrons, and I never got close to the aircrews at all.

Paul Stillwell: Captain Winters also mentioned the broadcasts of Tokyo Rose and how she mentioned that the *Lexington* had been sunk about four times.[*] Did you also hear her in the *Essex*?

Captain McCampbell: We heard some of that, but I wouldn't be surprised if three or four times she announced the *Lexington* was sunk. It may be exaggerated somewhat.

Paul Stillwell: He said the main reaction was one of amusement more than anything else.

Captain McCampbell: Right. Well, we didn't listen to it. I heard it once or twice but not often. I didn't pay attention to it.

---

[*] "Tokyo Rose" was the nickname of an English-speaking Japanese woman who made radio broadcasts during World War II. Full of Japanese war propaganda, they were aimed at U.S. servicemen in an attempt to demoralize them. For the most part, she was regarded as entertaining rather than effective.

Paul Stillwell: Were you concerned at all, during the later stages of your time there, with possibility of Japanese radar and its ability to detect you?

Captain McCampbell: Yes, we figured they had radar, and actually never knew whether they did or not. But they frequently acted like they had radar, whether they did or not. So, there again, we gave them the benefit of the doubt and would do such things as fly low on the water to keep under the radar range as much as we could, particularly if we were snooping or scouting. But that was about the only attention we paid to it.

Paul Stillwell: Did you ever drop any chaff to deceive radars?

Captain McCampbell: Oh yes, we did, although I think the only opportunity we had was during the Battles of the Leyte Gulf, because those were the only times that we had opportunity to attack large combatant ships or concentrated shipping. Those were the only two times I can think of. We attacked shipping all the time, but mostly cargo ships and troopships.

Paul Stillwell: Well, anything else to mention about Air Group 15 before we get back to the Sixth Fleet?

Captain McCampbell: No, we pretty well covered it.

Paul Stillwell: Well, you mentioned yesterday that you had three different admirals as Sixth Fleet commanders: Admiral Ofstie, Admiral Felt, and Admiral Brown. What comparisons would you draw about the operating styles and personalities of those three?

Captain McCampbell: Well, of course, I never got to serve under Admiral Ofstie when he was commander of Sixth Fleet. He had a disorder and then cancer of the intestine. He had to fly off to Germany to be operated on and, subsequently, he died from it.

Paul Stillwell: Was that just when you were reporting to the staff?

Captain McCampbell: Just before. I never got to meet him on the ship at all.

Paul Stillwell: I see.

Captain McCampbell: So then they quickly rushed in Admiral Felt, Don Felt, and he served about three or four, maybe five months. Then he was relieved to go back to serve as Vice Chief of Naval Operations, and Admiral Brown came aboard to relieve Admiral Felt. This change of command ceremony was held while we were anchored in Venice, Italy.

Paul Stillwell: What do you remember about Felt as the fleet commander?

Captain McCampbell: Felt was quite easygoing as a—he was strictly business, but he didn't interfere too much with the staff. We kept his notebook up to date for him on various actions and exercises. We had, of course, no combat action. Generally, a good naval officer, good sound naval officer.

Paul Stillwell: Do you remember any specific incidents involving him?

Captain McCampbell: No, no, I don't.

Paul Stillwell: We talked yesterday about a couple of things that were involved in the operational role, that is, in dispersing the ships to minimize detection and . . .

Captain McCampbell: Well, yes, that came into be when Admiral Felt was in charge, but we'd just gotten started in that, really.

Paul Stillwell: Then you said also that CinCNELM would put out the port visit schedule. Are there other operational type things you remember beyond those that fell under your direct interest/

Captain McCampbell: Well, yes, the Sixth Fleet staff was responsible for organizing, planning, and conducting the Sixth Fleet exercises, which were not too frequent actually. But when Admiral Brown came aboard, we developed this dispersal of the fleet to a pretty good degree, and we would practice that. We had exercises with British Bomber Command—two exercises, I remember in which we were testing our dispersal, wide disposition of the fleet in the Mediterranean. And the British bombers had a new type radar just coming into being at that time and, of course, they were anxious to test that out. So we held the two exercises. But in neither exercise did they ever discover the main fleet units of the Sixth Fleet, the aircraft carriers—which we normally had two all the time—or the Sixth Fleet flagship, the *Salem*.

Paul Stillwell: What was your interaction with the service force as far as scheduling rendezvouses and replenishment operations?

Captain McCampbell: Well, I guess Commander Sixth Fleet would dictate when we wanted the service force to provide the replenishment of ships and the disposition of the force. We weren't all necessarily in the same place or the same formation, so they would disperse their ships at our convenience, at the fleet's convenience.

Paul Stillwell: You mentioned the experience you had in Spain just when you began that tour. Another nation there in western Mediterranean was France, and that was sort of the homeport for the Sixth Fleet before de Gaulle kicked us out.[*] What do you remember about Villefranche and operations around that?

Captain McCampbell: Well, our homeport was Villefranche, which was quite near Nice, about eight or ten miles. That was a lovely bay in there and just a small town. We liked to be there; of course, our families were there. I wasn't married at the time so I didn't have a family there. But later on, when the action was moving to the eastern Med, like

---

[*] In 1966 and 1967 French President Charles de Gaulle gradually withdrew his nation's naval and military forces from NATO because he believed the United States had too much control over those forces. He also demanded that all NATO headquarters, bases, and troops be removed from France by April 1967, which was done. France remained a member of NATO politically but not militarily.

the Suez crisis and the Jordanian crisis—the Lebanese crisis came later—the action that was going on was mostly in the east Med. So that's where we kept our fleet.

At one point the commanding officer of the *Salem*—whose name skips me at the moment—wrote a letter to the Chief of Naval Operations. Of course, he wrote the letter and sent it up the line, so it arrived on the admiral's desk, Commander Sixth Fleet. He forwarded it with a few expertise words added. Unfortunately, the supply officer was responsible for putting Admiral Brown's endorsement on the letter, and it was not routed through CinCNELM. It was sent directly to Washington, and CinCNELM got a copy. He raised holy hell about that, because it had not gone through the chain of command. But the essence of the letter was that the home-porting of the *Salem* was kind of a useless thing, because we weren't spending enough time in the homeport to call it a homeport. It kind of blasted the Chief of Naval Operations too. So after that hullabaloo, CinCNELM began to pay a little more attention to getting the *Salem* back to the homeport. That's about the only thing I can remember.

Paul Stillwell: As the operations officer, were you responsible for making sure that ships got opportunities for maintenance and repairs?

Captain McCampbell: Yes, but we didn't have too much of that over there. They were supposed to come to us from ComAirLant and ComServLant after having had all the necessary overhauls and whatnot.[*] They'd come to us in good shape for a six-month tour and generally last through it. So there wasn't much of that; there was some. We had a maintenance ship equipped with all kinds of machine shops and whatever; it belonged to ServFor. That was first based in Naples and later more or less home-ported at Barcelona. She just sat there most of the time, and the ships that they needed a little repair would come to her.

Paul Stillwell: Did they have to check with you on that, or did they deal directly?

---

[*] ComAirLant – Commander Air Force Atlantic Fleet; ComServLant – Commander Service Force Atlantic Fleet. The other principal type commanders for ships were Commander Cruiser Force Atlantic Fleet, Commander Destroyer Force Atlantic Fleet, and Commander Amphibious Force Atlantic Fleet..

Captain McCampbell: No, the commander of Sixth Fleet would make the decision.

Paul Stillwell: Well, there are some things that are inevitable, such as storm damage or a piece of equipment breaks down, electronics, or what have you.

Captain McCampbell: Yes.

Paul Stillwell: What do you recall with you dealings with the amphibious force in the Mediterranean?

Captain McCampbell: We had a unit of Marines, and I've forgotten the size of it. It seems to me it was an understaffed regiment, and they would cruise around. We never had an exercise with them, to my knowledge. They were ready to go ashore anywhere, anytime, but we never had occasion. Even during the Suez crisis, we didn't put them ashore, although we evacuated maybe a couple hundred people out of Alexandria. The Jordanian, crisis, we didn't put them ashore. In the Lebanese crisis later on, they did put the Marines ashore.[*] That came after my tour with the staff of the Sixth Fleet.

Paul Stillwell: Are there any specifics you remember on that evacuation?

Captain McCampbell: I remember that CinCNELM had a plan to fly Air Force-type planes to evacuate by air, but that was never used in the case of the Suez and Jordanian crises. That was used later in the Lebanese crisis, when they flew in Air Force planes to take off people. Also, for emergency hospitalization, the Air Force had a group based somewhere in Germany, and they were available to us in case we needed them. For instance, Admiral Ofstie, if he had to go to the hospital up in Germany—at Wiesbaden, I think—he was flown out by Air Force people.

---

[*] On 15 July 1958, at the request of Lebanese President Camille Chamoun, two U.S. Marine battalion landing teams went ashore at Beirut. Their mission was to support the government of President Chamoun, who was threatened by both civil war and the prospect of foreign intervention.

Paul Stillwell: Did you have agreements with nations on the rim of the Mediterranean to provide divert fields for carrier aircraft?

Captain McCampbell: Italy, Greece, and Turkey were the only ones we had any agreements with.

Paul Stillwell: Libya was still friendly too.

Captain McCampbell: I was just going to mention Libya was still a growing concern and the Air Force had a training base there. I remember we went into Libya once, at Tripoli, and the skipper of the air base was Robin Olds.[*] He and his wife came out to the ship for lunch one day. And I played golf there at Wheelus Air Force Base.

Paul Stillwell: He was later a fighter pilot in Vietnam, I believe, wasn't he?

Captain McCampbell: Yes. And I played golf there once. I remember an unusual thing about it. It bordered right on a cemetery, and if you happened to slice a ball off into that cemetery, it was against the law to go in there and get your ball. That was not part of the base; that was off base.

Paul Stillwell: You just took a penalty stroke?

Captain McCampbell: You just took a penalty stroke, yes, and hit another ball.

Paul Stillwell: Did land-based patrol planes come under Sixth Fleet operational control?

Captain McCampbell: Yes. I think we called them air early warning squadron. They kept at least three planes at Port Lyautey all the time. We actually had exercises on

---

[*] Colonel Robin Olds, USAF, graduated from the Military Academy at West Point in June 1943; he served as a fighter pilot in both World War II and the Vietnam War but not in the Korean War. From 1956 to 1958 he was chief of the Weapons Proficiency Center at Wheelus Air Force Base, Libya. In that capacity he was in charge of all fighter weapons training for U.S. Air Forces Europe.

occasions with them. They would fly up with the fleet and operate with us. They were relieved on a regular basis. There were three always at Port Lyautey, and then they'd spend a tour, go back to the States, and send another three out.

Paul Stillwell: Do you remember anything specific about controlling the work of the cruiser-destroyer force?

Captain McCampbell: No, not really, except to, we operated with them. We'd call them together periodically, and they'd tag along.

Paul Stillwell: Did you get involved at all with the midshipmen summer cruises from the Naval Academy and NROTC?

Captain McCampbell: Yes, towards the last of my tour—this was in '58—we caught them one summer, but as I remember they were only attached to destroyers. We never saw them on the staff. But they would do their tour then go home.

Paul Stillwell: Anything else to wrap up the Sixth Fleet tour?

Captain McCampbell: We visited practically every country that bordered on the Mediterranean except Israel, Egypt, Tunisia, and Algeria. We visited all the others on a rest-and-recreation deal. Turkey. We even got into Beirut, Lebanon, when Chamoun was the President—a very delightful place, actually. We got in there twice. We got into Istanbul a couple of times. When I say "we," I mean the *Salem*.

Paul Stillwell: Did you visit Yugoslavia?

Captain McCampbell: Yes, we did on one occasion.

Paul Stillwell: What are your recollections of that?

Captain McCampbell: It was appeared to me to be a quite backward culture, although parts of it, I'm sure, were not. The part we saw seemed to be quite backward. We attended a couple of festivities that they put on while we were in there. But in all these different countries around the Med, I played golf in most all of them. Of course, in Villefranche, France, we had access to a golf club up over Monaco. They had no greens fees or dues, a delightful little course.

Oh, I remember in Lebanon I played golf once, and their golf course consisted of nothing but a sandlot, a little longer, maybe, than a sandlot, but that was about all. We teed off on rubber mats on top of the sand, and we'd drive down the fairway, they were all sand. And you'd have to run real quick to get your ball before the little Arabs would come out from under the trees to pick them up. Then we'd get to the greens and they were all sand, soaked with oil. They had a little Arab on each green with a rake, and after you'd putt, the little Arab would come over and smooth it out again so the next guy could putt. That was the most austere golf course I ever played on, I'm sure.

In Morocco, we flew down, played golf down there on the King's golf course, which is set out amongst a bunch of orange trees. And, there again, we had the sand greens soaked in oil. Played in Spain, where golf courses are few and far between. I played in Portugal. I don't think they had a golf course in Gibraltar. But, Italy, I played in two or three places; Greece; and Istanbul, we played against a Turkish team there, four on each team. We couldn't speak to each other, but we could have drinks with each other. I played in Libya. So that about covers the situation of my activities and recreation.

Paul Stillwell: Well, in early 1958 you went to command the fleet oiler *Severn*.* How did that come about?

Captain McCampbell: I was on the Sixth Fleet staff at the time and a letter came to

---

* USS *Severn* (AO-61), an *Ashtabula*-class fleet oiler, was commissioned 19 July 1944. She displaced 25,440 tons loaded, was 553 feet long, 75 feet in the beam, and had a maximum draft of 32 feet. Her top speed was 18 knots. She was originally armed with one 5-inch gun and four 3-inch guns.

Admiral Brown right out of the blue from Admiral Bill Davis, who was OP-05.[*]

Paul Stillwell: He'd been skipper of the *Franklin D. Roosevelt* when you were exec.

Captain McCampbell: Yes. And he asked Admiral Brown what Brown thought about sending me to the service force to take over the service force ship. Admiral Brown passed the letter on to me, and I answered for him. Admiral Brown was very much against it.

Paul Stillwell: Why?

Captain McCampbell: Well, because it was getting me out of the brown-shoe Navy to go to the service force.[†] So Admiral Brown sent the letter to me to answer for him, and I figured it was getting late in my career to get a deep-draft ship. But I knew Admiral Davis, and if he thought it was a good idea, I would go along with it. I think he mentioned in the letter that there was a program to get naval aviators more deep-draft ships to qualify and take over carriers. That was part of the program. So I answered the letter for Admiral Brown in the affirmative that, yes, it was probably a good idea, and I pointed out in the letter it would take me out of the sphere of the aviation Navy and publications like *Naval Aviation News*, which I was on the receiving end of regularly.

But, anyway, generally, for Admiral Brown I said, "Yes, it's probably a good idea." So it wasn't long after that I got my orders. And if I wasn't the first one, I was pretty close to it to get a service force ship for a naval aviator. I didn't know anyone that had gotten one previously. Anyway, I was assigned to the *Severn*. I knew the *Severn* would be a pretty sloppy ship, because we had replenished from it a couple of times in the Med. I thought, "Well, I've gotten into the mess now. It's better to accept that and go along with the program." So I was sent back home, and I joined the *Severn*. It was in the Todd shipyard in New York at the time for overhaul, so I reported in there.

---

[*] Vice Admiral William V. Davis, Jr., USN, served as Deputy Chief of Naval Operations (Air) from 1 August 1956 to 22 May 1958.

[†] In the early days of naval aviation, the aviators wore brown shoes with their khaki uniforms and green uniforms. They thus acquired the nickname "brown shoes" to distinguish them from the traditional surface ship officers, who are known as "black shoes."

I noticed when I went aboard that the ship had no commission pennant flying, and no one greeted me at the gangway. I walked aft; I figured the captain was up in the superstructure somewhere or in his cabin. I ran into a mess attendant, and I asked him to direct me to the captain's quarters. So I got up to his cabin, which was on the deck just above the well deck, and introduced myself. I didn't know him before; he was a black-shoe out of the class of '34. The first thing I asked him was if the ship had been decommissioned. And he said, "Oh, no, we're still in commission."

I said, "Well, I notice you don't have a commission pennant flying."

He said, "Oh, don't we?" So he called his communications officer up and told him to get a commission pennant up there. But there were lines all over the ship, getting water, electricity, and everything from the dock.

I said to him, "By the way, there was no one at the gangway when I came aboard."

He said, "Oh, I'll correct that real soon."

These two items indicated to me that the ship was being run in a pretty loose manner.

Paul Stillwell: This is where your Reeves training in the *Wasp* came in handy.

Captain McCampbell: Oh, yes. He took me on a tour of the ship. They'd been saving up most of the garbage and just putting it on the fantail. Figuring they were going to go out pretty soon, they'd drop it in the ocean. There was a hell of a pile of garbage. I later took a picture of it and sent it to Admiral Brown. And so, anyway, I found out the ship was supposed to have been out of the yard in three months, and now they were running to four months. They finally got out and under way for sea trials. Almost soon as soon as we got out from alongside the dock, the circuit board blew out. I've forgotten the details of it, but all the electricity went off the ship.

Paul Stillwell: Had you taken command before this happened?

Captain McCampbell: No, I'd not taken command yet. I was going out with him on his sea trials to check the thing out, and circuit board went out. Well, they got busy down there, and we didn't go out very far. We turned around and went back to the dock so they could fix the circuit board and give us some electricity. So we went back in for a day or two and then went out again. This time the circuit board was all right; we didn't have any blown fuses or anything.

We got out just beyond Fire Island Light, which is pretty well off, I'd say ten miles at least from the coast, and the ship sprung a steam leak in the main steam line. Well, then they had to shut down all the steam. Apparently the connections were such that if you had a bad leak in one line, you couldn't steam on the other one. Well, here we were, drifting out to the east in the Gulf Stream. We had no communications, steam line out, the emergency generator went out along with the steam line, and I guess no power to operate the emergency generator. So we drifted out there for an hour or so before they found out what the hell was happening. When they did, the captain said, "Well, I'll just put the motor whaleboat over the side. They'll go back to the lighthouse and report it, and they'll have to send a tug out, to pick us up." So he called away the starboard lifeboat. Well, the coxswain of the boat finally charged up the bridge and he said, "Captain, we ain't got no lifeboats; we left them all on the beach."

Oh, Jesus, we were really getting in trouble. So we floated around out there for two or three hours. They finally got the steam leak isolated and slowly we could get under way, get back into port. Well, that indicated to me that Todd Shipbuilding was doing a pretty lousy job on the ship. So we got back into port. As we were going in, now it was dark, and we had, of course, a docking pilot. We always carried an undocking pilot and a docking pilot. Going up the river, we got into a very tight squeeze, I admit, and most of the tankers are not very maneuverable in going alongside the dock. The docking pilot was going at too fast a speed, or at least he didn't stop to cut off the steam soon enough, and damn if we didn't hit the end of the dock. It didn't do any damage to speak of, but there we were again and we got tied up.

So we spent about another week, or maybe ten days, there. I told the skipper of the ship, "Look, I'm not going to relieve you until I find out whether this ship can run." And, of course, we had to report that back to the Service Force commander in Norfolk. He had been a roommate of mine on the old *Portland*. We didn't request any instructions. I just wasn't going to relieve him until I found out if the ship could run, meet her trials. So my predecessor had to ride with me up to Newport, Rhode Island, and we made the trip without mishaps. When we got up to Newport, I relieved him.

Paul Stillwell: Were you getting some ship handling training and experience during this process?

Captain McCampbell: No, not during that run. It wasn't too long a run. I think maybe one night, maybe two days, whatever. Anyway, I relieved him and took over, and then we hardly had arrived at Newport when we were ordered to Guantánamo for further training, gunnery and ship handling and refueling. We refueled other ships, of course. So we got under way and tripped on down to Guantánamo and had our training there.

We got a lousy score on gunnery. I came to find out the chief, who was the guy responsible for putting the gunsights on the target from the director, was half blind. [Laughter] He couldn't see. That was the reason, I guess, they got the lousy gunnery score. We did refuel a destroyer, just the one ship, successfully. Whenever went out at Guantánamo, we had an observer on board. Coming back to anchor, we were supposed to hit a certain spot within so many degrees, which was a pretty tight little spot, I'd say like 25-30 feet in diameter. You did that by taking bearings on at least two points ashore to get our bearings and try to gauge the spot. Then you'd have to allow for the time it takes to get the word from the bridge down to the first lieutenant, who then gives the order to drop the anchor, and the time it takes the anchor to go on the bottom. And you have to know how deep the water is, that sort of thing.

Paul Stillwell: So you were learning as you went along?

Captain McCampbell: Learning, yes. I hadn't had any of that training. So we missed the hole. The reason we missed the hole was because the guy up on the forecastle who was supposed to knock the pin out of the anchor chain, couldn't hit the goddamn pin. He had a sledgehammer, see, and he swung it three or four times, but he couldn't hit the pin. So we overshot the hole.

Paul Stillwell: Were you having some misgivings about the whole thing about this time?

Captain McCampbell: Oh, all the way through, all the way through. Larry Neville, who was the observer, was a classmate of mine at the Naval Academy.[*] I guess we missed the hole so far that he couldn't forgive us, even though he was a classmate. Well, we got a zero on that exercise; we had to do it over again, a couple times. Well, we got through Guantánamo in about two weeks. We'd go out every day and exercise, one form or another.

Paul Stillwell: How well did you do at refueling other ships?

Captain McCampbell: We had no problem there.

Afterward, we headed back toward Newport, but before we got there we were ordered out the middle of the Atlantic to refuel the *Lake Champlain*, which was on its way from Norfolk to the Mediterranean, and a couple of destroyers.[†] When we refueled the *Lake Champlain* and the destroyers, of course, we had rigs on both sides. After we refueled the *Lake Champlain*, she had separated from us, taken off on her way to the Med. During the retrieving of the span wire on the starboard side, the operator of the winch got his sleeve caught between the drum and the wire. It flipped him around three or four times like a rag doll, and he was unconscious. So I wired the *Lake Champlain* and told them we had had an accident; we had a badly injured crewman. I asked them to send over a helicopter to pick him, which they did. So we got him in the helicopter and it shoved off, took him to *Lake Champlain*. We never saw him again. He was first class boatswain's mate too.

Paul Stillwell: Did he survive?

Captain McCampbell: Apparently so, or we would have heard something. He was first class, so he was a pretty important cog in the whole situation. And then refueling one of

---

[*] Captain Lawrence R. Neville, USN.
[†] USS *Lake Champlain* (CVS-39) was an antisubmarine aircraft carrier.

the destroyers on the port side, apparently the shipyard had rigged up the winch, according to the story I got, anyway, so it was turned around and operated in the reverse direction. So the guy on the winch, who was supposed to retrieve the span wire, reeled it out instead of in. So, of course, that went right back to the propellers, and we got a prop hooked up. We noticed that because we were making so many turns and not getting that much speed out of it.

Paul Stillwell: So it fouled your port screw.

Captain McCampbell: Yes. And he reached the bitter end of the span wire. He couldn't reel out, and he couldn't reel in. So we had to shut down. Actually, I got in a motor whaleboat. We finally had our motor whaleboats aboard, and I got in one of them. I had a snorkel with me, and I went down and took a look. Sure enough, the span wire was around the prop. We had two props on there. So I wired the Norfolk and told them we had gotten a span wire caught in the port prop and requested permission to return to base. They wanted me to come into Norfolk rather than Newport. So I went back to them and said, "No, I prefer Newport," because they had deeper water there, and there's no dredged channel. In Norfolk there's a channel all the way in and then to the south, which I would have had to make if I had gone to Norfolk.

Paul Stillwell: So you figured you didn't need a shipyard?

Captain McCampbell: No, I didn't need a shipyard. I needed one of our repair ships that they had there at Newport for the destroyers. So we went into Newport, and we had orders by that time to report to Sixth Fleet as the fourth tanker. We went in at night, tied up to the dock, just forward of the repair ship. He sent divers over, and pretty quickly they used an underwater blowtorch, I guess, and got the span wire off the prop. So the prop, it was reported to me, was not damaged, so we had no strain.

Paul Stillwell: Did there come a point amidst all these mishaps that you called the officers and crew together and tried to straighten it out?

Captain McCampbell: Oh yes, I did, after that guy got caught in the winch. And maybe another time. Oh, after we missed the hole trying to anchor, and I called them together after our gunnery exposé.

Paul Stillwell: Did things gradually improve?

Captain McCampbell: Yes, but I was in the middle of something there.

Paul Stillwell: You were telling about pulling the wire off the screw at Newport.

Captain McCampbell: Yes, well, we got that all done, and we sailed the next morning for the Med. Because we'd been so busy since the overhaul, we hadn't had a chance to paint the ship. We had—from a previous tour in the Med, I think—oil over one side badly. We had to scrub the oil off and paint it. But we got into Straits of Gibraltar and went through and were in the Med off Algeria. I decided we'd concentrate one whole day just to paint the side of the ship. We got all the paint buckets and brushes out early so we could get to it, an all-hands evolution. So I anchored off Algeria and put them to painting. We painted the whole ship in one day—less than a whole day, as a matter of fact, because I remember we went swimming over the side afterwards for about an hour.

In the meantime, Algeria sent out a little patrol boat to check us out. I invited them aboard to have a cup of coffee with me, and they declined. But no trouble; they didn't come aboard at all. I waited a day until we got the ship painted before I reported to Sixth Fleet.

We went on in Sixth Fleet, and, as I remember, we didn't have any rest and recreation. We were the fourth tanker in the Med. Normally they only kept three, but they saw the Lebanese thing coming on, so they ordered us in. My first orders in the Med were to go to an oil depot in Pozzuali, right near Naples. We went there to top off and then proceeded to the island of Rhodes, which we did with no strain. We had been in Rhodes there for about four, five days, and we got orders one morning. I'd taken a room at the hotel, and the navigator came out one morning to my room, about 7:30, and announced we'd received orders to proceed immediately to Lebanon, and en route to refuel certain ships. In fact, as we left Rhodes, we refueled two or three destroyers en route out towards Lebanon.

Paul Stillwell: How would you assess the quality of the officers and crew that were assigned in the *Severn*?

Captain McCampbell: Well, I can't say too much against them, because I think you have to blame more on the skipper, who was a very lax operator. But I had a good pharmacist's mate. We didn't have a doctor, or dentist, or chaplain. I had to fire two officers. The warrant officer who was aboard when I got there, had been a prisoner of war over in Japan. He was a victim of Bataan Death March type, and he was crippled in his mind, I thought.[*] Because when we left the yard in New York, he failed to get us aboard enough proper lines to replace worn lines and that sort of thing. I turned him in down on our training cruise to Guantánamo, set him ashore to the hospital.

Then we had a young, grossly inexperienced ensign as the paymaster and supply officer. I had to fire him because he was very lax in handling his reimbursements for enlisted men and officers who had to go ashore for shore duty, or something of that type. He had one claim sitting on his desk that went back for nine months. We got investigated real thoroughly when I fired this guy. We had at least two of the investigations, possibly three. The Office of Management and Budget investigated us. They were the most senior people, I think. And then Commander ServForLant—or maybe it was the Division Commander, I've forgotten now—but I had an investigation by them. Anyway, I got rid of this paymaster and got a new one with a little more experience. The ensign was just green and incompetent all the way around.

And I had to get rid of one enlisted man, a radioman. They had sent him to the ship directly from the mental institution there in Philadelphia. He had been there for observation, or whatever. They released him back to duty, and he was sent to me. One day, shortly before we got into Athens, Greece, we were about 80-100 miles from shore in any direction. He dove off the ship there and struck out across the Mediterranean. He

---

[*] In late 1941 and early 1942, the Allies suffered heavy casualties and lost many troops to prison camps during operations on the Bataan Peninsula of the island of Luzon in the Philippines.

was going to fly, going to swim across the Med, I think. Anyway, we had to put a motor whaleboat in the water and about five people went to collect him. And he didn't want to be picked up. That was the only time I used the brig, which we had stuffed full of spare mattresses. We had to clean that up, make room for him, and then we turned him in when we got to Athens.

Paul Stillwell: What can you say about the disciplinary situation overall for the crew?

Captain McCampbell: Well, overall it was very good, I guess, because I don't remember holding captain's even once.[*] We never had any trouble ashore in the Med; we didn't get ashore enough. And we had no trouble there in Newport. I don't remember holding mast a single time.

Paul Stillwell: With your feeling that you had to exert so much personal attention in the command, did it make demands on your stamina?

Captain McCampbell: No, only that day that we fueled 13 ships and we worked around the clock. That really pooped me out.

Paul Stillwell: Did you make it a practice to be on the bridge during all replenishments?

Captain McCampbell: All replenishments. And I was on the bridge most of the time. The only difference was at night. There was a big fund-raising drive on then to build the Navy-Marine Stadium in Annapolis. I guess that still stands.

Paul Stillwell: It does, yes.

---

[*] Captain's mast is a sort of court in which the commanding officer of a unit listens to requests, awards non-judicial punishment, or issues commendations. Most often captain's mast is used for punishment of lesser offenses than those that merit courts-martial.

Captain McCampbell: We contributed our share to that, I thought. We'd hold bingo games every night. And when we could get them, we'd have movies and then followed by bingo, or vice versa. So that was about our only source of amusement, movies and the bingo games. I've forgotten how much we collected, but we'd take 10% out of the bingo profits every night. And that was another thing that disturbed me. I shouldn't have put the paymaster in charge of our profits. I strongly suspected that he was taking a little rake-off from it. I never proved it; I didn't try to prove it. But, we got rid of him anyhow.

Oh, I forgot to mention that in the first month that I had commanded the *Severn*, a chief petty officer came up to me on the bridge one day and said, "Captain, this ship is just infiltrated full of rats. Last night, two of us chief petty officers were bitten by them, and they're getting pretty hungry."

So I called up the chief pharmacist's mate, and said, "Look, it's been reported to me that we've got a ship full of rats. How are we going to get rid of them?"

He said, "Well, Captain, the only way I know to do it, is put out poison. The most effective poison is strychnine. And I know that's against Navy regulations to use it, but that's the best way." I instructed him to put out strychnine, and the first month we killed over 400 rats. I also put a prize on each guy that presented a rat tail to the pharmacist chief, to get a carton of cigarettes.

Now, when we were ashore, they had no rat guards on that ship. So I made them fabricate some rat guards, so whenever we were tied up, we could put the rat guards on. They weren't 100% effective, I know, but they were generally pretty good. They reduced the number we had, anyhow. We finally got rid of them; we cleaned up the garbage that was on the fantail, and I wouldn't permit anybody to put anything on there again, even in port. They had to take it ashore. So, we cleaned up the rats on the ship.

Paul Stillwell: Did there come a point after all these mishaps, that you began to feel comfortable with the ship?

Captain McCampbell: No, I can't say that that's true, that I ever became confident of the *Severn*.

Paul Stillwell: Well, did it serve the purpose for which it was intended, and that was to prepare you for carrier command?

Captain McCampbell: Oh, yes, sure did. Coming out of Norfolk, we always had an undocking pilot, and he usually had two or three tugs that would pull us away from the dock. Then he'd back out, and he'd put us in the channel. One day he put us in the channel and said, "Captain, I think you can make it okay from here. With your permission, I'll leave the ship." Now, this was before we made the turn into the channel heading east of Norfolk. He had hardly left his ship when there was a flat barge being pushed by a tug.

We were heading north generally, and this barge was coming right across our bow, heading for us. I sounded four blasts, emergency signal, and he didn't do anything, made no motion to change. So then I backed down full. He was getting so close on me that I turned and headed for the side of the channel. We always had our anchor detail up there on the bow when we'd come into port or leave port. I dropped both anchors, and then I hit the mud trap.

Now, the undocking pilot heard my four blasts and looked around to see what was happening. And we didn't have any trouble getting off from the side of the channel. Actually, we just backed down, and our props didn't get into the mud. We had our anchors out, so we hauled in on the anchors and backed down, no problem. The undocking pilot, seeing what was happening, he called on the eight tugs he had in the area at the time. They got this poor guy on the barge, and they had a tug in each quadrant. They just had him locked in. That was the last I saw as we went over the horizon; they still had this guy locked in there with the eight tugs around him.

Paul Stillwell: Did they escort him off to jail or something?

Captain McCampbell: I don't know whatever happened to him. I didn't even report it. I guess I was supposed to, but I didn't.

Paul Stillwell: Well, fortunately, your forecastle crew learned how to drop the anchors by that time.

Captain McCampbell: Right.

Paul Stillwell: You started to mention that you went to Olathe, Kansas, after that.

Captain McCampbell: Yes, I was sent over to the Olathe, Kansas. My detail officer by that time was Hugh Winters, who wrote the book. This was customary procedure before you took over a carrier, to go out there and qualify in one of the newest type planes you'd be flying or working with. I went out and spent almost three weeks inland, checked out on my F9F's, a two-seater, trainer, I guess you'd call it. I flew with them most every day and checked out thoroughly in it, no strain. As I told you before, I'd already flown one once anyhow.

Paul Stillwell: You probably enjoyed getting into the air again after that experience with the oiler.

Captain McCampbell: Yes. And then I went from there to join my carrier, the *Bon Homme Richard*.* I joined up with that out in Manila and relieved Dutch Close.† And I was there about three days. We had a plane I was flying in, a Constellation after we left Guam. We stopped there to replenish the fuel. We lost an engine, so we turned around and headed back to Guam and spent another day on Guam while they fixed the engine,

---

* USS *Bon Homme Richard* (CV-31), an *Essex*-class aircraft carrier, was commissioned 26 November 1944. She had a standard displacement of 30,800 tons, was 888 feet long, 93 feet in the beam, extreme width of 136 feet, and a maximum draft of 29 feet. Her top speed was 33 knots. Originally she had 12 5-inch gun mounts and could accommodate approximately 80 aircraft. On 1 October 1953 she was reclassified as an attack carrier, CVA-31. She went out of commission from 1953 to 1955 for a modernization that included installation of an angled flight deck, enclosed bow, and steam catapults. She remained in service until decommissioned on 2 July 1971.
† Captain Burdette E. Close, USN, commanded the aircraft carrier *Bon Homme Richard* (CVA-31) from 18 December 1957 to 5 February 1959. Captain McCampbell commanded the ship from 5 February 1959 to 15 February 1960.

changed it or something. Then went on in to Clark Air Force Base.* The ship sent a helicopter over to pick me up at Clark, and took me back aboard ship.

One thing I forgot to mention—when I had the *Severn* I was refueling, a destroyer in the Atlantic there once. The destroyer skipper obviously was a newcomer, and he collided with me, ran into me. He made two attempts, then came around on the third one and he came up directly astern of me, then swerved out and came around to my port side. What he was doing, I think, was directing the helmsman not by course, but by degrees of rudder. He turned in and came right into my side. His anchor put a nice little hole in my side, and my oil started leaking and that sort of thing. But those were the worst things that happened to me collision-wise, running into the side of the channel and then that.

Paul Stillwell: Was there an investigation?

Captain McCampbell: No, but the squadron commander of the destroyer asked me if I was going to report it. At first I answered him and said, "I haven't made up my mind. I don't know the extent of the damage." Later on I decided to report it because it caused an oil leak in the side, and I was going to have to get it repaired, so I did report it. Then he disclaimed hitting me. So I took a picture of it and when I got into Norfolk to the admiral, I showed it to the admiral, ComServFor.

Paul Stillwell: Were there any recriminations for the destroyer's skipper?

Captain McCampbell: No, not that I know of. So then back to the *Bon Homme Richard*. We left Manila for Yokosuka. About the third night out, the admiral, Bill Schoech, who was riding on the ship, called on me to refuel from a tanker.† I'm trying to place the name. I believe it was the *Juarez*; it was a Mexican name, anyway. The seas were quite rough. I guess they were running around eight to ten feet and a pretty good wind, maybe 25-30 knots. I came up on the tanker in good shape, but I overran him a little bit, and I cut back five revolutions on the engines, drifted back on him. As I drifted back, I guess

---

* Clark Air Force Base was about 50 miles north of Manila, on the island of Luzon in the Philippines.
† Rear Admiral William A. Schoech, USN, Commander Carrier Division Three from September 1958 to July 1959.

the wind blew me into him, and I collided with him, "kissed" him. I got out by going ahead and crossed his bow at about five degrees off his port, to keep my props from getting engaged in his side.

We had an investigation on that. The result of the investigation: the commander of the Seventh Fleet, who was the decision-making authority on that thing, gave me notice that he intended to issue a reprimand. He pointed out in the letter that I had recourse to appeal the decision, which he supposedly hadn't made yet. But I found out later that this information that he intended to issue had gotten back to the Navy, CNO or his staff.

Paul Stillwell: Who was the fleet commander?

Captain McCampbell: Vice Admiral Nappy Kivette.* I knew him because he'd been in Fighting Four. He was the gunnery officer just before I got there. Anyway, I appealed the decision and went back to my admiral riding the ship, Bill Schoech. It was passed through him and the only thing he put on there was "Forwarded." He wasn't giving me any support at all, although the investigation had been conducted on the ship, and it was obvious the tanker guy was three degrees off course. He was supposed to be making 11 knots, but he was making nine, which is, I claim the reason for my overshooting him. Also, before I came alongside, he was using, a five degree rudder on account of the wind and seas, shifting to hold the course. And, of course, when I came alongside, it took the wind off him and with this rudder on, it pulled it into my ship. So, it was, I figured, partially my fault and partially his fault.

Anyway, I appealed the decision and obviously Commander Seventh Fleet's attorney did his paper work. The fleets usually carried an attorney, and they did the legwork. The admiral signed it, even though he hadn't really read the report. Then the admiral must have read it because he cancelled the reprimand completely, and ultimately that cancellation got back to CNO and the Bureau of Personnel.

---

* Vice Admiral Frederick N. Kivette, USN, served as Commander Seventh Fleet from 30 September 1958 to 7 March 1960.

Paul Stillwell: Do you think that incident hurt you at all in your career?

Captain McCampbell: Could have been, because I had a later incident.

Paul Stillwell: Oh, I see.

Captain McCampbell: So, we went on into Yokosuka. We were there for a week or so, a little more. We came out of there, and then we started visiting various ports. We only had one or two possible fleet exercises out there. The first port we were to hit was Osaka, Japan, which is on one of the islands to the south. You go through the Inland Sea there and on into Osaka.

I had an incident there. It was about 6:00 o'clock in the morning; I'd been on the bridge since 4:00. Just shortly after we got into the Inland Sea, a small freighter came at me from the port side, left to right, which put me in a position of being the privileged ship, and he was the burdened ship.* And he kept coming, coming. I put the officer of the deck on the alidade to keep a bearing. If you get a steady bearing, it's a collision course. My officer of the deck was reporting the other ship's bearing, and it didn't change, didn't change, didn't change. So I reached the point where I figured I had to do something, and they call it "in extremis." So I sounded four blasts on the whistle, stopped all engines, and turned into him.

Now, I was carrying atomic weapons, and the other ship was headed for just about where they were. So I cut into him, which is contrary to custom. If you're further out, you turn away. But we were so close by then, I turned into him and just barely clipped his stern. I rushed over to the starboard side and saw him go down the starboard side. His lights were still burning brightly. He didn't appear to be damaged, although later we found out that he was. He had a little nick on the stern; maybe it was more than a nick. He claimed 30,000 bucks to repair it. The only injury was the chief engineer on this ship got a cut on his forehead from a broken porthole.

---

* In the Rules of the Road, the privileged ship is obligated to maintain course and speed, and the burdened ship is obligated to maneuver to avoid collision. Thus McCampbell's ship was not supposed to maneuver.

Well, as it turned out, my anchor on the starboard side caught his side when he got across the bow and then headed down. But, how that anchor got to his engine room, I don't know, because he was only about a 2,500-tonner, maybe 3,000-tonner.

Paul Stillwell: And that anchor's well above the water too.

Captain McCampbell: Yes. But the reason I say the anchor hit him, must have hit his masthead or something, if he got this broken porthole and injury to the chief engineer, then the bottom part of the bow must have hit him. But I can't tell. I didn't stick around to see if he was going to sink or anything because I figured he wasn't hurt. He'd gotten across the bow.

We got into port at Osaka, and I went over to call on the mayor. When I came back, Tony Schneider, the exec, met me and said, "Captain, there's a Japanese Coast Guard captain up topside your cabin, waiting for you. He wants to see you."[*] This guy spoke pretty good English, this Jap. He told me that I'd hit this little freighter; and that, as he came by to go aboard my ship, he noticed the paint on the anchor, which was the same color as the little freighter. So that's why I said the anchor hit him and whatnot. But we had an investigation on that.

Paul Stillwell: Who conducted the investigation? Admiral Schoech?

Captain McCampbell: No, it was Admiral Schoech's chief of staff. And, well, I have to take back and recount the first incident I had of hitting the tanker. The chief of staff of the admiral had the investigation. That was reported to Com7thFlt, but there was no action on his part. This is not an infrequent occurrence, sideswiping a tanker.

I remember Fitzhugh Lee had one on the *Franklin D. Roosevelt* when I was exec. And, there were two or three others when I was on the Sixth Fleet staff that were reported to Admiral Brown. Anyway, that was not the one they were going to issue the reprimand for; it was the second one. And ultimately Commander Seventh Fleet repealed it. My ship wasn't damaged; just a little paint on the anchor was all. So we spent about a week

---

[*] Commander Tony F. Schneider, USN.

in Osaka. While we were tied up alongside the dock, we put on a demonstration for a television company there. We launched a couple of planes there at the dock for them. Took them on a tour of the ship, everything except the special weapons compartment. Then nothing happened the rest of that cruise, except we visited various ports. The southernmost visit was to Sasebo.

After Osaka, not much else happened there. We went to a little place called Beppu, which is in kind of the center part of Japan, a beautiful little island. They gave us seven days there. You could play golf. It was not a big city, but a lot of scenery. And I remember the zoo, mainly monkeys. They're very fond of monkeys over there, the Japanese. I don't know why.

The first time we dressed ship was when we went into Beppu. I called the executive, and I said, "I think we ought to dress ship while we're here." We used to do a lot of that with Sixth Fleet. But it was new to him, and he said, "Captain, we've never dressed ship. We don't know what you mean, put up all the flags, all that stuff, we've never done it."

I said, "Well, we're going to do it." So he had them rig lines up to the top of the mast, fore and aft, so we got all the flags out and dressed up the ship. It was a most enjoyable little visit. The men enjoyed it, although there wasn't too much. There were a couple of nightclubs, dancing girls, and that sort of thing.

After that I guess we went back to Yokosuka. But later we got into Yokohama, just a little north of Yokosuka. Seems to me there was one other place, but I can't remember where it was. Oh, I guess it was Hong Kong I was thinking of. Got into Hong Kong. I remember the chief of staff, Paul Emrick, came down specifically to caution me.[*] He said, "Going into Hong Kong, it's a very crowded port. You're going to find these sampans. They'll see how close they can come to you. They'll cross your bow, and you'll lose sight of them while they're under the bow, they'll come so close." He said, "I wouldn't change course or speed for them."

Paul Stillwell: They try to transfer the evil spirits from their boat to your ship.

---

[*] Captain Paul E. Emrick, USN.

Captain McCampbell: Try to wipe them off their boat. They were just sampans. He said, "Now, the last time I came in here, it took me an hour and a half to get tied up to the buoy. You better get your people prepared and, if you can, cut down on that." Well, I called the first lieutenant up, and we got together on it. I said, "Look, you get all set to go. When we go in there, we're going to tie up to this buoy, and the tide will be right for us unless you take too long to tie up the buoy." So we got in, and we got tied up in 20 minutes, which made the admiral and chief of staff very happy. We spent about five days in there, five or six.

Paul Stillwell: That's always a real treat for the crew.

Captain McCampbell: Oh yes, a real nice treat. So then that's about all that happened. Now, this was the first tour I had out there. I joined the ship, as I told you, and we came back to the States in June. We had three months in the States to get a new air group and to train them off the coast. We made one trip down to San Diego to let the heads of department on the ship get acquainted with the people that they were working with on the staff, down in ComAirPac. We just spent about three days there, I think, and then we operated, both going down to San Diego and then going back towards San Francisco.

Paul Stillwell: You were based at Alameda, I believe.

Captain McCampbell: Based at Alameda, yes.

Paul Stillwell: What do you remember about flight operations when you were skipper?

Captain McCampbell: Well, they, more or less, were normal. We did a lot of operating, so much so that the second admiral that rode my ship—Andrew McBurney Jackson, that shitass—declared there'd be no flying on Sunday.[*] I kind of judged the flying by the

---

[*] Rear Admiral Andrew McB. Jackson Jr., USN, commanded Carrier Division Three from July 1959 to August 1960. The oral history of Jackson, who retired as a vice admiral, is in the Naval Institute collection.

good weather because we didn't always have good weather. But he said there'd be no flying on Sunday; he wanted to get some sleep. So, we stopped flying on Sunday.

We changed the air group while we were at Alameda and took them out and trained them. Then we left about around the first of December, I guess. Because I remember we were at Pearl Harbor on the seventh, which was a Monday. We just were going out for our operational readiness inspection. And we had the ceremony on the *Arizona* memorial December 7, 1959. I have a story about that. And, I guess that's about the next story to tell.

We were ordered to Pearl Harbor for operational readiness inspection on the way out to WestPac.[*] And this Monday morning, December 7—I knew what day it was, but I didn't know they were having a ceremony on the *Arizona*. Barry Goldwater was there for the ceremony, an old friend classmate of mine.[†] Don Felt, who was CinCPac, was there; Admiral Simmonds, commander of the naval shipyard, was there; and two or three others.[‡] Anyway, we were supposed to get under way at 8:00 o'clock, and Admiral G. B. H. Hall, whom I mentioned earlier who was the air group commander on the old *Wasp*, was to fly out by helicopter and ride the ship during the inspection.[§]

So I went down the flight deck to greet him. He got there promptly a quarter of 8:00. As soon as he got out of the helicopter, I met him and begged his permission to go up and get the ship under way. So I proceeded to do that, and I got up to, just eye-level of the bridge, and the exec leaned over the handrail and said, "Good morning, Captain, sir. The ship is under way."

I looked at my watch, and it was about eight minutes till 8:00. I said, "What do you mean, it's under way?"

The exec said, "Well, I don't know, Captain, but it's under way." We were tied up starboard side to pier 14, so I quickly dashed over to the starboard side, and, sure enough, the ship was under way. And it was worse yet; it was headed for Quarters K, the

---

[*] WestPac – Western Pacific.
[†] Barry M. Goldwater, a Republican from Arizona, served in the Senate from 3 January 1953 to 3 January 1965 and from 3 January 1969 to 3 January 1987. He and McCampbell were classmates in the 1920s at Staunton Military Academy in Virginia, as recalled in the first interview in this oral history.
[‡] Admiral Harry D. Felt, USN, served as Commander in Chief Pacific from 31 July 1958 to 30 June 1964. His oral history is in the Naval Institute collection.
[§] Rear Admiral Grover B. H. Hall, USN, Commander Fleet Air Hawaii.

admiral's quarters on Ford Island. About that time, I heard somebody yell out, "All engines stop; full left rudder."

Paul Stillwell: Who had the conn?*

Captain McCampbell: Well, I didn't know at that point, but it turned out it was the undocking pilot, and he had issued the orders all engines stop, full left rudder. I could see us wiping off the pier real good. As a matter of fact, we did get four or five pilings. But we got headed out in the stream with all engines stopped, and we had enough speed on to round Ford Island and pass the *Arizona* as they were having their one minute of silence. I found out later that Admiral Felt had turned to Admiral Simmonds and said, "Is the *Bonne Homme Richard* supposed to be in this celebration?"

He said, "Oh, no, sir, she's headed out to the first day of ORI. I don't know if Admiral Felt knew I was the skipper or not, but he said, "Well, they provided the perfect backdrop for the one minute of silence."

Of course, our bugler sounded attention, and all hands were at attention. All was quiet and serene. He said, "I think we ought to send the captain of the ship well done." But before the well done got to me, I got a report from a tug that had banged into the side of the ship. We got under way so fast, one of the tugs managed to slip his line. He cut it with an ax and got away, but the other one didn't slip his line; he banged into the side of the ship. And, by the way, they had to survey that tug.† But the undocking pilot said, "Well, don't worry about it. That was the oldest tug we had anyway. It was ready to be surveyed."

Paul Stillwell: Why had he gotten under way when you weren't even on the bridge yet?

Captain McCampbell: I'm going to tell you.

Paul Stillwell: Oh, Okay.

---

* The individual with the conn—normally an officer—directs the ship's movements in course and speed.
† In this case surveying means a determination that a piece of equipment is no longer able to be used.

Captain McCampbell: Of course, Admiral Hall had his chief of staff investigate. And this investigation went on the better part of the whole week we were doing our ORI. It turned out that in the early morning watch, a little third class fireman found out that when the engine-order telegraph was operated, the bells didn't ring in number-eight fireroom. So he reported to the first class, who went up and reported to the chief who was having breakfast. The chief said, "Well, for Christ sake, fix it." Didn't even get up from the table. So they go back down to the fire room and got it fixed.

About a quarter of 8:00, the word went back from the third class, to the first class, and to the chief. The chief said, "Well, call the bridge and have them actuate the engine order telegraph to make sure." So one of them called the little IC seaman on watch on the bridge, whose main job was to take complaints about the telephone not working, or something like that, just a seaman.* So whoever it was called the bridge and told them to go ahead and actuate the engine order telegraph. They wanted to check it out, see if they had fixed it so the bell rang in the number-eight fireroom.

So the little seaman went over, and everybody was now looking out the bridge at the admiral landing in the helicopter. He had a new type helicopter. So the little seaman went over and tested it. He signaled all ahead one-third, all ahead two-thirds, all ahead standard, all ahead full speed. Now we go to the engine room. The chief engineer was up on the hangar deck greeting the observers that were coming aboard; there were about 30 or 40 of them. So he was not in the engine room. Lieutenant Williams had the duty.

When the first class petty officer on the number-one throttle saw the engine order telegraph going ahead, he rushed back to Lieutenant Williams, who was in a cubicle, or a booth-like enclosure, to keep the noise out for him so he could talk over the telephone. He said, "Lieutenant Williams, I've just gotten orders from the engineer order telegraph to go ahead one third, go ahead two-thirds. Now, we have not received word from the bridge to answer all bells and signals. I know that they've singled up the lines to the dock. Should I answer it?"

Lieutenant Williams said, "Well, if they want to get under way this way, give it to them." So, of course, they had been instructed to answer the engine on the telegraph regardless whatever else happened, telephone-wise, otherwise. So he went back to

---

* IC – interior communications.

throttle. By now we were up to standard speed and then to full speed. So he cranked open the damn throttle, number-one throttle. The other three answered, and by five minutes to 8:00, why, we were under way. We weren't making full speed, but we were making about five knots and hadn't left the dock yet. So we were parting lines and so forth.

So that's what we found out as a result of the investigation. As I said before, we knocked out four or five pilings and clobbered this tug. There were no injuries; the people that were where the lines were parting, I think that only two or three lines were left to the dock and—oh, the guy hanging onto the accommodation ladder, he was hooked on, of course, at that time. So he quickly hoisted the accommodation ladder. It got away with no damage on that. So that was what happened.

Paul Stillwell: So the guy on the engine order telegraph evidently hadn't made it clear that it was just a test,

Captain McCampbell: Right.

Paul Stillwell: Was there any sort of reprimand out of that one, or how did that come out?

Captain McCampbell: No, it came out, I had to reprimand Lieutenant Williams, the engineering officer on duty, and the little IC seaman up on the bridge, and I didn't have guts enough to reprimand either one. I was supposed to give them an oral reprimand. So I just made like I did, and didn't.

Paul Stillwell: You mentioned the exec. Who was that?

Captain McCampbell: The second one was Charlie Brown, a guy I picked up from Alameda for the second tour of WestPac. The first one was Tony Schneider, who was an ex-dive bomber pilot in the war with a couple Navy Crosses. He's mentioned in Barrett Tillman's book.

Paul Stillwell: Do you have any other experiences to report with Admiral Jackson?

Captain McCampbell: Yes, one day we were coming in. It was when we were coming up from San Diego back to Alameda, and we were conducting operations all along the Atlantic. We had completed our operations just before we had to turn to go under the Golden Gate Bridge. The last four planes that were operating with us, I directed them to go back to the beach. So I'd been at, I don't know, I guess 20-22 knots. There was very little wind, frequently off San Francisco, no wind practically, so I kept my speed until after I'd made the turn to go under the bridge, into the bay.

He told me afterwards, "Dave, you've got to be more careful about expending your oil." And I know he'd pointed out about the experience where I'd sent the planes in to the beach, but I wanted to keep up enough speed in case they couldn't make the beach, or nearly—anyway, until they got over the land. So he said, "Yeah, when I had a ship in the Mediterranean, that's like a closed lake over there. We had a hell of a time not hitting the beach and couldn't carry too much speed. If we were going too fast we used up our sea room too quickly." You always got a lecture from him on that.

Well, the only thing, while he was riding the ship, we, on route from Alameda to Pearl Harbor, this Sunday when Admiral Jackson said he didn't want any flying. But that didn't eliminate, as far as I was concerned, respotting the deck. It was quite windy out there, it was Sunday, and I was lying down taking a nap. As they were respotting the deck, they lost one plane over the side. The ship rolled, and the plane went over the chocks and over the side.

Turned out there was a black plane handler in there, relatively inexperienced, and he didn't know how to swim. He was trying to jump out of the plane, so I guess when the plane hit the water, he was probably half in and half out. Anyway, we got the helicopter there in three minutes—Sunday morning everybody resting, which surprised the hell out of me. The helicopter went out trying to locate him in the water and couldn't. We searched around there for about four hours and we couldn't recover the body, so we finally proceeded onto Pearl.

Oh, the other thing I remember about Andy Jackson. He was our five-striper at the Naval Academy, class of '30. We would seek the wind during training operations, and often I would give a change of course two or three degrees, maybe working around to what would be a total of eight or ten degrees. But he told me that he didn't like that. He said, "Don't make any change of course under five degrees. You go all five degrees or none at all." Well, that's all right; that wasn't hard to live with, but I thought it was kind of picayunish.

Paul Stillwell: Sounds like he was trying to act as the skipper.

Captain McCampbell: Yes, that's exactly it. He was trying to run things.

Paul Stillwell: Getting in your business

Captain McCampbell: And didn't have the authority, that's right.

Paul Stillwell: Well, what happened once you got out to the Western Pacific on your deployment?

Captain McCampbell: It was pretty much the same. We hit a couple of ports and got into Manila and Yokosuka. We didn't get back to Hong Kong. Oh, a terrible thing happened. Commander Seventh Fleet had arranged on my first cruise in the WestPac—I had called on him there at Yokosuka, and he said, "Dave, on your way home, how would you like to stop by Guam for liberty port?"

I said, "Oh, no, I've been to Guam, and that's no liberty port." So, on the way back to the States that time we didn't stop at Guam. But then coming back to WestPac, we had in our instructions that we were supposed to stop at Guam for a four-day liberty port. So after Pearl Harbor, we went directly to Guam, and we were there, as I recall, over New Year's. The admiral there was Skee Erdmann—big, tall, egotistical, very self-important type.* Anyway, the admiral's wife had come out and was staying with Admiral Erdmann.

---

* Rear Admiral William L. Erdmann, USN, Commander Naval Forces Marianas.

Paul Stillwell: Admiral Jackson's wife?

Captain McCampbell: Yes. And he invited the admiral and me over for dinner one night, and of course his wife was there. After dinner, we were having a cordial, brandy or something, and he said, "Dave, how would you like to take a cruise box back to the States for me? It's a good BuPers-type cruise box. It's a metal thing, and I've got a bunch of knickknacks in it." He said it was rattan furniture that he picked up in Manila, and lamps, and knickknacks, ebony things, that sort.

So I said, "Sure, I'll be delighted to take it back. We're not going directly home now. We're going out for a six-month tour."

He said, "Well, that's all right."

I said, "Yeah, I'll put them down in 412A with the spare jet engines. I'll tell my relief that they're aboard, that it's your cruise box going back." He said that he was over his limit with household effects to take home. So this was a convenience for him, and just when the ship got to Alameda, I should have the skipper that relieved me turn them in to the supply depot there in Alameda.

So I thought no more about it. We went on out and did our cruise. I got relieved out in Yokosuka. The commander of the Seventh Fleet was there for the ceremony, and ComFAirJapan, I think he was called, was there and a few other dignitaries and staff officers. I was relieved there around the middle of February, which gave me almost exactly a year aboard the *Bon Homme Richard*.[*] I flew back to the States. I'd been ordered to report to the staff of the Joint Chiefs of Staff, you see. They would place me where they could best use me. So we were just where I had taken aboard Admiral Erdmann's cruise box, but that wasn't as easy as it sounds. We could handle the cruise box and the size. It was about, I guess, 12 feet long, give or take a foot or two, and about 5 feet high, and about 4 or 5 feet wide.

Paul Stillwell: That's bigger than the normal cruise box.

---

[*] The change of command was on 15 February 1960.

Captain McCampbell: Oh yes, it was a BuPers cruise box all right, and it was all metal. It came down to the dock at 7:30 Monday morning, when we were due to get under way at 8:00. I think it was purposely delivered at that time of day because Admiral Erdmann didn't want too much inquiry as to why it weighed 3,200 hundred pounds. So it came to the dock, and my supply officer, Commander Arrighi, was down to see it and receive it, be there when it came aboard.[*] And he came running up to my cabin. I was having breakfast, and he knocked on the door, but he didn't wait for me to say, "Come in."

He busted in the door of my cabin, and he said, "Captain, Admiral Erdmann's cruise box is on the dock and it weighs about 3,200 pounds, and it's a pretty big object. We can handle it okay. But he didn't send down a manifest with it, so we don't have any idea what's in it."

I said, "Well, you go to whoever's delivering that box down there and tell them get a manifest to us, or we don't take it aboard." So the manifest must have been prepared earlier but they had to go to the staff supply officer to get it. That took a little time, and they came down with it, almost 8:00 o'clock. The supply officer received it, and it said, furniture and knickknacks, lamps, and some ebony pieces. I don't remember it saying anything else. So we took it aboard, stashed it away down in 412A.[†]

The reason I happen to remember that number is that it was our engine compartment, and this incident engraved in my mind a good memory of this. So, anyway, we went on out. This was over New Year's, I remember.[‡] We picked up a hurricane, and we lost one day there, which didn't matter, really. We had to leave the little gulf there at Guam and go out the eastern side of the island. There was a hurricane coming in. And we stayed there until we were sure it was past, and then we came back into port again.

---

[*] Commander Norman L. Arrighi, Supply Corps, USN.
[†] Admiral Erdmann was indicted for smuggling, because the contents of the cruise box were not as he had listed on the manifest. He actually sent a large supply of liquor, more than 500 bottles, to the States and then stored it in a room in the house in Marin County, California, in which he lived after retiring from active duty. He evaded about $3,000 in taxes through the smuggling. An enlisted man informed on him to the Customs Service. He subsequently pled guilty and was fined $15,000 at a time when his Navy pension was $12,500. He also received a letter of reprimand from Secretary of the Navy William Franke. For details on the this case, see "The Big E," *Time* magazine, 26 September 1960; also *The New York Times*, 15 September 1960, 15 October 1960, 5 November 1960, and 26 November 1960.
[‡] The shipment was loaded aboard the *Bon Homme Richard* on 30 December 1959, and she returned to Alameda on 19 May 1960.

Paul Stillwell: Were you at Apra Harbor?

Captain McCampbell: Yes, and, oh, I went water skiing in Apra Harbor while I was there one day. Then we proceeded out to WestPac and did our tour. I didn't have any accidents and nothing very unusual happened there until I was relieved. Syd Bottomley relieved me.[*] I flew back to the States and then proceeded on to Washington. I was going to the Joint Staff there.

I had a couple of weeks' leave in there and joined the staff. At first, for about three weeks, I had no assignment. I was up in Navy Department most of that time studying up on the various planning documents, as to what the Navy's plan was and somewhat on the Joint Staff plan. Then I went down to Joint Staff, and I sat around in the office of the Chief of Plans for a couple weeks before I found out exactly where I was going to be assigned. Originally, I was supposed to be assigned as like an aide to the officer who was in charge of plans, J-5 Division. And finally they made up their mind. This officer who was chief of plans was relieved when he made general. So I went in and took his spot as Chief of Plans Division. Later we consolidated with Policy Division, and so I became the Chief of Strategic Plans and Policy; but it was mainly just paper work. I had 25 officers under me most of the time. It varied a little bit. I had two other Army colonels under me who fleeted up to. All these subordinates were Navy captains or colonels in the Air Force, Army, Marines.

The only couple of interesting things. One, that we put in long hours there, worked 14, 15, 16 hours a day sometimes. They had charge of formulating all the plans and later the plans and policies of the Joint Staff. And, of course, we did that in a way somewhat in conjunction with the individual services' staff officers who would come down and formulate a plan so that it was a joint plan.

I was there at the time of the initial blowup in Cuba, when we had to formulate contingency plans for the base in Cuba. I was there for the Bay of Pigs, but we had no

---

[*] Captain Harold Sydney Bottomley Jr., USN, commanded the *Bon Homme Richard* from 15 February 1960 to 21 December 1960.

part in that planning.* Bobby Kennedy had an office right across from me and all the information was being flown into him—what little, I guess, there was.† Anyway, it was an exercise of the CIA, and he was dealing with them.‡

Paul Stillwell: Kennedy had an office in the Pentagon for that?

Captain McCampbell: Yes. He was also, at that point, Attorney General.

Paul Stillwell: So how frequently did he come over to the Pentagon on that?

Captain McCampbell: Well, for two or three weeks he was there every day. I used to pass him in the passageway and I'd say good morning to him, and no answer out of him. He was a great thinker [laughter], thought all the time.

Paul Stillwell: How far along did that plan get to the invasion of Cuba?

Captain McCampbell: Well, we got our plan completed, but it was never, of course, implemented. I'd say we completed the plan, anyway.

Paul Stillwell: Did you work with Admiral Sharp on the Navy side?§

Captain McCampbell: I worked with his assistants, yes, and with him at one occasion. He was always trying to get more carriers for the Navy. I didn't do much of the legwork. My job was mainly to review what my staff had done, the papers that they'd crank out. To review it, make sure it made sense. And they, of course, would explain it to me

---

* In mid-April 1961 a force of 1,400 Cuban exiles, secretly trained by U.S. personnel in Guatemala, landed in the Bay of Pigs, on the southwestern coast of Cuba, in an attempt to overthrow Fidel Castro, that nation's Communist dictator. The invasion attempt was a disaster. President John Kennedy decided that U.S. naval intervention would worsen the situation, so ships and aircraft offshore were prohibited from taking part.
† Robert F. Kennedy served as Attorney General of the United States from 1961 to 1964.
‡ CIA – Central Intelligence Agency.
§ Vice Admiral U. S. Grant Sharp, USN, served as Deputy Chief of Naval Operations (Plans and Policy), OP-06, from August 1960 to August 1963. The oral history of Sharp, who retired as a four-star admiral, is in the Naval Institute collection.

frequently, that it was readable and understandable. There again, I was kind of the dumb sergeant, and I picked up grammatical errors and that sort of thing. It would go out as a piece of paper generated by the plans division of the Joint Staff.

Paul Stillwell: Where would the tasking come from to do various studies?

Captain McCampbell: From the director of the Joint Staff.

Paul Stillwell: Did you attend any meetings with the Joint Chiefs?

Captain McCampbell: Just one. As far as they were concerned, I was pretty far down the chain of command. The director of the Joint Staff, of course, always conducted the meetings. And the secretary to the Joint Chiefs, Champ Blouin, was always at the meetings, and, I think that was about all outside of the four Chiefs.[*] The Marine was not always included at the meetings of the three Joint Chiefs, but usually he was.

Paul Stillwell: Any other specific things you worked on besides the Cuban program?

Captain McCampbell: Yes, we worked on the Berlin situation.

Paul Stillwell: The Soviets built the Berlin Wall during that period.[†]

Captain McCampbell: Yes. And we worked up some plans there that if this continued— no, no, we actually put it into effect. We first tested out with a platoon of U.S. troops marched up to the gate and demanded a pass. And after some considerable time of one day there, they opened up the gate, they finally let the troops through. Next we sent, as I

---

[*] Rear Admiral Francis J. Blouin, USN, who had been a Naval Academy classmate of McCampbell.
[†] In 1961 the East German regime built a wall that separated the Soviet- and NATO-controlled sectors of the city of Berlin. It was a symbolic gesture at the height of the Cold War. A number of East Germans were killed in subsequent escape attempts. On the night of 9 November 1989 the East German government suddenly and unexpectedly opened the wall to permit free transit. The wall was subsequently torn down, this time a symbol of the easing of relations between the superpowers.

recall, a battalion and then a regiment, kept building up gradually. They all got through so there was no real confrontation. But that's about all that happened.

Paul Stillwell: There was also reactivation of reservists and also some mothballed ships being pulled out as a result of the Berlin crisis. Did you get into that?

Captain McCampbell: No. Although we did have a couple guys that worked on the situation over in Korea, mainly as regards the number of troops to keep there, the requirement for them and so forth. I didn't have too much part of it. It was kind of a minor problem to me, and I left it all to these two guys that had worked on it, that stayed right close with it. One of them made a couple of trips over to Korea in conjunction with this work on it. And we had another guy that worked on the reserve situation. Here again, as to how many combat-ready troops there were and in aviation. Very little of Navy in there; mainly it was Army and Air Force.

Paul Stillwell: Kennedy put emphasis on building up conventional forces. The previous reliance was on nuclear. Did you get into that buildup?

Captain McCampbell: Yes. Right at the tail end of my tour. Earlier we had 1,800 advisors in Vietnam, and Kennedy built it up to 18,000. That was just about in the end of my tour. We got in a little bit to the situation in Laos. At least we got in the political situation of it; no combat involved at the time we were with it.

Paul Stillwell: How did that billet compare in terms of job satisfaction to commanding an aircraft carrier?

Captain McCampbell: It can't compare in any way. I'd rather be skipper of a carrier than on that Joint Staff. The work was about equal. As I said before, we worked never an eight-hour day. We'd work 10 to 12, 14 hours, 16 hours. Maybe the whole of my Plans Division, but certain projects would come before us. The ones that were working on it would have to put in those long hours for a couple of weeks maybe.

Paul Stillwell: Well, the skipper of a carrier works 24 hours a day, but he's got a lot more control.

Captain McCampbell: That's right, yes. Well, we had all kinds of directives to prepare; there was no end to preparing contingency plans. You have a contingency plan for everything—whether you take your umbrella out with you today or not. So that wasn't, I'd say, not interesting. I had an apartment close, within walking distance of the Pentagon. That was convenient. And we'd work often on Sundays—not all the time, but often.

Paul Stillwell: Did you run into any nuclear weapons issues?

Captain McCampbell: Yes, I had a nuclear weapons division under me that handled all the nuclear weapons business, including the tests. They would attend, not all of them but quite a few of them.

Paul Stillwell: Another satisfaction with the carrier was that you were dealing with actual concrete operations instead of hypothetical things.

Captain McCampbell: Yes. And later on there, when we merged the policy and plans, I had a research and development team under me, three people. And in policy end of it, we had liaison with the State Department. I also was liaison with the, what they called the "Three Wise Men." You ever heard of them?

Paul Stillwell: No

Captain McCampbell: George Miller was one of them for a while.[*] There was a Navy, Army, and Air Force type. They sat out at the end of the hall there, and, hell, I don't know what they did. We collaborated with one of their papers. The State Department

---

[*] Rear Admiral George H. Miller, USN, who was a Naval Academy classmate of McCampbell. Admiral Miller's oral history is in the Naval Institute collection.

was part of it; it had to do with goals of the United States Government in a general sense. What are the goals at this point in time for our government? It was kind of like the work that the NSC was doing.*

Paul Stillwell: You certainly addressed a broad range of issues.

Captain McCampbell: Yes, but I didn't get in on that. Colonel Art West was the man who worked with the Three Wise Men, so that was about the end of that.

From there I was assigned to North American Air Defense Command out in Colorado Springs. Just before I left the Joint staff, I was given a choice of going to the Air War College at Maxwell Air Force Base, Alabama; Strategic Air Command in Omaha; or North American Air Defense Command, Colorado Springs. I favored the Colorado Springs deal because I'd been to Colorado Springs and I liked the area and figured that it would be a good experience for me. So I got married out there shortly after I arrived and planned to retire there. But my marriage lasted less than a year, so when I got a divorce, I came back south to Florida.

Paul Stillwell: Had you already been up for admiral at that point?

Captain McCampbell: I'd not been passed over at that point, no. But then it was getting real close. Of course, I ultimately was passed over. And I failed to make two selections, so that was the end of that. Actually, I finished 31 years of commissioned service.

Paul Stillwell: I just wondered how those three jobs compared in career-enhancing potential? Was that a factor in your decision at all?

Captain McCampbell: I don't think the Joint Staff helped me. I only know of one naval officer that had been on the Joint Staff, Whitey Moore, just ahead of me.† He was

---
* NSC – National Security Council.
† Rear Admiral Robert B. Moore, USN, of the Naval Academy class of 1932.

selected for admiral, but I don't know of any other captain selected for admiral out of there.

Paul Stillwell: Do you think that tour hurt you in that regard?

Captain McCampbell: Yes, it took me out of the Navy. Just like being in the fleet oiler. It took me out of naval aviation.

Paul Stillwell: Right.

Captain McCampbell: The North American Air Defense Command was the easiest job that I ever had. That didn't help me any either. I was like the assistant to the assistant in the outfit. I had a Canadian who, in our ranking system, would be like commodore. He was my boss, but there was an Army-type also. So we had both the Army brigadier general and myself as assistants. Then he reported to the—I can't remember the titles, but he has somebody. Well, of course, there was the chief of staff, but he had a Canadian either a three- or four-star general, as his boss. So I was kind of well down the line.

It was the Operations Division of the joint staff but not the operating part of the staff. There was a whole separate division set aside there for operations. It was kind of a screwy setup, I thought, all the way through. So I got out of that end of it as soon as I could, and I became the deputy chief of staff for programs. The chief of staff was the chief of staff to the four-star general. John Gunther was his name, a hell of a nice guy. I got along with everybody out there but I wasn't doing much work. As the deputy chief, programs, I had about 16 officers under me, and they didn't have much to do. Just a high-powered staff, as most of the Air Force staffs are.

Paul Stillwell: I think it would probably be helpful to explain to explain, at least in brief, general terms, the mission of the command that you were attached to.

Captain McCampbell: The North American Air Defense Command. Well, the purpose of the command was to set up a joint command staffed with both Canadians and U.S.

people. It was truly a joint staff; it had Army, Navy, and Air Force involved. And, mainly Air Force because it evolved into an Air Force function.

We had a big, elaborately equipped auditorium-like setup for large visual displays. That required a team of watch officers so they could give round-the-clock surveillance to either, well, submarines or air, any invasions of our area in the air, which then extended off the coast of Alaska to off the coast of Newfoundland, and, of course, to the south off the coast of Florida and Texas.

Paul Stillwell: The DEW line came under your supervision, didn't it?

Captain McCampbell: The DEW line was under the supervision of the defense command, yes.*

Paul Stillwell: Also, there were some radar picket ships, weren't there?

Captain McCampbell: The Canadians may have had some.

Paul Stillwell: I think at one point we had some converted liberty ships that fulfilled that role.

Captain McCampbell: Yes, but I don't recall those being used in the Air Defense Command.

Paul Stillwell: I see.

Captain McCampbell: The Canadians may have had some, though. And we had squatters stationed all around and, of course, we have some missile involvement, too, in that we were supposed to be able to detect any incoming enemy missiles. The Strategic

---

* DEW Line – Distant Early Warning Line, a chain of radar sites built 1,200 miles from the North Pole in the early 1950s as a means of detecting Soviet bombers approaching the United States over the Arctic.

Air Command had command of launching missiles, but we had interest in checking any incoming missiles or aircraft.

Paul Stillwell: Did you have a strong liaison function then with SAC on that?

Captain McCampbell: Yes, I visited their headquarters on one occasion, and, well, we had, well, let's say, communications. I also visited about four or five missile-launching sites as a part of the broad scope to get us to get acquainted with where the places were and see how they were set up and organized.

Paul Stillwell: I've seen the movies like *War Games* and *Dr. Strangelove* and so forth, where they had the big war room and the world projection. Was it somewhat similar to that?

Captain McCampbell: At the headquarters, yes. Well, with us, we had the large war room with visual displays, whatever we had to report on.

Paul Stillwell: To what extent what the operation computerized when you were there?

Captain McCampbell: It was pretty well computerized, I'd say. Another thing there—I keep calling it the Air Defense Command. Actually, it's North American Air Defense Command, which includes the Canadians. The Air Defense Command is a separate organization. That was entirely Army, and they had a small staff in Colorado Springs. I guess the Army had charge of the DEW Line. I'm not certain of that. But we were working on Cheyenne Mountain headquarters at the time I was there. It was mot completed when I was there, but shortly thereafter. It's a hole in the ground up at Cheyenne Mountain. I visited it on one occasion before it was complete. Personally, I had nothing to do with it.

Paul Stillwell: I'm still not quite clear on that first part of it when you were in operations but separate from operations. How do you draw that distinction?

Captain McCampbell: Well, we were the staff, and we were not the operating level. They had a separate Outfit for actually operating—like the war room was under this operational outfit.

Paul Stillwell: What sorts of things did you do in your staff function?

Captain McCampbell: Nothing. Practically nothing.

Paul Stillwell: Well, what sorts of things did you do in your program function then?

Captain McCampbell: Practically nothing, except maintain liaison with the Air Force in Washington. And, I visited the office there. My predecessor there visited so I continued and made a couple visits there.

Paul Stillwell: What did they need a naval officer for in that role?

Captain McCampbell: Nothing. Actually, about all we did and were supposed to do was report on advanced equipment that was coming into the Air Force in connection with the various air-defense squadrons we had around the United States and Canada. The Programs Division was the middleman between the Air Force and the Air Defense Command.

Paul Stillwell: Well, with these jobs that weren't too demanding, did they give you plenty of time off to enjoy the Colorado outdoors?

Captain McCampbell: Yes, regular hours and no work on the weekends. I enjoyed the tour there very much. Next to Argentina, it was the best tour I had.

Paul Stillwell: What sorts of things did you do in your off-duty time?

Captain McCampbell: Off-duty time? Elk hunting a couple of times. I fished all around the area; I'm a fly fisherman. I used to go to various spots, like Silver City; Lead, Colorado. That's up about 8,000 or 9,000 feet. I fished up there, had good fishing.

Paul Stillwell: You mentioned also you had to learn how to breathe in the high altitude.

Captain McCampbell: Yes, and I guess cigarette smoking didn't help any. It took me three or four months to be able to breathe freely at that altitude. In flying, when you get up to 6,000 feet you usually put your oxygen mask on. And we were at just about 6,000 feet. Denver claims to be a mile-high city, but actually Colorado Springs is a little higher than Denver, on average.

Paul Stillwell: You said that you had 31 years' commissioned service. Is that because you got the delay in commissioning back in the 1930s?

Captain McCampbell: Yes.

Paul Stillwell: When then did you retire from active duty?

Captain McCampbell: Nineteen sixty-four.

Paul Stillwell: Did you seek a second career then in business or something?

Captain McCampbell: I was pretty much into playing the stock market at that time. I continued that, and as I'd get a little more money stashed away, I'd put it in the market to the point where, to the last, about the last ten years I've been in, more or less, up to the hilt after I sold my other house, which I got a real good price for. I had some more money to throw in the market. So today I'm manly just living off my Navy retired pay.

On occasion, back in 1980, my income from investments amounted to $19,000 interest. Not from sales, from pure and simply dividends. But mostly from gold/silver stocks. Gold got way up there, about $850.00 an ounce, in 1980. With the additional income, I'd throw it back in the market. In 1980 I bought a new car—paid a nice big price for it—from the sale of 200 shares of one gold stock that I had. But I'm still fully invested in gold/silvers, mostly in the South Africa shares, which, by the way, are now doing quite well. Gold isn't doing much, just juggling around like a yo-yo, around $430.00 to $460.00. But the gold stocks are going up real good.

Paul Stillwell: Have you done any consulting work since your retirement?

Captain McCampbell: Yes, I was consultant to Merrill-Lynch, the local office over in Palm Beach. I wasn't getting paid for it, but my account executive—they don't call them brokers anymore—would call me occasionally, at least three times. She would get a client that wanted to buy some gold stocks and wanted to know which ones to buy, and she'd call me and ask my advice on it, because she knew that I was heavy in gold. That's the only consulting I've done except on these occasional visits to Maxwell Air Force. I've been called up there twice as an individual to observe their studies, what they had done by way of their curriculum and that sort of thing.

Paul Stillwell: This is a question that's out of sequence, but it just occurred to me. When you were the air group commander in World War II, you had the all-propeller air group. As the skipper of the *Bon Homme Richard*, you had a mixture of jets and propeller planes. How did that differentiate in the operation of the carrier?

Captain McCampbell: Pretty much the same, except the jet planes were considerably more short-legged. I had the F11F, which had an operational time of about 90 minutes.[*] They'd always take off last and come back aboard first. I'll put it that way. But we did have a stunt team out in that F11F squadron. I wouldn't say they were as good as the Blue Angels, but they were running a close second.

Paul Stillwell: They could do a lot for your ship's PR.

---

[*] The Grumman F11F Tiger was first delivered to Squadron VA-156 in March 1957. The F11F-1 model was 47 feet long; wingspan of 32 feet; gross weight of 22,160 pounds; and top speed of 750 miles per hour. It was armed with four 20-millimeter guns and four under-wing Sidewinder missiles.

Captain McCampbell: Right, except they had the CinCPacFlt came out once to, I guess, kind of inspect us casual, cursory inspection. I put on a show for him, and he didn't like it. He said wee were wasting of gasoline. But it's all part of a program of operations, you see. And he said, also, it was dangerous. He was a submariner. But he didn't go for that at all.

Paul Stillwell: Who was that, do you remember?

Captain McCampbell: I can't remember his name.

Paul Stillwell: Well, you talked about your investments since retiring, how have you spent the time for the last 23 years?

Captain McCampbell: Sitting on my fanny. Not really. I've made many trips around the country. I can't go to all the reunions by any way, but I've been to quite a few of them. And I always go to the inaugurations and the reunions of the Congressional Medal of Honor Society. They alternate, the inaugurations every four years and the Medal of Honor Society meets every two years. And I've been to the *Wasp* reunion, the *Essex* reunion, and one time, the *Portland* reunion. I belong to 22 different organizations. And, as I say, I can't begin to make all the reunions. There are the American Legion, Legion of Merit, the Naval Academy, various organizations that I belong to and pay dues to, but I don't attend the reunions.

Paul Stillwell: You have those stocks just to pay your dues.

Captain McCampbell: Yes. And I usually, anymore, I don't travel far to go to an event, whether it be a civic celebration or whatever, I don't go unless they pay my way.

Paul Stillwell: Have you lived in this area pretty much the whole time since you retired?

Captain McCampbell: Yes. I spent six months over in the Bahamas, in Freeport, when that was first coming on stream building up, trying to sell real estate and after six months I didn't sell any, so I came back to Florida.

Paul Stillwell: Well, this was your home before you went to the Naval Academy so it's a return.

Well, I know another thing—it's obvious from looking around your den here, that you do a lot of reading, both about current events and history.

Captain McCampbell: Yes, I do a lot of reading, historical. I've read all the books over in that bookcase. Some of these are novels up here or periodicals that I've saved mostly; there are some books in there. I've got a couple lying around here that I haven't read. Like, there's one right there.

Paul Stillwell: On the Civil War.

Captain McCampbell: Civil War. I've taken a series from Time-Life. I've read about four books, and I've got two that I haven't read yet.

Paul Stillwell: Just from my time that I've spent with you this week, I know you maintain a very active interest in the Iran-Contra hearings.[*]

Captain McCampbell: Yes.

Paul Stillwell: One thing we haven't talked about in too much detail, Captain, is your family. You mentioned in passing that you had two sons and a daughter. When were they born and what has become of them?

---

[*] Iran-Contra was a political scandal in the mid-1980s, during the Reagan Administration. The United States was selling arms to Iran, an avowed enemy. The proceeds from those sales were then diverted to the Contras, anti-Communist guerrillas in Nicaragua. Both the sale of the arms and the aid to the Contras violated stated administration policy and congressional legislation.

Captain McCampbell: My daughter's the oldest. She was born in 1941, before the war. I was married in '36 so '41 would be about right.

Paul Stillwell: What's her name?

Captain McCampbell: Frances. And she's married to an admiral, Stewart Ring, now based out in Honolulu.* My oldest son, David Perry McCampbell, is a commander in the Navy, and he has a command out in Honolulu also. The youngest son, unfortunately, I don't know where the hell he.

Paul Stillwell: What's his name?

Captain McCampbell: John C. McCampbell. Last I heard he was in Tampa, but I haven't had any communication with him in 10-15 years actually.

Paul Stillwell: You said your oldest son has a command.

Captain McCampbell: He has a command; I guess it comes under the service force because he's rescue and salvage. He took the training at Anacostia in deep-sea diving. He's a qualified deep-sea diver, and he's been in that work right on through the years.†

Paul Stillwell: Is he a Navy Academy graduate?

Captain McCampbell: He graduated in 1970. That's all I can tell you about him. He's building a house in Honolulu. I don't know where he's getting all the money. Guess he borrowed it, but he built a house, a duplex, in Panama City, Florida. He owns a condominium in Virginia outside, just outside of Washington, and now he's building a house out in Honolulu

---

* Rear Admiral Stewart A. Ring, USN, who was then Director for Plans and Policy, U.S. Pacific Command.
† David P. McCampbell retired from active duty as a commander on 30 June 1992, a few years after this interview.

Paul Stillwell: Well, naval officers today are considerably better paid than when you were on active duty.

Captain McCampbell: That's right. At one time when he had a salvage ship, he was getting regular pay, and they have a program now where, if you're in command of a fleet operating unit, you get additional pay. That's kind of like sea pay, I guess.

Paul Stillwell: I think it's called command responsibility pay or something like that.

Captain McCampbell: Yes.

Paul Stillwell: Then, of course, there's a generous housing allowance now.

Captain McCampbell: Well, he's doing all right. I guess he makes $45,000, $46,000 a year. I don't know. Honolulu is considered a hardship station, and my son gets $1,100 per month extra for being based there.

Paul Stillwell: What about your grandchildren?

Captain McCampbell: My daughter has two girls. They're about 18, 20 years old, along in there. I have a record in my address book, but that's about their age. And my son has a son who's eight years old.

Paul Stillwell: What's his name?

Captain McCampbell: Christopher David McCampbell.

Paul Stillwell: So that name David's been perpetuated?

Captain McCampbell: Yes, right. He goes by the name of Chris. My youngest son has one child, but he was divorced from the mother of the child, and she has been in contact with me about three or four years ago. She has a daughter who must be nine or ten by now. She asked if I had any objections to the daughter being adopted by her second husband. I said, "No. There are a couple of things you should consider. First is the name, and number two, inheritance and whether this marriage, or any marriage, is permanent or not. If you want to consider all those things, why, I have no objection. And legally I won't have any part of it anyway."

Paul Stillwell: In this generation, it's kind of hard to tell whether a marriage is permanent or not.

Captain McCampbell: That's right, but that's the decision she has to make.

Paul Stillwell: Well, Captain, these last six days have been extremely enjoyable for me, and fascinating. I very much appreciate the time and effort you put into this project. In a sense, it's a legacy to future generations to document the many noteworthy achievements of your career, and so I thank you very much.

Captain McCampbell: Well, thank you. I appreciate your taking the time to come down and interview me. I know you're getting paid for it, but that really doesn't enter into it. I'm delighted to have given what I can. I'm sorry I can't remember more of the details of my career. But it has been a very unusual career, I think. It hasn't been all bad at all. There's been some very good aspects of it, particularly when I was younger. But then as I grew in age and rank, I began to get more privileges and I enjoyed those as much as I could.

I'm not ashamed at all of not being selected for admiral, because along the way I've had considerable marital problems. I'm now on my fifth wife, and those things have been a hardship for me to go through. I blame the Navy itself, at least my duties, for two of the divorces—the first and the second—and, the third one just didn't work out. It lasted less than a year. The fourth one lasted about nine years. And this one is now over nine, so I feel like I'm over the hump.

Paul Stillwell: This one's permanent.

Captain McCampbell: Yes. But, anyway, thank you a lot for coming. And I appreciate the time you've spent with me.

Paul Stillwell: It's been a real privilege for me, sir, and an honor to talk to someone of your stature. Again, I thank you.

Captain McCampbell: Well, thank you again.

Launched in 1969, the U.S. Naval Institute's award-winning oral history program is among the oldest in the country. Used in combination with documentary sources, oral histories offer a richer understanding of naval history through candid recollections and explanations rarely entered into contemporary records. In addition, they help depict the atmosphere of a particular event or era in a manner not available in official documents.

The nonprofit Naval Institute accomplishes its history projects solely through contributed funds and gratefully accepts tax-deductible gifts of all sizes for this purpose. This support allows the Institute to preserve the life experiences of today's service men and women so they may enlighten and inspire future generations.

For information about opportunities to underwrite Naval Institute oral history projects, please contact the Naval Institute Foundation at 291 Wood Road, Annapolis, Maryland 21402; by phone at (410) 295-1054; or by e-mail at foundation@usni.org.

Index to the Oral History of
Captain David McCampbell, U.S. Navy (Retired)

A6M Zero (Japanese Fighter)
   Operations in combat against U.S. forces in 1944, 129, 161-162. 172, 182, 308

Air Force, Atlantic Fleet (AirLant)
   Logistics of supplying weapons to the Sixth Fleet in the early 1950s, 229-230, 277, 283-286

Air Force, U.S.
   Plans in the mid-1950s for evacuating U.S. personnel from the Mediterranean region, 322
   Role of Wheelus Air Force base in Libya in the 1950s, 323
   Role of the North American Air Defense Command in the early 1960s in preparing for possible Soviet attack, 357-362

Air Group 15
   Training ashore on the East Coast in 1943-44, 111-118, 314-315
   Training operations with the aircraft carrier *Hornet* (CV-12) in 1944, 119, 129-132, 140
   In early 1944 did training flights from Pu'unēnē Naval Air Station on the island of Maui, 126-127, 141, 314
   Combat operations in 1944 from the aircraft carrier *Essex* (CV-9), 123-220, 273-274, 307-318
   Role of combat intelligence officers, 154-157, 169
   Enlisted men in the air group, 162-163, 217-218

Air Group 19
   Operations from the aircraft carrier *Lexington* (CV-16) in 1944, 166-168, 200, 206, 208

Alaska
   Visited in 1937 by the heavy cruiser *Portland* (CA-33), 43-44

Alcohol
   Medicinal brandy provided to pilots on board the aircraft carrier *Essex* (CV-9) in 1944, 191
   On board the aircraft carrier *Bunker Hill* (CV-9) in late 1944, 220-221
   Commander Naval Forces Marianas, Rear Admiral William Erdmann, smuggled liquor to the United States in 1959-60, 349-351

Antiair Warfare
   Japanese antiaircraft fire at U.S. planes over Marcus Island in May 1944, 123-125, 148-149, 315

At Iwo Jima in June 1944, 173-175
In Manila in the autumn of 1944, 214

Argentina
Living conditions in Buenos Aires for the McCampbell family, 1948-51, 261-263

Argentine Navy
McCampbell's role in 1948-51 as aviation adviser and war college instructor, 252-268
Capabilities of the Navy, 259-260
Rivalry with the Argentine Army in the late 1940s-early 1950s, 260-261
Falklands War in 1982, 260

Arkansas, USS (BB-33)
Midshipman cruise to Europe in 1930, 23-25

Armed Forces Staff College, Norfolk, Virginia
McCampbell was in the first class of students in 1946, 229
Curriculum and joint-service training in the late 1940s, 244-251
McCampbell's role on the staff as assistant intelligence officer in the late 1940s, 250

Army, U.S.
Training at Camp Meade, Maryland, in the 1920s, 5-6
Role in nuclear weapons storage in the early 1950s, 229-230, 283-284

Arrighi, Commander Norman L., Supply Corps, USN
Served in the late 1960s as supply officer of the aircraft carrier *Bon Homme Richard* (CVA-31), 351

Atlantic City (New Jersey) Naval Air Station
Site of training in 1943-44 of Fighting Squadron 15 (VF-15), 111-117, 314

Awards, Naval
In early 1945 McCampbell received the Medal of Honor and toured the country, 221-227, 300-301
Public appearances and other events over the years that resulted from McCampbell's Medal of Honor, 232-244, 271-272

Baroja, Commander Pio
Argentine naval officer whom McCampbell befriended in the late 1940s, 253-258, 264-268, 275

Beakley, Lieutenant Commander Wallace M., USN (USNA, 1924)
As air group commander of the aircraft carrier *Wasp* (CV-7) in the early 1940s, 81, 83-84, 106

Beckmann, Lieutenant Alcorn G., USN (USNA, 1931)
    In September 1942 was executive officer of the destroyer *Farenholt* (DD-491) when she rescued survivors from the aircraft carrier *Wasp* (CV-7), 105-106

Berlin, Germany
    Work of the Joint Staff's Plans Division in connection with Berlin in the early 1960s, 354-355

Bermuda
    Visited by the aircraft carrier *Wasp* (CV-7) during Neutrality Patrol in 1941, 71-72. 94

"Betty" (Japanese Bomber)
    Attacked by U.S. fighters in operations in 1944, 18-19, 135, 177, 213-215

Bogan, Vice Admiral Gerald F., USN (USNA, 1916)
    Served as ComAirLant in the late 1940s, 230

Bombs/Bombing
    By planes from Air Group 15 of the aircraft carrier *Essex* (CV-9) in 1944, 141-142, 207-208, 311

***Bon Homme Richard*, USS (CVA-31)**
    Deployment to the Western Pacific in early 1959, 338-343
    Operations off the West Coast in mid-1959, 343-344, 348-349
    Deployment to the Western Pacific in late 1959-early 1960, 344, 349-352
    The ship got under way unexpectedly early while in Pearl Harbor on 7 December 1959, 344-346
    Collisions in 1959, 338-341, 345
    Nuclear weapons on board, 340, 342
    Enlisted men in the crew, 1959-60, 346-348
    Commander Naval Forces Marianas, Rear Admiral William Erdmann, smuggled liquor to the United States on board the ship in 1959-60, 349-351
    In the late 1950s the air group included F11F Tigers, 363-364

Bradley, Captain Willis W., Jr., USN (USNA, 1907)
    In the mid-1930s commanded the heavy cruiser *Portland* (CA-33), 34, 36, 44

Brewer, Lieutenant Commander Charles W., USN
    Served in 1944 as commanding officer of Fighting Squadron 15 (VF-15), 119, 136-138, 179-181

Brown, Vice Admiral Charles R., USN (USNA, 1921)
    In late 1944 served as chief of staff to Rear Admiral Frederick Sherman, Commander Task Group 38.3, 300-301
    Commanded the Sixth Fleet, 1956-58, 300-304, 306, 319-321, 325-326

Browning, Captain Miles R., USN (USNA, 1918)
In 1943-44 served as the first commanding officer of the aircraft carrier *Hornet* (CV-12), 112, 119-122, 129-130, 137, 140-141

***Bunker Hill*, USS (CV-17)**
Took Air Group 15 back to the United States in late 1944 after its combat deployment, 220-221

Burnham, Ensign W. T., USNR
McCampbell's wingman who was killed by antiaircraft fire during an attack on Marcus Island in May 1944, 148-149

Callaghan, Commander Daniel J., USN (USNA, 1911)
In the mid-1930s was executive officer of the heavy cruiser *Portland* (CA-33), 41, 45

Camp Meade, Maryland
Site of Army training in the 1920s, 5-6

Carrier Aircraft Service Unit (CASU)
Support of Air Group 15 in the aircraft carriers *Hornet* (CV-12) and *Essex* (CV-9) in 1944, 111, 120

Carter, President James E., Jr. (USNA, 1947)
McCampbell's impressions of as President, 242-244

Cassady, Commander John H, USN (USNA, 1919)
Served in the early 1940s as air officer of the aircraft carrier *Wasp* (CV-7), 85

***Chitose* (Japanese Aircraft Carrier)**
Attacked by U.S. carrier planes on 25 October 1944, during the Battle of Leyte Gulf, 207

CinCNELM
In the mid-1950s exercised command over the U.S. Sixth Fleet, 304, 319, 321-322

Clifton, Lieutenant (junior grade) Joseph C., USN (USNA, 1930)
Service in the late 1930s in Fighting Squadron Four (VF-4), 55, 59, 61

Collins, Lieutenant John J., USNR
Pilot from the aircraft carrier *Essex* (CV-9) who was wounded in May 1944 and given relatively safe assignments after that, 192, 315

Collisions
Between the aircraft carrier *Wasp* (CV-7) and the destroyer *Stack* (DD-406) in March 1942, 94

Between the fleet oiler *Severn* (AO-61) and a destroyer in 1958, 338
The aircraft carrier *Bon Homme Richard* (CVA-31) and a fleet oiler in 1959, 338-339
The *Bon Homme Richard* and a small freighter in 1959, 340-341
The *Bon Homme Richard* and a tugboat in 1959, 345

Communications
Use of radio by planes from the aircraft carrier *Essex* (CV-9) in 1944, 132, 139, 165-166

Congress, U.S.
Involvement in McCampbell's appointment to the Naval Academy in 1929, 11

Connally, John B. Jr.
Served on board the aircraft carrier *Essex* (CV-9) in World War II and was later Secretary of the Navy and Governor of Texas, 145-146

Cuba
Guantánamo Bay was the site of training for Fighting Squadron Four (VF-4) in the late 1930s, 62
The crew of the fleet oiler *Severn* (AO-61) was trained at Guantánamo in 1958, 329-330
In the early 1960s the Joint Staff developed contingency plans for Cuba, 352-353

D4Y "Judy"
Japanese dive-bomber that operated against U.S. Navy forces in 1944, 179

Davis, Vice Admiral William V., Jr., USN (USNA, 1924)
Commanded the aircraft carrier *Franklin D. Roosevelt* (CVB-42), 1950-51, 275, 277, 279-280
Served 1956-58 as DCNO (Air), OP-05, 325-326

Denton, Lieutenant Jeremiah A., Jr., USN (USNA, 1947)
In the mid-1950s experimented with dispersed formations for Sixth Fleet operations, 302-303, 320

Dew, Lieutenant Commander Irwin L., USN (USNA, 1933)
In February 1944 was removed as commanding officer of Bombing Squadron 15 (VB-15) on board the aircraft carrier *Hornet* (CV-12), 119-121

Dickey, Commander Fred Clinton, USN
Served as executive officer of the aircraft carrier *Wasp* (CV-7) in the early 1940s, 83, 103

Doyle, Lieutenant Austin K., USN (USNA, 1920)
On the Naval Academy staff in the early 1930s, 17, 21

Drane, Commander William M., USN (USNA, 1930)
In February 1944 was removed as Commander Air Group 15 (CAG-15) on board the aircraft carrier *Hornet* (CV-12), 119-120

Duncan, Lieutenant Commander George E., USN
Fighter pilot who flew from the aircraft carrier *Essex* (CV-9) in 1944, 135

Einstein, Professor Albert
In the early 1950s declined to have a building at the Technical Training Center in Jacksonville named for him, 290

Eisenhower, President Dwight D. (USMA, 1915)
As NATO Supreme Allied Commander in the early 1950s visited the aircraft carrier *Franklin D. Roosevelt* (CVB-42), 241
As President, 242

Emrick, Captain Paul E., USN (USNA, 1932)
In 1944 was navigator and mess treasurer of the aircraft carrier *Essex* (CV-9), 187-188
In 1959 served as chief of staff to Commander Carrier Division Three, 342-343

Enlisted Personnel
On board the aircraft carrier *Essex* (CV-9) in 1944, 162-163, 217-218, 316-317
In the aircraft carrier *Franklin D. Roosevelt* (CVB-42) in the early 1950s, 282
At the Naval Air Technical Training Center in Jacksonville, 1953-54, 286-294
On board the fleet oiler *Severn* (AO-61) in the late 1950s, 330-335
In the crew of the aircraft carrier *Bon Homme Richard* (CVA-31) in 1959, 346-348

Erdmann, Rear Admiral William L., USN (USNA, 1924)
As Commander Naval Forces Marianas, smuggled liquor to the United States in 1959-60, 349-351

***Essex*, USS (CV-9)**
Combat operations in 1944 with Air Group 15, 123-211, 227, 273-274, 307-314, 316
Enlisted men on board the ship in 1944, 162-163, 217-218, 316-317
Hit by kamikaze in 1944, 227
Lack of cleanliness in World War II, 281

F3F
Grumman fighter flown by Fighting Squadron Four (VF-4) in the late 1930s, 55-68
Flown by Captain John Reeves of the aircraft carrier *Wasp* (CV-7) in 1940, 77-81

F4F Wildcat
Landing characteristics, 113

F6F Hellcat
    Used in Fighting Squadron 15 (VF-15) in 1943-44, 113, 307-310
    Combat operations in 1944 from the aircraft carrier *Essex* (CV-9), 123-126, 137-138, 141-150, 160-164, 171-220, 273-274, 307-314
    Nicknames of McCampbell's planes, 126

F8F Bearcat
    Hot new Grumman fighter that McCampbell flew shortly after World War II, but not in combat, 271-273

F9F/F9F-6/8 Cougar
    Grumman fighter that provided jet training for McCampbell in the mid-1950s, 297-298, 337
    Pilot killed in the mid-1950s while testing an F9F, 299

F11F Tiger
    Formed a stunt team in the air group of the aircraft carrier *Bon Homme Richard* (CVA-31) in the late 1950s, 363-364

Fairbanks, Lieutenant (junior grade) Douglas E., Jr., USNR
    Actor who served for a time in 1942 as a reserve officer on board the aircraft carrier *Wasp* (CV-7), 93

***Farenholt*, USS (DD-491)**
    Rescued survivors from the sinking of the aircraft carrier *Wasp* (CV-7) in September 1942, 104-107

Felt, Admiral Harry D., USN (USNA, 1923)
    Briefly commanded the Sixth Fleet in 1956, 300, 305-306, 319
    As CinCPac in 1959, 344-345

Fighting Squadron Four (VF-4)
    Operations in 1938-40 from the aircraft carrier *Ranger* (CV-4), 55-68

Fighting Squadron 15 (VF-15)
    Training of in 1943-44 in preparation for combat, 111-120, 126-127, 129-130
    Equipped with F6F Hellcats, 112-113

Flight Training
    As Pensacola in 1937-38, 26, 47-54

Foltz, Lieutenant (junior grade) Ralph E., USNR
    Flew as part of Air Group 15 in the aircraft carrier *Essex* (CV-9) in 1944, 213-214

Formosa
    U.S. carrier air operations in the area in 1944, 195-196

Fort Campbell, Kentucky
    Role in nuclear weapons storage in the early 1950s, 229-230, 283-285

France
    The Sixth Fleet flagship *Salem* (CA-139) was home-ported in Villefranche in the late 1950s, 320-321

***Franklin D. Roosevelt*, USS (CVB-42)**
    Visited in the early 1950s by General of the Army Dwight Eisenhower, 241, 277
    Nuclear weapons on board in the early 1950s, 241, 277
    Sixth Fleet operations in the early 1950s, 241, 277-280, 282
    East Coast operations and overhaul in the early 1950s, 281-283
    Enlisted crewmen in the early 1950s, 282

Freeman, Captain Charles Lawrence, USN (USNA, 1927)
    Served in the mid-1950s as Sixth Fleet chief of staff, 305

Fuller, Lieutenant (junior grade) Harold D., USN (USNA, 1934)
    Served in the aircraft carrier *Wasp* (CV-7) in the early 1940s, 76-77

Germany
    Work of the Joint Staff's plans division in connection with Berlin in the early 1960s, 354-355

Goldwater, Barry M.
    As a student at Staunton Military Academy in the 1920s, 3-7

Gregg, Walter
    Enlisted pilot who flew from the aircraft carrier *Wasp* (CV-7) in the early 1940s and became a landing signal officer, 73

Grumman Aircraft Corporation
    Paid expenses for McCampbell to stay in New York City after his combat exploits of 1944, 221-222
    Visited by McCampbell in early 1945, 224, 227

Guadalcanal
    Support of by the aircraft carrier *Wasp* (CV-7) in August-September 1942, 96-100

Guam
    Air operations in the vicinity during the summer of 1944 by planes from the aircraft carrier *Essex* (CV-9), 128-129, 182-183, 311
    Visited by the aircraft carrier *Bon Homme Richard* (CVA-31) in late 1959, 349-352
    Commander Naval Forces Marianas, Rear Admiral William Erdmann, smuggled liquor to the United States in 1959-60, 349-351

Guantánamo Bay, Cuba, Naval Base
    Site of training for Fighting Squadron Four (VF-4) in the late 1930s, 62
    Site of training for the crew of fleet oiler *Severn* (AO-61) in 1958, 329-330

Gunnery—Naval
    Shooting by the .50-caliber machine guns of the F6F Hellcat during combat in 1944, 172-174, 309-310, 313-314

Hall, Rear Admiral Grover Budd H., USN (USNA, 1921)
    Served as air group commander when the aircraft carrier *Wasp* (CV-7) was commissioned in 1940, 74-76
    In 1959 was ComFAir Hawaii, 344-346

Harrill, Rear Admiral William K., USN (USNA, 1914)
    During part of 1944 served as Commander Task Group 58.4 with his flag in the aircraft carrier *Essex* (CV-9), 170-171, 177

Hawaii
    In early 1944 pilots of Air Group 15 did training flights from Pu'unēnē Naval Air Station on the island of Maui, 126-127, 141, 148, 314-315
    The aircraft carrier *Bon Homme Richard* (CVA-31) got under way unexpectedly early while in Pearl Harbor on 7 December 1959, 344-346

Hipp, Ensign Jacob E., USNR
    Officer who abandoned the aircraft carrier *Wasp* (CV-7) after she had been torpedoed in September 1942, 102

Hong Kong
    Visited by the aircraft carrier *Bon Homme Richard* (CVA-31) in 1959, 342-343

Hornet, **USS (CVS-12)**
    Shakedown training near Bermuda in early 1944, 119, 129-132, 140
    Air group training in Hawaii in 1944, 140-141
    Shot at planes from the aircraft carrier *Essex* (CV-9) during the Battle of Leyte Gulf in October 1944, 204

Houston, **USS (CA-30)**
    As President in the mid-1930s, Franklin Roosevelt made a fishing trip in the ship, 37-39

Iceland
    U.S. Navy ships escorted convoys to Reykjavik early in World War II, 88

Intelligence
    Role of combat intelligence officers in Air Group 15 in 1944, 154-157, 169

Ise (Japanese Battleship)
  Attacked by U.S. carrier planes on 25 October 1944, during the Battle of Leyte Gulf, 207

Iwo Jima
  Attacks on by Air Group 15 from the aircraft carrier *Essex* (CV-9) in June 1944, 173-175

Jackson, Rear Admiral Andrew M., Jr., USN (USNA, 1930)
  Served in 1959-60 as Commander Carrier Division Three, 343-344, 348-349

Japan
  In 1959 the aircraft carrier *Bon Homme Richard* (CVA-31) collided with a small freighter in the Inland Sea of Japan, 340-341
  Visits to various Japanese ports in 1959 by the *Bon Homme Richard*, 342

Japanese Aircraft
  In combat against Americans in 1944, 18-19, 129, 135, 142-144, 152-153, 156, 161-162, 167, 171-172, 177-180, 194-197, 202, 213-214

Japanese Navy
  Target of air actions on 25 October 1944, during the Battle of Leyte Gulf, 206-209

Joint Staff
  Work of the plans division in the early 1960s, 352-357

Jones, Lieutenant (junior grade) Robert F., USN (USNA, 1931)
  Aviator in the mid-1930s in the heavy cruiser *Portland* (CA-33), 34-35

Kamikazes
  Use of by the Japanese in the Battle of Leyte Gulf in October 1944, 142-143, 146-147, 218
  Hit the aircraft carrier *Essex* (CV-9) in late 1944, 227

Kane, Lieutenant Commander William R., USN (USNA, 1933)
  Pilot who was shot down during the Marianas campaign in June 1944, 184-185

Kennedy, President John F.
  Events connected with his inauguration in January 1961, 236-239
  McCampbell met Kennedy at receptions in the early 1960s, 240-241

Kernodle, Commander Michael H., USN (USNA, 1921)
  Served as air officer of the aircraft carrier *Wasp* (CV-7) at the beginning of World War II, 79, 85

King, Fleet Admiral Ernest J., USN (USNA, 1901)

Had a natatorium in Jacksonville named for him in the early 1950s, 289-290

Kivette, Vice Admiral Frederick N., USN (USNA, 1925)
As Commander Seventh Fleet in 1959, reviewed collisions involving the aircraft carrier *Bon Homme Richard* (CVA-31), 339, 341

Klinsmann, Commander George Otto, USN (USNA, 1933)
As Commander Air Group Four, was lost in action on 15 January 1945, 124-125

Konrad, Lieutenant (junior grade) Edmond G., USN (USNA, 1932)
Served as LSO in the aircraft carrier *Wasp* (CV-7) in the early 1940s, 69-70, 72-74
In 1942-43 ran pilot training at Cecil Field in Jacksonville, 109

Lake Champlain, **USS (CVS-39)**
Refueled from the fleet oiler *Severn* (AO-61) in 1958, 330

Lambert, Lieutenant Commander Valdemar G., USN
Commanded Torpedo Squadron 15 (VT-15) on board the aircraft carrier *Essex* (CV-9) in 1944, 132-133, 207, 273-274

Landing Signal Officers
McCampbell's service in the aircraft carrier *Wasp* (CV-7), 1940-42, 69-100
In 1942-43 McCampbell ran the landing signal officer school in Melbourne, Florida, 66-67, 69, 109-110

Langley, **USS (CVL-27)**
McCampbell landed on board after his successful mission of 24 October 1944 in the Battle of Leyte Gulf, 203-205

Lebanon
Relationship with the U.S. Sixth Fleet in the late 1950s, 321-322, 324-325, 332-333

Lee, Captain Fitzhugh, USN (USNA, 1926)
Was one of McCampbell's flight instructors in the late 1930s, 47
In World War II was executive officer of the aircraft carrier *Essex* (CV-9), 281
Commanded the aircraft carrier *Franklin D. Roosevelt* (CVB-42), 1951-52, 279-280, 341

Lentz, Lieutenant August W., USN (USNA, 1926)
Served in the aircraft carrier *Wasp* (CV-7) in the early 1940s, 78-79
Killed when the ship sank in September 1942, 79

Lexington, **USS (CV-16)**
Actions against the Japanese in 1944, 166-168, 185-186, 200, 206, 208, 215-216

Leyte Gulf, Battle of
    Participation in by Air Group 15 from the aircraft carrier *Essex* (CV-9), 139, 142-147, 192-193, 198-209, 218
    Role of U.S. submarines, 198-199
    Use of kamikazes by the Japanese in the battle, 142-143, 146-147
    On 24 October 1944 McCampbell and his wingman Roy Rushing shot down 15 Japanese planes between them, 142-145, 160-161, 199-206, 218, 300-301
    Activities of Air Group 15 against the Japanese on 25 October 1944, 164-167, 192-193, 206-210

Libya
    Site of Wheelus Air Force Base in the 1950s, 323

Litch, Captain Ernest W., USN (USNA, 1920)
    Navigator of the aircraft carrier *Ranger* (CV-4) in the late 1930s, 65
    During World War II was involved in naval aviation training at Jacksonville, Florida, 65-66
    Commanded the aircraft carrier *Lexington* (CV-16) in 1944-45, 66

***Long Island*, USS (CVE-1)**
    In late 1943 was used for carrier qualifications for the pilots of Air Group 15, 118, 126

Malta
    Delivery in 1942 by the aircraft carrier *Wasp* (CV-7) of British Spitfires to the Mediterranean, destined for Malta, 80, 90-94

Marcus Island
    Attacked by planes from the aircraft carrier *Essex* (CV-9) in May 1944, 123-125, 148-149, 153-154, 192, 315

Mariana Islands
    Support of the U.S. invasion in 1944 by Air Group 15 from the aircraft carrier *Essex* (CV-9), 147-148, 152, 154-155, 172, 176-185, 187-188, 190, 314
    Commander Naval Forces Marianas, Rear Admiral William Erdmann, smuggled liquor to the United States in 1959-60, 349-351

Marianas Turkey Shoot
    Actions by Air Group 15 from the aircraft carrier *Essex* (CV-9) on 19 June 1944, 147-148, 172, 179-182, 187-188

McCaffree, Captain Burnham C., USN (USNA, 1926)
    Commanded the aircraft carrier *Wasp* (CV-18) in 1952, 293-294
    Commanded Jacksonville Naval Air Station in the early 1950s, 291, 294

McCain, Captain John S., USN (USNA, 1906)
    Commanded the aircraft carrier *Ranger* (CV-4), 1937-39, 61, 63

McCampbell, Captain David, USN (Ret.) (USNA, 1933)
    Parents, 1-2, 4, 9, 11, 45, 225-227, 268-270
    Wives, 23, 36-37, 44, 249, 262, 266, 325, 368
    Daughter Frances (Mrs. Stewart Ring), 64, 266, 366, 367
    Son David P., 261, 366-367
    Son John C., 261, 366-368
    Boyhood in Alabama and Florida, 1910s and 1920s, 1-3
    Prep school in Staunton, Virginia, late 1920s, 2-8
    One year at Georgia Tech, 1928-29, 8-10
    As a Naval Academy midshipman, 1929-33, 9, 11-27
    Civilian work, 1933-34, 27-28
    Duty in 1934-37 in the heavy cruiser *Portland* (CA-33), 29-46
    Flight training at Pensacola in 1937-38, 26, 47-54
    From 1938 to 1940 served with Fighting Squadron Four (VF-4), based on the aircraft carrier *Ranger* (CV-4), 54-68
    From 1940 to 1942 was landing signal officer of the aircraft carrier *Wasp* (CV-7), 69-109
    In 1942-43 ran the landing signal officer school in Melbourne, Florida, 66-67, 69, 109-111
    Served as commanding officer of Fighting 15 (VF-15) in 1943-44, 111-120
    Commanded Air Group 15 in 1944, 18-19, 121-211, 273-274, 307-318
    In early 1945 received the Medal of Honor and toured the country, 221-227
    Public appearances and other events over the years that resulted from McCampbell's Medal of Honor, 232-244, 271-272
    Served 1945-46 at Oceana Naval Air Station as representative of ComFairQuonset, 228-232, 271-272
    In 1946-48 was a student and then a staff member at the Armed Forces Staff College, 229, 244-252
    From 1948 to 1951 was senior aviation advisor to the Argentine Navy, 252-268
    Served as executive officer of the *Franklin D. Roosevelt* (CVB-42) in 1951-52, 241, 275-283
    Served 1952-53 on the staff of Commander Aircraft Atlantic, 229-230, 283-286
    Commanded the Naval Air Technical Training Center in Jacksonville, 1953-54, 286-294
    From 1954 to 1956 served as flight test coordinator at the Naval Air Test Center, Patuxent River, Maryland, 294-299
    Served 1956-58 as operations officer on the staff of Commander Sixth Fleet, 299-306, 318-326
    Commanded the fleet oiler *Severn* (AO-61), 1958-59, 325-338
    Commanded the aircraft carrier *Bon Homme Richard* (CVA-31), 1959-60, 338-352, 363-364
    Served 1960-62 in the plans division of the Joint Staff, 352-357

Served 1962-64 on the staff of the North American Air Defense Command in Colorado Springs, 357-362

Activities after retiring from active duty in 1964, 362-369

McCandlish, Commander Benjamin V., USN (USNA, 1909)
In the mid-1930s was executive officer of the heavy cruiser *Portland* (CA-33), 41

McCorkle, Lieutenant (junior grade) Francis D., USN (USNA, 1926)
Service in the mid-1930s in the heavy cruiser *Portland* (CA-33), 32-33

McDonald, Commander David L., USN (USNA, 1928)
During World War II was involved in naval aviation training at Jacksonville, Florida, 65-66, 151
Served in 1944 as executive officer of the aircraft carrier *Essex* (CV-9), 151, 221, 281, 316

McFall, Commander Andrew C., USN (USNA, 1916)
In the late 1930s was executive officer of the aircraft carrier *Ranger* (CV-4), 64-65

Medal of Honor
In early 1945 McCampbell received the Medal of Honor and toured the country on behalf of the Navy, 221-227, 300-301
Public appearances and other events over the years that resulted from McCampbell's Medal of Honor, 232-244, 271-272

Melbourne, Florida, Naval Air Station
Site of landing signal officer school in World War II, 66-67, 69, 109-110

Miller, Rear Admiral George H., USN (USNA, 1933)
As a Naval Academy midshipman n the early 1930s, 24

Millett, Lieutenant Charles R., USNR (USNA, 1922)
Survived the sinking of the aircraft carrier *Wasp* (CV-7) in September 1942, 108

Mini, Lieutenant Commander James H., USN (USNA, 1935)
Commanded Bombing Squadron 15 (VB-15) in 1944, 121-122, 133, 196-197, 217-218

Mitchell, Ensign John J., USN (USNA, 1942)
Badly wounded in the sinking of the aircraft carrier *Wasp* (CV-7) in September 1942, 106

Mitscher, Vice Admiral Marc A., USN (USNA, 1910)
While commanding the Fast Carrier Task Force during 1944 operations against the Japanese, met with McCampbell, 185-186

Morehouse, Rear Admiral Albert K., USN (USNA, 1922)
    Commanded Fighting Squadron Four (VF-4) in the late 1930s, 56, 59
    Helped McCampbell while serving in Norfolk in 1950, 267

Morris, Lieutenant Bert DeWayne Jr., USNR
    Movie actor who was a fighter pilot in Fighting Squadron 15 (VF-15) during World War II, 114-115, 188, 206

Morocco
    Port Lyautey Naval Air Station provided support for the Sixth Fleet in the 1950s, 229-230, 275-276, 323-325

Nall, Ensign Raymond L, USNR
    Served in Air Group 15 during operations from the aircraft carrier *Essex* (CV-9) in 1944, 180

"Nate" (Japanese Fighter)
    Actions against U.S. aircraft in 1944, 194-195

Naval Academy, Annapolis, Maryland
    Plebe summer in 1929, 12-13
    Academics in the late 1920s-early 1930s, 9, 14
    Discipline in the late 1920s-early 1930s, 13-14
    Athletics, 15-18
    Professional training, including summer cruises, 20-26
    Only half the class of 1933 was commissioned on graduation, 20, 26-27
    In 1948 McCampbell made a trip to the academy that indirectly resulted in his father's death, 268-270
    The Naval Academy Museum declined to exhibit a bust of McCampbell while he was still alive, 268-270

Naval Air Technical Training Center, Jacksonville, Florida
    Role of in 1953-54, 286-294

Naval Air Test Center, Patuxent River, Maryland
    Different types of testing during the mid-1950s, 294-299

Naval Aviation Museum, Pensacola, Florida
    Agreed to exhibit a bust of McCampbell that the Naval Academy Museum declined to put on display in the late 1940s, 268-270

Navigation
    Direction finding by carrier pilots to find their way back to their ships during World War II, 131

Negros, Philippine Islands
 Site of air operations by pilots from the aircraft carrier *Essex* (CV-9) in 1944, 135, 194

Neville, Captain Lawrence R., USN (USNA, 1933)
 Served as an observer for training of the crew of the fleet oiler *Severn* (AO-61) in 1958, 329-330

Night Operations
 By Fighting Squadron Four (VF-4) from the aircraft carrier *Ranger* (CV-4) in the late 1930s, 67-68

North American Air Defense Command
 Role in the early 1960s in preparing for possible Soviet attack, 357-362

Noyes, Rear Admiral Leigh, USN (USNA, 1906)
 Was embarked in the aircraft carrier *Wasp* (CV-7) in the summer of 1942, 75, 96, 104

Nuclear Weapons
 Logistics of supplying weapons to the Sixth Fleet in the early 1950s, 229-230
 On board the *Franklin D. Roosevelt* (CVB-42) in the early 1950s, 241, 277, 283-286
 On board the aircraft carrier *Bon Homme Richard* (CVA-31) in the late 1950s, 340

Ofstie, Vice Admiral Ralph K., USN (USNA, 1919)
 Commanded the aircraft carrier *Essex* (CV-9) from November 1943 to August 1944, 139, 151, 177, 210-211
 Commanded the Sixth Fleet in 1955-56 and left prematurely because of cancer, 305, 318-319, 322

Okinawa
 U.S. carrier air operations in the area in 1944, 197-198

Olds, Colonel Robin, USAF (USMA, 1943)
 In the mid-1950s ran the Weapons Proficiency Center at Wheelus Air Force Base in Libya, 323

Ormoc Bay, Philippines
 Strike operations against the Japanese in November 1944 by planes of Air Group 15 from the aircraft carrier *Essex* (CV-9), 166, 215-216

Pearl Harbor, Hawaii
 Site of failed eye exams for potential naval aviators in 1936, 39-40
 The aircraft carrier *Bon Homme Richard* (CVA-31) got under way unexpectedly early while in Pearl Harbor on 7 December 1959, 344-346

Pensacola, Florida, Naval Air Station
    Site of flight training in 1937-38, 47-54

Personnel
    Abundance of U.S. naval officers in the years shortly after World War II, 231

Philippine Islands
    Air operations in the area in 1944, 18-19, 135, 155-156, 194-195, 198-210, 212-214, 273-274, 300-301

Photo Reconnaissance
    By Air Group 15 of the aircraft carrier *Essex* (CV-9) in 1944, 155, 213

Pirie, Rear Admiral Robert B., USN (USNA, 1926)
    Commanded a carrier task group in the Mediterranean in the mid-1950s, 304

Pittard, Ensign George F., USN (USNA, 1934)
    Injured while serving in the heavy cruiser *Portland* (CA-33) in the mid-1930s, 35

Planning
    Air Force plans in the mid-1950s for evacuating U.S. personnel from the Mediterranean region, 322
    Work of the Joint Staff's Plans Division in the early 1960s, 352-357

***Portland*, USS (CA-33)**
    Operations in the Pacific and Caribbean in the mid-1930s, 31-46
    Ship's officers, 32-45
    Ship's teams in sports, 46

Port Lyautey, Morocco, Naval Air Station
    Served as a support station for the Sixth Fleet in the early 1950s, 229-230, 275-276, 323-324

Public Relations
    In early 1945 McCampbell received the Medal of Honor and toured the country, 221-227
    Public appearances and other events over the years that resulted from McCampbell's Medal of Honor, 232-244, 271-272

Pungo Naval Auxiliary Air Station, Virginia Beach, Virginia
    Site of pre-combat training in 1943 for Fighting Squadron 15 (VF-15), 116-117, 315

Pu'unēnē Naval Air Station, Hawaii
    In early 1944 was the site for training of pilots of Air Group 15, 126-127, 141, 148, 314-315

Racial Issues
    Segregated barbershops at the Technical Training Center, Jacksonville, Florida, in the early 1950s, 291-292

Radio
    Use of by planes from the aircraft carrier *Essex* (CV-9) in 1944, 132, 139, 165-166

Ramage, Commander Lawson P. (Red), USN (USNA, 1931)
    Received the Medal of Honor from President Franklin D. Roosevelt in January 1945, 224-226

Reeves, Captain John W., Jr., USN (USNA, 1911)
    Served as first commanding officer of the aircraft carrier *Wasp* (CV-7), 1940-42, 76-82, 88

Replenishment at Sea
    By the fleet oiler *Severn* (AO-61) in 1958, 330-331, 334, 338

Rescue at Sea
    The destroyer *Farenholt* (DD-491) rescued survivors from the sinking of the aircraft carrier *Wasp* (CV-7) in September 1942, 104-107

Rhodes, Greece
    Visited by the fleet oiler *Severn* (AO-61) in 1958, 332-333

Rigg, Lieutenant Commander James F., USN
    In 1943-44 served as executive officer and commanding officer of Fighting Squadron 15 (VF-15), 111-112, 114, 134, 181

Robertson, Lieutenant Commander Carl J., MC, USN
    Ship's doctor in the mid-1930s on board the heavy cruiser *Portland* (CA-33), 39-40

Rockets
    Used by pilots of Air Group 15 on board the aircraft carrier *Essex* (CV-9) in 1944, 273-274

Roosevelt, President Franklin D.
    As President in the mid-1930s made a fishing trip in the heavy cruiser *Houston* (CA-30), 37-39
    Awarded the Medal of Honor to McCampbell and Commander Lawson P. Ramage on 10 January 1945, 222-227

Royal Air Force
    Delivery in 1942 by the aircraft carrier *Wasp* (CV-7) of British Spitfires to the Mediterranean, destined for Malta, 80, 90-94
    Exercised with the U.S. Sixth Fleet in the mid-1950s, 303, 320

Royal Navy
Operations in the Mediterranean during the Suez Crisis in 1956, 300

Runyan, Commander Elmo C., USN
Warrant officer who abandoned the aircraft carrier *Wasp* (CV-7) after she had been torpedoed in September 1942, 102
Served on the ComAirLant staff as an officer following World War II, 231

Rushing, Lieutenant (junior grade) Roy W., USNR
Served as McCampbell's wingman during combat in 1944, 18-19, 142-144, 148-150, 160-161, 199-206, 212-214, 218, 273-274, 308, 311
Left the Navy in 1950, 266-267

Russell, Lieutenant Hawley, USN
Served as landing signal officer in the aircraft carrier *Wasp* (CV-7) in the early 1940s, 81-82

SB2C Helldiver
Flown by Bombing Squadron 15 (VB-15) in 1944, 122, 127

SB2U Vindicator
Flown by the aircraft carrier *Wasp* (CV-7) in the early 1940s, 75
Initially was used by Bombing Squadron 15 (VB-15) in 1944 but replaced before combat, 122

SNJ Texan
Used in flight training at Pensacola in 1937-38, 47, 51, 113
Familiarization flight in 1943 by pilots of Fighting Squadron 15 (VF-15). 126

Saipan, Mariana Islands
Support of the U.S. invasion in June 1944 provided by Air Group 15 from the aircraft carrier *Essex* (CV-9), 176-178, 184-185

***Salem*, USS (CA-139)**
In the mid-1950s served as Sixth Fleet flagship, 301-302, 320-321

San Blas Islands
Visited in the mid-1930s by the heavy cruiser *Portland* (CA-33), 37

Scapa Flow, Orkney Islands
Base for the aircraft carrier *Wasp* (CV-7) while operating with the British Home Fleet in the spring of 1942, 78-79, 85-86, 89-90

Schneider, Commander Tony F., USN
In 1959 served as executive officer of the aircraft carrier *Bon Homme Richard* (CVA-31), 341, 344, 347

Schoech, Rear Admiral William E., USN (USNA, 1928)
   As Commander Carrier Division Three on board the aircraft carrier *Bon Homme Richard* (CVA-31) in 1959, 338-341

Seligman, Lieutenant Commander Morton T., USN (USNA, 1919)
   In the late 1930s commanded the air group of the aircraft carrier *Ranger* (CV-4), 64

Semmes, Lieutenant (junior grade) Benedict J., Jr., USN (USNA, 1934)
   Served in the aircraft carrier *Wasp* (CV-7) in the early 1940s, 76-77, 99

***Severn*, USS (AO-61)**
   Shipyard period in New York City in 1958, 326-329, 331
   Operations off the East Coast in 1958-59, 327-332, 336-338
   Enlisted crew members in the late 1950s, 330-335
   Officers in the crew in the late 1950s, 334
   Deployment to the Mediterranean in 1958, 331-334
   Ship handling, 336-338
   Collision with a destroyer in the late 1950s, 338

Shea, Lieutenant Commander John J., USN
   Killed in September 1942 during the sinking of the aircraft carrier *Wasp* (CV-7), 86, 221

Sherman, Captain Forrest P., USN (USNA, 1918)
   Commanded the aircraft carrier *Wasp* (CV-7) from May 1942 until her sinking in September of that year, 96, 104, 107
   Served as Chief of Naval Operations, 1949-51, 275-276, 278

Sherman, Rear Admiral Frederick C., USN (USNA, 1910)
   Commanded Task Group 38.3 during the Philippine campaign in 1944, 189-190, 199-201, 216

Ship Handling
   On board the fleet oiler *Severn* (AO-61) in the late 1950s, 336-337

Sixth Fleet, U.S.
   Logistics of supplying nuclear weapons to the fleet in the early 1950s, 229-230, 277, 283-286
   Vice Admiral Ralph Ofstie left the fleet command in 1956 because of cancer, 305, 322
   Vice Admiral Harry Don Felt briefly commanded the fleet in 1956, 300, 305-306, 319
   Vice Admiral Charles R. Brown as fleet commander, 1956-58, 300-304, 306, 319, 321, 325-326
   Experiments in the late 1950s with dispersed formations, 302-303
   Villefranche, France, was the homeport of the fleet flagship in the 1950s, 320-321

Ship maintenance and repair, 321-322

Various crises in the mid-1950s, including Suez, Jordan, and Lebanon, 321-322, 332-333

Slack, Ensign Albert C., USNR
Combat operations in 1944 as part of Air Group 15 in the aircraft carrier *Essex* (CV-9), 145

Smith, Commander Daniel F. Jr., USN (USNA, 1932)
Commanded Air Group 20 of the aircraft carrier *Enterprise* (CV-6) in 1944, 199, 206, 215-216

Smith, Commander Donald F., USN (USNA, 1921)
Served as navigator in the aircraft carrier *Wasp* (CV-7) in the early 1940s, 79-80

Smith, Ensign James A., USN (USNA, 1933)
As a Naval Academy midshipman, 18
Flew a floatplane from the heavy cruiser *Portland* (CA-33) in the mid-1930s, 35, 42

Smith, Pilot Officer Jerrold Smith, RCAF
Spitfire pilot who made an unusual landing on board the aircraft carrier *Wasp* (CV-7) in the spring of 1942, 90-94

Snowden, Lieutenant Commander Ernest M., USN (USNA, 1932)
Commanded Scouting Squadron 72 (VS-72) on board the aircraft carrier *Wasp* (CV-7) in 1942, 97-98

Spain
McCampbell visited Barcelona and Valencia in 1951 in connection with Sixth Fleet duty, 275-276

Spitfire
British fighter plane delivered to Malta by the aircraft carrier *Wasp* (CV-7) in 1942, 80, 90-94

Squantum, Massachusetts, Naval Air Station
Base for the air group of the aircraft carrier *Wasp* (CV-7) when she was first in commission in 1940, 77-78

Staunton Military Academy, Staunton, Virginia
As a boys' prep school in the late 1920s, 2-8

Stillman, Major General Robert M., USAF (USMA, 1935)
Attended Armed Forces Staff College in the late 1940s, later commanded Sheppard Air Force Base in the 1950s, 251-252

Swimming and Diving
    McCampbell's prowess, 3-4, 10, 15-17, 33
    At the 1932 Olympic Games, 28-29
    Crew members of the aircraft carrier *Wasp* (CV-7) in the water after their ship was torpedoed in September 1942, 101-105

Switzer, Lieutenant Commander Wendell G., USN (USNA, 1921)
    Commanded Fighting Squadron Four (VF-4) in the late 1930s, 56, 59
    As Chief of Naval Tactical Training in Memphis in the early 1950s, 287, 290-291

Test Pilots
    At the Naval Air Test Center, Patuxent River, Maryland, in the mid-1950s, 294-299

Thach Weave
    Used in 1944 by pilots of Fighting Squadron 15 (VF-15), 126-129

Training
    At the Naval Academy in the early 1930s, including summer cruises, 20-26
    Flight training at Pensacola in 1937-38, 26, 47-54
    Landing signal officer school in Melbourne, Florida in 1942-43, 66-67, 69, 109-110
    Training of Fighting Squadron 15 (VF-15) in 1943-44 in preparation for combat, 111-120
    In the mid-1940s McCampbell was at Oceana Naval Air Station to train air groups, 228-230
    Role of the Naval Air Technical Training Center in Jacksonville, 1953-54, 286-294
    Post-shipyard training for the crew of fleet oiler *Severn* (AO-61) in 1958, 329-330

Turner, Lieutenant Commander Frank, USN (USNA, 1927)
    In the early 1940s commanded Scouting 72 (VS-72), based on board the aircraft carrier *Wasp* (CV-7), 77, 87-88

Ulithi Atoll, Caroline Islands
    Fleet anchorage for the aircraft carrier *Essex* (CV-9) and other warships between operations in 1944, 218-220

VF-4
    See: Fighting Squadron Four (VF-4)

VF-15
    See: Fighting Squadron 15 (VF-15)

Villefranche, France
    Homeport of the Sixth Fleet flagship in the 1950s, 320-321

Wasp, USS (CV-7)
    Operations in the Atlantic in 1940-42, including Neutrality Patrol, 69-81, 86-89, 94
    Collision with the destroyer *Stack* (DD-406) in March 1942, 94
    Operations with the British Home Fleet in 1942, 85-86, 89-90
    Delivery in 1942 of British Spitfires to the Mediterranean, destined for Malta, 80, 90-94
    Operations in the Pacific in mid-1942, 95-99
    Sinking of on 15 September 1942, 78-79, 83-84, 99-108

White, Byron R. "Whizzer"
    Supreme Court justice who served on the staff of Vice Admiral Marc Mitscher during World War II, 312-313

Wieber, Captain Carlos W., USN (USNA, 1918)
    Commanded the aircraft carrier *Essex* (CV-9) in 1944-45, 189-190, 201

Winters, Commander T. Hugh Jr., USN (USNA, 1935)
    During World War II commanded the air group of the aircraft carrier *Lexington* (CV-16) and afterward wrote a book about his experiences, 66, 167-168, 200, 216, 307, 312, 315-317
    Officer detailer in the late 1950s, 337

Wright, Lieutenant (junior grade) Spencer D., USN
    In 1942 served in Scouting Squadron 71 (VS-71) on board the aircraft carrier *Wasp* (CV-7), 101

Yugoslavia
    Visited by the Sixth Fleet flagship *Salem* (CA-139) in the mid-1950s, 324-325

Zero/"Zeke"
    See: A6M Zero (Japanese Fighter)